S.H. Fazan, CMG, CBE, 1888–1979, was a Provincial Commissioner in Kenya. A classical scholar of Christ Church, Oxford, in 1911 he sailed to British East Africa (Kenya) where he worked continuously for the next 31 years in agricultural and political development, being latterly also an *ex-officio* member of the Legislative Council. After war service he returned to Kenya between 1949 and 1963. His most notable appointments in these years were as a special magistrate, official historian of the Kikuyu 'loyalists' and member of both the Mau Mau Detainees Appeals Tribunal and the Committee for the Study of the Sociological Causes of Mau Mau.

John Lonsdale is a Fellow of Trinity College, Cambridge, and Emeritus Professor of Modern African History at the University of Cambridge.

'Sidney Fazan was Britain's most important colonial officer serving in Britain's most important African colony. His voice is to be heard in every key discussion in Kenya's history from before the First World War until the Mau Mau rebellion. This edition of his personal writings, selected and superbly edited and annotated by John Lonsdale, will be an indispensible asset for any student of Kenya's colonial moment. This is a wonderful and immensely useful volume.'

David M. Anderson, Professor of African History, University of Warwick

'For students of British Colonialism and especially development to independence this is an invaluable record. We are fortunate that the editor has revealed the importance of S.H. Fazan's work. I was fortunate to meet him, long after retirement, working on his colonial records in happy seclusion in Muguga near his home. Increasingly Fazan pointed to the rising population of Africans and the grievances which led to the Mau Mau insurrection. Renewed calls for change came from the United Nations and newly independent countries like Ghana exerted pressure. The United Kingdom decided to accelerate the programme with independence in East African countries, in Tanganyika in 1961, Uganda in 1962 and Kenya in 1963. Fazan's work had helped prepare the ground successfully for African rule.'

Sir John Johnson, former High Commissioner to Kenya

S.H. FAZAN

Colonial Kenya Observed

British Rule, Mau Mau and the Wind of Change

Edited and with a Foreword
by John Lonsdale

BLOOMSBURY ACADEMIC
LONDON • NEW YORK • OXFORD • NEW DELHI • SYDNEY

BLOOMSBURY ACADEMIC
Bloomsbury Publishing Plc
50 Bedford Square, London, WC1B 3DP, UK
1385 Broadway, New York, NY 10018, USA

BLOOMSBURY, BLOOMSBURY ACADEMIC and the Diana
logo are trademarks of Bloomsbury Publishing Plc

First published in Great Britain by I.B. Tauris 2015
Paperback edition published by Bloomsbury Academic 2020

Cover design: Eleanor Rose
Cover image © Vince Cavataio/Getty Images

A catalogue record for this book is available from the British Library.

A catalog record for this book is available from the Library of Congress.

ISBN: HB: 978-1-7807-6865-6
PB: 978-1-3501-5536-7
ePDF: 978-0-8577-2555-4
eBook: 978-0-8577-3784-7

CONTENTS

List of Illustrations vii
Foreword by John Lonsdale ix
Preface xxxviii
A Note on Names xl
Map: Fazan's Kenya 1911–1942 xliii

Part I British East Africa
1 Historical Background 3
2 Early Days of the Protectorate 14
3 First Impressions 27
4 Races and Migrations 36
5 The First World War 49

Part II The Colony During the Inter-War Years
6 The Coast 61
7 Principal Events and Politics 74
8 Changes 88

Part III Government in the African Lands
9 The Field Administration 101
10 African Authorities 117

14 A coastal street, 1920s.

15 Unroadworthy car, 1920s.

16 Uncarworthy road, 1920s.

17 The District Commissioner's new house, Machakos, *c.* 1927.

18 S. H. Fazan with Kamba women charcoal burners, 1920s.

19 A District Commissioner's Baraza, 1920s.

20 Kikuyu Ngoma [dance], almost certainly in 1928, to celebrate the visit of Edward Prince of Wales.

21 The Aga Khan's Golden Jubilee, celebrated in Kisumu, 1937. Left to right, outside the Provincial Commissioner's House: The Aga Khan, Sir Sultan Muhammad Shah; Anthea Fazan, Stephen Fazan, Eleanor Fazan, the Begum Andrée Aga Khan, S. H. Fazan, Mrs Fazan, Mrs Cochrane, Cecil Davenport (a fellow Provincial Commissioner).

22 S. H. Fazan in full tropical fig with the Governor's lady, Lady Brooke-Popham, 1937.

23 The new Governor, Sir Robert Brooke-Popham, with his senior officials, 1937. S. H. Fazan, as the senior Provincial Commissioner, is seated at the Governor's right-hand side.

All images, courtesy of the Fazan Estate.

FOREWORD[1]

An official life

Historians who work in the Kenya National Archives, housed in Nairobi's old National Bank of India, sit up when they see a report from S. H. Fazan. He is always worth reading, one of the most interesting of colonial Kenya's officials. As a fellow historian has put it, 'clever and determined, [...] diligent, serious and scholarly, he had little time for colleagues who refused to grapple with the complexities of African life.'[2] He had that irritating habit, hard to forgive, of reaching the right conclusion before his seniors. In the opinion of a colleague he could speak Swahili and 'do nearly everything else better than most'.[3] Some complained that his memoranda were too long but they could not ignore his intellect. At critical moments in colonial history it was indispensable. Unusually, he was appointed to the Order of the British Empire, OBE, in 1930, when not yet a senior district commissioner (DC); and no civil servant was better suited – by ability, stamina and moral courage – to be secretary to the Colony's most controversial official enquiry, the Kenya Land Commission of 1932–3, the Carter Commission, chaired by Judge Morris Carter. Fazan's labours in this task, which aimed to secure agreement to the allocation of land

1 I am indebted to Dr Juliet McMaster and Gillian Fazan, daughters of S. H. Fazan, for much detailed help in producing this edition of their father's memoir. I also owe much to my colleagues David Anderson and Richard Waller, and friends who were there, Peter Fullerton, Chris Minter and Ian Parker, for comment on an earlier draft. They will all, for different reasons, disagree with some of the use I have made of their advice.

2 David Anderson, *Histories of the Hanged: Britain's Dirty War in Kenya and the End of Empire* (London: Weidenfeld & Nicolson, 2005), p. 143.

3 H. E. Lambert to T. H. R. Cashmore, 6 April 1964: Rhodes House Library, Oxford: Mss.Afr.s.919.

between black and white, got him promoted to CBE, a Commander of the Order. Kenya's white settlers came to regard the commission's report as their Magna Carta, a pun difficult to avoid; 20 years later Mau Mau's African insurgents, most of them members of the Kikuyu people of central Kenya, saw it as a charter of injustice. They had lost about 7 per cent of their land to white settlement; the commission had failed to give all but a tiny fraction back, and its other forms of compensation were scarcely satisfactory. The counterinsurgent war against them, under 'emergency' laws that abrogated many legal protections, was the bloodiest of Britain's several wars of decolonisation. Fazan, now in retirement, advised on this counterinsurgent campaign and then recorded one of its key aspects in his last report, the *History of the Loyalists*.[4]

If this Foreword is to do justice to Fazan the man, it must range as widely as his own intellectual interests and manifold career. Nonetheless, if his memoir of a life's work spent in Kenya colony's progress has a core, it is found in his reflections on these two reports. The first, the report of the Carter Commission, was almost entirely his own enormous labour, within terms of reference set by British politicians. Fazan instigated the search for evidence, collated it for the commissioners' consideration, and arranged for its publication in three fat volumes before then drafting the commission's recommendations.[5] The second, his history of the Kikuyu who, under British command, fought Mau Mau, their kinsfolk, was little more than a compilation of other men's work. With hindsight – but it was argued by many at the time – one may say that the failure of the first report to secure African consent, in particular the consent of Kenya's most politically alert people, the Kikuyu, had made the second inevitable, a record of counterinsurgency against angry rebels. Fazan never publicly admitted to that connection nor did it occur to him to openly blame the commission's contradictory instructions, to which he had objected confidentially at the time. Carter's first five terms of reference had all been concerned with African needs and the 'adequate settlement' of their claims to land previously alienated, or not yet alienated, to white settlement. In an

4 Colony and Protectorate of Kenya, *History of the Loyalists* (Nairobi: Government Printer, 1961).

5 Colonial Office, *Report of the Kenya Land Commission* (London: HMSO, Cmd 4556, 1934); hereafter Carter Commission, *Report*. In 1972 Fazan told Dr Breen that he had drafted most of the report apart from sections on the Rift Valley and the chapter on African livestock. The *Report*, of over 600 pages, has 45 chapters; Fazan may have drafted 37 of them, depending on how one interprets 'Rift Valley'. See Rita M. Breen, 'The politics of land: The Kenya Land Commission, 1932–33, and its effects on land policy in Kenya' (Michigan State University: PhD thesis, 1976), p. 61, footnote 3.

afterthought a sixth term had been added, the one to which Fazan objected, to define the Highland area in which whites enjoyed a privileged position. This instruction had been secretly reinforced by colonial office 'advice' for the commissioners to accept the 'facts' of white settlement. The land commissioners started to take evidence from Kikuyu, in well-attended public meetings, in November 1932. A month earlier Fazan had advised one of their district commissioners to warn his people not to entertain any 'extravagant expectations'.[6] Expectations of restitution were scarcely extravagant but were dashed all the same.

Within its contradictory and restrictive terms the commission, Fazan always maintained, had been more than fair to Africans; so in his view Mau Mau insurgents were later recruited less by legitimate grievance than by exaggeration, intimidation and superstition. But they were not solely to blame for the tragedy of the Mau Mau war. In Fazan's reflections one finds rumination on the character of Kenya's white colony, how its members might have changed and why they did not do so. Why did not more of them come to see when (quite when is not clear) their racial privilege, possibly the colony's necessary foundation stone, had become both an intolerable injustice to Africans and a hindrance to Kenya's general progress? This memoir represents, among its other merits, an extended meditation – summarised in Appendix I – on the practical compromises demanded of all executive power, especially colonial power, when pursuing policies favoured by some major civil interests, but to which others, less influential but with an acute sense of injustice, are bitterly opposed. An outline discussion of Fazan's professional career is required before such a meditation can be properly understood.

The colonial government needed Fazan; historians of the colonial period need him too. We use his data, learn from his insights and quote his reports; we trust him. This memoir helps us to know him better, especially his stringent sense of what made the politically practicable morally desirable in a context where official powers of persuasion were laughably lacking. Scholars of the pre-colonial era have found him equally valuable as an alert and curious observer. In his classic history of the Luo people before 1900 the doyen of Kenya's historians, Bethwell Ogot, relied at several points on what the young district officer, an 'indefatigable recorder of traditional history', had noted in his district record book in 1913, only two years after arriving in Kenya.[7]

---

6 Carter commission, *Report*, pp. 1–2; Breen, 'The Politics of Land', pp. 61–6, 74–8.

7 B. A. Ogot, *History of the Southern Luo, Volume 1: Migration and Settlement 1500–1900* (Nairobi: East African Publishing House, 1967), pp. 229–33.

Fazan's sharp mind, clear prose and calm judgment mean that this memoir, finished in 1969 when he was 80 years old, remains a fascinating and important read. A senior official's history of colonial Kenya, it is a remarkable tribute to its author's wide experience and intellectual grasp. When he had finished writing, however, no publisher could be persuaded to take the manuscript; the mood of that Beatles era was too guiltily anti-imperial. His family has now resurrected it and with today's greater distance from events we can be more objective. We can be more like Fazan. He could understand both the African native subjects of his day and the often more troublesome, certainly noisier, minority of white settlers. He could blame white intransigence as well as African sedition for the horrors of Mau Mau. Such balance was unusual; Kenya's turbulent history tended to divide white opinion between the 'pro-native' and the 'pro-settler'. Readers whose letters were published in the settlers' paper, the *East African Standard*, sometimes sheltered under the pseudonym 'non-pro-native' when criticising their fellow whites. Fazan's even-handedness is all the more valuable, a product of the official's often unenviable position as 'man in the middle'.

Fazan brings a uniquely well-informed perspective to Kenya's colonial history. A sceptical younger generation may also meet here a wiser, more humane, economically and sociologically literate imperial servant than they may have been led to expect. Fazan was not afraid to condemn abuses of the system he was proud to serve, but as a civil servant he also knew when to keep silent. Never a sentimentalist, he was one of the Empire's practical intellectuals, a thinker but also a doer, duty-bound to steer a responsible way through the moral maze of an imperial enterprise that was mixed in motive, practice, and effect – generous and greedy, authoritarian and liberal, humane and brutal, culturally self-confident to the point of racial hubris but often and increasingly assailed by self-doubt. His family have done well to bring the manuscript of such a man, in his time, once again to light.

Sidney Herbert Fazan, CMG, CBE, 1888–1979, was a doctor's son from the southern English home county of Sussex. Schooled at Epsom College, he won a Classics scholarship to Christ Church, Oxford, an early indication of his intellectual distinction, although his college thought him still better at cricket. Before 1900 colonial officials had been a motley crew, often picked up locally from a range of adventurous backgrounds. Early in the twentieth century, the Colonial Office in London turned to the old universities of Oxford and Cambridge in order to recruit field administrators from the professional middle class, more able to manage the complexities of peaceful and productive overseas rule. Fazan responded to this opportunity soon after graduating. Choosing to serve in the new East Africa Protectorate, he sailed out in 1911, aged 23, with little further training.

Kenya Colony, as the Protectorate became in 1920, was notorious as the most excitable and one of the least profitable territories of British Africa. Its government provided African land, labour and revenue to support a tiny, vocal, white minority whose farmers and planters, with few exceptions, failed to find profitable markets before the 1940s. London sent out repeated commissions to enquire into the equity of this relationship; these did more to ease the imperial conscience than to reach a more sustainable political economy. Public controversy centred on whether the settlers – of whom never more than a quarter were farmers – were a benefit to the native population as tutors in industrious civilisation; or a hindrance, in absorbing public attention and expenditure; or mere parasites, sapping African energies by denying them resources and opportunity. One's answer to that question answered the next: how far was it justified to make Africans work for white profit after the state had expropriated much, if not always the best, African land for white farms? Before 1930 this coercion was sometimes direct, by force; normally, and later, it operated indirectly through the gross racial imbalance that existed, before the 1940s, between the taxes paid by Africans and the value of public services performed for settlers.

A third argument followed, and continued in various forms from the early 1920s until 1960. How far, if at all, could white settlers be allowed to share the responsibility of rule with the Crown's overseas civil servants, Fazan among them? After settlers had won a share of responsibility in the 1920s, on the plea that that was their right as propertied, free-born Englishmen, the question widened: how far should the much larger South Asian immigrant community or even the overwhelming majority of African subjects be associated with this power? As late as the 1940s some settler leaders dreamed of inheriting a white minority ruling power at independence, following the earlier example of their counterparts in South Africa. That was always a fantasy, although the British government could seem to waver from its policy, stated in 1923, that Kenya was 'primarily' an African territory. Kenya's whites had neither numbers nor wealth. White South Africans were one fifth of their country's total population around 1950; Kenya's settlers were never more than 1 per cent. South Africa also had, as Kenya did not, a mining sector that needed and could finance an industrial economy that was able to employ a growing African population.

Fazan spent most of his career in the all-African areas of the Colony; he rarely had charge of white farmers. His life in the 'native reserves' clearly gave him a respect for Africans, based on his astonishing knowledge of their way of life, learned as an observant junior official when away from his desk, on foot, 'on safari'. Historians owe much to the percipience of district officers whose interest in African lives was every bit as attentive as our own. Fazan did not condemn white settlers; they brought a welcome social energy– but they were also too reluctant, once they had achieved economic success, to share it with Africans. They should, in his view, have been more ready to open up inter-racial access to the 'white' land that the Carter Commission, his commission, had guaranteed them. At what date he came to this conclusion it is difficult to say. Towards the end of his story can one see a growing sympathy for them as Britain seemed intent on denying their children an African future; wearied by war, by the 1950s it wanted to drop the increasingly unpopular burden of empire. In the view of many of Fazan's class and generation, the hurried exit from imperial responsibility broke faith with both white citizens and African subjects, and its pension arrangements were as mean as only the British Treasury knew.

Fazan served his formative first years in the almost entirely African province of Nyanza, Kenya's western region, on the shores of Lake Victoria. His provincial commissioner (PC) was John Ainsworth, one of the founders of modern Kenya. A Manchester man, he had first come to Africa to trade in African products, an experience that shaped his later outlook. With little social grace or standing but possessed of great energy, also given to writing over-lengthy reports, Ainsworth was convinced that Kenya's future lay in a combination of African peasant cultivation and white commercial farming, each compatible with the other. Cadet Fazan clearly absorbed his PC's 'pro-native' vision. New officials had no training manuals; they learned by observing their seniors. In this, his official's history, the best evidence for Fazan's loyalty to his mentor is seen in his resort to anonymity when telling how Ainsworth's humane principles – which had always required Africans to work their own salvation – appeared to give way to settler demands for more African labour after the First World War.[8] Fazan does not

8 Robert M. Maxon, *John Ainsworth and the Making of Kenya* (Lanham MD: University Press of America, 1980); idem, *Struggle for Kenya: The Loss and Reassertion of Imperial Initiative 1912–1923* (London and Toronto: Associated University Presses, 1993), pp. 145–58, 193–9. See Chapter 12 of this book.

confide in us to the extent of criticising named colleagues. He does, however, sometimes reveal his feelings, as when remembering that his first major move, in 1915, to the desert frontier district of Turkana, only recently and ferociously conquered, led to a sense of isolation and frustration that made him ill.[9]

After the war Fazan endured short-term postings in different districts – a failing for which the government was often censured but of which it was never cured. There was some perverse logic at work too: officers who spent too long in one district might become more 'their natives' champion, and less the government's agent; but it also reproduced much ignorance and personal idiosyncrasy in policy that was difficult for Africans to predict, faults that Fazan seems to have avoided.[10] From 1918 to 1925 he helped to rule the largely Muslim Coast province, with an interlude in Central Nyanza in 1921–2. Staff shortages in a pauper colony meant that he was repeatedly transferred between three of the coastal districts, Malindi, Tana River and Mombasa town. He witnessed what was widely seen as the demoralised torpor of a previously slave society, with its former Arab masters and former black slaves. The experience must surely have stimulated his later thoughts about what policies made for economic growth and social vitality.[11]

Fazan spent the rest of his career 'upcountry'. In the late 1920s he had almost three years with the Kamba people, mixed farmers and herders, in both the Machakos and Kitui districts, important recruiting grounds for police and army – the King's African Rifles.[12] In December

9 For the conquest of Turkana, see John Lamphear, *The Scattering Time: Turkana Responses to Colonial Rule* (Oxford: Clarendon Press, 1992).

10 For the Kenya administration's official culture, see Bruce Berman, *Control and Crisis in Colonial Kenya: The Dialectic of Domination* (London: James Currey, 1990), Chapter 3. Data for Fazan's postings are derived from district and provincial annual reports and handing-over reports, located in the Kenya National Archives.

11 For this era of the Kenya coast's agrarian history, see Frederick Cooper, *From Slaves to Squatters: Plantation Labour and Agriculture in Zanzibar and Coastal Kenya 1890–1925* (New Haven, CT; London: Yale University Press, 1980).

12 Timothy H. Parsons, *The African Rank-and-File: Social Implications of Colonial Military Service in the King's African Rifles, 1902–1964* (Portsmouth, NH: Heinemann, 1999). For Kamba colonial history, see J. F. Munro, *Colonial Rule and the Kamba: Social Change in the Kenya Highlands, 1889–1939* (Oxford: Clarendon Press, 1975); Myles Osborne, *Loyal Sons of Kenya: Virtue, Ethnicity and Martial Race among the Kamba, c. 1800 to the Present* (Cambridge: Cambridge University Press, 2014); Katherine Luongo, *Witchcraft and Colonial Rule in Kenya, 1900–1955* (Cambridge: Cambridge University Press, 2011).

1928, aged 40, he became DC of the northernmost Kikuyu district, Nyeri – later a core area of Mau Mau insurgency. Within the year he moved to southern Kikuyu, to Kiambu, fast becoming a suburb of Nairobi and the centre of African politics, with its market gardeners, commuting clerks, and women traders.[13] Proximity to Nairobi meant that he could at last join a cricket club – the Kenya Kongonis. Fazan's first official task here, however, was scarcely cricket; it was to calm both Kikuyu and white opinion over the 'female circumcision crisis' when some Protestant missions tried to get their married converts to renounce the practice of clitoridectomy for their pubescent daughters. It was the most dramatic clash of cultures in colonial Kenya. Conventional Kikuyu opinion regarded the surgery and its rituals as a necessary initiation into the painful responsibilities of womanhood; whites thought it revolting, cruel, and often dangerous to future mothers. As DC, however, Fazan could not allow cultural revulsion to overrule administrative judgment.[14]

Fazan was also plunged into the no less contentious question of Kikuyu land tenure. Land was Kenya's key political issue then, as it is today. Government wanted to put an end to the endless argument over how far white settlement had expropriated which Africans and what remedy, if any, was called for. Fazan calculated that Kikuyu had lost 7 per cent of their land, almost all of it from Kiambu. The question of how much land had been expropriated, however, was the least of the issues. More difficult to answer was the question 'from whom?' It needed an understanding of African tenures. Did individual Africans own property or did they merely enjoy the use of communal land by virtue of their tribal membership? Most whites believed the latter to be the case: 'primitive' people could surely never conceive of private ownership. Kikuyu protested, to the contrary, that family groups or individuals did indeed own land, that the British had stolen from known persons, that these deserved specific compensation for private loss, and

---

13 For Nyeri in Fazan's time, see Derek R. Peterson, *Creative Writing: Translation, Bookkeeping, and the Work of the Imagination in Colonial Kenya* (Portsmouth, NH: Heinemann, 2004); for Kiambu, Marshall S. Clough, *Fighting Two Sides: Kenyan Chiefs and Politicians, 1918–1940* (Niwot, CO: University Press of Colorado, 1990).

14 This crisis has generated a large literature. For an account that notices that Fazan appreciated that Kikuyu feelings were 'primarily and consciously nationalist' – a calmer perspective than that of some missionaries – see Robert L. Tignor, *The Colonial Transformation of Kenya: The Kamba. Kikuyu, and Maasai from 1900 to 1939* (Princeton, NJ: Princeton University Press, 1976), Chapter X. A fuller bibliography and discussion are given in the notes to Chapter 7 of the memoir.

that the remaining land they still possessed needed the protection of legally-secure title deeds.

As DC, Fazan was appointed to a committee of enquiry. Disagreeing with the other two committee members, one being the young Dr Louis Leakey, white Kenya's most famous intellectual, he submitted a minority report. Both Leakey and Fazan understood the underlying principle of Kikuyu land law to be 'seigniory'. They used this term, a dubious borrowing from feudal England, to characterise the authority that lineage elders – not the Kikuyu people as a whole – held over the usage and disposal of their extended families' land. Leakey accepted that change was needed but called for more research before there was any attempt to reform this social web of entitlement to property. Fazan – hearing frequent land cases between Kikuyu – wanted greater urgency: government must register individual title when asked and, in due course, encourage an African market in land, with little regard for the historical accidents that, in his view, protected unequal indigenous power over property. Only such reform could, he believed, promote the more efficient use of what would always be limited land – even had there been no white settlement – and so fight the spectre of destitution in a rapidly growing population.[15]

Four years later Fazan got the Carter Commission to adopt his view. Politically daring, it was the conventional agrarian wisdom – inasmuch as agricultural officers, charged mainly with the health of white farming, were able to spare thought for the 'native reserves'. The commission recommended, accordingly, that while African land tenure rules should respect local 'custom', this should 'be progressively guided in the direction of private tenure, proceeding through the group and the family towards the individual holding.'[16] Even such a gradual revolution was beyond Kenya's administrative capacity or official courage at the time. Little was done to implement Fazan's views until a more drastic reform, jumping straight from 'customary' to private tenure, was adopted in response to the Mau Mau rising.

Whether Fazan's step-by-step privatisation of land would have bought off rebellion with increased productivity is doubtful; it might have provoked resistance all the sooner. It would have widened the already apparent gulf between a comfortable upper peasantry, even a 'gentry', with full lineage rights, and a growing landless class among the

15 M. P. K. Sorrenson, *Land Reform in the Kikuyu Country* (Nairobi: Oxford University Press, 1967), pp. 30–31; Anderson, *Histories of the Hanged*, pp. 144–7.

16 Carter Commission, *Report*, p. 420, paragraph 1650.

committees. One was asked to enquire into the social composition of the movement; the other heard appeals from detainees, the tens of thousands of Mau Mau suspects held behind wire without trial. Most British opinion saw these as psychologically deluded rather than justifiably aggrieved; colonialism was still widely thought to be a civilising mission that 'disturbed' rather than exploited indigenous peoples.[24] On the first committee Fazan argued that land-hunger could not be accepted as a legitimate grievance; government, following Judge Carter's recommendations, had amply compensated Africans who were dispossessed by white settlement.[25] On the second committee he interviewed detainees, securing better conditions in at least one case and commending the sincerity of a man's 'fanaticism' in another.[26] He also acted as special magistrate, trying Mau Mau offences and, as a final service to the colony, compiled the official history of the so-called 'loyalists' – Kikuyu who had fought their Mau Mau neighbours under British command but in their own cause.[27] The clarity of his *History of the Loyalists* shows that, in his 70s, Fazan's mind was as sharp as ever; but its silences pose a difficult question.

When may one's personal knowledge of official misdeeds, learned in government service, be denied public communication? It happens all the time, of course, and can sometimes be justified as a defence of national security. It is also how officials protect themselves from scrutiny, saving themselves embarrassment at the cost of proper accountability and even, at times, of rank injustice. In 1960, when compiling his *History* from accounts submitted by different DCs, Fazan must have pondered such editorial questions; his 1969 memoir gives proof of this rumination. In Chapter 15 he summarises his account of the Kikuyu Guard (KG), the militia raised from the ranks of chiefs' retainers and led by young white men, most of them Kenya-born. It is a faithful summary; it gives the authentic flavour of the 1961 *History*. We

24 John Lonsdale, 'Mau Maus of the mind: Making Mau Mau and remaking Kenya', *Journal of African History* 31 (1990), pp. 393–421.

25 Anderson, *Histories*, pp. 281–4. The adequacy of the commission's recommendations is discussed in the notes to Chapter 11.

26 See further in the notes to Chapter 15.

27 The use of inverted commas for the term 'loyalist' reflects that these Kikuyu fought not so much to save British rule as to regain from Mau Mau the initiative in leading the Kikuyu contribution to African politics, but 'loyalist' has stuck in the literature. In the 1950s African majority rule became an increasingly feasible alternative to the British policy of 'multi-racial' power sharing. Fazan acknowledged this self-interest, inadmissible in 1961, when he came to write his memoir in 1969.

learn that the KG served without respite for two years on the Mau Mau war's front line – never a line but a knotted web of private rivalries. The British use of local auxiliaries had, as officials must have known was inevitable, cemented local feuds into an imperial conflict. While Kikuyu fought Kikuyu in their own internal cause, one must doubt if their rivalries, which were largely over land, would have reached so lethal a level had they not also been fighting for or against the British. The KG killed more insurgents, often their neighbours, than any other military unit, numbering nearly half the total recorded Mau Mau dead; it also suffered the heaviest casualties. Fazan's *History* and, eight years later, his memoir tell of loyal courage, crucial to British victory. In 1969 the original work was at his elbow. When he came to finish Chapter 15, however, he had to admit that its heroic tale was not the full story.

As Fazan acknowledged by 1969 but not in 1961, the KG – along with the other security forces – had not only fought bravely in open combat but had also perpetrated private abuses, often in revenge for Mau Mau atrocity, even at times murdering captives. Knowing how difficult it was to fight a 'clean' counterinsurgency war when the enemy was difficult to distinguish from a sullen but unarmed civil population, the British general in charge, George Erskine, tried to confine his British and Kenyan army units to operations against Mau Mau fighters in the mountain forests of central Kenya, 'prohibited areas' where it was permissible to shoot on sight. The KG was given chief responsibility for the densely-populated Kikuyu 'reserves' where high officials admitted that, even with the best will in the world, and best discipline – neither of which conditions applied – murderous mistakes were all too likely.[28] A general amnesty given by the governor, Sir Evelyn Baring, to Mau Mau and KG alike in early 1955 had put both their criminal records beyond further legal scrutiny but not out of mind. Fazan made no mention of this in his 1961 *History*. Did his silences, like those of other official statements at the time, cover up criminal deeds that were best forgotten?

That suggestion raises in acute form the issue of the historian's responsibility to the past and its people. Before levying such a charge in this case he or she must first not only know, but also feel, the political and moral dilemmas of the colonialism that Fazan had served long, loyally, and well. He will have been pulled in different directions by conscience and duty, as most of us are from time to time. Looked at

28 Huw Bennett, *Fighting the Mau Mau: The British Army and Counter-insurgency in the Kenya Emergency* (Cambridge: Cambridge University Press, 2013), pp. 129–33, 158–9, 223, 225, 248–52, 260, 261, 269.

with these considerations in mind, and remembering his official loyalties – but lack of official responsibility – his editorial rather than authorial role, and the governor's amnesty, his *History* prompts a rather different question: when, why and how far may one expect any individual to dissent from the conventional thought and behaviour of his or her friends and colleagues? How far might one then expect him or her to go in trying to expose or change that behaviour? Public dissent used to be almost unthinkable for civil servants, duty-bound to air any doubts through 'official channels' rather than in public. Fazan was a pensioner civil servant, steeped in this tight-lipped culture. Like any other official in Kenya he was no stranger to controversy, to a conflict of loyalties. He had not publicly aired his doubts about the Carter Commission's contradictory task in the 1930s. He was the same man 30 years later, facing a similar dilemma.

When he compiled his official history, the war against Mau Mau had been won; notorious crimes on both sides had been pardoned. Two battles for the meaning of the war remained to be decided. First, had its ethnic terror disqualified any claim for Mau Mau to be included in a legitimate Kenyan nationalism? Second, had Mau Mau, no matter what its barbarity, proved that a 'white man's country' was no longer sustainable? Fazan's *History* was, inevitably, a weapon in both battles of interpretation. In the first contest, the British attempt to incriminate a militant nationalism, Fazan questioned the official view; in the second, in which settlers faced the inconvenient truth that the war could not have been won without the British Army and its Kikuyu allies under the administration's command, he stood by his friends in that administration, black and white. Both these points require elaboration, so that readers may begin to appreciate the moral tensions beneath Fazan's apparently calm detachment.

First then, the provincial administration, Fazan's old service, was determined to pin the blame for a terrible war on a Kikuyu political leadership that could never be accepted as nationalist. The Carter Commission, so their argument went, had met all legitimate African claims to restitution; post-war prosperity had benefited Africans as well as whites; most black Kenyans seemed content; only the Kikuyu had turned to violence. Bewildered by social change, they must have been manipulated into rebellion by their leaders' lies and a play on their superstitious fears. In the second battle for Mau Mau's meaning, however, many white settlers – particularly those too old to have fought alongside them – were equally determined to demonize Kikuyu 'loyalists'. However helpful they may have been in war, they must not be allowed to win the peace; after all, the KG could have done nothing without white leadership and its barbarous excesses proved that even the best of Africans could not be trusted with power. Fazan, despite his official status in the first instance and because of it in the second, wrote against the grain of both these popular white views. His portrayals of both Jomo Kenyatta, alleged 'manager' of Mau Mau, and of the Kikuyu 'loyalists', must be understood in context as the acts not only of a loyal pensioner but also of an independent moral agent.

The times were difficult to read for Kenyan whites, the audience Fazan had most in mind. Hitherto British rule had seemed secure in well-doing. Mau Mau proved otherwise. After the first critical months there was no risk that the insurgents would win in battle. The risk, rather, was that unbridled counter-terror would forfeit British rule any remaining legitimacy. By 1959 the colonial regime was indeed twice disgraced. Many white settlers thought it culpably weak, not least in relying on the 'loyalists'. The locally recruited Asian Home Guard seemed equally dangerous to them; sacrifice in war represented far too potent a political claim.[29] In contrast, many British politicians, not only of the Left, were appalled by the vengeful ferocity of colonial self-defence. This was where official abuses had 'political consequences', to use Fazan's own words.[30] Harold Macmillan's Conservative government accepted both the Empire's moral weakness in the face of African nationalism and the political impossibility of further violent resistance to its wind of change. Britain decided, accordingly, to negotiate an African exit as soon as decently possible – in the view of Kenya's settlers and officials, with indecent haste.[31]

Fazan, then, was writing in changing times; previous conceptions of right and wrong, justifiable and unjustified force, were in question. This volatility perhaps gave him greater freedom to exercise independent judgment. At all events, he broke ranks, discreetly, with the highest official in Kenya (the governor) in his assessment of Kenyatta, but stuck to the line his juniors (the DCs) had given him over the KG. He had good reason in both cases.

First then, the official struggle to bar Mau Mau's alleged leaders from the right to be called legitimate nationalists reached its height in

---

29 Gerard McCann, 'Sikh communities in Southeast Asia and East Africa, *c.* 1870–1970' (Cambridge University: PhD dissertation, 2010), p. 246.

30 In Chapter 15.

31 Ronald Hyam, *Britain's Declining Empire: The Road to Decolonization 1918–1968* (Cambridge: Cambridge University Press, 2006). Britain was well advanced in decolonising its West African territories, Ghana, Nigeria and Sierra Leone, none of which were colonies of white settlement.

1960, precisely when Fazan was compiling his *History*. Early in the year a constitutional conference in London had ended all prospect of multiracial power-sharing and set Kenya on the path to African majority rule. Despite this, high colonial officials recoiled from having to negotiate terms with the supposedly satanic Kenyatta, still in detention, and were determined to exclude him from Kenya's future. That was an unstated purpose of the authorised history of Mau Mau, published in May. Its author, Frank Corfield, another retired official but from the Sudan, had concluded, without any qualification, that 'Kenyatta and his associates' had callously *imposed* the horrors of Mau Mau on the Kikuyu and Kenya.[32] A new governor, Sir Patrick Renison, pressed the message home on the radio, calling Kenyatta the 'leader to darkness and death'. Despite such announcements, British control over the future was evaporating; in 1961 they had to concede that Kenyatta must soon be released.[33] He would almost certainly assume the nationalist leadership (as indeed he did) and so become the man with whom the British would have to deal.

In his only original contribution to the *History*, its introductory pages, Fazan softened Corfield and Renison's verdict on Kenyatta with deliberately less excited prose, perhaps with an eye to this changing political weather. Equally possibly (we do not know) Fazan may have recalled his opinion of 30 years' earlier, during the comparable 'female circumcision crisis' – to the effect that Kikuyu leaders had been shaken by the mass enthusiasm they had aroused. He had had experience of how easily protest could gather a crowd. Fazan scarcely mentioned Kenyatta in his analysis of Mau Mau origins and, while not absolving him of responsibility, hinted that he too might have been swept along by popular anger.[34] This substantial modification of the official line, incidentally, made it easier to talk to

---

32 Colonial Office, *Historical Survey of the Origins and Growth of Mau Mau* (London: HMSO, Cmd 1030, May 1960), p. 28, and many similar passages, especially 284 – but it is not true (p. 317) that Kenyatta's name 'appears on almost every page' of the *Survey*, which was Corfield's excuse for not including his name in the index.

33 For narratives of this period, see Keith Kyle, *The Politics of the Independence of Kenya* (Basingstoke: Macmillan, 1999) and B. A. Ogot, 'The Decisive Years 1956–63', in B. A. Ogot and W. R. Ochieng' (eds), *Decolonization and Independence in Kenya 1940–93* (London: James Currey, 1995), pp. 48–79.

34 *History of the Loyalists*, Chapter II. For Fazan's earlier view of Kikuyu leadership in crisis, see 'Political situation report by District Commissioner Kiambu', 12 January 1930: Kenya National Archives, DC/MKS.10B/12/1.

a man who had no longer led but had been hustled by others along the path to darkness and death.

Fazan's approach to the second battle for meaning, for the honour of the KG was, by contrast, true to his official culture of silence, to his British colleagues – some of them his former juniors – and to the chiefs on whom they all relied. The provincial administration had used its emergency powers to regain the authority it had lost to the government's technical departments in the years of post-war development.[35] The fight against Mau Mau 'brought all the house captains to the top'.[36] These, the DCs in the thick of the fight, had written their own district histories of the KG.[37] Fazan, a house captain himself, knew where his loyalties lay: with his chaps. It was not up to him to query his successors' accounts but to stitch them together in a single intelligible story. Chiefs, deputy school prefects, had been among the first of Mau Mau's victims. Their retainers, the Tribal Police, always under the administration, not the Kenya Police, had also suffered terrible losses and in self-defence had formed the nucleus of the KG. All whites knew that Mau Mau could not have been defeated so quickly without them. That the Tribal Police should have been 'the rallying point' was in Fazan's view 'a source of the greatest gratification to the several generations of the officers of the district administration'.[38] Not all settlers shared Fazan's gratification; some hardliners had publicised KG atrocity, comparing one case to the Nazi death-camp Belsen[39] – just the sort of thing to expect if Africans

35 Berman, *Control and Crisis*, Chapter 8. Huw Bennett, *Fighting the Mau Mau: The British Army and Counter-insurgency in the Kenya Emergency* (Cambridge: Cambridge University Press, 2013), pp. 34–6, qualifies this argument by concluding that Kenya administration and British army co-operated as equals.

36 The late Tom Colchester, retired official, in conversation, 9 February 1977. House captains are senior prefects in British private schools with considerable disciplinary power including, in Fazan and Colchester's (and your editor's) day, the authority to administer, with a bamboo cane, corporal punishment on their fellow pupils.

37 For the Fort Hall (Murang'a) story, see David Lovatt Smith's edition of Jock Rutherford, *A History of the Kikuyu Guard, 1953–1955* (Herstmonceux: Mawenzi Books, 2003, second edition 2006). For the role of Kenyan-born white officers in the Kikuyu Guard, see Ian Parker, *The Last Colonial Regiment: The History of the Kenya Regiment (T.F.)* (Milton Brodie: Librario Publishing, 2011), pp. 207–8, Chapters 13, 25 and 26.

38 Fazan, *History*, p. 13; Fazan thought Kenyatta nursed a particular hatred for the tribal police.

39 Anderson, *Histories*, p. 305.

should ever gain power. Fazan would have none of that racial meanness. His *History* was, above all, an uncomplicated tribute to brave men, the provincial administration's men, his men, to whose 'high courage' not only settlers but also Kikuyu owed a debt. By resisting Mau Mau's 'brutality, terrorism and atrocity' the 'loyalists' had rescued their fellow tribesmen from the 'depth of ignominy', so redeeming 'the name and prestige of their tribes from oblivion'. That was one reason why government had raised the 'loyalist' force in the first place. Had there been no KG, how could Kikuyu 'ever again be trusted or respected after the horrors and bestialities *Mau Mau* had committed? Or how could one endure to live among them?'[40] A tribute was no place to ask awkward questions.

In any case KG atrocities were, as Fazan says in Chapter 15, 'common knowledge'. In 1961 there was nothing to hide. There had been legal prosecutions, even if many had been abandoned, that were reported in the press and raised in question time at Westminster. As a magistrate Fazan will also have known more than most about the outrage in police and legal circles over the complicity of officials who betrayed the rule of law by covering up, in court or before trial, the KG's 'crimes of punishment'.[41] It was no defence to say that Mau Mau had been the first to enter this 'competition in crime' and so, when scores were settled by the KG, deserved little sympathy.[42] Mau Mau was not committed to uphold the rule of law; the administration, in contrast, had no higher – and in Kenya's history often no more irritating – duty.[43]

---

40 *History of the Loyalists*, Foreword and p. 79. Fazan refers all too briefly (in Chapter 15) to another Kikuyu claim to redemption, in European eyes at least, in the way in which 'pseudo gangs', composed increasingly of 'turned' Mau Mau alone, helped to destroy insurgent morale at the end of the war; see Parker, *The Last Colonial Regiment*, pp. 183–4, 230–1 (Mau Mau recruited into Kenya Regiment), 288–314, 331–2.

41 Anderson, *Histories*, Chapter 7.

42 To adopt Lord Lytton's description, in *The Desert and the Green* (London: Macdonald, 1957), p. 93, of acts by Irish republicans and their 'Black and Tan' opponents in the Irish War of Independence, 1922. As a young officer he asked himself questions (p. 74) that a younger generation must have pondered when fighting the Mau Mau: 'What was a just war? Could both sides be waging a just war at one and the same time? Were the laws and usages of war morally binding? Was it right to make war on savages because one British official was murdered?' For the settling of scores, see Parker, *Last Colonial Regiment*, p. 171.

43 For the often acerbic relationship between 'administrative justice' in which district commissioners used 'local knowledge' and the impersonal assessment of evidence proven in court required by the colonial judiciary, see H. F. Morris and James S. Read, *Indirect Rule and the Search for Justice: Essays in East African Legal History* (Oxford: Clarendon Press, 1972), especially pp. 98–103, 295–301.

Fazan said nothing of this dark side of the war. It was already known to his most likely readers; the governor's amnesty had deleted KG crimes from the legal agenda; the DCs' accounts had written them out of history. It was not up to him to reopen cases that had been closed five years earlier and on which his sources were silent.

He had two further reasons for selective silence that had nothing to do with either legal or editorial obstacles. First, the 'loyalists'' story simply deserved to be told; an account of gallant sacrifice and hard-won success. The sort of men whom he had trained and on whom he had relied throughout his career should not be forgotten 'in the surge of progress and development' to come,[44] in which – as Fazan did not say – a settler fear of too strong an African ally might well be replaced by a nationalist desire to punish black traitors. No one else was going to tell their story. Settlers found it hard enough to argue their own case for consideration; African politicians could not yet be certain that that future was theirs. Neither had reason to speak up for 'loyalists' – least of all any among the rising nationalists who owed their educational advantage to 'loyalist' fathers or uncles. But Fazan need not have worried. Poorer 'loyalists', it is true, probably fared no better than poorer insurgents. Younger, educated men, however, were recruited into the provincial administration, the instrument of future nationalist rule as much as it had been of past colonial control.[45] Second, a simple record that his DC contributors had created by silencing its intimate complexities was also needed to make the Mau Mau war intelligible. Fazan set out to create a readable narrative rather than a confusing medley of episodes, and one that was fit to be told. Like all wars, much of what went on in Kenya's Emergency was unspeakable in the opinion of both the British and the insurgents.[46] Fazan had his own reasons for thinking some things unmentionable. Judging by the rarity of their mention in his memoir, he found it difficult – and it was not easy for any British officer – to understand African beliefs in witchcraft or magic, which were deliberately exploited on both sides of the Mau Mau war.[47]

---

44 Fazan, *History*, Foreword.

45 Daniel Branch, *Defeating Mau Mau, Creating Kenya: Counterinsurgency, Civil War, and Decolonization* (Cambridge: Cambridge University Press, 2009), Chapters 5 and 6.

46 Luongo, *Witchcraft and Colonial Rule in Kenya*, pp. 167, 168.

47 Ibid., Chapter 7. More generally, see Richard Waller, 'Witchcraft and the law in colonial Kenya', *Past & Present* 180 (2003), pp. 241–75.

Also, as he emphasises, he was personally distressed by the way in which Mau Mau – but also, he might have added, the British use of the KG – had divided Kikuyu whom he had known and liked, even to the point of murder.[48] All civil wars reproduce intimate violence many times over; loyalist atrocity was often retaliation for Mau Mau atrocity.[49] To recall such unspeakable local, even familial, complications would make the story incomprehensible and re-open wounds that were better left to heal – especially at a time, although he did not say so in 1961, when the rise of nationalism and its inherent competitions might well have re-opened those wounds, causing them to fester.

Those who might be expected to have most resented Fazan's partisan picture should have the last word. After the Emergency was ended and their freedom of movement restored, a party of former Mau Mau detainees came unannounced to his Tigoni home. Mrs Fazan was nervous: were they seeking revenge? Fazan went out to meet them. They had come, they said, to thank him, a special magistrate during the Emergency, for his even-handed justice.[50] For one who had steered as straight a course as any through Mau Mau's moral minefield, this was a healing gesture indeed. A cricketer, he had played a straight bat.

As a Cambridge research student, looking into the history of the Nyanza Province, I was fortunate to interview Fazan in 1963, two years after his *History of the Loyalists* had appeared and a few months before independence. He was hoping that the outgoing colonial regime would repatriate him to England because of his roles in the Carter Commission, which most Kikuyu saw as an imperial betrayal, and in the subsequent inter-Kikuyu politics that had led, among other bitter disputes, to the Lari massacres, the bloodiest twin episode of the war.[51] Fazan was thought to be at risk from an independent government that, under Kenyatta, would surely seek revenge. He lent me another of his reports, written in the 1930s, on relations between central and local government in Britain and how these might be adapted for Kenya.[52] This research lay behind his encouragement of Nyanza's African local councils. It was my first encounter with his formidable mind. It is a

48 See note 61.

49 Branch, *Defeating Mau Mau*, Chapter 2.

50 Gillian Fazan, personal communication, 7 June 2013.

51 Anderson, *Histories*, Chapter 4.

52 *Report on the Relations between Government and Local Native Councils* (Nairobi: Government Printer, 1938).

pleasure to meet it again in the pages that follow. Here one can read, among much else, of his admiration for the forgiving nature of Jomo Kenyatta's post-colonial rule. Fazan was not to know that the new regime had deliberately destroyed an achievement for which he had been partly responsible, Kenya's emerging tradition of strong local government.[53]

Fazan's Kenya

Fazan tells little of his personal story in this quasi-official history. Anyone who has had read him in the archives, however, will recognise his analysis as very much his own. It stems directly from what we know of his observations in the field. No other official could have told the story with greater intellectual grasp. This is particularly true of the three appendices. The first two were written at the same time as the memoir, long after retirement. In one he reflects on the difference between colonial theory and administrative practice; in the other he dissects the complexity of African laws and customs, especially those relating to marriage and property. These alone make his memoir essential reading for anyone wishing to understand the colonial official's mind and the dilemmas that district officers faced daily. Readers will soon recognise Fazan's respect for the intellect of the Africans he and his colleagues thought they ruled. After explaining the moral economy of bride price he exclaims: 'Tribal custom could seldom be faulted on a point of logic!'[54]

Appendix III is still more important, as it was composed during his active service. Fazan did not include it in his memoir. It has been added here to reinforce the value of this publication. All economic histories of Kenya rely on his 'Economic Survey of the Kikuyu Reserves', written in 1932 with the help of fellow officers, to guide the Carter Commission's thoughts on land allocation and usage. No other attempt to analyse an African agricultural economy at this date can rival Fazan's attention to detail and the range of his enquiry – into what a family needed to earn in order to meet its growing needs and ambitions, what knowledge and tools it commanded, how far its land could meet its needs with those techniques, and so on. The original memorandum ran to nearly 70 closely-printed pages. Here there is room only for a heavily edited version. Fazan's account of the situation in his own time, which he

---

53 For a firsthand account, see B. E. Kipkorir, *Descent from Cherang'any Hills: Memoirs of a Reluctant Academic* (Nairobi: Macmillan Kenya, 2009), Chapter 7.

54 See below, Appendix II.

markets. Investment in African smallholder farming gave substance to ideas that Fazan had advocated 20 years earlier. Kenya began to decolonise internally before formal independence. In recording such colour-blind market reform, however, Fazan also continues to meditate on what changed least: the fierce white settler attachment to protected property that turned his Carter Commission's pragmatic proposals into a sacred text not open to critical reinterpretation.[58]

Second, this is change and continuity seen through official eyes, and very keen Fazan's were. He can explain the otherwise puzzling rise in the number of 'punitive expeditions' (PEs) that took place, even as the British succeeded in 'pacifying' more of Kenya in its early days. The reason is obvious enough to an official: for as one acquired more African allies, so one gained more local enemies. He may have had a particular sequence of 'PEs' in mind, in the northern part of the Nyanza Province, what is now Western province or Buluyia. While still learning his trade, two years after his arrival, Fazan recorded local memories of a PE less than 20 years earlier, on the border between the Luyia and Luo peoples. The British had intervened in 1896 to protect their main local ally, the Luyia chief Mumia, against a colonising Luo clan, the JoKager. In Luo memory the British Maxim gun 'quickly despatched 200 of the Luo'. The remainder fled, all save their chief, Gero. In a passage that makes one wish all district officers had been Oxbridge classicists, Fazan recorded, in an analogy not known to his Luo informant, that Gero 'sat outside his house, alone, in his bracelets and ornaments and waited, like a Roman Senator, for death'. The British only took him hostage, releasing him when the refugee Luo returned to their homes and so assented to British rule.[59]

Official eyes had to be trained to see through African eyes, but it was by watching one's seniors, men like Ainsworth, that one learned how to apply such knowledge. By the same rule of thumb, one had to allow for

58 The East African Royal Commission of the 1950s, with its advocacy of non-racial free markets, was deeply critical of the Carter Commission's 'tribal standpoint' – just as Fazan was critical, in his 1969 memoir, of racial protectionism. When the commission's chairman, Sir Hugh Dow, interviewed Fazan in Nairobi on 19 December 1953, he found him 'a very discursive witness'. The interview transcript, of only about 320 words, records Fazan's criticism of particular decisions taken by the earlier commission, but no comment on its overall tribal (and racial) premises. See *East Africa Royal Commission 1953–1955 Report* (London: HMSO, Cmd 9475, 1955), Chapter 6 and, for Fazan's interview, UK National Archives: CO.892/7/3/27.

59 Quoted from Central Nyanza Political Record Book Vol II by Ogot in *Southern Luo*, pp. 232–3.

the different executive capacities of African chiefs; some had hereditary authority behind them; others did not. Such practical wisdom had its drawbacks, however, as Fazan admits, in sometimes obscuring the need for change – such as the desirability of paying chiefs larger salaries as the economy diversified and as educated men, who might have become more progressive chiefs than their fathers, found better paid opportunities elsewhere. But some problems seemed beyond solution: like the complications of African land tenure set out in Appendix II.

Fazan's perspective was coloured by an official self-interest that saw itself as entirely disinterested. His was a life called to be a work in progress for all Kenya's peoples, regardless of race. The pursuit of what officials saw as the common good can be seen in three different aspects of his account. Like many officials, first, he found some aspects of Christian missionary work too otherworldly in pressing for cultural changes that Africans resisted, so making difficulties for their white rulers. One consequence, already discussed, was the greatest cultural clash in colonial Kenya, the 'female circumcision crisis', found in Chapter 7. Like all whites, Fazan thought clitoridectomy – today counted by many as female genital mutilation – cruel and degrading. For an administrator charged with keeping the peace, however, it was something Kikuyu would have to decide for themselves, in due course.

For much of his career, next, Fazan felt that his colleagues' work of progress in the African lands, the 'reserves', was not appreciated in the white settler community among whom many officials looked for off-duty recreation, friendships and, indeed, wives. This racial ignorance contributed to the settler determination to hang on to what privileges they could, a matter to which Fazan returns again and again, especially in relation to land, the core issue on which he had exercised more influence than most. This sense of being undervalued by white Kenya is as nothing to Fazan's anger against British policy at the end of empire. London's haste to get out put at risk all that the Kenya administration felt it had achieved in 70 short years. In Chapter 18 he finds it contemptible that, because Britain 'anticipated ticklish problems' between different local communities, it seemed 'advisable to hurry on with independence'. London was following what Fazan deplored as 'Kashmir lines' – that unresolved problem created by the partition of the British raj into India and Pakistan in 1947. In East Africa, similarly, Britain was leaving Africans to sort out problems for which they themselves were scarcely responsible, with some created and others aggravated by British rule. Fazan the colonial official despised the abdication of imperial responsibility.

As a third and final characteristic of this memoir, Fazan's judgment is stern, not reactionary. Indeed, one is struck by the modernity of his thought. He never reduces 'tribal' or 'racial' characteristics, as many did, to some unchanging cultural essence. This comes across most clearly in Appendix II, on African laws and customs. Here his analysis focuses on the moral and ethical relations between Africans and the dilemmas they faced, rather than, as conventional European opinion would have done, on their supposedly superstitious fears. One finds the same appreciation of the variety of human rationality and energy, responsive to circumstance, throughout his memoir – often subversive of conventional colonial wisdoms. He is uncertain, for instance, as are today's academic anthropologists, how far the various Dorobo or Okiek groups were Kenya's aboriginal peoples, as was a common colonial view, or more recent refugees from other, stronger, ethnic groups. He points out – contrary to the prejudicial pamphleteering that settler leaders engaged in after the First World War – that not all Kenya's South Asian immigrants were descended from low-caste railway-building 'coolies' but often, also, from intrepid traders who were the hardy pioneers of the African crop and livestock markets. He recognises that the hardships suffered by African porters in the First World War, without whom German East Africa (now Tanzania) could not have been conquered, constituted a ghastly rebuke to any British claim to conduct a 'civilising mission'. Later on Fazan acknowledges that the African way of interplanting different crops together, so offensive to tidy-minded Britons, was ecologically sounder than any monoculture. Most historians would also agree, in broad terms, with his analysis in Chapter 14 of the often tense relationship between the legal politics of the post-1945 Kenya African Union and the secretive Mau Mau movement. The official line in the 1950s and early 60s had been very different, as we have seen: the former was little more than a wickedly deceptive cover for the latter. Fazan had begun to have doubts in his *History of the Loyalists*; further reflection and, possibly, new reading, seems to have confirmed them.[60]

60 See Chapter 14. Carl G. Rosberg and John Nottingham's *The Myth of 'Mau Mau': Nationalism in Kenya* (New York, NY; London: Praeger & Pall Mall, 1966) appeared in 1966, three years before Fazan completed his memoir. His revised interpretation of the pre-Emergency years was similar in many respects but it is not now possible to say if he read this book. Nottingham did not know Fazan, so much more senior to him in the administration (personal communication, 24 June 2013).

Fazan's sober account of the subsequent 'Emergency' in Chapter 15, better termed internal war, is in marked contrast to some white hysteria of that recent past. And there was no need for him, as he did in 1969, to face up to the atrocities committed by government personnel, white and black, during the counterinsurgent campaign. Ten years after the Emergency ended, they were fading from British consciousness; independent Kenya's own policy was one of national amnesia; and historians had no access to the relevant archives so soon after the event. Despite this, memory clearly nagged. Furthermore, and still more worthy of note, he could understand how a British emergency played out in an African trauma of civil war, being personally distressed 'that of the two leading Africans I knew best and, perhaps, respected most, one should have been allegedly implicated in the plot to kill the other'.[61]

Above all, Fazan is readable. This Oxford Classics scholar has a delightful wit, often at the expense of official pretentions, as when he sums up the meagre government effort at the coast in the 1920s: 'it was possible at least to keep up appearances, if not to make progress.' He attributes to his African subordinates an equal keenness of mind. At some point in the same decade he warned a Kamba chief that a reservoir, which would have to be built with unpaid communal labour, might not solve the local water shortage. The chief nonetheless agreed to cooperate with his district commissioner: 'If a man has a barren wife, does he refuse to sleep with her? We will try.'

Conclusion

A personal conclusion is needed. I have tried to understand the most difficult aspect of Fazan's career, the perspective from which he wrote his *History of the Loyalists*. Many historians would blame the Mau Mau war in the 1950s on the failure of the Kenya Land Commission in the 1930s to deal justly with African complaints of 'stolen lands'. Fazan

61 Fazan refers to the murder of Waruhiu, a senior Kikuyu chief, in October 1952. As the most dramatic in a series of Mau Mau murders of fellow Kikuyu it persuaded the new governor, Sir Evelyn Baring, to ask London's permission to declare a state of emergency. Ex-Senior Chief Koinange was among those charged with conspiracy to commit the murder, on evidence that, in the deeply divisive atmosphere of the time, was bound to be partisan. While not convicted he was nonetheless detained. Fazan was instrumental in getting his conditions of detention improved. See Kenya National Archives file JZ. 7/17: Advisory Committee on Detainees, courtesy of Daniel Ostendorff, now working on his Oxford DPhil dissertation 'The Koinange dynasty and the development of Kenyan politics'.

believed, he had to believe, that within his contradictory terms of reference substantial justice had been done. If policy was to blame for Mau Mau, it was the fault of later white intransigence, not of the pragmatic realism of the Carter Commission, Fazan's commission, in trying to deal justly with two opposing interests.

I have focused on these core tensions in Fazan's text so that readers of this official's history, this memoir of a life's work in progress, may see more clearly some of the strains beneath the reflective calm of his Oxford-trained prose. But what of my own perspective? How has that shaped my attempt to understand him? Historians rightly admit the need to explain 'where they come from'. I would not have agreed to introduce and annotate his memoir were I not already fascinated by the man, by his rigour and complexity. He had a forbidding sense of the 'severity' with which alien rule must at times pursue what it believes to be beneficial measures; but he could also be angry at the injustice this could cause. Equally, he took a companionable pleasure in learning how other people lived, people he seems not to have thought of as subjects; he also researched into social conditions in all their detail before proposing changes in policy, intended for his subjects' benefit.

The man Fazan, however fascinating, can be understood only in the imperial context in which he lived and worked: one of extreme inequality in which personal relations, with all their mutual respect and sense of honourable obligation, were nonetheless possible between rulers and ruled. The calls on personal integrity were all the more severe. The challenges met by his generation might well have tested my own – and can be as gripping for us, therefore, as histories of the Second World War. How, we ask, would I have done? As a young man, between school and university, I briefly experienced the closing years of Fazan's Kenya. I did my British national service in the King's African Rifles in 1956–8, shortly after the regiment, white-officered with black other ranks, had been withdrawn from fighting the Mau Mau. My 'active service', in which not a shot was fired, was to defend northern Kenyan pastoralists from cattle rustlers and testicle raiders (so it was rumoured in the ranks) from across the Ethiopian frontier. Fazan had served in a neighbouring area 40 years before. My schoolboy command of a platoon of battle-tested Africans was in reality an extempore piece of theatre in which they coached me in how to act and speak my leading role. Hierarchical structure dissolved into joint enterprise, a tacit negotiation of what was permissible to both.

Fazan was made of sterner stuff than me but also knew the need 'to keep up appearances'. The British Empire was as much accident as design, both weak and strong, a mix of bluff and determination, dialogue and dictation, a performance as well as an intention, full of mixed motives and consequences – like any other human enterprise, especially one so vast and varied in its social and economic jigsaw.

Above all, the Empire was lived by real people, whether rulers or ruled, who tried to live justified lives in testing situations. Only propaganda – whether imperial, anti-imperial, or nationalist – can pretend to simplify the morality or immorality of the colonial situation. It could be as hard to justify one's rule over native 'others' as to be a native, subject to alien rule. An occupational hazard of the first role was fury at failure, at loss of face; and of the second, anger or shame at one's humiliation. Individual lives were built within sometimes horrifying contexts that individuals could rarely choose or hope to alter. Considered lives were built nonetheless and with self-reflective discipline, even behind a detention camp's wire, in a refusal to be defeated, or haunted by the violence of war.[62]

Both sides of the imperial divide hungered for conversation; life was intolerable without it. Rulers could not bear their natives to be silently sullen. Native subjects could not bear to be unheard; to make their rulers accessibly human they gave them shrewdly apposite nicknames. Blanket condemnation or praise for imperial rule are both too simple and the counterfactual – what would Africa be like had there been no European imperialism? – does not convince. In any case, the texture of colonialism differed greatly over space and time; no two colonies were the same, least of all in their degree of racial tension. Not many British officials in West Africa had to face the sort of tests that confronted Fazan and his colleagues in Kenya.[63]

Still fewer historians have been tested with the severity that could be a daily ordeal for imperial rulers or colonial natives. We cannot claim any moral superiority. To try to understand humanity in face of all its bewildering tests is our more modest vocation.

John Lonsdale

---

62 For reflective self-conduct under stress by a Mau Mau detainee and a Zimbabwean community, see Derek R. Peterson, *Ethnic Patriotism and the East African Revival: A History of Dissent, c. 1935–1972* (Cambridge: Cambridge University Press, 2013), Chapter 10, and Heike I. Schmidt, *Colonialism and Violence in Zimbabwe: A History of Suffering* (Woodbridge: James Currey, 2013), Chapter 7.

63 As Richard Rathbone, historian of the Gold Coast–Ghana, has reminded me.

PREFACE

Colonial Kenya was a place of extraordinary vitality and the story of the sixty-eight years of British rule is probably unique. No other African colony had so intricate a fusion of social and political interests and in few others did nation and nationalism grow up in circumstances of such rapid change in the lifestyle and awareness of the people as a whole. This book is conceived, therefore, not only as an account of Kenya's colonial history, but also as an analysis of development in the country at large – i.e., of those events and tendencies with which the administrative officer was especially concerned. Subject to the exception which I shall mention below, it is an account of colonial days as seen through the eyes of an administrative officer, myself, who came to the country in 1911 and remained to see it independent; and it is well to say at the outset that the administrative officer in Kenya was expected, while devoting most of his attention to his own province or district, to obtain a good working knowledge of the policies and problems of the entire country.

The exception is the account of historical background with which I begin. It was added after the rest of the book had been virtually completed, because it was evident that the achievements of colonial rule in Kenya could not be properly assessed without an examination of what the country was like before the British came and why Britain had proclaimed a Protectorate there at all. There is nothing original about it, but it is written with an understanding enriched by the conversations I had as a young man with coastal Arabs and old stagers who had some recollection of that time. As for the bulk of the book, I have not been limited by the same inexperience, but, while I have always tried to keep the balance true, some allowance must be made for the angle of vision from which particular events were regarded. A very large proportion of my service was spent in the African tribal areas, and consequently I am able to write with more authority about them than I can, for instance, about the White Highlands.

I have been much helped in the writing of certain chapters by various assignments of special duty which I have been fortunate enough to receive in the course of my service. For instance, a treatise which I wrote in 1928 on the tribal system of land tenure resulted in my being appointed to the Kikuyu Land Tenure Committee, and that again to my being sent to the Transkei for a period of comparative study, after which I served as secretary to the Kenya Land Commission of 1932/33. As well as the problem of land tenure, I also took a keen interest in the systems of administration in African lands, with the result that in 1937 I was seconded for a few months from the province of Nyanza to investigate and report on interrelations between African local councils and the central government. Another appointment of special interest I had was when for a few months in 1942 and continuously from the beginning of 1943 until the end of the war, I was seconded for liaison duties with the East Africa Forces overseas. Then, having retired, and returning to Kenya as a settler in 1949, I was given several assignments, the most interesting of which was with the Mau Mau Detainees Appeal Tribunal and the committee on the sociological causes of the outbreak.

These, in a sense, were highlights, but it was the long years spent in the normal business of district and provincial administration that provide the essential background to this book.

S. H. Fazan
c. 1969

A NOTE ON NAMES

The philosopher Heraclitus found great difficulty in the fact that all things were subject to constant change, so that before you had time to complete a statement about anything, it had changed into something else. But, as far as I know, he did not have the parallel difficulty that, even when things continued the same to all outward appearance, they were constantly being given different names. Africa has these problems to an exceptional degree. Fast as things themselves have changed, their names have changed still faster.

Countries — The Protectorate of British East Africa was proclaimed in 1895 but the country was not given the name Kenya until 1920, when it became Kenya Colony. The name Tanganyika was given after the First World War to that part of the former German East Africa which became a mandated territory under British protection. Since gaining independence it has amalgamated with Zanzibar and changed its name to Tanzania. Nyasaland and Northern Rhodesia have, since independence, changed their names to Malawi and Zambia respectively. Somaliland is now Somalia, the former Belgian Congo has become Zaire,[1]

1 Now (2014) the Democratic Republic of Congo.

while the country that used to be known as Abyssinia is now officially Ethiopia.

Natives: Africans

The word 'native' was universally used until 1931 to describe the indigenous population, but the African witnesses called to London to give evidence to the Joint Select Committee thought, when they heard themselves called natives in Britain, that there must be something derogatory about the term. The word 'African' shall, therefore, normally be used but if occasionally it is convenient to use the term 'Native' there will certainly be no intention to disparage. It was only rather slowly that the titles Native Tribunal, and Local Native Council were changed to African Court and African District Council respectively.

African Lands: Native Reserves

When the policy of making grants of land to non-Africans was started at the beginning of the century, it became necessary to ascertain what land was available for the purpose and what must be protected from alienation as being in effective occupation by African tribes. These tribal areas were first called Native Reserves or simply Reserves. Later, however, a distinction was made between Native Lands – later, African Lands – which were held to belong to African tribes on grounds of historical right and Reserves, which were deemed to have been added on grounds of economic need. In practice, the word 'Reserve' remained in general use, unless it was necessary to be precise.

Highlands

The word written with a capital 'H' refers to the land specially reserved to settlement by Europeans. When written with a small 'h', unless it has the prefix 'white' or 'European', it means simply high land –

PART I

British East Africa

1

Historical Background

The first known record of the East African coast occurs in a document of about the year 60 AD, *The Periplus of the Erythrean Sea.* It is there called Azania, and there is a reference to market towns, and to trade in gold, ivory, spices, incense, tortoise shell and slaves. It seems that trade with the coast had been carried on by dhows from India and Arabia from time immemorial, but it was not until the seventh century that written records of Arab immigration began. The first wave of Arab settlement was not Mohammedan – it is probable that many of the immigrants were fugitives from the wars of the Caliph – but, by 900 AD, Islam had begun to establish itself on the coast, and at the close of the fifteenth century the whole coast population were followers of Mohammed and inclined to resent the infidel. All the way between Mogadishu in Somalia to the north, and Sofala, centre of a flourishing gold trade, in Mozambique to the south, there were well-established, prosperous Arab towns, largely independent of each other but most of them owing a somewhat grudging allegiance to the Imam of Oman as their overlord.[1]

Ever since the capture of Constantinople by the Turks in 1453, which severed the main trade highway between Europe and India, keen interest had been aroused among European nations in establishing a sea

1 This 'Historical Background' is the most dated chapter in Fazan's account, reflecting the interests and knowledge of his own day. While factually correct, by today's historical canons it concentrates on European actors and actions, some of them ephemeral. The reading suggested in this and later notes is chosen, principally, to indicate how historians think they can show how local, African and Arab life was conducted, with more lasting legacies, in earlier centuries. See Randall L. Pouwels, *Horn and Crescent: Cultural Change and Traditional Islam on the East African Coast, 800–1900* (Cambridge: Cambridge University Press, 1987) for a standard history. For the sophisticated, socially unequal, urban commercial life of the coast, observed by a leading anthropologist, see John Middleton, *The World of the Swahili: An African Mercantile Civilization* (New Haven; London: Yale University Press, 1992).

Seyyid Said had become the ruler of Oman in 1806. Having secured his position in Muscat, he turned his attention increasingly towards the control of East African interests, gaining control of Mombasa in 1837, and his shrewd political and commercial instincts, coupled with energetic fiscal reform, were to do much to bolster the prosperity of the coast in the 50 years of his rule. Accepting the agreements his predecessors had made with the British, his attitude regarding the major European powers was, nevertheless, equivocal until after 1815 and the defeat of France; but in 1822, entering into a further agreement with Britain – the Moresby Treaty – he made a decree applying to his African dominions prohibiting the sale of slaves to subjects of Christian powers. The treaty, however, had little effect as it did not interfere with the trade in slaves between Zanzibar and Oman, and it depended for its enforcement on British naval patrols. In 1845, five years after Seyyid Said had moved his capital to Zanzibar, he therefore made another agreement with Britain, the Hamerton Treaty, which ended the export of slaves from Zanzibar to Oman, but the means of enforcement remained inadequate.[7]

In 1823, there occurred an incident of considerable historical interest for Kenya although it had no permanent effect.[8] The Mazrui Arabs of Mombasa, alarmed at the rapid growth of Omani power and being, as usual, at almost open war with them, determined to seek the protection of the British Crown. Accordingly, when Captain Vidal in *HMS Barracouta* put in at the port in December of that year, a deputation waited upon him and besought him to declare Mombasa a British protectorate. Mindful of Britain's treaty with Oman, he declined the request and sailed away, but the Mazrui, refusing to take 'no' for an answer, hoisted an improvised Union Jack over Fort Jesus. Shortly afterwards Captain Owen of *HMS Leven*, acting without orders and with more zeal than prudence, called on the Imam in Muscat, virtually gave him an ultimatum that slavery must be ended in three years, and announced his intention of sailing to Mombasa and granting it British protection. This he proceeded to do. In February 1824 he reached Mombasa while it was actually being bombarded by

7 For a Zanzibari view, see Abdul Sheriff, *Slaves, Spices, and Ivory in Zanzibar 1770–1873* (London: James Currey, 1987).

8 Fazan's account appears to rely on a reading of Sir John Gray, *The British in Mombasa 1824–1826, being a History of Captain Owen's Protectorate* (London; New York, NY: Macmillan, 1957). Unfortunately we do not know what literary aids to his memory Fazan will have had in his bookshelves as he wrote this manuscript.

an Omani fleet and, after hoisting an authentic Union Jack over Fort Jesus, he drew up a treaty guaranteeing, on Great Britain's part, that the post of Sheikh of Mombasa should be hereditary in the Mazrui family and, on the part of the Mazrui, that the slave trade should be abolished.

Captain Owen then proceeded on his way, leaving Lieutenant John Reitz, 21 years old, as first commandant, with the assistance of George Phillips, midshipman, a corporal of marines and three seamen. Attempting a short voyage of exploration down the coast, Reitz was struck down with malaria and the party had to return, carrying him on a stretcher. He died within sight of Mombasa but Midshipman Phillips carried on manfully. On one occasion he confiscated a dhow found to be carrying slaves and settled them at English Point, the first of the ex-slave settlements in Kenya. In September Commodore Nourse put into the port leaving Acting-Lieutenant Emery in command, but after little more than a year all told this first British Protectorate in Kenya came abruptly to an end. On proof that Mombasa was part of the Imam's dominions, the British Government repudiated Captain Owen's 'treaty' and evacuated the last survivors of the party. So ended a gallant, if misguided, episode.

The period of the great explorers came about 20 years later. The first in Kenya was the redoubtable Ludwig Krapf, a German who arrived under the auspices of the Church Missionary Society (CMS) in 1844, together with his wife, Rosina. They suffered terribly from malaria, and though his wife died in childbirth soon after they arrived, Krapf resolved to carry on. After staying in Mombasa long enough to master Swahili and begin his dictionary and translation of the Bible, he proceeded to Rabai on the borders of the Nyika country with his fellow missionary, Johann Rebmann. There they founded the first of an intended chain of mission stations and undertook a series of journeys into Taita, Chagga, and Kamba lands. On one of these journeys in 1848 the snow-capped mountain of Kilimanjaro was seen by Rebmann and in the following year Krapf had his first view of Mount Kenya from the Kamba country around Kitui.[9]

Tales of snow-capped mountains in the tropics were not easily credited when they first reached England, but a third German named

9 For what Krapf, Rebmann and their missionary successors at the coast achieved in terms of establishing a local Christianity, see Colin Reed, *Pastors, Partners and Paternalists: African Church Leaders and Western Missionaries in the Anglican Church in Kenya, 1850–1900* (Leiden: Brill, 1997).

Erhardt, who had joined Krapf and Rebmann, had carefully recorded their discoveries on a map, on which he also showed a large lake and a range of mountains – the Ruwenzori. Their position was the same as that for the 'mountains of the moon' which the ancient geographer Ptolemy had shown on his famous map of 150 AD, and this so excited the interest of the Royal Geographical Society that they equipped an expedition with a view to discovering what they presumed to be the source of the Nile.

This expedition was led by two officers of the Indian Army, Captains Burton and Speke. They made first for Lake Tanganyika, which they reached at Ujiji, but, hoping to find a northerly river flowing out of the lake, they had, somewhat crestfallen, to retrace their steps to Tabora. Thence Speke, leaving Burton behind unwell, proceeded north, reaching Lake Victoria in July 1858 at the place afterwards called Speke's Gulf near Mwanza. Some half a dozen years later he returned with James Grant, the naturalist, and worked up the western and northern shores of the lake until he reached the Falls, which he named after Lord Ripon, President of the Royal Geographical Society, correctly assuming that they were the source of the Nile.[10]

Soon after these events, the geography of the African hinterland from the Zambezi to Lake Tanganyika was being revealed by that greatest of all missionary explorers, Dr David Livingstone, in a series of journeys undertaken between 1859 and his death in 1873 at the age of 60.[11] He conceived his task as being 'the wide diffusion of better principles' rather than 'going about with a Bible under the arm', and the object of his journey was to open up the interior of tropical Africa to Christianity and trade. If the slave markets were supplied, he wrote, 'with articles of European manufacture by legitimate commerce, the trade in slaves would become impossible'. One notable success that crowned his work was that, in 1873, following his death, the slave market in Zanzibar was finally closed. This happened when Sir John Kirk, the British Resident General, through patient and skilful diplomacy, at last succeeded in persuading Sultan Barghash to ban all transport of slaves in or from his

---

10 Alan Moorehead, *The White Nile* (New York, NY: Harper, 1960 and many subsequent editions) remains a most readable account.

11 As one of the greatest of Victorian heroes, Livingstone has attracted many biographers. But there were African heroes too, for whom see Donald Simpson, *Dark Companions: The African Contribution to the European Exploration of East Africa* (London: Paul Elek, 1975); Chapter 8 tells of the 'faithfulness and heroism' with which Livingstone's African companions ensured that his body would return home.

dominions, but the threat of blockading Zanzibar had to be added before the Sultan gave way.[12]

It was trade, however, rather than any decree, that defeated slavery in the long run, just as Livingstone had foretold.[13] A protagonist of this method was Sir William Mackinnon, founder of the British India Shipping Line. General Gordon, Governor of Equatoria in the southern Sudan, was also enthusiastic, sending an expedition to Formosa Bay to prospect a route from Lamu to the Upper Nile, both for trade purposes and as a means of protecting the Sudan against encroachment by the French, who were actively extending their influence in that direction from French Equatorial Africa. Although the project was frustrated, very similar objects were to inspire the inception of the Uganda Railway a score of years later.

In 1873, about the same time as the Gordon expedition, the explorer H. M. Stanley reached Uganda by the southern route through Tanzania and visited Mutesa, the Kabaka of Buganda. Finding him then favourably disposed towards Christianity, he wrote a letter, with Mutesa's consent, inviting missionaries to come. This he sent to General Gordon, who forwarded it to the *Daily Telegraph* in London, in prompt response to which a party of CMS missionaries arrived in 1877 and were followed ten years later by a party from the French White Fathers' Mission on the Nile.[14]

In 1883, the young explorer and naturalist Joseph Thomson was chosen by the Royal Geographical Society to seek a route through the Kenya highlands to the Lake. Passing through Masai country peacefully and unmolested, he only achieved this with some ingenuity – producing his false teeth as a sign of magic powers when the occasion demanded. That he succeeded in his hazardous journey without any display of force was important for future prospects of opening up the country to trade. In this respect his journey was to be of more abiding

12 Alastair Hazell, *The Last Slave Market* (London: Constable, 2012) is a gripping account. For a more general history of the Indian Ocean slave trade and its abolition, see R. W. Beachey, *The Slave Trade of Eastern Africa* (London: Rex Collings, 1976).

13 Fazan was only partially correct, for trade was not enough by itself. For the surprisingly slow death of slavery under colonial rule and legislation, see Frederick Cooper, *From Slaves to Squatters: Plantation Labor and Agriculture in Zanzibar and Colonial Kenya, 1890–1925* (New Haven, CT; London: Yale University Press, 1980).

14 The consequences were momentous for the history of Christianity in Africa. Buganda's martyrdoms and religious wars of the late nineteenth century have attracted a large historiography. For a vivid account, see John Iliffe, *Honour in African History* (Cambridge: Cambridge University Press, 2005), Chapter 10.

raids. There appears to be no record of any serious fighting in the open, but the post which Captain F.D. Lugard had established at Dagoretti was subjected to frequent raids and had to be abandoned. Fort Smith, which succeeded it, was intermittently raided and it was not until 1893, when Francis Hall was in charge there, that hostilities came to an end after a peace-making ceremony with the local Kikuyu headmen and Masai elders. This ceremony was arranged with the help of Kinanjui, a remarkable man of mixed Kikuyu and Dorobo blood, who, from being a servant at Fort Smith, rose in after years to become paramount chief of the Kikuyu.[18]

In 1890 Lugard received orders to proceed to Uganda and take charge. Refusing to pay tribute, *hongo*, to the Masai or other tribes encountered on the way, he explained how very different his caravan was from those of the Arabs and Swahili. He pointed out that he was well provided and would pay fair prices for any food his men might require, and that though he desired only peace, he would fight hard if attacked. Consequently, he had no trouble. The further advance of the company beyond Kikuyu through Ravine and the Baringo district to Lake Victoria was achieved with no great difficulty. The only tribe to offer sustained opposition was the Nandi, against whom punitive measures had to be undertaken before they stopped raiding their neighbours and pillaging passing caravans.

Much success had been gained by the company in pacification among most of the tribes encountered and, if they had not been able to stop slavery altogether, they had at least denied the route to the slavers' caravans and forced them to seek alternative routes in the North, thus protecting the tribes over which the company's influence extended and preventing them from raiding each other and selling their captives to the slavers. The essentials for the development of legitimate trade had been thus created but, by 1892, it had become clear that the company was facing a task beyond its financial capacity. It could not hope to administer and control the immense extent of the British East African sphere of influence with its very limited resources, especially as there was never any hope of quick financial returns to be had from the East

---

18 Godfrey Muriuki, *A History of the Kikuyu 1500–1900* (Nairobi: Oxford University Press, 1974) would agree with this account, adding only that Hall and Kinanjui (sometimes Kinyanjui) together exercised considerable force in order to establish a peace among the Kikuyu that was also agreeable to the British. Lugard's diaries are essential source material: see Margery Perham and Mary Bull (eds), *The Diaries of Lord Lugard*, 3 vols (London: Faber, 1959).

African hinterland. There was little beyond ivory of any export value, except perhaps for rhino horn, hippo teeth, ostrich feathers, beeswax and the hides of fallen cattle and, as for cereals and pulses, all that the company could do, and that with difficulty, was to buy enough with their trade goods to feed their own troops and carriers. Nor did the funds available or in prospect permit them to contemplate a programme of slow and methodical development. Regarded, therefore, as a private trading enterprise, the company could not have carried on but, as a pioneering effort, it was a gallant and successful venture. It was now inevitable, however, that if the British sphere of influence was to be developed, the government should step in and declare a protectorate.

2

Early Days of the Protectorate

Being unable to raise further capital, the company decided that it must withdraw from Uganda – an action which would have left the missionaries there in a very precarious position – or else it must ask the British Government to vote the funds for a railway. In the upshot, after much hesitation and under much public pressure, the British Government voted the funds and took over the company and its officers. Two protectorates were declared: one, called Uganda, was proclaimed in 1893 and the other (Kenya) was called the British East Africa Protectorate and was proclaimed two years later. There was an alteration of the boundary between them in 1902, making them, in respect of their common boundary, substantially as they are at present.[1]

While authority was being transferred to the government there was trouble at the coast between two rival sections of the Mazrui Arabs who, turbulent as ever, were disputing about the sheikhdom of Mombasa. The company's ruling, which had awarded it to Rashid bin Salim, Liwali of Takaungu, was disputed by a kinsman named Mabruk bin Rashid. Fighting broke out and spread along the coast and the first Commissioner of the British East Africa Protectorate, Sir Arthur Hardinge, took over with a rebellion on his hands. The trouble lasted ten months, and troops had to be called over from India before order was restored.

Upcountry, matters went on much as before, the company's officers having been converted to government servants. There was now more money available and, with it, more activity, particularly in survey expeditions and preparations for the railway. The increased tempo of

---

1 G. H. Mungeam, *British Rule in Kenya 1895–1912: The Establishment of Administration in the East Africa Protectorate* (Oxford: Clarendon, 1966) is the standard narrative of the establishment of British rule in the years before Fazan arrived as a young cadet. Mungeam would not dissent from Fazan's account.

activity, however, was not matched by any corresponding increase of staff, and trouble resulted. The system of head-load porterage was wasteful and quite unsuitable for long-distance journeys, for a porter carrying maize meal would consume his own load in 30 days. Donkey transport had been tried but the death rate among the pack animals was enormous. Efforts were being made to improve the tracks and make them fit for wagons, but there were as yet no wagons or trained oxen to dray them. Meanwhile, the porter caravans became larger and larger.

In November 1895 a caravan consisting of 1,100 men was sent forward from Fort Smith with food supplies for Ravine. A young Swahili headman was in charge of the safari. All went well enough on the outward journey, and Ravine was reached with the loads intact. It was in the Kedong Valley on the return journey that disaster occurred. Some Masai elders, who had accompanied the caravan from Naivasha, had warned the headman to be sure to keep his porters well in control because a large Masai *manyatta* lay close ahead. The first half of the caravan passed it without incident but some of the rest got out of hand, attempted to drive off Masai cattle, and even forced their way into the *manyatta* itself and started molesting the girls. The Masai *moran* were enraged and, in a few moments, the place was a shambles. There followed a merciless butchery; the pursuit along the Kedong valley lasted for miles and 555 Kikuyu and 90 Swahili from the caravan lost their lives. In the aftermath a trader named Andrew Dick was also killed while taking severe reprisals in the company of two French sportsmen.

This was the worst but not the only serious disaster which occurred in connection with the carriage or requisitioning of supplies. To guard against a recurrence, a government station was opened at Naivasha in 1896, where there was already the beginning of a trading post, to serve as a half-way halting place for caravans between the Kikuyu centre at Fort Smith and Ravine on the route to Uganda. The fort at Naivasha was built by Major Eric Smith, who had also built the fort bearing his name, and half a company of Sudanese troops was stationed there, with the other half at Ravine.

Early in the following year signs of discontent were noticed among these troops. The grounds of complaint, which were duly reported but without any effective action being taken at headquarters, were short rations and inadequate pay received at irregular intervals. The pay, when it came, was only 5 rupees a month, compared with 15 rupees being paid at Machakos. It was explained to the men that an increase of rations was impossible until fresh supplies arrived from Kikuyu: meanwhile, they would receive an issue of cloth which, presumably, they were expected to barter with the local natives for food. In

place. Thus a new station called Nairobi opened on the railway near the Kikuyu/Masai border, and soon eclipsed the company's posts at Ngongo Bagas and Fort Smith. Because of fortunate circumstances, including a long halt called while the route ahead was being surveyed, Nairobi grew rapidly until, in 1907, the administrative headquarters of government were moved there.

It must have seemed very unlikely that the railway could be made to pay its way for many years to come, and the best chance of finding revenue appeared to be in the cultivation of the highlands by European settlers.[5] This was the view of Sir Charles Eliot who was governor, then called commissioner, from 1901 to 1904. He was much struck by the emptiness of the highlands and the fact that their climate seemed eminently suitable for white settlement. He was an enthusiast for the project both for its economic potential and for its own sake, and from that time onwards it became the policy of successive governors to encourage and foster white settlement. Subject to certain safeguards, this policy had the full support and approval of government in the United Kingdom. In 1901 there were only a dozen settlers in the country, but from then on they began to arrive in considerable numbers and were soon accorded a share, which was to become very prominent, in the councils of government. The influx of settlers was not without its difficulties, however, particularly in securing labour for the farms. The first major settlers' indignation meeting, the precursor of several, was held in 1908 and the first Labour Commission sat in 1912. It was a problem that was to be perennial.[6]

While white settlement was being established as the bedrock of the government's plans to make the economy self-sufficient and the railway a paying proposition, the administration was being expanded and

---

5 The standard account remains M. P. K. Sorrenson, *Origins of European Settlement in Kenya* (Nairobi: Oxford University Press, 1968).

6 A full account of Kenya's often notorious labour history is provided by Anthony Clayton and Donald C. Savage, *Government and Labour in Kenya 1895–1963* (London: Frank Cass, 1974). The root cause of 'the labour problem' and its sometimes coercive remedy was the inability of an undeveloped white settler agricultural economy with costly access to distant markets to attract enough labour from out of the generally self-sufficient African peasant economies that Fazan spent his career trying to improve. Plantations which produced coffee or tea – which Africans were prevented from growing until the 1930s and 1950s, respectively – were, by contrast, generally profitable enough to attract sufficient labour with acceptable pay and conditions. In the early 1920s, however, even coffee needed the forced labour of women and children in the picking season, recruited by British officials and African chiefs.

taxation introduced.[7] From the earliest years of the protectorate the country had been divided into four provinces under sub-commissioners. The East African Rifles had also been formed and the courts system organised. In 1901 hut tax regulations were issued and nine years later provisions for poll tax were also introduced. The Village Headman Ordinance of 1902 resulted in many prominent Africans being enlisted as government servants, and the Order in Council which came out in the same year gave the commissioner specific authority to make a wide range of appointments. Departments of government were subsequently created and municipalities set up. The executive was further expanded in that the heads of the departments and two nominated non-officials were appointed to the Executive Council, which was, in theory, an advisory body, but in fact served as the chief organ of policy. In 1907 the Legislative Council also came into being with five officials from the Executive Council and three nominated European non-officials. This followed the move in 1905 whereby responsibility for the protectorate passed from the Foreign Office to the Colonial Office.[8]

It was not only in the burgeoning administration that government expanded, for ever more extensive areas of territory were also being brought under its control. In the days of the company there had been neither the resources nor the inclination to establish any more control over the land than was necessary to protect the caravan route to Uganda. Initially this meant simply the building of strongpoints along the way, but during the 1890's the local influence of officers stationed at these forts grew steadily wider. This was achieved largely by patient

---

7 The best studies of Kenya's British administration and its officials are T. H. R. Cashmore [himself a former district officer in Kenya, after Fazan's day], 'Studies in district administration in the East Africa Protectorate (1895–1918)' (Cambridge University: PhD dissertation 1968, available from the Cambridge African Studies Centre as an occasional paper), and Bruce Berman, *Control and Crisis in Kenya: The Dialectic of Domination* (London: James Currey, 1990), especially Chapter 3. Fazan was the first former official Berman interviewed when doing his doctoral research in 1968. Charles Chenevix Trench [a former district commissioner], *Men Who Ruled Kenya: The Kenya Administration 1892–1963* (London; New York, NY: Radcliffe Press, 1993), is stronger on the later years of colonial Kenya and has disappointingly little to say of Fazan, quoting him only as a commentator on his junior officers' actions (pp. 86, 102–4).

8 The best political histories of colonial Kenya's early decades are George Bennett, *Kenya, a Political History: The Colonial Period* (London: Oxford University Press, 1963); and Robert M. Maxon, *Struggle for Kenya: The Loss and Reassertion of Imperial Initiative, 1912–1923* (London: Associated University Presses, 1993).

work in negotiating treaties and building up friendly relations with the Africans, but it also involved punitive expeditions to protect the caravans and later the railway. Nor were these officers merely the guardians of the trade routes, for they also had a civilising intent. Slavery was still a problem and the expansion into the Kitui district of Akamba country was prompted largely by a desire to deprive the slaving caravans of their northern route. The expansion into Nyanza was likewise in part intended to deprive Arab and Swahili slavers of a hunting ground, but Hobley's work there from 1894 to 1900 also showed clearly how the assertion of the *Pax Britannica* was seen increasingly as a worthy end in itself, curbing the internecine warfare which seemingly had for centuries restricted African development. Even so the Protectorate government, under the auspices of the Foreign Office, was very reluctant to impose its authority over the country at large and it was not until 1901 that F. D. Hall at last received permission to establish the post at Murang'a that was to bear his name.

Meanwhile punitive expeditions were assuming a different character.[9] In the early days of protecting the trade routes they were simply a show of strength and fitted easily into the pattern of African hit-and-run warfare. Later, as British authorities increasingly undertook to guarantee the safety of local African populations, punitive expeditions were undertaken in retaliation for raids, not only on trading caravans and railway construction gangs, but on protected African communities as well. This led inevitably to a rise in their frequency and, sometimes, in their scale. The first expedition against the Nandi in 1895 had been provoked when tribesmen raided land of the Abaluhya and killed a trader named Peter West. Thereafter, the armed forces were to be kept fairly busy, principally in action against the Nandi, but also against the Kikuyu and Embu of the Mount Kenya area and westwards in Sotik, Kisii and against the Bugusu, the most northerly section of the Abaluhya.

The wider responsibilities of protecting friendly Africans cast on government the obligation of ensuring that the raids of hostile neighbours were not repeated, and so, instead of withdrawing after each expedition, strongpoints were built and strategic gains consolidated. This in turn stretched the commitments of government forces, with the result that in 1902 the army and the police were separately constituted,

---

9 Fazan's analysis of the changing character of 'punitive expeditions' is confirmed by John Lonsdale, 'The Conquest State of Kenya, 1895–1905', Chapter 2 in Berman and Lonsdale (eds), *Unhappy Valley*, pp. 13–44.

one as the KAR under officers seconded from the British Army, and the other as the British East Africa Police, similarly constituted, with Africans up to the rank of sergeant, but with higher ranks from Britain and India.

These measures were an indication of the changing nature of government control – now far more thorough than in the days of the company, though still very far from being a military occupation. Despite all the military activity in the early days of the protectorate, conquest was never contemplated and there was no case of unprovoked invasion of African lands. Indeed, with its meagre resources, it was important for government to maintain as low a military profile as was possible. By 1908 punitive expeditions had virtually ceased and, thereafter, with the exception of two minor rebellions – of the Giriama in 1914 and the Masai incident in 1918 – military activity was confined to the Northern Frontier province where stock thieving was endemic and where well-armed raiders from Abyssinia were already making their presence felt.[10]

In the course of little more than a decade, protectorate rule over the hinterland had thus replaced tribalism and tribal warfare with a much more thorough system of authority. Nowhere was this more clearly demonstrated than with the 'Masai Move'.[11] This comparatively small tribe had terrorised the country far and wide for generations. Their warriors were well trained and organised, both in open fighting and especially for night raids in which they fell upon their enemies unawares, slaughtered men and women without mercy and plundered their cattle. It happened that, in the closing years of the nineteenth century, a very severe outbreak of rinderpest had killed vast numbers of their cattle and the tribe itself had been weakened by internal fighting. By the time the protectorate was declared in 1895 their power had been seriously diminished.

---

10 For these episodes of resistance, which are important today in justifying ethnic claims to be included in Kenya's national story, see Cynthia Brantley, *The Giriama and Colonial Resistance in Kenya, 1800–1920* (Berkeley; Los Angeles, CA: University of California Press, 1981); Lotte Hughes, *Moving the Maasai: A Colonial Misadventure* (Basingstoke: Palgrave Macmillan, 2006); John Lamphear, *The Scattering Time: Turkana Responses to Colonial Rule* (Oxford: Clarendon, 1992).

11 Fazan's account of Anglo–Maasai relations which follows, especially his imputation of 'mixed motives' to the British, would not be disputed, other than in some details, either by R. D. Waller, 'The Maasai and the British, 1895–1905: The origins of an alliance', *Journal of African History* 17 (1976), pp. 529–53, or by Hughes, *Moving the Maasai.*

well have played too great a part, the land to which the Masai were moved was ample enough to provide, on average, more than a square mile per family of five, and the quality over all was well up to the Kenya average. The government also took steps to improve watering facilities for livestock by boring wells in the more arid eastern areas; there was no problem in the west.

It might have been wiser, in the light of after experience, to have devoted a larger share of the land vacated in the first move to extending other tribal areas – although it is doubtful if the Masai would have agreed to the move if they had thought this would be done – and rather less of it to European settlement.[13] But there was no evidence of congestion among any local tribe and, the total land in Kenya in relation to population at that time being only about 11 persons to the square mile, no problem in that direction was apprehended. It was regarded as axiomatic that the best economic use for vacant land in the highlands was to make it over to European settlement, and the British government had specifically approved the policy. The individual settler, while pursuing his own ends like everybody else, regarded himself as playing a patriotic part in the general development of the country.

As to the land vacated in the second move, the Samburu, a neighbouring and kindred tribe from the north, moved in on a large part of it as the Masai moved out, and in the event they were never disturbed. A special issue arose over the part known as the Leroki Plateau, an attractive highland area of some 850 square miles suitable for stock farming. Representations made to the governor by the European members of the Legislative Council were sent on to the secretary of state, claiming that this land had been promised for settlement at the time of the Masai move, but he replied in a dispatch of 1929 that he was not convinced, and the matter was held over for consideration by the Kenya Land Commission of 1933/4. The Commission recommended that the Leroki Plateau should be classed as land over which the natives should have a prior but not exclusive right. This was accepted and, in point of fact, no alienation ever took place.[14]

---

13 Here is an early indication of Fazan's meditation, discussed in the Foreword, on the rights and wrongs of Kenya's land allocation, for which, as this paragraph shows, there was no easy answer.

14 White settler politicians felt that this decision over rights to the Leroghi Plateau, as it is now spelled, was an imperial betrayal. As secretary of the Kenya Land Commission, Fazan was heavily involved in this decision and it was doubtless important to him to record this example of a refusal to bow to settler demands.

Following the Masai moves, in 1913 an event took place which was destined to have important repercussions later on, though it passed without much comment at the time.[15] It was the demarcation of about 50 square miles of the Limuru area for European settlement in addition to the land in the Rift Valley vacated by the Masai. The name *Limuru* was of Masai origin but the land sequestered, although sparsely occupied at the time, was definitely in the area of effective occupation by the Kikuyu tribe. As elsewhere, land in the actual occupation of natives was deemed to be excluded from the lease when the land was let for settlers' farms, but most of the occupants preferred to take their compensation and go.

In conjunction with the entrenchment of European settlement, the years immediately preceding the outbreak of the First World War were also important for a number of measures designed to consolidate the protectorate government. Two enactments of cardinal importance for the internal administration of tribal lands were the Native Tribunal Rules of 1911 and the Native Authority Ordinance enacted in the following year. They gave closer definition and direction to the system of rule – through chiefs and headmen, councils of elders and tribunal courts – which was already being fostered by the provincial and district administration. For some districts it meant no more than the development of an organisation already existing; in others much had to be improvised but there was always something on which to build.

At this time an ordinance was also prepared – but not enacted until 1915 – which gave definition to government control of land. In the early 1900's doubts had arisen as to the legal power of the governor to make grants of land either by lease or in freehold –except in the Coast Strip where the right had been conferred by treaty with

15 The meditation on land continues: Fazan here refers to what turned out, in retrospect, to be the deep historical origins of the two Lari massacres of March 1953, the bloodiest episodes of terror and counter-terror in the Mau Mau war; for later references, see below, Chapters 12 and 15. David Anderson, *Histories of the Hanged: Britain's Dirty War in Kenya and the End of the Empire* (London: Weidenfeld & Nicolson, 2005), Chapter 4 would concur with Fazan on the need to understand the massacres within a long history of land alienation to white settlers and the consequent disputes between Kikuyu as to how they should respond. Fazan himself lived at Tigoni, in the disputed area, after his retirement – which may be interpreted as a statement of faith in the justice of his resolution of the border dispute between black and white, on lines he had proposed in 1930 and were then adopted in the *Report of the Kenya Land Commission* (London: HMSO, Cmd 4556, 1934), pp. 114–18 (hereafter Carter commission, *Report*).

the Sultan of Zanzibar.[16] Legal opinion obtained by the Foreign Office from the law officers of the Crown was that the governor had such power where land was not occupied by any native population by virtue of the Protectorate, but to make assurance doubly sure, the East Africa (Lands) Order in Council was issued in 1901 which defined Crown lands in terms of public, as distinct from private, i.e. tribal, rights. This was amended in 1915 by the Crown Lands Ordinance which declared, in effect, that all land in British East Africa outside the Coast Strip was Crown land. In practice what it did was to add to the definition contained in the 1901 legislation the words '... and shall include all lands occupied by the native tribes of the Protectorate and all other lands reserved for the use of the members of any native tribe'. There was no intention, of course, to extinguish tribal and individual rights. These were protected by special clauses in all grants and leases, but it was plainly intended, nevertheless, that the ordinance should give the government a clear right of land disposal. This was, in many respects, a response to settler pressure. There had been a good deal of settler resentment occasioned by the limitations on title imposed by the Crown Lands Ordinance of 1902, which not only restricted the length of leases and the size of holdings, but also imposed strict conditions as to minimum development, payment of taxes, transfer only with specific permission and security for native homes and villages. The system had been designed to prevent speculation in land but the settlers argued that limitation on title served only to check legitimate business and investment. More fundamentally, they simply objected to having the government as overlord.[17] The upshot was that although many of the conditions remained, provision was made under the 1915 ordinance for grants of 999-year leases of agricultural land and, subject to specific approval of the secretary of state, the governor was empowered to dispose of land as he saw fit.

---

16 For the history of colonial Kenya's land law and other agrarian laws see Y. P. Ghai and J. P. W. B. McAuslan, *Public Law and Political Change in Kenya: A Study of the Legal Framework of Government from Colonial Times to the Present* (Nairobi, Oxford University Press, 1970), Chapter 3.

17 Historians would here agree with Fazan, who is also setting out some of the constraints of which he had to take note when secretary of the Carter Land Commission. The most eloquent statement of a leading settler view, critical of government and doubtless on Fazan's bookshelf, is Elspeth Huxley's two-volume *White Man's Country: Lord Delamere and the Making of Kenya* (London: Chatto & Windus, 1935).

3

First Impressions

The pioneer days had ended with the nineteenth century, and the first dozen years of the twentieth had set the pattern for future development. The Protectorate of British East Africa had been proclaimed in 1895 and, seven years later, the boundaries had been enlarged so as to include certain territory previously administered from Uganda. The seat of government had been moved to Nairobi, and executive and legislative councils had been set up. Peace had been established among the East African tribes and pledges had been given concerning the reservation of an area in the highlands for European settlement. The country had been mapped into provinces and districts, and effective administration had been established. It was a good time to be looking round.

One day in December 1911, there arrived at Kilindini by the little Union Castle steamer *Guelph* nine new administrative cadets for East Africa, fresh and raw from Oxford and Cambridge. Not a very significant event in the history of East Africa, it was a thrilling moment for the nine concerned, the point of first impact. Our ignorance of the country until that moment was profound. One had an uncle who had been a judge in Zanzibar and another, a brother in Somaliland, but the rest of us started with no more than the three weeks' instruction we underwent before sailing, the precursor of a far more elaborate full-time course. It was limited to short lectures on law (good), tropical diseases (frightening), the colonial system of accounts (adequate but uninspiring) and plane table surveying – on Saturdays and mostly skipped.

There were no alongside berths at Kilindini in those days so we were rowed ashore to the rudimentary steps and landing stage. There, those cadets who were bound for Uganda left by train for upcountry, and the remainder of us proceeded by trolley car the two miles to Mombasa. The trolley on rails was then one of the island's more eccentric features. Until it was removed during the war to support the army's advance, it served to connect house and office as well as Kilindini and the town;

and, alongside the track, where sisal had been planted, uncomfortable upsets at sharp bends were a common experience.

For three or four days after our arrival we enjoyed the hospitality of the chief justice, Sir Robert Hamilton, and of Judge Bonham Carter. The seat of government had been moved to Nairobi some five years earlier, but the High Court remained in Mombasa for the time being. In tribute to the old capital an annual session of legislative council was held at Mombasa, and this happily coinciding with our arrival, we were fortunate to meet some of our future superior officers in congenial surroundings.

After attendance at the magistrate's court in the mornings there was leisure time to wander around the town. Fort Jesus then dominated the Mombasa scene even more than it does now. It had been built at the end of the sixteenth century by the Portuguese and, except for a short period, was held by them continuously for just on 100 years until, after a siege which lasted three years, it was taken by storm by Omani Arabs after the garrison had been decimated by plague. It seemed a good justification for Mombasa's alternative name of M'vita, war, in contrast to that other port to the south in German East Africa, Dar es Salaam – haven of peace.

Mombasa port and harbour – not to be confused with Kilindini[1] – was reserved then as now for dhows, and presented an animated and colourful scene. The Old Town, with its narrow streets, teemed with the exotic variety of its people, *hamali* carts, goats and chickens and a pervasive smell which was mostly copra. The population appeared predominantly Arab and Arab-type Swahili, with Indians next. It was estimated at some 33,000, compared with 19,000 in Nairobi. The Europeans in Mombasa numbered about 300. There were few up-country Africans to be seen in the town but many were, no doubt, employed on the railway and at the port.

The first part of the 300 miles of the train journey to Nairobi was uninspiring, except for the majestic sight of Kilimanjaro some 60 miles away on the German side of the border. Once the palm fringe of the coast belt lay behind us, the land rose through the red dust and scrub of the Taru desert over which night was falling. It was in the early morning that the thrilling scene opened out over the wide plains of the highlands, revealing herds of antelope and, for background, the

---

1 Mombasa harbour, used for centuries, was along the northern shores of Mombasa Island. Kilindini docks, which were built in the twentieth century – and now generally called the Mombasa docks – run along much of its southern shore.

abruptly rising hills of the Akamba and Masai. Yet the abiding thought which the journey left in my mind was not the game or scene; it was the closeness of Kilimanjaro and the German border. It was the year of the Agadir incident and there was much speculation on the chances of war.[2]

Arriving in Nairobi a few days before Christmas, we lodged at the Norfolk Hotel, then a single storey building of modest appearance, but renowned as the meeting place of settlers and already rich in diverting stories. Nairobi had a makeshift look then and contrasted sharply with the historic town of Mombasa, where even the houses of officials were substantial coral-built dwellings. Little more than a decade had passed since it was an advanced railway headquarters depot where, construction having temporarily caught up with the survey, there was a prolonged halt while the difficult route ahead was being determined. It was at the very end of the plains before the land rose into the hills and forest fringes of the Kikuyu country. There had been nothing but pasture land on the site before, intermittently grazed over by Masai herds before they had been decimated by rinderpest.

The encampment had grown gradually until, with the arrival of government headquarters there in 1907, the place began to show evidence of a town to come. It was laid out spaciously with streets and avenues, planned and marked out with angle irons, but, so far as actual construction went, there was very little. Offices and officers' bungalows were of wood and corrugated iron raised on stilts to keep out vermin. Shops, with very few exceptions, were no better than ramshackle *dukas* to be found in any little Kenya township. I doubt whether, in 1911, there were as many as a dozen really substantial buildings of two or more floors high. Hired transport was by rickshaw. There were also mule carts, some horse-drawn traps and hand-pushed *hamali* carts for luggage. All longer-distance road travel was by ox-cart. No motor cars were to be seen, though I learnt afterwards that Sir Percy Girouard, the governor, had one. Nairobi was a jog-trot town then; scarcely that. Yet

2 The 'Agadir crisis' of 1911 was indeed one of the successive international crises that prepared Europe's leaders to accept the likelihood of war. In 1911 the French had taken greater control over Morocco – ostensibly in order to protect its Sultan from rebellion – than had been previously agreed between Germany, France and Britain. Germany sent the gunboat *Panzer* to Morocco's Atlantic port of Agadir in order to persuade France to reconsider. There was fresh talk of European war – temporarily postponed by negotiations over a Franco-German re-division of insignificant stretches of western Africa.

there was a distinct impression of liveliness about the place and a conscious air of 'going to be'.

After Christmas, and now alone, I travelled on by train through the highlands and, after a night stop at Nakuru in the heart of European farmland, I proceeded for a further 100 miles to lake level at Kisumu, the railway terminus and headquarters of Nyanza Province.[3] It matched Nakuru for size. Both were small towns a long way behind Mombasa and Nairobi, but in purpose and development they were strongly contrasted. Nakuru served and depended upon the European farmers, while Kisumu depended entirely on African production and its position as the centre of the lake transport to Uganda.

The original intention had been to carry the railway on further into Uganda, but an outbreak of malaria and sleeping sickness among the construction workers forced the management to alter the plan and make for the nearest feasible point on the lake. The point was at the head of the Kavirondo Gulf.[4] A suitable site for a moderate-sized town was found in the neighbourhood, and, fortunately, it was uninhabited, although there were many Africans in the surrounding area. It was therefore possible to lay out the town in an orderly way. There was time to plan and, to this day, Kisumu has a neat appearance. By the time of my arrival it had developed to an extent that there were five steamers on the lake, plying to Uganda ports and the German ports at Mwanza and Bukoba. They had been pre-constructed in England and reassembled locally; the docks and workshops were already impressive for so young a port.

The total number of Europeans in Kisumu at that stage was about 130. Nearly all were officials, of whom the railway and marine were about half. There were adequate administrative, police and medical services but, except for one Jamaican,[5] there were no educational or agricultural officers in the whole province of 12,000 square miles with a population of more than a million. As for the Asiatics, they considerably outnumbered the Europeans. Practically all the trade and clerical posts were in their hands and it was not until after the First World War that Africans participated beyond the level of interpreters and domestic servants. Nevertheless, the whole town depended for its existence on African produce and African labour.

---

3 The lake was Lake Victoria.

4 Now called Winam.

5 Henry Holder, agricultural assistant, the best cricketer in the province and on that account doubtless known to the cricketing Fazan.

The name Kisumu given to the town was that of the surrounding Luo clan.[6] It was no bad place for a young man to begin his administrative career, under one of the most renowned of East African administrators, John Ainsworth.[7] It was the headquarters of a fertile province which, at that time, was almost entirely African. The people were numerous, friendly, and trusting and there was a straightforward job of steady development to be done.

★★★

It was noticeable how very recently even senior officers had come to East Africa. Still more recent comers like myself would hang on their lips as if they were oracles as they told of doings away back in what, between ourselves, we irreverently called 'the prehistoric days of nineteen hundred and eight'. It was, though, a time of extremely rapid change. Quite how rapid this change had been was brought home to me within my first days at Kisumu, when I was asked by Ainsworth to accompany him to the station to bid farewell to an old stager who was leaving the country for the last time. It turned out to be James Martin, the former Maltese sailor who had travelled with Thompson on his momentous journey of exploration through Masai and the highlands less than 30 years before.

That such extraordinary changes had been effected during these years owed a great deal to the work in the 1890s of a few remarkable pioneers. Most notable of these were the efforts of Ainsworth in Akamba and Hobley in Nyanza.[8] Kikuyu was more of a joint enterprise: the early work of Lugard was consolidated by Hall, and useful connections were also established by the trader-adventurer, John Boyes, eastwards towards Mount Kenya.[9]

---

6 A more common view is that Kisumu means a place of hunger.

7 For whom, see R. M. Maxon, *John Ainsworth and the Making of Kenya* (Lanham, MD: University Press of America, 1980).

8 Ainsworth, who retired to South Africa in 1920, never wrote a memoir. C. W. Hobley's *Kenya, from Chartered Company to Crown Colony* (London: Witherby, 1929) is still worth reading, despite his reticence about some of the major disagreements he had with his superiors over the general direction of Kenya's pro-settler development. As he warned in his Preface: 'no old controversies will be revived, all the decencies will be preserved, and I shall not even abuse the Government I had the honour to serve.'

9 See Perham and Bull, *Lugard Diaries*. Fazan's praise for John Boyes, self-proclaimed 'King of the Wa-Kikuyu', is somewhat surprising. Boyes was an ivory trader and a bit of a brigand, charged with but cleared of banditry in 1900.

As an example of their enterprise and of the life of a district officer in the 1890s, one need only consider the brief career of Francis Hall. He was born in 1860 and lived the life of a rover during his early adult years. In 1892 he arrived in East Africa as an employee of the IBEA Company and by the middle of the next year was in charge at Fort Smith. On his arrival at the fort he found the Kikuyu so hostile that at times he felt himself almost a prisoner in his own station, yet by the end of his first tour of duty, with very limited resources, but with great patience and force of character, he had won the confidence of both the Kikuyu and the Masai in the neighbourhood, had virtually put an end to local traffic in slaves, could move about more freely, and by the making of roads and in other ways had greatly extended his influence. He had also made safe the route for well-conducted caravans and saw to it that food and labour were provided. All this was accomplished at no little risk to himself, and he had indeed been ambushed in a shower of poisoned arrows, gored by a rhino and mauled by a leopard.

Hall's second tour of duty was more peaceful and he put to good use the farming, veterinary and medical skills he had acquired in his roving days. He experimented with crops and livestock at Fort Smith, organised a vaccination campaign against smallpox to keep the caravan route open, and provided relief for the Akamba in the famine of 1898. Later he established a new station at Murang'a but, in February 1901, returning from a small punitive expedition, he caught fever and dysentery and died. He was a resolute man and may have been severe at times, but that his word was well respected there was no doubt. Thirty years later when I was at Kiambu I found that a land dispute could generally be settled at once if it could be shown how Hall had decided on a similar matter.[10]

By 1912 things were very different. Peace and order had been secured and the basics of government, public services, farming and trade had been established. Yet pioneering work did not disappear overnight, and I was to have some experience of it myself as government penetrated into the remoter regions. Shortly after the outbreak of war I was posted to Kisii, where a battle had taken place only two weeks before my arrival. Situated on the border of German East Africa, the Germans remained in occupation of about a third of the district, and for the next year and more I was to serve there under W.F.G. Campbell, one of the country's ablest district commissioners. From Kisii I was then sent to remote North Turkana to set up a station.

---

10 Hall's 'severity' cost scores of Kikuyu lives in a number of 'punitive expeditions'.

To this end the caravan of 40 porters which I took with me on the long walk north[11] included 16 who were carrying a safe. I had nothing like a station to go to, however, not even a hut so, with the help of a police officer, I chose a site at Lokiriama on which to build.

Turkana was a vast land, sparsely inhabited, and with a resident staff consisting of a single interpreter and a handful of *askaris* there was not much that one could reasonably achieve other than to see that order was maintained. Indeed that was the essential part of the job, for at that time the Turkana were about the most bellicose tribe in the country, and their constant raids on their southern neighbours, the Samburu and the Suk, had meant that an expedition had recently been sent against them when forces could ill be spared. Although the expedition had only gone into southern Turkana, the problem of lawlessness was general, and very much exacerbated by the extensive activities of Abyssinian and Swahili gun-runners. Nor should it be imagined that it was merely a local matter, for the Turkana were capable of raiding over literally hundreds of miles and they sometimes stole thousands of head of cattle in a single raid. Shortly before my arrival a post had been established at Kalosia on the river Kerio and, once the post at Lokiriama had also been built, more concerted efforts could be made to contain the problem. It was a problem, though, which could not be resolved until more resources were available to check the activity of the Abyssinians crossing the northern frontier. For this reason it was frustrating work, and, on top of the uncertainty and danger, one had to cope with the relentless heat, the monotony of food and landscape, and months on end without speaking a work of English. Finally, cut off through no lack of effort on my part from the momentous events happening on the world stage in 1916/17, my isolation felt complete, and after a year I returned to be sent home on sick leave.[12]

Fortunately, there was not much field work of so uncompromising a nature, and if it was often hard, there were always many compensations, as I learnt from my earliest days in Nyanza. Office work was not arduous, and about two thirds of my time was spent on

11 Approximately 160 miles, 250 kilometres.

12 Fazan understates the violence that marked this period and place in his career, when both Turkana and British were mobilising larger forces against each other – for which see Lamphear, *The Scattering Time*. The Earl of Lytton's *The Desert and the Green* (London: Macdonald, 1957) is a vivid memoir of soldiering in the Turkana area in the early 1920s, in conditions similar to Fazan's.

tour in the district. Travel was by head-load porterage and I generally walked along with the porters, but those who preferred could ride one of the station mules or use a bicycle. All rather hot work in the Nyanza sun, but one soon got used to it, liked it and kept very fit. For those who didn't like safari it would have been better to give up the job altogether.[13]

Having got the district commissioner's covering instructions, one was allowed and encouraged to use imagination and ingenuity in carrying them out, learning meanwhile about the tribes around, preaching the gospel of cotton planting, road making or something of the kind, making ludicrous mistakes, laughing them off, and plodding happily on. Even an unpleasant task like collecting hut tax could be a colourful experience, for, when taxpayers used to come into camp from early morning onwards, they literally danced and sang and brandished their tally tickets which they held in cleft sticks.[14]

One soon learnt, however, that the specific object for which a safari had been undertaken was seldom the most valuable part of it. The overriding duty was to keep in close touch with the people, note what was going on, be available to listen to any grievance or matter that might be causing concern, explain the reasons and remove misunderstandings. That was the most essential work, and the method was by discussion with the headmen and elders both in *baraza* and outside. General contact too was easy, for the district was densely populated by the Nilotic Luo tribe in the areas nearest the lake and the Bantu Maragoli, Kisa and Tiriki further inland.[15] They thronged around, a seemingly happy and carefree people, especially the Luo, clad in their bare skins and little else. At set meetings, however, they made more of a spectacle, for many of the elders were arrayed in ostrich feathers and hippo ivory ornaments on their cowrie-covered caps. Quite a number

---

13 District officials had to make an annual return of their days spent on safari, away from their desk. In these early years they were expected to spend at least half their time away from the office – in an era not only long before mobile telephony but also, in many cases, before the official motorcycle, let alone car.

14 Those taxpayers who chose to turn up may have danced; other former colonial officials remember seeing villagers running from their homes before their tax-collecting safari arrived. The skill of Kenyans in tax evasion (as well as British underestimates of the number of children in African families) was proven when the first official African census of 1948 showed that the population was about 30 per cent larger than had been estimated from the previous tax registers.

15 The district in question appears to be Central Kavirondo, later Central Nyanza.

also had ear-fringes with jade insets which their ancestors had brought with them from the Nile.

The chiefs in Nyanza were disposed to be friendly and helpful. Ruling as they did over large compact clans, often from 20,000 to 50,000 strong, they measured up pretty well to one's preconceived ideas of what an African chief might be. Though they owed their appointments to government recognition, many had also hereditary claims and could count their ancestry through several generations.[16] I expect allowances were made for newcomers like myself and the path made easy. At any rate, a junior officer had the one great advantage: that he did not cause inhibitions, so he learned much in casual conversation about tribal customs and the like, which would not have been so readily forthcoming later on.

16 Kenya's historians agree that Luo colonial chiefs had better claims to a hereditary status than the chiefs appointed among other peoples in the colony whose traditional leaderships were not so closely related to lineage position.

4

Races and Migrations

The African population of Kenya at this time was estimated to be around 3 million, containing a great diversity of tribes.[1] No statistics are reliable but there were believed to be about 3,000 Europeans, possibly 4,000 by the time the 1914 war broke out. Asians outnumbered Europeans heavily and can be credibly guessed at about 20,000. There were round about 10,000 Arabs at the coast and a few up-country, but it was a very difficult matter to draw a dividing line between Arab and Swahili in the very mixed population at the coast.

The total area of the British East Africa Protectorate in 1914 was 210,750 square miles, not counting the province of Jubaland, which was ceded to Italy at the end of the war, to become part of Italian Somaliland. A little more than half of the whole area was taken up by Turkana and the Northern Province. With a few attractive exceptions such as the neighbourhood of Mount Marsabit, the land to the north was arid and bare, sparsely occupied by desert tribes at a density which was then probably not more than two persons to the square mile on average. It was a region where the keeping of the peace between tribe and tribe was the major preoccupation of British rule. Only very limited material progress was made, and potentialities for development were never fully explored. The inhabitants were stockmen, keeping camels, donkeys, cattle, sheep and goats. The principal occupant tribes were the Nilotic/Hamitic Turkana and Samburu, the Hamitic Galla and the

1 Kenya's population would have been between 2 million and 3 million in 1900, at a time of terrible mortality due to drought, smallpox among famine-weakened populations, and cattle plagues. The population did not start growing again until the 1920s. Although Kenyans still talk of tribes, with the connotation of 'descent group', scholars prefer the term 'ethnic groups' since this conveys a looser form of cultural association, more faithful to the mixed origins and interrelations of so-called 'tribes'. Nonetheless, Fazan's use of 'tribe' reflects the understandings of his day.

Somali, regarded as being of Semitic origin, although obviously with a considerable Hamitic admixture.[2]

The remainder of the country, the southern half of Kenya, was just over 100,000 square miles. The climate was hot and moist at the coast and hot and dry at Lake Victoria level. The intervening area, including the Highlands and the major African tribal lands, with the exception of the Luo and Abaluhya near the lake, and the Nyika in the coast hinterland, was high and healthy, often cold and misty in the early morning, but nearly always sunny at midday, with two fairly well defined but often capricious rainy seasons.

The native inhabitants of the country, excluding the Somalis and Galla of the Northern Province, were nearly all of three races: Bantu, Nilotic and Nilotic/Hamitic. Whence these peoples came is largely a mystery, particularly in regard to the Bantu.[3] The proportions were roughly two thirds Bantu, Nilotic a sixth and Nilo/Hamitic a sixth. If they were to be classed by the amount of land they occupied instead of by their numerical strength, the last named, being much more thinly spread, would show much higher.

The word *bantu*, which simply meant 'men', was the generic name applied to a group of tribes who spoke related languages, a characteristic of which was that they used this word or some variant of it, such as *watu* in Swahili or *wantu* in Kikuyu or plain *bantu* in Luganda, for 'men'. These related languages were all synthetic, admitting of inflections both before and after the verb stem, but mainly before, to signify differences of person, tense and mood and also a positive or negative connotation. The most widely known language of this group was Ki-Swahili, the language of the Swahili of the East African coast. Although it was widely used as a lingua franca, it was not really typical, having a large number of Arab words in it.

It is not certain whether all the tribes who spoke Bantu languages were of one race or whether there was an invasion of a people so dominant that it was able to impose its language in the course of

2 The term Hamitic has been replaced by Cushitic; scholars now emphasise what Fazan calls 'admixture' in the makeup of all African peoples. Fazan's Galla are now called Oromo and/or Borana.

3 'Bantu expansion' is still not fully understood. Bantu-speakers probably originated in the forests of what is now the Nigeria–Cameroun frontier; some of their pioneer colonists may have reached East Africa's Great Lakes region around 1000 BCE. The most accessible recent knowledge is found in John Iliffe, *Africans: The History of a Continent* (Cambridge: Cambridge University Press, second edition 2007), pp. 16, 34–6.

generations upon tribes of other races. One theory is that they came in waves from the north east from about the fourteenth to the eighteenth century, and while most Bantu tribes in Kenya admitted to having come into their present homes from somewhere vaguely in that direction, there was at least one tribe – the Kitui Akamba – who professed no recollection whatever of having been anywhere at any time except where they were.[4] Another theory was that they came from central Africa, the Abaluhya along the northern shores of Lake Victoria, and the other tribes from the direction of Kilimanjaro. Wherever they came from, the Kenya and Uganda Bantu were about the northernmost of the Bantu tribes in this part of Africa. In Kenya they were just over two thirds of the population but occupied very much less than half of the land. Going south into Tanganyika the proportion increased until, by the time the central Tanganyika railway was reached, the African population was almost entirely Bantu right down to the Cape. In East Africa they were mixed farmers, with the accent on agriculture rather than livestock, although they might well have preferred the latter if they had had the space available. The principal Bantu tribes in Kenya were the Kikuyu, Akamba, Abaluhya, Meru and the group collectively known as the Nyika – the Giriama, Chonye, Kauma, Jabana and others, nine sections in all[5] – who inhabited the rather barren and uninviting area behind the coast belt. The word *nyika*, incidentally, was not a tribal name but merely meant grassland, as typifying the area in which they lived. The Arabs in the days of slavery used to call them *wa-Toro* or runaways.

The second largest racial group was the Nilotic, of which the only true representative in Kenya was the large Luo tribe, who were closely akin to the Acholi and Lango in Uganda. They were an agricultural people, having insufficient land for stock rearing on any large scale, and showed little proclivity that way. They were not particularly tall but were big-boned and thick set. They had a fondness for fish and fishing. The Luo were believed to have come into Kenya from the Nile during

4 By the 1920s, when Fazan served among them, Kamba will have become nervous lest more of their land be expropriated for white settlement; in these circumstances many Africans believed that their best defence was to claim 'indigeneity' or 'autochthony', namely, to deny that they had ever migrated from elsewhere, having been settled where they now were from time immemorial.

5 Now known collectively as the Mijikenda or 'the nine villages'. For their pre-colonial history, see Thomas T. Spear, *The Kaya Complex: A History of the Mijikenda Peoples of the Kenya Coast to 1900* (Nairobi: Kenya Literature Bureau, 1978).

the seventeenth century.[6] As they seemed to have kept their sub-tribal organisation and traditions intact, it would appear that they had come in units of some strength. Their move southwards was still continuing and they were making considerable penetration into Tanganyika, but they were doing this individually or by small family groups.

Except as regards language, there were many points of similarity in the way of life and, to some extent, in appearance between the Nilotic Luo and the Bantu group of tribes – Maragoli and others – who lived next to them in Nyanza Province and now call themselves Abaluhya.[7] For some reason that is not very plain the Luo and Abaluhya were lumped together officially as Kavirondo, sometimes with the prefix Nilotic or Bantu to distinguish them. The name Kavirondo was said to be a combination of *Kaffir* and *Murono*, the latter being the local nickname for the muzzle-loading muskets that had been introduced into North Nyanza by Swahili filibusters about 1900. But that is as may be, there were other common features which the Kavirondo shared at this time. There was a high degree of nakedness among both men and women, but the Luo women wore fringes in front and tails like horses behind. The Abaluhya of Kakamega location in North Kavirondo or North Nyanza, to give it its later name, were the only known instance in Kenya where absolute nakedness prevailed among both men and women, without even a cord around the waist. The elders on both sides, however, especially the Luo, wore skins and elaborate headdresses of cowrie shells and ostrich feathers. The warriors, too, were imposingly adorned, with more apparent regard for show than for fighting. A further common feature of the Kavirondo was that all adult males had lower jaw teeth extracted: the Luo, six, and the Abaluhya four. Neither was accounted very warlike but they made good labourers for heavy work and offered themselves with less reluctance than any other Kenya tribe at this time, except perhaps for the Kikuyu. The Kikuyu, however, were seldom prepared to travel far from home.

The Nilotic/Hamitic element, apart from the purely Hamitic Galla who had penetrated south to the Tana River area from their tribal home in Abyssinia, consisted of the Masai and Nandi groups. They were

---

6 The doyen of Kenya's (and Luo) historians, Bethwell Ogot reckons that the first Luo pioneers arrived in their present location in the late fifteenth century CE. See B. A. Ogot, *History of the Southern Luo* (Nairobi: East African Publishing House, 1967), 28.

7 For the mixed ethno-linguistic origins and history of the Abaluhya, now more commonly called Luyia, see Gideon S. Were, *A History of the Abaluyia of Western Kenya, c. 1500–1930* (Nairobi: East African Publishing House, 1967).

believed to have entered Kenya from the north between the fifteenth and nineteenth centuries, the Nandi group, now often called the Kalenjin, coming first.[8] The Kalenjin comprised the Nandi and Kipsigis, who were virtually one tribe, and several smaller elements such as the Elgeyo. They were a small-boned, athletic people, comparable to the Masai, but not closely related. They had a similar organisation for war, but, unlike the Masai, were not averse to progress. Although mainly stock-owners and good herdsmen, they also cultivated *shambas*. All the tribes of Masai and Nandi groups were much given to cattle stealing, regarding them as fair game. When caught they would commonly admit the offence readily and regard the term of imprisonment which followed as a distinction rather than a stigma – a very likeable people.[9]

The Masai, who were related to the Samburu, were traditionally a purely stock-owning people. They were a handsome tribe with a dignified and unselfconscious carriage, very brave and loyal to their word. They were the only tribe in East Africa to respect the wild animals, being content to share their land with them without considering that they spoiled the grazing for their cattle. Something like a mutual tolerance had developed between cattle and game, but they were kept away from areas where the wildebeest had calved down. Otherwise there was little avoiding action. Living almost exclusively on blood and milk, the Masai seldom ate meat and, until recently, no grain or vegetable food at all, except roots. There was, however, one section which practised agriculture and, since the Masai had begun to marry Kikuyu wives, some cultivation was seen. Thus things were changing, but the Masai were very slow to adapt. They still kept their tribal dress and, so far as was allowed, their warlike organisation. Although they were warriors, there were few in the army

8 Nandi and Maasai pioneers probably reached 'Kenya' about 500 years earlier than was realised in Fazan's day. For Maasai see (with a fine bibliography of earlier work), Thomas Spear and Richard Waller (eds), *Being Maasai: Ethnicity and Identity in East Africa* (London: James Currey, 1993). *Kalenjin* means 'I say to you', a greeting first widely heard in the Second World War when the colonial government appealed to African loyalties by means of vernacular radio broadcasts. For the process in which 'Nandi-speakers' became 'Kalenjin', see Gabrielle Lynch, *I Say to You: Ethnic Politics and the Kalenjin in Kenya* (Chicago, IL; London: University of Chicago Press, 2011).

9 Stock theft was more than 'fair game', although it was also that. See David Anderson's two articles, 'Stock theft and moral economy in colonial Kenya', *Africa* 56 (1986), pp. 399–416, and 'Black mischief: Crime, protest and resistance in colonial Kenya', *Historical Journal* 36 (1993), pp. 851–77.

or police force, largely because they did not take kindly to individual discipline outside their own tribal authority. Their warriors still went about in traditional dress, carrying spears and with their hair and bodies covered in red ochre. Although it is true that their name and fame were known all over the country, and nowhere west of the Tana River had been safe from their raids, there were, nevertheless, tribes who had been their match. The Masai were night raiders but, in the daylight and in the open, the Nandi and Kipsigis were at least their equal, and the Akamba, although not an aggressive people, had always been ready and able to defend their borders against Masai spearmen with their bows and arrows.

The Dorobo, Sanye, Boni, Dahalo, Mukogodo and others came to be known collectively as the Dorobo. It was a Masai word meaning tsetse fly, but they called themselves the Okiek.[10] They were the forest tribes. If one had to assign them to one of the racial groups one would probably say Hamitic. They may have been aboriginals of East Africa, but more likely they were tribal offshoots. It seems that some tribes had, as it were, a forest-dwelling section barely or grudgingly recognized as fellow tribesmen. The Dorobo, for instance, claimed affinity with the Masai, and some with the Nandi, while the Sanye at the coast and the Boni up the Tana River may well have been of Galla origin. There were, no doubt, also tribal outcasts and others amongst them who, with their descendants, had taken to life in the bush. Their common feature was that they lived by hunting and bee-keeping. Although they were often said to have lived in or under trees, it is unlikely that this was ever wholly true. Rather they moved about very freely as their occupation demanded, and did not much encumber themselves with permanent huts. As time progressed they became more settled.

After the period of the great migrations was over, the tribes had settled down in their lands in comparative security. Inter-tribal fighting, where it occurred, was mainly confined to cattle raiding and wanton attacks on border villages. In such raids the Masai were the chief aggressors until the later years of the nineteenth century. Otherwise, at least with the Bantu and Nilotic groups, relations were normally peaceful and, when fighting occurred, it was more likely to be between

10 It is now thought that the Maasai name for Okiek, *iltorrobo*, indicated their perceived poverty, shown in their lack of livestock. Fazan's comments on their varied origins are, however, supported by modern scholarship, for a summary of which see Spear and Waller, *Being Maasai*, pp. 5–9.

clans of the same tribe disputing a boundary than between one tribe and another. After the Nandi expeditions and settlement with the Masai, the protectorate government had no great difficulty in establishing general peace.[11]

***

The Arabs and the people known as Swahili inhabited the coast belt. Practically without exception they were Mohammedans, although the earliest waves of Arab settlement dated from before the Prophet. Coming from all parts of Arabia but mostly from Oman, the Arabs belonged to two main groups: the Swahili in the Malindi area and the Mazrui around Mombasa. The Lamu Arabs were more mixed and there was a suggestion of a Persian element. The word *swahili* meant a coast-dweller. It was probably applied, in the first instance, to Arabs of an earlier wave of settlement who had come so long ago as to have acquired a local character, by mixture of blood or otherwise. In the course of time, however, all the Arab stock became much diluted by the practice of slave-owners taking concubines from among their freed slaves.[12]

The Swahili language must have taken several generations in its development. It was an amalgam of Bantu grammar with a considerable assortment of Arabic expressions and words, and it differed from one area to another, so that Zanzibar, Mombasa, Malindi and Lamu all had different versions.[13] The variations depended, at least in part, on the African language of the neighbourhood and the language spoken in the area from which the slaves were drawn. Swahili was, nevertheless, very much a language in its own right, pleasant sounding and softer than most of the Bantu group. Although it was a difficult language for Europeans to master correctly, it stripped down easily into simplified

11 Fazan's calm reflections on the relative absence of pre-colonial 'tribal war' – very different from some of his more prejudiced contemporaries – is borne out by modern scholarship. See Richard Reid, *War in Pre-Colonial Eastern Africa: The Patterns and Meanings of State-level Conflict in the Nineteenth Century* (Oxford: James Currey, 2007), in which the area that became 'Kenya' is largely omitted from consideration, thanks to its lack of state-building violence or military elites.

12 For recent scholarship on coastal history, see the references cited in Chapter 1, 'Historical Background'.

13 Fazan's thoughts on the origins and history of Swahili are not contradicted but vastly expanded in the currently standard work by Derek Nurse and Thomas Hinnebusch, *Swahili and Sabaki, a Linguistic History* (Berkeley; Los Angeles, CA: University of California Press, 1993).

versions, one being sometimes called *ki-settla.*[14] Swahili was a genuine lingua franca in the sense that one could get by with it almost anywhere, but it was not the first language of any tribe outside the immediate coastal strip. It was not much used between Africans upcountry except in the towns or on European farms where there was a mixture of race or tribe. It came easily to the Bantu, but the Nilotics had to learn it like anybody else.

The coast was going through a period of deep depression at this time.[15] Although the Arabs had been compensated in cash for the loss of their slaves, they were lost without them, and they had little to barter with the dhows from Oman. Many mortgaged their houses to Indians and then found themselves unable to pay the interest. The Indians who foreclosed on them were left with useless, empty houses on their hands, and trade was at a standstill. The freed slaves, too, were elderly and bewildered. Government kept a vote, curiously called 'Maintenance of Slaves', to provide doles to the most distressed. Half a generation had to pass before the coast began to look up again.

Some Indians had been at the coast for generations as traders, but they only came upcountry with the railway construction.[16] Although most of the original coolies were returned to India at the end of the work, there were many of clerical and artisan grades who stayed on, as did some others, particularly Sikhs, as carpenters, masons, and builders. Some rich Indians at the coast operated in a big way as merchants, having in some cases amassed their initial capital from profitable deals in ivory and, in others, by money-lending transactions with Arabs. But upcountry they were generally earning a precarious livelihood by petty trading from corrugated iron shacks. They were capable of holding on in their little *dukas* through years

---

14 It is well worth trying to find a copy of F. H. Le Breton, *Up-country Swahili* (Richmond: Simpson, 13 editions from 1936 to 1956), which could be called *Teach Yourself Ki-settla*, not least for its paranoid conversations with one's cook.

15 For which see Cooper, *From Slaves to Squatters.*

16 Fazan again shows his unusual lack of prejudice here: many Europeans in colonial Kenya held the self-serving belief that the South Asian community was descended mainly from lower caste 'coolies', the navvies who built the railway, and who therefore deserved little political recognition. Robert G. Gregory has contributed most to the history of East Africa's Indians – more properly South Asians since the partition of India and Pakistan in 1947. See especially, his two books both published in 1993: *South Asians in East Africa: An Economic and Social History, 1890–1980* (Boulder, CO: Westview Press), and *Quest for Equality: Asian Politics in East Africa 1900–1967* (New Delhi: Orient Longman).

of very slender profit, often in remote and unprotected areas in circumstances of great discomfort and no little risk. These people were certainly the pioneers of trade in the African tribal areas. Although any person could take up a shop plot in the trading centres established at about 15- to 20-mile intervals along ox-wagon routes, they were, in practice, an Indian monopoly, and it was many years before Africans were able to compete. As for the Goans, they were officially ranked as Asiatics, but they were Roman Catholics and proud of their Portuguese ancestry. For many years they filled nearly all the clerical posts in government offices loyally and without complaint. As clerks, artisans and retail shopkeepers, the Indian and Goan communities were thus performing a useful service to the country at large at a time when Europeans had not the numbers and Africans had not the experience to do these jobs themselves.[17]

Before 1914 Kenya was for the European an ox-cart and foot-slogging country.[18] Motor cars were so much out of the question along those muddy tracks that they were hardly even imagined. Horses could only be kept in a few fly-free and favoured areas, but if kept at all, they were mainly for pleasure and did not come much into the working picture. Mules, perhaps, but not horses. And hardly anywhere were the roads really fit even for ox-carts. There was a demand for laws to keep cartwheel rims wide but, whatever was done, the roads were always deeply rutted and churned up in the rains.

Probably the only export crop which had been established at this time, and was able to bear the cost of transport and make a profit, was coffee.[19] Wheat had been planted but had not yet developed on any scale. Other cereals, such as maize, were only grown for internal use in the country. Cattle ranching and dairy farming, which were to become key industries, could only be established slowly and at great cost, for farms had to be fenced and precautions taken against East Coast fever, pleuropneumonia, and rinderpest. There was also

---

17 Mervyn Maciel, *Bwana Karani* (London: Merlin Books, 1985) is a charming autobiography of a Goan clerk.

18 Officials travelling by ox-cart might hope to average 12 miles per day.

19 The best economic history of Kenya's white farming is Paul Mosley, *The Settler Economies: Studies in the Economic History of Kenya and Southern Rhodesia 1900–1963* (Cambridge: Cambridge University Press, 1983); for economic history more generally, see R. M. A, van Zwanenberg, with Anne King, *An Economic History of Kenya and Uganda 1800–1970* (Basingstoke: Macmillan, 1975).

pasture to be improved and deficiencies in the soil discovered and remedied. Bank overdrafts grew. Fortunately there were a few European settlers who had access to capital and were bold enough to venture it on new enterprises and experiments of doubtful outcome. Such, outstandingly, were Lord Delamere and Captain Grogan. They set a lead which at a much later date government was able to follow and expand, for there were no financial resources available at that time for the establishment of agricultural or research services in any effective degree.[20] Some of the Christian mission stations also did useful experimental work.

Of plantation crops, coconuts were fairly extensively cultivated at the coast, an enterprise which was mainly in the hands of Arabs and seldom brought much reward. The few Europeans who tried it had disappointing results. Others tried rubber in the Malindi area, but none of them succeeded. Sisal, both at the coast and upcountry, was showing more promise. Coffee was doing well in the Highlands below 6,000 feet and was the only permanent crop that could yet be pronounced a success. Gums and wattle trees were fairly extensively planted but, at this stage, mainly for wind breaks or as fuel for the railway. It was already clear that cattle, sheep, cereals and mixed farming were to be the dominant feature of the highland farms above the area of the coffee zone.

Few of the settlers were farmers before they came. They had to learn an unaccustomed job in an unaccustomed country, and not least of their troubles was the management of totally unskilled labour, mostly Luo for heavy work, Kikuyu for coffee, and, provided that a friendly connection had first been established, Nandi or Masai for herding. It was for the European settlers a young and vibrant country – young in every sense. The age, even of the veterans, was seldom over 40. Few were married. Most, except the newly arrived, had fought in the South African war – including an element of Cape Dutch on the Uasin Ngishu Plateau who had fought on the other side. Many of these Afrikaners had come in a party by sea, complete with ox wagons and household goods, and, after a period of refitting at the Nakuru railhead, had trekked onwards to their farms. Starting

---

20 For Delamere, see Huxley, *White Man's Country*; for Grogan, Edward Paice, *Lost Lion of Empire: The Life of 'Cape to Cairo' Grogan* (London: HarperCollins, 2001). Fazan gives here the practical justification for Kenya's foundation in racial inequality, an essential assumption in his meditation on the politics of land.

in a hand-to-mouth way, they were to become a very staunch section of the settler community.[21]

Both for settlers and officials it was a hardy, outdoor life. Clothing was mostly bush shirts and shorts and the ubiquitous double *terrai* hat. The cowboy type of attire, seen for a brief period in later years, was not yet in favour. Game was plentiful in most areas, and, though shooting was mostly for the pot, hunting safaris were not uncommon when other forms of sport were not easily come by. Trophies in the shape of horns and skins were typical adornments of settlers' houses but, despite appearances, it was essentially a work-a-day life, seldom admitting of holidays, and, in any case, travelling was difficult, slow and expensive. The settler not only farmed his land, but was architect of his house and chief builder too. He had also to be his own doctor and to treat minor ailments of those in his care, being required by law to keep a supply of drugs for this purpose.

Malaria was the chief enemy, sharing that distinction with dysentery and similar ailments. To cope with these troubles a box of medicines was issued on payment of 2 rupees to government officials on safari, and most of all the drugs in it I remember the 'Livingstone Rouser'. The assumption was that one might be so ill and confused with malaria that one would not remember in what order or in what quantity to take aspirin, quinine, cascara and so forth. The 'Livingstone Rouser' was for just such an emergency. It was superb, and of most grateful memory.

The missions were a most significant part of European endeavour, and might well have been mentioned before, for they provided not only the early explorers, but also the first Europeans to settle upcountry in permanent homes. The majority of them, however, arrived after the

---

21 Kenya's white settler community has attracted a large literature. See especially, Dane Kennedy, *Islands of White: Settler Society and Culture in Kenya and Southern Rhodesia, 1890–1939* (Durham, NC: Duke University Press, 1987). William Jackson, *Madness and Marginality: The Lives of Kenya's White Insane* (Manchester: Manchester University Press, 2013) reminds us that not all settlers were masterly. John Lonsdale, 'Kenya: Home County and African Frontier', in Robert Bickers (ed.), *Settlers and Expatriates: Britons over the Seas* (Oxford: Oxford University Press, 2010), pp. 74–111, is brief; a fuller narrative is given in C. S. Nicholls, *Red Strangers: The White Tribe of Kenya* (London: Timewell Press, 2005). The most eloquent and prolific author among those who were once white settlers was Elspeth Huxley; of her two semi-autobiographies *The Flame Trees of Thika* (London: Chatto & Windus, 1959) is better known than its sequel, *The Mottled Lizard* (London: Chatto & Windus, 1962). Her edition of her mother's letters, *Nellie: Letters from Africa* (London: Weidenfeld & Nicolson, 1980), presents a lively picture of an observant farmer, liberal by the standards of her day.

first waves of settlement. Two British missions, the CMS and the Church of Scotland, were among the earliest and firmest established as also were two Roman Catholic missions, the Mill Hill mission, with priests from Holland and Ireland in about equal parts, and the White Fathers from France. The Africa Inland Mission, the Friends Africa Mission, the Seventh Day Adventists and others were mainly American or Canadian. In fact, if it were not for a zoning policy which only slowly became effective, they might have been in danger of treading on each other's heels. Today they need no champion, for the immense value of their work is clear for all to see, but in the early days the practical results of their work were not so obvious. Indeed, it was a popular attitude among the know-alls of the settler community to warn newcomers against engaging a 'mission boy' as a servant, as he would probably be dishonest and tale-bearing. There were times, too, when mission dignitaries did not see eye to eye with the provincial administration as to what was fair dealing towards the Africans, and they occasionally fulminated in the *Manchester Guardian.* But the issues would right themselves and the comparison of views was often of value.[22]

Europeans did not figure prominently in trade because it was mostly in Asian hands, apart from a few established firms such as Smith Mackenzie and the IBEA Corporation. Nevertheless, there were a few British stalwarts starting in a small way at about this time who were later to found firms of considerable importance. As for the public services, the members of the medical department were devoted and skilled, but few. Education was left almost entirely to the missions and agricultural services were undeveloped. Occasionally one met a stock inspector on safari or a surveyor mapping out the land. The port and railway services, remarkable in the existing circumstances, were soon to be put

22 Again, there is a large literature on Kenya's missionaries. For the early missions at the coast, see Reed, *Pastors, Partners and Paternalists.* For coast and interior, see Robert W. Strayer, *The Making of Mission Communities in East Africa* (London: Heinemann, 1978). For highland Kenya, see John Karanja, *Founding an African Faith: Kikuyu Anglican Christianity 1900–1945* (Nairobi: Uzima, 1999); Lawrence M. Njoroge, *A Century of Catholic Endeavour: Holy Ghost and Consolata Missions in Kenya* (Nairobi: Paulines, 1999); and Derek R. Peterson, *Creative Writing: Translation, Bookkeeping, and the Work of the Imagination in Colonial Kenya* (Portsmouth, NH: Heinemann, 2004). For the political disagreements to which Fazan refers, mostly to do with the coercion of African labour for both private and public purposes, the best source documents are in John W. Cell (ed.), *By Kenya Possessed: The Correspondence of Norman Leys and J. H. Oldham, 1918–1926* (Chicago, IL; London: University of Chicago Press, 1976). Not all issues righted themselves, especially when concerned with land.

to a very severe test when war broke out in 1914, and the efficiency of the police and the post office was beyond anything to be expected in so young a country. The armed forces in East and Central Africa at that time consisted of the KAR, native African troops officered by seconded British Army officers, and organised in four battalions, of which the third was Kenya's own.

5

The First World War

The provision in the Congo Basin Treaties ensuring the neutrality of African dependencies in the event of war between metropolitan powers proved of no avail when the test came.[1] It is difficult to see how such an arrangement could have held for long in the circumstances of a world war because the necessity of protecting sea communications and denying the use of ports to enemy shipping made involvement inevitable. The shelling of the wireless mast at Dar es Salaam by a unit of the British Navy was the first overt action on the East African coast. The governors on both sides, Herr Von Schnee and Sir Henry Belfield, were anxious to keep their charges out of it and the Germans in the coast towns were of the same mind, because of British sea power; but Europeans on each side desired to help their parent countries, as shame at the idea of holding aloof was too much for them. Skirmishes were therefore taking place on the inter-territorial border from the outset. There was no sign anywhere upcountry of an intention to be otherwise than hostile. It should be noted, however, that the strength of the armed forces raised and trained by either side up to the outbreak of war was no more than was necessary for purposes of internal security, and there seemed to have been no active preparations until war was imminent.

The immediate effect in Kenya of the declaration of war was that the settlers, practically to a man, left their farms and hurried to Nairobi to join up.[2] The East African Mounted Rifles (EAMR) was hastily formed as a European unit and did valuable work in patrolling the

---

1 The best account of the East African campaign of 1914–18 is now Edward Paice: *Tip and Run: The Untold Tragedy of the Great War in Africa* (London: Weidenfeld & Nicolson, 2007); it has an admirable bibliography for those who wish to read further. William Boyd's *An Ice Cream War* (London: Hamish Hamilton, 1982) must surely be the best fictional account, with a superb portrait of a then ramshackle Nairobi.

2 Ian Parker, *The Last Colonial Regiment: The History of the Kenya Regiment (T.F.)* (Milton Brodie: Librario Publishing, 2011), Chapters 1 and 2.

border, mainly in the central section, during the early months of the war. Later, when reinforcements arrived and the initiative passed to the British side, the unit was used to provide officers for the new battalions of the KAR or supporting arms and services. Also formed in Nairobi in the first few weeks were Ross's Scouts, a unit which operated for some 15 months in the Kisii district, and Bowker's Horse, which was soon disbanded. They were intended to reinforce the EAMR. In Mombasa, an irregular and untrained force known as the Arab Scouts, mainly consisting of Arabs, was formed under the command of Major Wavell for scouting operations on the German border between the coast and Taveta. It gave a gallant account of itself in the opening hostilities until Wavell was killed, after which it held on until reinforcements arrived from India and the situation became more stable, when it was dissolved.

These hastily assembled and untrained formations were a most useful supplement to the KAR who were the only regular troops at the outbreak of war.[3] The regiment at that time consisted nominally of four battalions, but the Second Battalion had recently been disbanded and had to be reformed. Some companies of the First Battalion (Nyasa) were in Kenya, where they had been operating on the Northern Frontier. The Third Battalion, which had been raised and trained in Kenya, was its own, and the Fourth Battalion was Uganda's and arrived very opportunely in September. Further battalions were formed as the war proceeded, some of them forming part of General Northey's column which later attacked the Germans from the south. The Kenya police also gave the KAR valuable support, especially in the two battles at Kisii and Gazi.

Although the forces available to the Germans at the outbreak of war substantially outnumbered those of the British, their position vas scarcely enviable – with the British to the north, Belgians to the west, Portuguese and Rhodesians to the south, and the sea routes blocked against them. Their plan of campaign was consequently dictated by necessity: they must strike early before the Allies could coordinate their strength and before reinforcements could reach Kenya by sea. Their land forces, therefore, directed their attacks towards cutting the Uganda railway while, by sea, the cruiser *Koenigsberg* sought to harass the

3 An exhaustive account of the KAR's early years and actions in the Great War (and Second World War) is given in H. Moyse-Bartlett, *The King's African Rifles: A Study in the Military History of East and Central Africa, 1890–1945* (Aldershot: Gale & Polden, 1956).

transport routes. She had an initial success in trapping the small British cruiser *Pegasus* in Zanzibar harbour and quickly put her out of action by shellfire from superior range. This, however, was her last success. She was soon tracked down by the cruisers *Chatham* and *Weymouth*, took refuge up the Rufiji River, and was bottled up there for the rest of the war. Later she was immobilised, both by shellfire from monitors and by air attack.

The first engagement by land forces in the campaign was the attack on the small district sub-station of Taveta on the Kenya side of the border in the first month of the war, and its occupation by a small German force under Captain Von Prince.[4] The object, presumably, was to use it as an advanced base for raids against the railway which, at Voi, was only some 60 miles distant. Indeed, for the next two months, the Germans made several raids and two or three larger attacks, always with the idea of cutting the railway. At Longido, a border point south of Nairobi on the way towards Moshi, a sharp engagement took place with moderate forces, which was possibly intended as a probe rather than a penetration in force. Bold action by the EAMR, however, forced the Germans to retreat.

The most ambitious of these German attacks was staged in the Kisii district in September 1914. The advance was made by about 400 African regular troops strengthened by white ranks. They were accompanied by a large number of tribal spearmen who ran at the first shot, so their number is not known – spearmen were not used on any other occasion by either side and it may well be that they had joined in uninvited. By chance, news of the attack reached Kisumu at the same time as a double company of the Fourth KAR with two machine guns was passing through from Uganda en route for Nairobi. They were at once diverted and were conveyed by lake steamer to Kendu Bay. As they marched up the 19-mile road to Kisii, they met the district commissioner and a small party of evacuees. The district commissioner with his 40 African police at once turned about and went along with the troops, leaving his assistant in charge of the rest of the party of civilians. The troops reached the environs of Kisii overnight and Major Thorneycroft, in command, disposed them along a hillside overlooking the station, with a narrow valley in between.

At daybreak next morning Richard Gethin, a storekeeper who had elected to stay, emerged in pyjamas from the hut where he had slept, to

4 An evocative and perceptive fictional account is to be found in M. G. Vassanji, *The Book of Secrets* (Edinburgh: Canongate, 2006).

find himself in full view of the Germans coming down the opposite ridge. Making off through the bush he came upon the KAR and was able to give useful information and served as guide through the rest of the day. What happened in the battle, quite shortly, was this: it appears that the Germans learnt of the KAR position from an African and sent a party to reconnoitre. They marched down the road in close formation, presenting an easy target for the machine gunner who opened fire. In the ensuing battle, fought from static positions in the long grass and scrub across the little intervening valley, German askaris were at a disadvantage because they were using black powder in their rifles, thus clearly revealing their whereabouts. Exploiting the advantage, the KAR advanced. Crossing the valley they went up the hill through a wattle plantation and charged the German command post. Major Thorneycroft was killed as he shouted to them to surrender, but they had had enough and did not wait for more. The German troops killed amounted to 21 white men and 110 Africans. They evacuated their wounded, but three machine guns and part of their stores were captured.

The third and last penetration of consequence was the German attack in October 1914, which reached the neighbourhood of Gazi about 16 miles from Mombasa. The forces engaged were not large but there was a serious threat to the railway and, possibly, to Mombasa itself, which was very inadequately defended. An African corporal, afterwards decorated for his gallantry, was the hero of the final engagement: at a critical moment during close and confused bush fighting, he ordered his men to charge and restored morale and eventually the Germans withdrew.

It was during these initial engagements that the defence of Kenya depended on its own and Uganda's resources. After that, Indian Expeditionary Force B and the Loyal North Lancashire Regiment took over the major role for a time, to be followed later still by larger forces from South Africa, which vastly outnumbered the Germans.

The first action in which these new forces were engaged was the unsuccessful attack on Tanga in November 1914, with a force landed from transports. It was a dismal failure. A further reverse was sustained in January 1915, when the Germans attacked and surrounded a body of Indian troops at Jassin on the Kenya side of the border in the coast region. After putting up a strong resistance and holding out for three days, the Indian force was compelled to surrender when all their ammunition had been exhausted. The total loss was 400 men, but the Germans also sustained heavy losses which they could ill afford. General Von Lettow-Vorbeck, who was in command of the German forces throughout the campaign, decided that, for the future, they must avoid pitched battles in the open.

The remainder of 1915 was occupied chiefly, on the Kenya side, in building up strength, in expansion, training, and administration of reinforcements arriving from South Africa. In order to encourage an offensive spirit, however, an attack was made in June on the German port and district station of Bukoba across Lake Victoria. It was taken without much difficulty.

The Germans too had been building up strength. A supply ship, the *Rubens*, successfully ran the blockade, carrying arms, ammunition and other war material. They also obtained reinforcements of 300 men from the *Koenigsberg*, and managed to salvage her naval guns and mount them on wheels as field pieces. Later in the war another blockade-runner got through. They contrived, furthermore, from natural resources and their own ingenuity, to supply themselves with boots, quinine, a whiskey substitute and other provisions.

In February 1916, General Tighe, the General Officer Commanding in Kenya, launched an offensive against Salaita Hill near Taveta in an endeavour to capture Moshi before the arrival of General Smuts from South Africa to take command. He found the Germans strongly entrenched, and the attack had to be called off after heavy losses. It was the first serious engagement in which South African troops participated and it forced them to revise their opinion of the quality of the native African troops opposing them.

General Smuts, arriving soon afterwards, adopted, with certain modifications, a plan which he found already drawn up. It was designed to encircle the German forces by an attack in the Taveta region to the east of Mount Kilimanjaro, combined with a rapid advance from westerly Longido. The operation started on the 4th March and, within ten days, the two encircling forces had joined hands, Von Lettow-Vorbeck, though compelled to retire from Moshi and Arusha, managed nonetheless to extricate his forces. The advance was pressed forward to Tanga and then via Handeni, southwards to cut the central Tanganyika railway at Kilosa. Dar es Salaam fell without a battle. Mwanza, on Lake Victoria, fell to the Belgians and Tabora, where Governor Von Schnee had made his temporary capital after leaving Dar es Salaam, fell soon afterwards.

After the spectacular campaign of Smuts and the South Africans the war resolved itself into a series of attempts to split the German forces and bring them to battle. During these last two years of the war the East African forces, organised and expanded under General Hosking, again had the major role. The Germans, on their side, were brilliantly handled by General Von Lettow-Vorbeck who, although for the most part compelled to take evasive action and at one time forced to seek refuge in Portuguese territory, nevertheless succeeded in preserving his army in being, in apparent good heart, undefeated and capable of offensive action when opportunity arose. The end of the war found him with a striking force reduced to some 1,400 askaris and a handful of Germans in south-west Tanganyika where, news of the German defeat in Europe having been received, he surrendered with the honours of war. In spite of Von Lettow-Vorbeck's evasive skill, however, the British victory could not have been much longer delayed. The KAR and Allied reinforcements were firmly in occupation of most of German territory, the Belgians had taken Mwanza and General Northey's column of Nyasaland and Rhodesian troops had forced its way up from the south. Although the actual battle casualties incurred in this campaign were moderate, the losses from malaria and other diseases were extremely severe and the losses to horses, mules and donkeys were appalling. The Carrier Corps on both sides suffered especially badly. Had it been realized how great these casualties were going to be it is doubtful whether a full-scale invasion into German East Africa beyond the Tanga–Moshi line would ever have been attempted.

★★★

The war in East Africa was a sideshow, with little appreciable effect on the Great War as a whole, and it seems a pity that it should have had to be fought at all. One can be thankful, at least, that, as between the combatant forces it was fought with mutual respect and very little bitterness. There are, however, some graver reflections. It is a sobering thought, having regard to the high civilising ideals with which the administration of British East Africa had begun, that the protectorate was less than 20 years old before Africans were being enlisted in large numbers to fight in a campaign far more deadly than any of their tribal wars and in a quarrel with which they had nothing to do.

In the previous war between Europeans in Africa, the Boer War, the Africans had been largely kept out of it by both sides, at least from combatant roles. But no such course, however desirable, was open in 1914. During all the early months Kenya was under active invasion by German forces, there was no opinion anywhere, black or white, opposing its defence. It may have been a fact that the fate of the protectorates would depend on the result of the war in Europe, not on local efforts, but that was not the spirit prevailing. The truth is that there was a strong feeling of pulling together, soldiers and civilians of all races, to see the crisis through. The settlers had volunteered to a man and as for the askaris, they were a credit to themselves and their training. They were keen from the first and, with their strength expanded in the course of the war to about 18 battalions, preserved their morale to the end. Their loyalty to their side and to earning their pay was such that, as was noticed in the Kisii district where the inter-territorial boundary ran regardless through the Tende[5] and other tribes, those on one side fought for the British and those on the other fought for the Germans, even in battle against each other.

The tragedy of the African Carriers must be considered in more detail.[6] It cannot be denied that, because of the rapidity with which British defences and, afterwards, the advance into German East Africa had to be organised, supporting services were improvised very hurriedly. Supplies for the fighting troops had to be conveyed long distances through bush country with roads no more than tracks. Head-load porterage, supplemented by pack donkeys and mules where available, was frequently the only practicable means. Even where the South Africans were able to use their motor transport, it was very often bogged down and had to be manhandled out of the mud. A Carrier Corps, getting larger and larger as the advance proceeded, was a first essential of the campaign.

The task of raising it, equipping it, and finding officers for it was assigned to the civil administration. In the opening months, while operations were still taking place on the British side of the border, demands were not large and the task could be adequately performed, but to provide for the advance into German East Africa it was obvious that a vast expansion of the Corps would be required. It is the greatest pity that the Army did not take it over completely at this stage and make proper provision for documentation and records, pay, equipment, supplies, and a suitable staff of British officers and non-commissioned

5 Now known as Kuria.

6 The following account of one of colonial Kenya's major scandals is strikingly honest and passionate, indicating the continued strength of Fazan's feelings many years after the event. Fazan was one of the sources interviewed by Geoffrey Hodges for his essential book, *The Carrier Corps: Military Labor in the East African Campaign, 1914–1918* (New York, NY: Greenwood Press, 1986). Fazan's memory here was doubtless assisted by reference to the angry opinion he had written in 1933, in the Kenya Land Commission's *Report*, pp. 512–15. He and the other commissioners denounced the 'callous violation of the principles of trusteeship' committed by the British War Office in refusing to pay the £50,000 unclaimed balances of pay owed to dead or missing carriers, and called for that sum to be spent on measures to improve the condition of the African lands. For the British government's equally angry response see note 8 below.

officers, leaving to the civil administration only the initial recruitment, the secondment to the Army of such selected civil officers as could be spared, and appropriate functions of liaison and welfare. The failure to do these things resulted in much grave and avoidable hardship.

The civil administration did its best. A senior district commissioner, O. F. Watkins,[7] was seconded as staff officer to the Corps with the rank of colonel and a registration section was set up under Major Gray, another seconded officer of the administration. When, in the last two years of the war, the Corps had swollen to an active strength beyond 150,000, a very senior provincial commissioner in the person of John Ainsworth was seconded to take charge as Director of Military Labour. Recruitment may have been voluntary at first, but was afterwards by conscription, conducted through the chiefs under supervision of the district commissioners, all recruits being subject to medical inspection. Inevitably, though, the numbers of the Corps and their wide distribution quickly outran the capacity of the civil administration to provide from local resources either a sufficient base organisation or officers for the field. From first to last upwards of 400,000 men passed through the books of the Carrier Corps, although the period of conscription was initially short and, I believe, never exceeded 18 months, so that fewer than half the book total would have been on the strength at one time.

Apart from known casualties, which were extremely heavy, some 39,000 men were reported missing and there was about £50,000 of pay outstanding where relatives could not be traced. The fair thing would have been to have paid the money to the Native Trust Fund. The Kenya and Uganda governments argued the case with persistence, but the War Office, although apparently admitting the claim, contended that overpayments to relatives of other carriers who had died or deserted would have to be set off against it and, in the end, no payment was made.[8]

---

7 See the biography by his daughter, Elizabeth Watkins: *Oscar from Africa: The Biography of O. F. Watkins* (London: Radcliffe Press, 1995).

8 Fazan's criticism of the non-payment of the £50,000 outstanding carrier pay, angry and cogent in itself, must also be read as a part of his meditation on the justice, or otherwise, of Kenya's land allocation. The Carter Commission, following earlier Kenya government efforts to get the moneys refunded for general African benefit, recommended that the sum owed should help to improve African agriculture (see note 6 above). The British War Office and Treasury were furious, and the £50,000, not acknowledged as a debt to the carriers, was absorbed in meeting the general expenses of the commission. Fazan must have been as angry with this evasion of responsibility as his chairman, Judge Carter; see Breen, 'The Politics of Land', pp. 116–19.

The privations of the Carrier Corps were an experience that nobody could wish to see repeated. In future, a proper system of registration and record would therefore be essential. The lesson was taken to heart. The record of the Pioneer Corps and the Military Labour Force in the 1939–45 war was a very different story, though there was much more time then to foresee that war was coming and make adequate provision in advance.[9]

At the very end of the war came another affliction: the Spanish influenza. It arrived in Kenya soon after it had attacked South Africa and about the same time as it reached Europe. The number of deaths will never be known. They were probably exaggerated in the reports circulated at the time, but the onslaught was certainly severe and sudden, passing as rapidly as it came.

The effects of the war in Kenya were far reaching, the most important being the increased understanding and respect which developed between the races. But two other effects were more immediately apparent. The first in time, and arising directly out of the campaign itself, was the arrival of the motorcar as a practicable means of transport to replace the head-load porter and ox-wagon. They came progressively into the picture as General Smuts's advance into German East Africa developed. The fact that they could be used at all in the frightful condition of the roads in those days was a revelation. Those that survived the very heavy treatment they endured in the campaign were sold off cheaply and pioneered a revolution in Kenya's economy. Within half a dozen years motor cars, lorries, and tractors were in everyday use and, although for many years after that the state of the roads made driving an adventure, the days of the ox-wagon were over and the way was open for a new and progressive economy. With it came a new outlook, with the accent not so much on cheap labour but on good quality produce and modern methods. The other far-reaching effect of the war was that it saw the white population at least doubled within four years of the armistice to a figure round about 9,000. There had been only about 3,000 Europeans in 1911, said to have increased to about 4,000 at the outbreak of war.

There had been much speculation during the war as to what would happen to German East Africa when Germany surrendered.

9 In 1942 or 1943 Fazan, as civil liaison officer with the East African forces and accompanied by chief Josiah Njonjo from Kikuyuland and other chiefs from Uganda and Tanganyika, visited the soldiers posted to the Middle East in order to ensure that a proper administrative system was indeed in operation (Hodges, *Carrier Corps*, p. 200).

Considerable pressure was being exerted from India for it to become an extension area to absorb surplus population.[10] The hope in Kenya was that it would become a British protectorate to form a single block with the other East African territories. Uncertainty continued for some time, causing hesitation in the investment of capital in all these territories. The final settlement, drafted in 1920 and confirmed when the League of Nations was established in 1922, gave Ruanda and Urundi to Belgium and the rest of German East Africa to be administered by Britain under mandate from the League.[11] Also, whether as part of the general peace settlement or for administrative convenience, Kenya's province of Jubaland, inhabited by Somalis, was handed over to Italy to be administered by them as part of Italian Somaliland.

10 See Robert G. Gregory, *India and East Africa: A History of Race Relations within the British Empire 1890–1939* (Oxford: Clarendon, 1971), Chapter V.

11 For which see Michael D. Callahan, *Mandates and Empire: The League of Nations and Africa, 1914–1931* (Brighton: Sussex Academic Press, 1999).

PART II

The Colony During the Inter-War Years

6

The Coast

The Coast Strip stretched the full length of the Kenya shoreline but extended inland to a depth of only 10 miles. This was the Kenya Protectorate as distinct from the Colony and, except for the small enclave of the Sultanate of Witu, was leased from the Sultan of Zanzibar. Though the pace of development lagged, the coast had its own special features and administrative problems, arising from past history and the mixed character of its population. Indeed, it was the only part of Kenya that had a written history before the British came.[1]

There was a quiet calm about the coast quite different from the rest of Kenya. A vivid sense of the past could be felt in what was seen around in ruins haunted by the spirits of the baobab; in ancient mango trees planted by slaves for Arab masters and owned today by the grandsons of those slaves; in mangrove swamps where slaving dhows used to hide from vessels of the British Navy; in the old harbour at Mombasa where the dhows came in from Muscat; in Arab streets flanked by once proud buildings, their embossed doors and ornate carved lintels sadly in decay, but streets still alive with the happy-looking faces of children of many races. There were also the great monuments: Fort Jesus to the Portuguese, the fort at Lamu built by Seyyid Said for resisting the Mazrui and the mysterious ruins of twice sacked and abandoned Gedi, long lost in

1 The best guides to the historical status of the coastal strip and how it then affected coastal politics in the colonial period are A. I. Salim, *Swahili-speaking Peoples of Kenya's Coast, 1895–1965* (Nairobi: East African Publishing House, 1973) and James R. Brennan, 'Lowering the Sultan's flag: Sovereignty and decolonization in coastal Kenya', *Comparative Studies in Society and History* 1 (2008), pp. 831–61.

the forest of Mida and leaving not even a memory behind to tell what happened.[2]

None of the Arab towns were as populated or prosperous when the British Protectorate started as they had been 400 years earlier when they first excited the attention of the Portuguese. Their ruthlessness in sacking Kilwa, Mombasa and Lamu started the decline of Arab power and raids by African tribes from the interior added to the destruction.

The failure to make any lasting recovery during the years after the Portuguese left must be ascribed partly to the rising influence of Zanzibar, but mostly to the turbulence and ceaseless bickering of the Arab towns. The essential unsoundness of a slave-based economy must have been a contributory cause and the fact that many wells along the coast turned brackish may also have had something to do with it. When Sir Arthur Hardinge, the first commissioner, took charge in 1895, quelled the Mazrui rebellion and put a final stop to the traffic in slaves, he was faced with the formidable task of arresting the tide of decline and getting a free-labour based economy started.

Slave ownership on the coast was fully abolished in 1907 and the Arabs were compensated for their slaves, but they soon ran through the money, lacking the skill and enterprise to engage labour or to work the land themselves. Many of them mortgaged their land to Indians; the mortgage money went the same way, and they were ruined. In matters of ownership of plantation land, which slave labour had formerly cultivated, the Protectorate government was bound by the treaty with the Sultan to honour all titles which he had conferred, and a recorder of titles was appointed to ascertain them. There were very few cases, however, outside the towns and their immediate neighbourhood, where clear title could be established or where boundaries of land were defined. As for the released slaves, not many of them went home. Here and there, especially at Freretown on the northern mainland opposite Mombasa Island, a few of their descendants lived and traded in special reservations near Christian mission stations, and other settlements intended for them were established in Kilifi and Malindi districts. The

2 For the international commercial history of the coast, see the references to Chapter 1 above. For the history of the local peoples and their settlements, the most enthusiastic is James de Vere Allen, *Swahili Origins: Swahili Culture and the Shungwaya Phenomenon* (London: James Currey, 1993); for more sober assessments, see John Sutton, *A Thousand Years of East Africa* and Mark Horton, *Shanga: The Archaeology of a Muslim Trading Community on the Coast of East Africa* (London: British Institute in Eastern Africa, 1990 & 1996, respectively).

great majority, however, stayed on to cultivate the land abandoned by their former masters.[3]

Although many of the people living on the coast strip were ex-masters or ex-slaves, the general Swahili population was neither the one nor the other, but was of mixed Arab/African blood, living in the towns or in village settlements along the coast and cultivating the neighbouring land as of squatter right. Many of those near Mombasa claimed to be of Arab descent through membership either of the *Tisa Taifa* (nine tribes) or of the *Thelatha Taifa* (three tribes) and presumably belonged to a very early wave of settlement of coast Arabs, scarcely recognised as such by the later immigrants. They engaged in petty trade, but retail trade in the towns had passed into the hands of Indians, some of whom had been on the East African coast for generations.

Among other elements in the population there was, in the Kilifi and Malindi districts, an increased infiltration of Nyika from the hinterland. Further north, in the area beyond Malindi – between Mambrui and the Tana River – there was a stretch of fly-free country where a section of the Galla, who were originally from Ethiopia, lived and kept cattle. The Pokomo inhabited the Tana Delta and upriver along the banks for about 200 miles while, in the off-shore islands of Lamu and in parts of the adjoining mainland lived elements of the Bajun, of whom there were only a few thousand in Kenya. They were lighter skinned and straighter-haired than other East African tribes and they divided their time between agriculture, fishing and cutting poles in the mangrove swamps, which they transported to Lamu for export to Oman. The Sultan of Witu was himself a Bajun.

In the first decade of the Protectorate, while the seat of government was still at Mombasa, the commissioner travelled freely in the coastal districts and was able to give them a large share of his attention. A telegraph line was laid through the bush to connect them with headquarters, and staff for administrative, medical, police and even agricultural services was provided on a scale which, modest indeed, was

3 The authoritative work on this process, Cooper's *From Slaves to Squatters*, adds to this analysis the initiative shown by ex-slaves in exploiting the uncertain property rights to which Fazan refers. For a wider social history of the coast in Fazan's day that argues that internal struggles between Africans, between generations or between patrons and clients, were the motor of what Fazan and his colleagues saw as decline, see Justin Willis, *Mombasa, the Swahili, and the Making of the Mijikenda* (Oxford: Clarendon, 1993). Fazan's memories are especially useful here, since historians have not paid as much attention to the coast in the colonial period as to upcountry Kenya.

generous in proportion to the tiny revenues of the country. By their efforts, combined with those of the Arab officers, it was possible at least to keep up appearances, if not to make progress. Thus encouraged, several European firms ventured capital on coconut, cotton and rubber plantations, to be followed later by sisal and at least one sugar plantation. But when the seat of government was moved to Nairobi the coast again fell into decline. Much of the land between the towns and village settlements reverted to bush, especially in the Kilifi district. Sanye bushmen again ranged the scrub in search of elephants and hunted and trapped small game. Elephants came down to the coast in June to bathe in Kilifi creek to rid themselves of mange. Over large stretches of country tsetse fly was returning and rendered wide areas impossible for keeping cattle.

It was not, however, a total collapse. Several of the wealthier Arabs, especially those around Lamu and some near Mombasa and in the neighbourhood of Witu, managed to keep their former plantations under some degree of cultivation. Others sold their plantations to Europeans or Asians, while there were many cases in which plantations, once of considerable size, had been split up under the Mohammedan system of inheritance into quite small pieces where the heirs eked out a precarious livelihood. This was seen especially in the Tana River delta, where the fragments were so small as to be scarcely even worth the cost of registration.

Efforts by Europeans to start plantations on a wider scale had had, at this date, little or no success. Rubber was a failure and so was cotton at that time. Coconuts were proving a very poor investment, and the price of sisal was dangerously low. As I went up the coast road in 1918 I met the last of the Malindi rubber planters on his final way out. Shortly after this the fortunes of the coast reached about their lowest ebb, with conditions of acute food shortage almost amounting to famine, followed by the outbreak of Spanish influenza. Maize had to be imported from South Africa, and it was dealt out, partly, by issue to selected traders who had to be trusted to distribute it fairly under supervision of the *liwali*, and partly by road construction relief works, the pay for one day's work being a pot of heaped maize. This pot, called a *pishi*, was a recognised measure holding six pounds of maize when heaped or six pounds of rice when cut off flat. The day's pay, therefore, was calculated to provide a full ration for the worker himself and enough for three other adults besides, which was the surplus which he took home to his family. The year became known as *N'daa ya pishi moja*, while the former famine of 1898 was the *N'daa ya mahunia* – the pot famine and the gunny-bag famine. The Spanish influenza, following soon afterwards, proved much the greater affliction of the two, because there was no known remedy. Tea drinking was advised for those who could afford it; and hot water for those who could not. Doses of kerosene oil were held by some to be efficacious but, perhaps fortunately, this advice did not arrive until the epidemic was virtually over. In spite of rumours to the contrary I do not think the mortality was very serious at the coast, certainly not nearly as grave as it was with the Kikuyu upcountry. The only exception to the general depression along the coast at this time was Mombasa Island itself, which enjoyed comparative prosperity through being the port and railhead for upcountry.

In all other district stations of the Kenya coast – reduced to five by the secession of Jubaland – administrative staffs had dwindled until there was only one British officer in charge of each of them in addition to the Arab officers maintained under the treaty. Departmental officers were almost non-existent except for an occasional posting on temporary duty. When extra help was needed it had to be obtained from provincial headquarters at Mombasa or from Nairobi.

With staff so low and almost no money available, there was little the district administration could do to arrest the process of decay. It was easier to see what was required to be done than how to do it, how to tackle the principal sources of decline, among which apathy, disease, drink and debt were prominent; to get the land, including abandoned plantations, back into agricultural use; to improve the quality of produce; to foster the dhow and fishing industries and the small local handicrafts and check the decline in coastal trade. Often the only weapon was hope, but at least the coast was peaceful and the people friendly.

Of the Arab officers maintained under the terms of the treaty, there was an average of about three per district. The *kathi* was the one with the most clear-cut duties to perform. He was concerned with matters of Islamic law, arising chiefly in connection with marriage, divorce, inheritance questions, and the administration of *wakf*, or consecrated lands.[4] The other Arab officers – *liwalis* and *mudirs* – had titles which, except in the case of the senior *liwali* for the coast, were higher than the nature of their duties warranted. They appeared to regard their duties in different ways. Some seemed to consider their small salary as a pension, and sufficiently earned by acting as social head of the local Arab community. It was a defensible point of view, for there was

4 For the Islamic legal system in coastal Kenya, see also Ghai and McAuslan, *Public Law and Political Change*, Chapter IV.

nothing prescribed; but they were more useful when, besides giving special attention to their own communities, they undertook also to cooperate in the general administration of the coast population, African as well as Arab. There was so much fusion of blood amongst them that I recollect no difficulty in getting the African headmen to accept it. They were practically all Mohammedans in the Coast Strip, except the Nyika encroachers, who usually became so before long.

Except for a short period when the Nyika tribe[5] was administered from a centre inland, the boundaries of all the coast districts extended far into the hinterland. It was essential that produce from the interior should have easy access to the small coast ports as well as to Mombasa and the railway, so road communications were gradually improved and, as they lost their fear of slavery, many of the Nyika infiltrated into the Coast Strip and settled on vacant land. They were in fact trespassing on land which, in most cases, was under some form of claim and awaiting adjudication, but, on the other hand, they were clearing it of bush, putting it to good agricultural use and, in the process, opening up the landscape and warding off infestation by fly. Seeing that the main problem of administration was how to check the decline of the coast, get some heart into the thoroughly dispirited population, and try to restore some measure of prosperity, these encroachments were accounted an asset and best left undisturbed, at least until a specific issue for adjudication of the land arose.[6]

The Africans in this part of the coast were unenterprising compared with most upcountry tribes and lacking in political cohesion. The Arab domination had gone and their headmen had little authority. Order had therefore to be effected, mostly following upcountry lines with native councils and tribunals. But the tempo of progress was slow. Many Africans were extremely improvident, especially the Nyika from the hinterland, and were constantly in debt to Indian shopkeepers who advanced them loans. These loans were mostly of food in the hungry season, given against the security of growing crops, and were usually advanced on a basis of sevenfold repayment. Rescuing these people from this state of economic servitude was a chief preoccupation.

---

5 Now called Mijikenda. Historians differ as to when the Mijikenda first became aware of themselves as one people. Spear, *Kaya Complex*, argues that this consciousness grew in the nineteenth century while Willis, *Mombasa, the Swahili, and the Making of the Mijikenda*, believes it to have been a colonial phenomenon.

6 The indeterminacy of title at the coast made land-grabbing easy for political elites in the 1990s, for which see Karuti Kanyinga, 'The land question in Kenya: Struggles, accumulation and changing politics' (Roskilde University: PhD dissertation, 1998).

Attempts to deal with the matter by regulation were never successful, for there was as yet no usury ordinance so framed as to cover such transactions, so the best hope was to show to fair minded Indians that their methods must cease if agriculture and, consequently, their own businesses were ever to prosper on the coast.

Apart from the Arab community, which was generally abstemious, drinking among the Africans was often carried to great excess. Palm wine could be very strong, especially when laced with Nubian gin, and the places where it was brewed, though usually hidden in the bush, were easily traced by the smell. Because they were often the scene of violent crime they had to be kept under control, so the experiment was tried of bringing them out into the open where they could be licensed and easily inspected. Fear that this policy would increase drunkenness rather than diminish it proved groundless and, as the idea was developed in later years, these places became social clubs and a valuable source of local government revenue. It also proved possible, by regulation, to give the owners of the palms and tappers a better deal.[7]

Agriculture, forest produce, fishing and the dhow-carrying trade were the chief economic activities. Ivory, once significant, was now of minor importance. Few could afford the fee for an elephant licence and 'found' ivory had by law to be handed in, payment being withheld until the circumstances of the find were proved. There was some smuggling and poaching of ivory and rhino horn but it seemed not to be in any great quantity.[8] Rope, sails, mat bags, lace caps, carpet mats attractively coloured with local vegetable dyes, well made locally, and some weaving, carpentry and wood carving were also sent. There were silversmiths too, but they were mostly Indians, often working in Indian rupees illegally melted down.

The coast belt was rich in the diversity of its agricultural produce. The plantation giants – coconut palms, mangos, and cashew nut trees – dominated the scene as they must have done for centuries. All were of great value in the general life of the countryside, and every part of the coconut palm had its local uses. However, it had little export value. The market for copra showed no expansion and excessive tapping of the trees for palm wine had spoilt the yield. Although limited use of the oil was made in Mombasa soap factories, started about this time, and

7 For a history of what was of as much concern to African elders as to colonial officials, see Justin Willis, *Potent Brews: A Social History of Alcohol in East Africa 1850–1999* (Oxford: James Currey, 2002).

8 Unlike the twenty-first-century threats to both elephant and rhino.

fronds for thatching were sold upcountry, the planting of coconuts beyond the requirements of local needs had had its day. Neither mangos nor bananas were of good enough quality to have much export potential but there was more hope for cashew nuts. The quality of the nuts was excellent and there was no lack of demand, but the problem here was that the trees were so scattered as to make collection and processing difficult. Nevertheless, at a later stage, a processing plant was started. It seemed, however, that the less conspicuous crops would have to be relied on to bring prosperity to the coast. They included rice from the Tana River (the planting of which could be much extended through irrigation), sesame, groundnuts, castor and other vegetable oils, beans, cotton, chillies and a little tobacco. There was also fruit – oranges, limes, pineapples, grapefruit, mangustines and pomegranates – all of which grew well.

There was not much that could be done about these things in the early years before agricultural officers arrived. But a start was made by constant exhortation and attention to such matters as the better selection of seed so that produce coming to market should be more uniform. Further, it was ensured that sales should be for cash and not barter which had generally meant a double profit to the traders at the expense of the growers. Strenuous efforts were also made to get more of the land back into use. As for livestock farming on the coast, it was entirely in African hands, and was confined to the hinterland and the fly-free areas of the coast belt. Its problems were no different from what they were in the tribal areas upcountry.

***

The year I spent among the Pokomo on the Tana River was a light charge among a pleasant and contented people.[9] The district commissioner at Lamu told me when I was on my way there, 'You've got a most absurd district, four hundred miles long and two miles wide'. This was, of course, an exaggeration, but it may have been true that the river was as long as that, with all its windings, and that nearly all the cultivation was along its banks. All the Pokomo lived there, while the plains of the right bank were sparsely occupied by Galla and an influx of Giriama from the Nyika country. A few miles away on the left bank lay Witu and the Lamu district and inland of that was Somali country, part of the Northern Frontier province. With the

9 Another under-researched people, in whom Fazan clearly took great interest.

latter I had nothing to do beyond providing them with fly-free access routes to the river for their cattle.

The district station for Tana River was Kipini at the mouth of the Ozi Creek into which the river flowed. There was practically nothing there beyond the official quarters and a small customs post, a shop or two and the huts of a few aged ex-slaves drawing government pensions as having no other means. There had been a mission station close by but this had been abandoned, and there was practically no native habitation within several miles. There were a few privately-owned dhows, a government launch, a lighter which it could tow, and a fleet of about 40 dug-out canoes. The main function of the station was as a base to rest and refit and enter up the books and accounts between up-river safaris. In order to avoid too frequent visits I fixed up the lighter as an office and took a clerk with me up the river so that wherever I happened to be at the time became the district office. When the river was in flood the launch could go the whole length of the Tana Valley almost to the rapids; at most other times one could generally reach the middle river and then proceed by canoe or on foot.

The Pokomo of the lower and middle river were Swahili-speaking. They mostly appeared to be of no professed religion. Those of the delta, however, tended towards Islam, while along the middle river there was a chain of Methodist mission stations exercising some local influence. Further up the river were people of other speech and, probably, other stock. They were known by the Pokomo as *korokoro*, but they may well have been Tharaka like those of Embu district. There was also a settlement of the Boni, who were akin to the Sanye and Dorobo.

The staple food of the Pokomo was rice and bananas, though maize and millets and all the usual coast crops grew well. There was no lack of palm wine made both from coconuts and also from *mkindu* and *mtwapa* palms growing wild on the plains, although the use of the latter two was restricted to prevent wasteful destruction. The presence of 'fly' prevented the keeping of livestock beyond chickens and very few goats, but there was occasional barter with Galla from the hinterland. These Galla – and the Boni too – would sometimes come in with ivory which they alleged to have been 'found'.

As a rule the Pokomo had no great difficulty in feeding themselves, but the river, flooding twice a year, was apt to play tricks. It would sometimes alter course for a few miles or would heap a man's land not only with silt but sometimes with sand. From time to time the river failed to flood and there was drought. More often floods were excessive and would carry all before them, causing widespread devastation. It was therefore obvious that, if ever proper use was to be made of the great potentials of the Tana Valley, extensive irrigation and protection works would have to be undertaken. The need was the more urgent having regard to the pressure of growing population and expansion amongst the Kikuyu and other large tribes.[10] But such development was far beyond the resources then available. All one could do was to study and promote the methods of self-help that the Pokomo themselves were employing to protect their villages. This they did with little ramparts built along the banks. They also dug conduit trenches, which they called *m'belezo*, which led off over the dead-level plains to depressions further back in which temporary lakes were formed, some of them almost permanent. In some of the worst flooded areas of the middle reaches of the river the Pokomo built their huts on stilts and communicated by canoe. In these places rice was planted on rafts ready to be transplanted to seed beds when the river subsided; later it was transplanted a second time into the paddy fields.

The Pokomo had no money to speak of and not much need of it. Apart from occasional finds of ivory, their only source of wealth was the export of rice and bananas to Lamu and a little tobacco, roped and coiled, to Italian Somaliland. These things they transported by *sangalis*, rafts holding about a ton and a quarter weight constructed over two canoes placed side by side. Rice to a European palate is rice, but the Arabs were very fastidious about it. There were just three of the many varieties grown on the river that had any value for them. It was thus very necessary to keep the seed unmixed, and much attention had to be devoted to that end.

Mosquitoes existed in such hordes up the river that they had to be swept off rather than swatted. The Pokomo had acquired a tolerance of malaria and seldom exhibited its symptoms, but constant biting may have affected their bloodstream causing lethargy. The worst disease plaguing the Pokomo however was yaws, a disfiguring complaint causing hideous growths. There was practically no treatment available, although a little could be done by sending a man to hospital at Lamu for treatment, but I never saw any marked result. I felt so strongly about the matter that I made a special journey to Nairobi to persuade the authorities to undertake a campaign of inoculation. Happily they yielded to my importunities and a team of two doctors was sent to tour the whole length of the river giving inoculations. Whether this had any

10 Since independence the large settlement of Kikuyu in the Tana River basin has caused great political controversy.

permanent effect in reducing the spread of the disease I am unable to say, but I am quite sure that the immediate effects were extremely beneficial.[11]

When I had been on the river a year or so, the Tana and Lamu districts were combined and I found myself in charge. The two areas had been so interdependent that the combination was logical and to the advantage of both. The Arab community of Lamu, especially their elders, lived in an atmosphere of sedate resignation, addicted to ceremonial and acutely conscious of the dignity of life. It was a pleasant enough change to be there, provided one could get away on safari.[12]

It was well after 1920 when the first motorcar reached Malindi, and none had as yet got as far as Lamu. As there were no lorries on the coast, the transport of produce was by sea-going dhow and the occasional steamer; the only alternative was by head-load porterage. Large dhows from Oman still visited the coast ports to sell carpets and other merchandise and generally, on the return journey, they carried mangrove poles for Arabia. Dhows of that size, however, were now seldom built on the Kenya coast. In 1923 there were, I believe, only three of 60 tons or more on the register at Lamu and only one in the course of construction. There were also about a dozen on the 40 tons register, but most were under 20 tons. While the ownership of the dhows remained in Arab or Swahili hands they were usually run on family lines and paid off, if not handsomely, at least well enough. There was a happy-go-lucky spirit and well-understood rules about the respective shares and responsibilities of owner, captain and crew, and they worked well so long as they had a common interest. But Indian traders with a keener sense of business had bought out many of the owners and squabbles arose with the crews. All too often they ended with crews taking advances and getting deeper and deeper in the owner's debt. It was necessary, therefore, to negotiate an amnesty from time to time, if the industry was not to be ruined.

As for the fishing industry, it carried on using its traditional methods of traps, nets and boats. Regulations were made from time to time but on the whole it went on without much innovation or control except for

11 The eradication of yaws, latterly with the aid of penicillin, was one of the indisputable benefits of colonialism.

12 Lamu, now a UNESCO World Heritage site under threat from oil-related development, is thought to be the oldest continually inhabited town in Kenya, dating from the twelfth century CE. See Patricia Romero, *Lamu: History, Society and Family in an East African Port City* (Princeton, NJ: Markus Wiener, 1997).

some improvement in the better organisation of the fish markets. It was not until about the 1930s, with Japanese and other non-Africans taking an interest, that signs of expansion began to appear.

The slow pace of change on the coast had its exception in Mombasa. By 1924, the date of my first posting there, a period of considerable economic and constructional expansion was already in progress. With the assistance of substantial loans, the first two deep-water berths at the port of Kilindini were nearing completion and the whole of that area was being redesigned and reconstructed.[13] At the same time a new town plan was being worked out, and a little later a substantial sum was provided for road widening and such other improvements in the Arab old town as were practicable without destroying its original character.

***

When I renewed my acquaintance with the coast in 1933 there were signs of moderate, but definite, improvement in all coast districts, particularly in the fields of agriculture and public health. A new hospital had been built at Kilifi with two British doctors and a nursing sister, and all up and down the coast there was evidence that health measures, combined with bush clearing and cultivation and the consequent opening up of the landscape into wider prospects was having good effect. Malaria was well under control, and disfiguring diseases such as yaws and elephantiasis were far less commonly seen. The general African population, among whom were now large numbers of Luo from Nyanza Province employed on public works or on European sisal plantations, appeared better fed and more alert. Cotton at Malindi, once a failure, was now being grown with success under supervision of the agricultural department. Sisal plantations under corporate ownership had survived a series of poor prices and were also expanding. Road transport facilities had been much improved. Even the livestock

13 Fazan here passes over one of the several Kenya controversies – some say scandals – over the triangular relationship between concession, capital investment and profit in pursuit of 'development'. Government concessions of (African) land were intended to attract private investors; if private capital were then risked in developing the land the question then became one of how the subsequent utility and profit should be shared between (white) private and (white) public interests. The case here relates to the creation of Mombasa's port facilities, initially on the shorefront of a concession earlier made to Ewart Grogan. For opposing views, the first focusing on scandal and the second emphasising the risks and costs of entrepreneurship, see William McGregor Ross, *Kenya from Within: A Short Political History* (London: Allen and Unwin, 1927), Chapters IX and XV, and Paice, *Lost Lion*, Chapter 20.

industry was not being entirely neglected: a fly-free route had been found through Lamu district for the export of slaughter stock to Zanzibar and at Mazeras on the railway a cooperative dairy, established by the joint efforts of the Nyika native council and the veterinary department, was taking an increasing part in the Mombasa milk supply. Every year more holiday-makers, both European and Asian, were coming from the highlands to the coast in search of 'sea air and sanity'. In short, the corner had been turned and there was no more fear of the Coast 'going back'.

7

Principal Events and Politics

A most valuable feature of the influx of new settlers to Kenya at the end of the First World War was that a large proportion consisted of young and keen men who came either newly married or shortly to be married, and eager to settle on the land. They were home-builders and a welcome addition to the vigour of the colony. Land for them was made available at low rental and stand premium charges under a soldier settlement scheme. Some of it, for instance the Trans-Nzoia, had already been set apart and demarcated for farms before the war and had not been taken up. Other land was surveyed for them in the Kipkarren and Kaimosi areas on the Nandi border and in the Kericho and Sotik areas bordering the Kipsigis. The last considerable alienation was in 1919. After that it was declared that, to all intents and purposes, no further land was available for settlement except by subdivision of existing holdings. Not all the newcomers bought farms. Many thought it advisable to take employment as managers or even as learner-apprentices before entering upon land of their own. And, of course, the new immigrants were not entirely confined to would-be farmers. There was a small professional and business element. To provide for medical attention in rural areas, farms were granted free to doctors who were willing to take them up.

It was not a particularly good time to begin farming, because there were, as yet, no established markets for export produce except coffee and sisal. One large soldier-settlement cooperative made an unfortunate venture in flax but the members were eventually able, through the good offices of the director of agriculture, to offload the property without loss and to find openings in other areas or take employment with the tea company that had succeeded to their land. In one way or another, most of the soldier settlers made good, in spite of hard times ahead.

One particularly hard stroke of fortune was the change in East African currency which had until then been a rupee currency linked to the Indian at 15 rupees to the pound sterling. With the increase in the price of silver during the war, however, the Indian rupee had risen in value until it reached something like Shs. 2/3d. The Kenya currency was then changed and linked to the pound sterling. Rupees were called in at the exchange rate of one florin note for 1 rupee, and shortly afterwards an East African currency was introduced at 20 shillings to the pound. The effect was that mortgage debts increased overnight to the tune of 50 per cent. This obstacle was eventually surmounted, but it was a drag on development for several years.[1]

In 1920 Kenya was proclaimed a Colony in recognition of the fact that British people had made their homes there in considerable numbers. At about the same time the composition of the Legislative Council was changed so that the unofficial members had henceforth to be elected, although the nominated official element still held the majority. The elections were to be on a community basis with 11 seats for Europeans. Originally there were only two seats assigned to Indians, both nominated, but this was later increased to an elected five, plus one nominated and one elected for the Arabs. The representation of Africans was entrusted primarily to the chief native commissioner and to one European non-official, later two, nominated by the governor.

During the ensuing ten years or so the European population increased at an average rate of barely a thousand a year, although the extent of the alienated land could have accommodated many more; there was room on the farms for subdivision, bearing in mind that the lorry and the tractor did not require acres of grazing land to be kept for their depasturage as their oxen forerunners had done. After 1931 the increase, in which children born in the country were a significant factor, was a little faster, and the probable total figure for European residents in 1939 was around 25,000.

There were not wanting among other races objections against the privileged treatment of European soldier settlers and, indeed, against the whole policy of the White Highlands. Although the Africans showed little resentment over the soldier-settler scheme as such, it gave a new argument to the growing political element who were casting their eyes on empty spaces in the Highlands on the fringes of their own reserves. They could now claim that, while white ex-servicemen were given land, the

1 These were critical years for colonial Kenya. The future of white settlement was in question, thanks to the difficulties that Fazan relates, added to which there were imperial controversies over the use of forced African labour for private white profit and the civic status of Indian immigrants. There is a large literature. See especially, Maxon, *Struggle for Kenya*, Chapters 5–7; Clayton and Savage, *Government and Labour*, Chapter 4; Berman, *Control and Crisis*, Chapter 4; Huxley, *White Man's Country*, Chapters XVI–XX; C. J. Duder, '"Men of the officer class": Participants in the 1919 Soldier Settlement Scheme in Kenya', *African Affairs* 92 (1993), pp. 69–87.

African's only reward for his war service was the widely resented *kipande*, a combined identity and registration card bearing fingerprints, which all adult males were obliged to carry under the terms of the 1920 Native Registration Ordinance. There was also suspicion about the change-over from Protectorate to Colony, as there was about the currency change, the depression and the temporary reduction of wages that had followed. As a special issue among the Kikuyu, a demand was also being put forward for registration of clan and family right-holdings within the area of the Kikuyu reserve, as well as for the demarcation of its boundaries.

The prime mover in voicing these grievances on behalf of the Kikuyu was the newly-formed Young Kikuyu Association with a handsome young man named Harry Thuku at its head. Through Kikuyu agents and, indeed, through Thuku himself, who made a visit to Kisumu, the discontent spread to Nyanza Province among the Luo and Abaluhya.[2] These latter tribes had not lost any appreciable area of land to white settlement, but with the Kikuyu there was a genuine issue deserving investigation.[3] Meanwhile the Indians, with the support of the government of India, were claiming the right to purchase land in the Highlands. They had not liked the policy from the start and common cause was made between them and Kikuyu agitators in an attempt to form a militant East African Association. In subsequent proceedings against Thuku, evidence was adduced by the chief native commissioner purporting to show that the main theme of the movement was 'to stimulate enmity between black and white and to get people to consider that they are in a state of slavery which had been imposed upon them by the Europeans'. The result was that the governor, convinced that Thuku's activities were prejudicial to peace and good order, had him placed under restriction in a remote part of the colony. The immediate outcome of his detention was a serious riot in Nairobi.[4]

---

2 Thuku never visited Nyanza but one of his associates, James Beauttah, did. Fazan almost certainly picked up this minor factual error from Bennett, *Kenya, a Political History*, p. 45, although we cannot now know to what reading matter Fazan referred when writing this memoir.

3 Again, it is impossible for Fazan not to return to the issue of land.

4 The government admitted to 25 killed by police rifle fire; African estimates were much higher. The African politics of these years have also generated a large literature. See especially, Carl G. Rosberg and John Nottingham, *The Myth of 'Mau Mau: Nationalism in Kenya* (New York, NY; London: Praeger & Pall Mall, 1966), Chapters II and III; Robert L. Tignor, *The Colonial Transformation of Kenya: The Kamba, Kikuyu, and Maasai from 1900 to 1939* (Princeton, NJ: Princeton University Press, 1976), Chapter X; John *Spencer, KAU: The Kenya African Union* (London: KPI, 1985), Chapter 2; Marshall S. Clough, *Fighting Two Sides: Kenyan Chiefs and Politicians, 1918–1940* (Niwot, CO: University Press of Colorado, 1990), Chapters 2–5.

While all these issues – and particularly the Indian claim to the right to buy land in the White Highlands – were awaiting the secretary of state's ruling, feelings were running very high in Nairobi. There was great apprehension among the settlers' leaders, and much scheming and hot-headed talk, but the restraining influence of the imperturbable governor, Sir Robert Coryndon, prevented anything very serious from occurring. And, as it happened, there was no need for their alarm. The decision of the secretary of state, conveyed in the 'Devonshire white paper' of 1923, reaffirmed the existing administrative practice of restricting land grants in the Highlands to Europeans and ordained its continuance both in initial grants and transfer.[5]

There was great relief among the settlers at this decision and it is doubtful if even the Indians were seriously disappointed. Their complaint was largely political, for when given the opportunity to farm in lower-lying areas, they showed little inclination to do so. The fear among European settlers, however, had not been so much that local Indian tradesmen would rush to take up farms as that, if the Highlands were opened up to Asiatics, the colony would be swamped by an influx from India. It was widely believed that the Indian government, besides supporting the present claim, had, during the war and after, asked for Tanganyika as an area for the relief of India's expanding population, and Kenya was not felt to be safe. Some, too, remembered that, when Joseph Chamberlain had been secretary of state, the British government had offered the Kenya highlands as a national home for the Jews.[6]

As part of a general statement of policy in the White Paper of 1923 it was declared that: 'Primarily Kenya is an African territory and His Majesty's Government think it necessary definitely to record their considered opinion that the interests of African natives must be paramount, and that, if, and when, their interests and the interests of the immigrant races should conflict, the former should prevail.' The European settler community was not too happy about this but accepted its general purport. The conception of partnership rather than conflict

---

5 The phrase 'existing administrative practice' is important here, referring to the 'Elgin pledge' of 1906, for which see Chapter 2, note 12. One of the most contentious outcomes of the Carter Land Commission was the translation of 'administrative practice' into the legal protection of white privilege in the Highlands under the Highlands Order in Council of 1939.

6 For which see Robert G. Weisbord, *African Zion: The Attempt to Establish a Jewish Colony in the East Africa Protectorate, 1903–1905* (Philadelphia, PA: Jewish Publication Society of America, 1968).

would have made more appeal but, nevertheless, a real effort was made to proceed on these lines.

After this dispatch tempers cooled down. Explanatory *barazas* took place in the Kikuyu and Nyanza districts on all questions of substance that had been raised, including the question of clan or family group rights and the gazettement of the native reserves. The boundaries of the latter were ready for gazettement in 1926 but legal enactment was delayed, presumably to allow time for objections. On the question of private rights inside the reserves, it soon became evident to all parties that the matter required much more study, both as to what the Africans really wanted and how far it was practicable. District commissioners in Kikuyuland and Nyanza made investigations and, in 1929, a committee appointed by the governor reported on *The Kikuyu System of Land Tenure*. This inquiry was well received by the Kikuyu and they gave useful cooperation.[7]

Just as the horizon appeared serene, another trouble broke out. Traditionally among the Kikuyu, both boys and girls were circumcised after reaching puberty. This ceremony had profound significance, both religious and civic, as admitting the initiates to full membership of the tribe. To interfere with it would be an extremely rash act, only justified if the effects of the practice could be shown to be wholly evil.

7 Fazan leaves much unsaid here – but see further below, Chapter 11. As district commissioner of Kiambu, he was a member of the three-man committee of enquiry, the others being Chief Native Commissioner G. V. Maxwell, who knew almost nothing about the Kikuyu, and the 26-year-old Louis Leakey. Leakey had been born at the Kabete Anglican mission station near Nairobi and was now at the start of his famous palaeontological career; he was considered by himself and by other Europeans to be the leading white expert on Kikuyu life. The 'useful cooperation' given by Kikuyu included much invented history, designed to promote their unchallengeable claim to the land. The enquiry's majority report, by Maxwell and Leakey, was indeed 'well received' since it supported the authority of lineage elders to continue to allocate land usage while acknowledging that 'rules' would be needed in future. Fazan thought that the relationship between complex African land tenures and poor productivity was sufficiently urgent for government to undertake measures to grant individual title to improving smallholder farmers, to guard against both undue land concentration in the hands of lineage elders and uneconomic fragmentation. Chief Koinange, whom Fazan much respected, later denounced this proposal for greater government intervention as 'communist'. Fazan returned to the argument again soon after, as Secretary of the Kenya Land Commission. See further discussion in the Foreword and John Lonsdale, 'Contests of Time: Kikuyu Historiographies, Old and New', in Axel Harneit-Sievers (ed.), *A Place in the World: New Local Historiographies from Africa and South Asia* (Leiden: Brill, 2002), pp. 201–54.

To European eyes, the practice of circumcising girls seemed revolting and barbarous. It was represented with truth by those who wished government to interfere, that the female operators were often in such a state of religious or alcoholic frenzy that they sometimes caused grievous harm, rendering their victims unfit for child-bearing. It was also sincerely, though wrongly, represented that these cases were so frequent as to threaten the tribe with slow extinction. Suddenly the Church of Scotland Mission (CSM), without any warning or consultation, announced that parents who allowed their daughters to be circumcised would not be admitted to Holy Communion. The Gospel Mission and the African Inland Mission joined them in condemning female circumcision, but the CMS and the Roman Catholics held aloof.[8]

The result of the CSM action was that they lost most of their mission outschools, and a number of their African pastors seceded. Seeing that the outschool churches had been built and furnished from Sunday School collections at those outschools, the local elders were in a strong

---

8 Again, the 'female circumcision crisis' of 1929–30 has generated a large literature. As district commissioner, Fazan did all within his professional power to maintain the peace in a highly emotive situation – not least in his capacity as resident magistrate when investigating the murder and forced circumcision of an elderly female missionary (for which see David Anderson and Richard Waller, *Colonial Crimes*, forthcoming). Fazan was misinformed, however, if he thought the Church of Scotland's decision 'sudden': the CSM and other Protestant missions had been discussing the matter for many years, and the official Local Native Councils had been trying, ineffectually, to reduce the physical reach of the operation. The CSM blamed the crisis on a court decision not to press a charge of grievous bodily harm on a circumciser for operating on a young Christian woman – to the consternation of many white missionaries and some Kikuyu Christians; see Church of Scotland, *Memorandum Prepared by the Kikuyu Mission Council on Female Circumcision* (Kikuyu, 1931), pp. 34–8. In an extraordinarily interesting analysis written in January 1930 (copy in Kenya National Archives, DC/MKS. 10B/12/1) Fazan conceded that hasty missionary action was not entirely to blame. He thought that educated young Kikuyu were in any case increasingly opposed to authority, whether British or African, thanks to 'primarily and consciously nationalist' motives, and that the circumcision issue was therefore a catalyst for action rather than its cause. Recent scholarship agrees with Fazan here, since parental authority over young women – concerned to see that they were rendered marriageable by initiation and circumcision – was closely linked to control over land, a never-ceasing Kikuyu concern. See Strayer, *Making of Mission Communities*, Chapter VIII (with Jocelyn Murray); John Lonsdale, 'The moral economy of Mau Mau' in Berman and Lonsdale (eds), *Unhappy Valley*, pp. 386–95; Peterson, *Creative Writing*, pp. 103–12; and Tabitha Kanogo, *African Womanhood in Colonial Kenya 1900–50* (Oxford: James Currey, 2005), Chapter 3.

position in claiming the property and asserting that it was the Mission station and not they who had introduced a new doctrine.

In the midst of this furore the government found itself in the position of a mediator and slowly straightened the position out. The local native councils in two of the three Kikuyu districts passed resolutions requiring the licensing of operators and their restriction to a comparatively mild form of operation. To the extent which these resolutions took effect the CSM may have done some good by their protest, but it started a secessionist movement both among the churches and the schools. Those who broke away on the religious side became known as the *Karing'a* or Orthodox. They broke into two sections, the more extreme of which sponsored an association of independent schools known as the Kikuyu Karing'a Education Association (KKEA), which was anti-government and anti-mission from the start. The more moderate section, although continuing to be independent, maintained a comparatively friendly liaison with the CMS and became known as the Pentecostals. They started, with others, another and more genuinely educational association of independent schools known as the Kikuyu Independent Schools Association (KISA). Both KKEA and KISA were destined to play a prominent part in the formative period of the Mau Mau rising some twenty years later.[9]

The Young Kikuyu Association, which had been the chief organ for the expression of Kikuyu political opinion under Harry Thuku, had ceased to exist after his detention and had been succeeded, in 1925, by the Kikuyu Central Association. On his release from detention, Thuku had no difficulty in getting himself elected president but, disapproving of their intransigent course, he resigned and formed the Kikuyu Provincial Association, which sought to achieve aims by peaceful negotiation. The move was not a success, and after the failure

9 Independent Kikuyu Christianity in fact pre-dated the 'female circumcision crisis', being first inspired by the publication of the vernacular New Testament in 1926. Reading scripture for themselves gave some Kikuyu their own theology. Otherwise Fazan's summary account is correct; he could have added that the Church of Scotland mission soon recovered its pre-crisis numbers, thanks both to divided Kikuyu opinion on the significance of clitoridectomy and to the advantages conferred by mission education. *Karing'a* means unmixed or pure. See John Lonsdale, 'Kikuyu Christianities: A history of intimate diversity', Chapter 6 in David Maxwell and Ingrid Lawrie (eds), *Christianity and the African Imagination: Essays in Honour of Adrian Hastings* (Leiden: Brill, 2002), pp. 157–97.

of his new association, he settled down to farm his own land and became a most respected citizen and a wise and moderate counsellor in times of trouble.[10]

By now a new figure had appeared on the political scene. He was a man in his mid-30s, an ex-employee of the Nairobi town council named Johnstone Kenyatta, but better known by the name of Jomo which he afterwards assumed. Jomo Kenyatta became vice-president of the Kikuyu Central Association in 1928 and, later, its president. He was away in Europe during the time of the circumcision issue and probably had no part in it, for it was to the land question and political equality for Africans that his energies were devoted.[11]

Towards the close of 1929 the industrial depression first made itself felt in Kenya through a steep fall in prices for export produce and difficulty in finding markets. Government revenues fell disastrously and it was difficult to find money even for essential services. Recovery, following that in Europe, came slowly, but by the end of 1934 the colony was back to normal. The gold rush to Kakamega in Nyanza Province, which began in these years and soon dwindled, gave a little relief to the economic strain. It brought a certain amount of capital from speculators and introduced a much-needed element of hope. A small number of settlers made a little by panning alluvial gold, although pegging claims and selling prospects was more lucrative. About a dozen real mines were started, of which I believe not more than four were still working after a decade.[12]

The question of the closer union of the three East African territories of Kenya, Uganda and Tanganyika together with Zanzibar was engaging close attention both locally and in Britain. It was increasingly

---

10 Harry Thuku, with Kenneth King, *An Autobiography* (Nairobi: Oxford University Press, 1970) is one of the few autobiographies of Africans active in this inter-war period.

11 Yes, Kenyatta – general secretary rather than vice-president of the Kikuyu Central Association, and never its president – almost certainly played no part in stirring up opposition to the missions. In public he looked to education to change attitudes in due course. He was guarded in his book, *Facing Mount Kenya: The Tribal Life of the Gikuyu* (London: Secker & Warburg, 1938), Chapter VI, not only emphasising the cultural importance of the rite of initiation but also appealing for educated Kikuyu to be allowed to decide for themselves whether to continue the practice. Kikuyu opinion remains divided to this day.

12 Fazan was correct; see Hugh Fearn, *An African Economy: A Study of the Economic Development of the Nyanza Province of Kenya 1903–1953* (London: Oxford University Press, 1961), Appendix D.

becoming a commercial reality and it seemed that political union must follow.[13] The Hilton Young Commission of 1927–8 got as far as recommending the immediate appointment of a high commissioner, to be succeeded in due course by a governor-general. Meanwhile, Kenya had acquired a new Government House which was completed in about 1928 when Sir Edward Grigg was governor. Its proportions were so imposing as to leave no doubt in anybody's mind that it was meant for a governor-general, but the tendency to let things slide or pass them on from one commission to another kept the question rolling slowly on for a number of years until initial enthusiasms had cooled off. By the time it reached the Joint Select Committee of Parliament in 1931, the most favourable moment for any decisive steps had passed.

The report of the Joint Select Committee was a most important document,[14] for it covered not only the immediate issue of federation but also the principal questions of policy involved, such as the relations between races, the principle of trusteeship, the composition of the Kenya legislative council, the encouragement of native African councils, questions of the burden of taxation as between the races, and so on. It passed in review the previous reports and White Paper pronouncements on these subjects: the Ormsby-Gore report of 1925, the Hilton Young report of 1929, Sir Samuel Wilson's report of 1929, and the secretary of state's White Paper entitled *Future Policy in East Africa* – and explained away, or modified expressions in them which sometimes, being quoted out of their contexts, had caused resentment and misunderstanding.

To the disappointment of some and the relief of others they advised against federation in existing circumstances but recommended extended functions for the Governors' Conference, with closer organisation and a permanent secretariat. It is possible that the committee might have gone much further and at least recommended a high commission, but for the apprehensions of the African witnesses with whom I had travelled to London, especially those from Tanganyika and Uganda, who were worried about the influence of the Kenya settlers.[15] It was unfortunate, however, that the question of

13 Apart from underplaying the obstacle of Tanganyika's legal status as a League of Nations' Mandated Territory, Fazan's account of the 'closer union' controversy accords with recent research, see Callahan, *Mandates and Empire*, Chapter 9.

14 House of Commons (HC) *Paper 156* and House of Lords (HL) *Paper 184* (1931).

15 For Fazan's role as guide to the African delegation to London, see Clough, *Fighting Two Sides*, pp. 155–6.

Kenya settler influence should have weighed so heavily, for, with the increasing power of commerce and industry, which was bound up with black interests as well as white, the voice of the Kenya settler farmer in politics was already finding its own more appropriate level.[16]

Apart from inter-territorial jealousy, the essential issues before the committee were as follows. Would the countries in combination have a greater attraction for the investment of outside capital than any of them would have separately? What would be the advantages or disadvantages of unifying essential services, and what services, if any, should be embraced besides those such as currency, which had been unified already? Thirdly and lastly it had to consider how far unification should go and under what form of central structure. The question of what would be the result of not settling these matters firmly before independence was granted was not considered. The possibility that these countries, disunited, might one day become Balkans for the Great Powers to exploit and contend for in a renewed and more subtle scramble for Africa is not after-wit, for it was mentioned by Lord Hailey many years ago.

The Joint Select Committee finally decided against federation because of the wide differences in the composition, degree of development and aspirations of the respective territorial populations. They recommended that the Governors' Conference, with its extended functions, should be regarded as in perpetual session and should deal principally with the subjects of transport, customs and administration, post and telecommunications, scientific and technical research, commercial law and defence. They contemplated that, when in the process of time the value of the organisation should have proved itself in respect of the transferred subjects, further functions might be added and a greater degree of unification emerge by consent.

This decision went about as far as it could have been expected to go in the circumstances for, while official opinion was divided, scarcely any of the unofficial witnesses had wanted federation. The fact that Tanganyika was a mandated territory may also have weighed with the committee for, although one article of the mandate expressly allowed administrative union, another forbade political union. Thus, while a high commission dealing only with transferred subjects would have

16 This is an important observation. After the Second World War British commerce became increasingly interested in the African produce and consumer markets, and accustomed to African trades unionism. British businessmen were therefore less perturbed than settler farmers at the prospect of African political advance.

been constitutionally acceptable, any association closer than that would certainly have invited protest.

These proposals were implemented almost in their entirety. The time came more quickly than the committee had imagined when the organisation proved itself. When war broke out in 1939 the secretariat of the Governors' Conference became, in effect, the central secretariat of the War Council. It remained a compact body and proved competent to shoulder an astonishing amount of work in the coordination of the war effort in all its aspects in the East African territories. It was also the principal instrument of liaison with Northern Rhodesia and Nyasaland. In fact, by the end of the war it had become so indispensable that a high commission and a central legislative assembly seemed inevitable.[17]

As well as its constitutional proposals, two inquiries were recommended by the Joint Select Committee as a matter of urgency. The first was upon the burden of taxation as between the races and financial matters generally. This was entrusted to Lord Moyne.[18] The broad conclusions, contained in his report of 1934, were that Africans were contributing more than their fair share to the revenue and receiving less than their fair share of services. He, therefore, recommended the introduction of income tax, the burden of which would fall almost exclusively on Europeans and Asians, and a readjustment of expenditure so that a greater proportion should go to African advancement. The Income Tax Ordinance passed legislative council after protracted debates and became law in 1937. The Colonial Development and Welfare Act, although not enacted by the British Parliament until 1940, also stemmed from Lord Moyne's report, for he insisted that young undeveloped colonies could not provide from their own resources the basic services which were essential for their own development, nor could they cope, unassisted, with economic slumps.[19]

The other inquiry which the committee advised was on the question of land. The recommendation was expressed as follows: 'in view of the nervousness among the native population as regards the land question, a full and authoritative enquiry should be undertaken immediately into the needs of the native population, present and prospective, with

17 This, again, is a fair account of the process that gave birth to the East African High Commission after the Second World War, the administrative core of a potential (as yet unrealised) East African Federation.

18 Assassinated in 1944 by Zionist terrorists when he served as the British minister of state in the Middle East.

19 See further, Stephen Constantine, *The Making of British Colonial Development Policy 1914–1940* (London: Frank Cass, 1984).

respect to land, within or without the reserves, held either on tribal or on individual tenure.'[20]

The Kenya Land Commission was accordingly appointed by the secretary of state under the chairmanship of Sir Morris Carter with corresponding terms of reference, but with one extra term added, namely: 'to define the area, generally known as the Highlands, within which persons of European descent are to have a privileged position in accordance with the white paper of 1923.'[21]

It was obvious from the first that the way in which the commission dealt with these matters would profoundly affect the development of the colony.[22] In the end it recommended that land in the permanent occupation of tribes having historical rights thereto – and also land

---

20 Joint Select Committee, *Report* (HC Paper 156), 44, paragraph 105 (ii).

21 As secretary to the commission Fazan was deeply worried by this added term of reference. It contradicted the Joint Select Committee's recommendation that any proven African need for land might be met 'within or without the reserves'. The committee must have had in mind the possibility of returning some White Highland land to African cultivation since almost all land that was neither in the White Highlands nor in the 'native reserves' was unsuitable for agriculture, being too low, hot, and dry or too high, cold, and wet. This restriction on the Carter Commission's freedom of action was reinforced by secret instructions that effectively transformed privileged white access to the Highlands from convenient administrative practice to a legal right, as affirmed by the Highlands Order in Council 1939. See Breen, 'The Politics of Land', pp. 74–8 and Chapter VI.

22 In this account of the (Carter) Kenya Land Commission's enquiry and report, Fazan scarcely does justice to his own role as secretary in what historians think to be the most significant and controversial of the many official enquiries conducted in colonial Kenya, the colony's Domesday Book. The published *Evidence* amounted to over 3,400 pages, in three volumes; the *Report*, published as a Command Paper (Cmd 4556, 1934), added a further 600 pages. Fazan was the driving force in organising and presenting this huge amount of data. The evidence of 487 African witnesses, heard in public meetings from August 1932 to February 1933, represents one of Africa's most important collections of oral history. The Commission's terms of reference assumed racial and tribal segregation and, as explained in the previous footnote, were contradictory – both to preserve the privileged position of white farmers in Kenya's highlands and to do justice to African land claims and provide for future population growth. White settlers thereafter felt justice had indeed been done – and therefore saw the later Mau Mau rising as ungrateful black treachery. Africans, especially Kikuyu, felt to the contrary, that they had been betrayed by the imperial government, since almost no individual African claimants had their land returned. Moreover, the additional land allocated to ethnic groups whose land had been expropriated for white settlement was available for settlement only because its higher altitude or lack of water or presence of human or cattle disease had made it unattractive for earlier human habitation. Fazan's discussion of the Commission's findings continues in Chapters 11, 12 and 16.

which the commission recommended to be given to them in compensation for land, formerly theirs, which had been alienated – should cease to be Crown Land and become 'native land' to be held by the occupant tribes, groups, families, or individuals in accordance with their customary methods of tenure. It also recommended that the integrity of the boundaries of the African Lands should be entrusted to a specially appointed Lands Trust Board whose approval would be necessary for any agreed modifications or exchanges, but that the direction of development inside the boundaries should rest with the government. The commission was also emphatic that development of land tenure practices must not be left to unguided evolution, but that government must have power to make rules. This, in the long view, was its most important recommendation.[23]

Besides the land awarded as native lands on grounds of historical right, the commission considered that, in some cases, there was need for extra land beyond the boundaries to provide for economic needs. They recommended that such land should continue to be Crown Land but should be earmarked as 'native reserve', permanently or impermanently according to need. The total area so set apart was 1,555 square miles, so that the total of 'native lands' and 'native reserves' combined was 52,095 square miles. Besides this, the commission recommended that native tribes should have prior rights in the Northern Frontier and Turkana districts, but, in view of the sparseness of the population, not exclusive right.

In determining the boundaries of native lands and reserves the commission made allowance for the requirements of isolated African families who had been found to be living on land subsequently alienated and for compensation for loss of land and disturbance.[24] Also, for the

23 This statement is a modest blast of triumph. It means that Fazan had persuaded the Commission to adopt his view of the need for government action 'to make rules', against the view of Maxwell and Leakey, on the Kikuyu Land Tenure Committee of three years earlier, that more research on African tenures was first needed. It took the later crisis of Mau Mau for the government to summon up the political will to act on Fazan's recommendation in anything more than a piecemeal fashion. Agricultural officers shared his view for technical reasons but the provincial administration, Fazan's own service, was reluctant to push the policy through because of the anticipated African hostility to any challenge to their family control of land. See further, Chapter 11, and M. P. K. Sorrenson, *Land Reform in the Kikuyu Country* (Nairobi: Oxford University Press, 1967).

24 This appears to be a reference to the fate of the several thousand Kikuyu 'right-holders' living on land that had been alienated under them but from which they had not subsequently moved. This turned out to be far more contentious than Fazan indicates here, and is discussed further in Chapter 12, footnote 11.

benefit of Africans who might not wish to live in the tribal lands, they recommended that land totalling 939 square miles be set apart as African leasehold areas. This was without prejudice to their right to obtain leases in any part of the colony (e.g. Coast province) in which there was no special privilege. In order to palliate, as far as possible, the rigidity inherent in the allocation of specific land to tribes, the commission made proposals for tribal leases and did not exclude the possibility of such leases in the Highlands, subject to safeguards.

The commission then set itself to define the boundaries of the White Highlands which, together with the 3,950 square miles of forest reserves contained therein, were found to comprise 16,700 square miles. Well over 90 per cent of this land had been either previously uninhabited by any permanent population or only intermittently grazed over by Masai herds. Most of it was open savannah plain but where it was arable its over-all quality was generally not first rate.[25]

The recommendations of the commission were accepted[26] and the boundaries of the Native Lands and the Highlands were safeguarded by Order of the King in Council. The succeeding years were for Kenya a period of peaceful and orderly progress. In 1935 Italy invaded Abyssinia but in spite of the gathering war clouds daily lives were not much affected until 1938.

---

25 Maasai grazing was not so much intermittent as seasonal, determined by the suitability of different altitudes and vegetations in the alternation of rainy and dry seasons. Fazan is correct that most of the White Highlands had been under pastoral use, largely by the Maasai and Kalenjin peoples, being too dry for reliable peasant agriculture. Less than 2 per cent of the land under settler farms had previously been owned by Kikuyu cultivators, a major factor in Fazan's – and others' – belief that the Carter Commission's recommendations for their compensation had been just. Kikuyu had lost less than 7 per cent of their land to whites, about 125 square miles, almost all of it from Kiambu district. While these figures were historically true, policies based on them failed to take account of new realities, particularly population growth and the Kikuyu colonisation of what had been Maasailand, as labour-tenants of the new white owners. By the mid-1930s nearly two generations of Kikuyu 'squatters' (in their own eyes, pioneer colonists, as white settlers also saw themselves) had made large areas of the supposedly 'White' Highlands their own – something that no British official seems to have understood. For Fazan's discussion of the remedial land allocations made to Kikuyu, see Chapter 14.

26 Not by Kikuyu and only reluctantly by the colonial office, which was especially criticised by the India Office for the now legal exclusion of Indian ownership on the Highlands. Settlers, also, as already noted, felt betrayed by being denied expansion on to the Leroghi Plateau, 'the promised land'. That the Commission had displeased all the contending claimants could be said to be its chief merit – but the settlers were well placed to derive the maximum benefit.

8

Changes

There was all-round development in the inter-war years. The population increased and public services were improved. By 1939 Nairobi had grown into a fair-sized town but, in spite of a good sprinkling of presentable buildings, it still had something of a pioneer look. Mombasa too had developed and had acquired modern docks comparable with the best in Africa. After the First World War the railway was extended from Nakuru over the Uasin Gishu Plateau to Uganda and communications of all sorts were fast improving. They could hardly be called good though, except for air travel, which boasted not only aeroplane and flying boat services to the United Kingdom, but internal charter services too.

Agriculture and labour

Farming was now far better established in all areas, white and black. By trial and error, both privately and at the experimental and seed-raising stations of the agricultural department and at veterinary centres, appropriate farming practice had been ascertained for the particular conditions in each district. Kenya thus established a much greater variety of crops than either of its neighbours and in the dairying and ranching industries, too, it easily led the field. Though as yet the landscape viewed over large stretches of the Highlands was hardly a smiling prospect of well-cultivated farms, the initial unspectacular work of setting fences and improving pasturage was well in hand and by and large the outlook was good.

In spite of a greatly increased demand for labour there was not much shortage. As settler's farms improved, so did quarters, rations and conditions of work, by the efforts of a young and conscientious labour department. Whereas most labour before the First World War had been recruited on short-term contracts, there were now two methods used for farm employees. They could either be recruited on contracts for a period varying from about six to 18 months, or they could sign squatter contracts – officially, 'resident native labour' contracts. These gave them a right to have their family with them and to cultivate a piece of land assigned by the employer, and they were generally allowed to keep a specified number of livestock, in return for which they had to do 30 days' work within a calendar period of 42 days, on the completion of which they received their wage. The former method was usually preferred for labour-intensive plantations, while the latter method became general for most mixed farming and ranching areas. The essential provision of squatter contracts was decreed in a succession of Resident Native Ordinances, the first of which was issued in 1918. Essentially they were intended to protect the well-being of squatters, but the restrictions on any form of consideration other than labour were initially designed also to curb the problem of absentee landlords and uneconomic subdivision among what were, in effect, African sub-tenants on white farming land.[1]

Public health

Great strides were made in improving public health everywhere. In respect of hospitals and medical staff, African areas had priority and, within the limits of resources, district headquarter stations were well provided. Health services in towns had almost eliminated the major tropical diseases, and much had been done to purify water supplies.[2]

Africans suffering from yaws and elephantiasis used to be a common sight at the coast before 1914 but had became a rarity. The pneumonia which attacked the Kikuyu was now held in check as were the epidemics of bubonic plague which used to cause havoc in the lake areas of

---

1 This is too rosy a view of 'the squatter problem', arguably the most fertile seedbed of Mau Mau insurgency. Undercapitalised white farmers had initially offered attractive freedoms to their incoming Kikuyu labour tenants. These entitlements to grazing and family cultivation on large, undeveloped, white farms – more valuable than the pay offered for seasonal farm labour – were gradually withdrawn as more machinery was used on increasingly profitable farms from the later 1930s. At first a necessity, squatters became an agrarian nuisance and a political threat. Most were Kikuyu. These bitterly resented their loss of 'squatter rights', especially after the Second World War. See Tabitha Kanogo, *Squatters and the Roots of Mau Mau*; Frank Furedi, *The Mau Mau War in Perspective*; and David Throup, *Economic and Social Origins of Mau Mau*, Chapters 5 and 6 (all London: James Currey, 1987, 1989 and 1987, respectively); see also Clayton and Savage, *Government and Labour*, Chapter 10, 'The Squatters' Revolt'.

2 For Kenya's public health history, see George O. Ndege, *Health, State and Society in Kenya* (Rochester, NY: University of Rochester Press, 2001).

Nyanza Province. Similarly, too, the sleeping sickness on the shores and islands of Victoria Nyanza was now susceptible to treatment, and, subject to proper precautions, the menace could be controlled. Amoebic dysentery, one of the major troubles afflicting Europeans, was likewise beginning to yield to resolute attack. Intestinal diseases and parasitic worms caused less comment because they were less obvious but they were, in fact, extremely widespread among the African population, and other races were by no means immune. Less well-known diseases, such as bilharzia and onchocerciasis, the latter causing blindness, were also a menace in certain areas. These, too, were being gradually overcome as their causes and means of prevention were being ascertained. In all this work the efforts of the public health services deserved the highest praise. Looking back from 1939 to the days before the First World War, when malaria was inevitable and blackwater a constant menace, one was astonished at the magnitude of the change and sometimes wondered how one had survived to see it.[3] That it was possible at all was in no small part due to the high degree of international collaboration that existed between departments working in this field.

Education

Educational services had been in a very embryonic condition before the 1914 war and developed only slowly for several years afterwards.[4] It was not until 1924 that the government devised a comprehensive programme which planned separate schools for racial and religious communities. Such a proposal did not then attract any criticism, as after 1924 there was a speeding up of educational advance. Government gave education its proper place in the priority of its obligations and devoted to it a much increased proportion of its still very modest

3 Fazan's astonishment at his survival was well justified. In 1918 and 1919, when white officials (of all branches of service) in post averaged fewer than 700 in number and most were young, their deaths (not in combat) totalled ten and 15, respectively. Their in-service death rates in the 1920s averaged about five per annum: R. R. Kuczynski, *Demographic Survey of the British Colonial Empire*, Vol II (London: Oxford University Press, 1949), p. 228.

4 For white education, see Nicholls, *Red Strangers*, pp. 101–5, 172–5, 197–8, 249–51; for African education, see John Anderson, *The Struggle for the School* (Nairobi: Longman Kenya, 1970) and Kenneth J. King, *Pan-Africanism and Education: A Study of Race, Philanthropy and Education in the Southern States of America and East Africa* (Oxford: Clarendon, 1971); for Asian education, see J. S. Mangat, *A History of the Asians in East Africa, c. 1886 to 1945* (Oxford: Clarendon, 1969), pp. 132–6, 172–4.

revenues. Many of the schools, however – government, mission, grant-aided and private – were built to serve only the immigrant communities, and the cost of education for the children of Europeans was considerably more than was covered by fees. An allocation from government revenue was therefore necessary, which meant that the Europeans were getting more than their fair share. To obviate this, a special education tax was levied on all white adult males and the Asian communities also contributed to the upkeep of their schools by donations and bequests.

The biggest development, by far, was in the African schools. Mission schools, with government grants to help them, were still the most numerous, but there were now a few schools run by the government directly. The Africans themselves showed great enthusiasm, being just as keen for their girls to be educated as their boys. The result was that their district councils voted more money for the purposes of education than they really could afford. Despite these advances, however, neither the quality nor the quantity of education for Africans was anywhere near the demand. There were a few good schools at the top of the pyramid and the quality of the missionary teachers was high, but the spread of education to the generality of the population was still, by 1939, at an elementary stage.

Clothing

Among the many remarkable changes of the inter-war period was the altered appearance of the Africans.[5] Before 1914 the men, when not wearing full tribal dress, mostly appeared in skins, blankets or near nakedness, although occasionally they were embellished with pieces of cast-off European kit, like helmets or puttees or umbrellas. Conservative tribes like the Masai still kept to their tribal dress but,

5 District commissioners can show more cultural curiosity than scholars; historians have been slow to take an interest in clothing. See E. S. Atieno Odhiambo, 'From warriors to *jonanga*: The struggle over nakedness by the Luo of Kenya', in Werner Graebner (ed.), *Sokomoko: Popular Culture in East Africa* (Amsterdam: Rodopi, 1992), pp. 11–22; Donna Klump and Corinne Kratz, 'Aesthetics, Expertise and Ethnicity: Okiek and Maasai Perspectives on Personal Ornament', Chapter 10 in Spear and Waller, *Being Maasai*, pp. 195–221; Luise White, 'Work, Clothes, and Talk in Eastern Africa: An Essay about Masculinity and Migrancy', in E. S. Atieno Odhiambo (ed.), *African Historians and African Voices: Essays Presented to Professor Bethwell Allan Ogot* (Basel: Schlettwein, 2001), pp. 69–74; and Margaret Jean Hay, *Fashioning a Modern Identity in Colonial Western Kenya: Struggles Over Clothing in the Interwar Period* (Boston, MA: African Studies Center, Occasional Paper 35, 2002).

with the advent of employment and town life, khaki drill shorts and a shirt became the general attire for African men. The women mostly took to wearing *lesos* in Swahili fashion[6] or, in the case of the Luo, a work-a-day garment not unlike a tennis dress. Although clothing, when worn constantly, was apt to bring chest complaints, it was not long before the quantity was increased and dealers in second-hand clothing were doing a roaring trade. African women, meanwhile, were turning out large numbers of neat dresses for sale in the native markets. Another side effect of the clothing revolution was that the custom of oiling the body was falling into disuse. The practice, however, had had its purpose for as there was a deficiency of fat in the African diet, oiling the body served to keep the skin moist. Eventually the problem solved itself, for with the planting of soya beans and vegetables a greater variety was introduced into the food supply.

Apart from the change in clothing, there were other inroads being made into long-established tribal custom. The younger generation was abandoning practices such as the filing of teeth among the Akamba, the extraction of lower-jaw teeth among the Luo and Abaluhya, and the elongation of ear lobes among the Kikuyu and several other tribes. All these customs were disappearing fast or slowly, according to the degree of contact with the towns and centres of European life. Such contact also facilitated changes in employment and diet, which also had some effect in altering the appearance of the people.

Housing

African housing improved little during the inter-war period. Only in trading centres and the homes of a few progressive Africans had tolerably well-built rectangular structures replaced the old round huts of up-country areas. There were enough of them, however, to suggest that wholesale change was about to come. They were built mainly with wattle and daub, and had beaten-out four-gallon petrol tins for roofing but, with the coming of the petrol pump, the supply was getting scarce. The generality of the population, however, was still living in the huts customary to each tribe, although there were many who could have afforded better. The reason why the change was so slow was to be found in tribal custom for, when a man wished to build a house, he called upon his neighbours to help, and each contributed his share of the labour according to a well-understood plan. It was also accepted

6 Also known as *kanga*: printed calico cloths that can be worn toga-fashion.

what the obligations of owner, as host, should be. Departures from the normal were disapproved, and the owner, who knew that his turn would come to perform a like service for others, was careful not to exceed in his demands. The principle of equality, although admitting exceptions, was often very potent in tribal life.

Newspapers

It was remarkable how the horizon of African thought was expanding. A close interest was taken in the news reported in the *East African Standard*. The first vernacular newspaper, *Mwigwithania*, was started by the Kikuyu, with Jomo Kenyatta as editor, and others followed both in the Central and Nyanza Provinces.[7] The prevalent tone could be described as tribal patriotic, but there was inevitably a tendency towards political agitation. To try and strike a balance, the government therefore entered the field with *Baraza* in Swahili, and, having been taken over by the *East African Standard*, it was not long before *Baraza* sales were exceeding those of the English language paper.

Trade

Plots on the trading centres in the African Lands had originally been taken only by Indians.[8] Although there were then no Africans with the flair or desire to engage in trade, this mood quickly passed. Nevertheless, Africans still had difficulty in securing connections with wholesalers willing to supply them with trade goods for retail. They received some help, however, from European settlers in 1921 at the time when anti-Indian feeling was running high. Much as the underlying motive may be deplored, it did have the effect of enabling African shop-keeping to get started. It was about 1928 when African-owned shops first began to appear in any numbers outside the coastal region. By 1929 they were quite common and had begun to compete

---

7 For *Mwiguithania* see John Lonsdale, '"Listen while I Read": Patriotic Christianity Among the Young Gikuyu', Chapter 24 in Toyin Falola (ed.), *Christianity and Social Change in Africa: Essays in Honor of J. D. Y. Peel* (Durham NC: Carolina Academic Press, 2005), pp. 563–93.

8 Gavin Kitching, *Class and Economic Change in Kenya: The Making of an African Petite Bourgeoisie 1905–1970* (New Haven, CT: Yale University Press, 1980), Chapters VI and VII, traces the growth of African trade, its competition with Asian traders sometimes assisted by Local Native Councils loans and bye-laws. For a businessman's account, see Oginga Odinga, *Not Yet Uhuru* (London: Heinemann, 1967), Chapter 5.

with Indians both in the retail trade and the produce market. The Indian traders, not to be outdone, contrived to keep level by advancing capital and by employing more African salesmen in their own shops. This caused more friction, but the government watched the situation unconcerned, except to preach the doctrine that there should be no racial discrimination in trade. Although it was obviously right in principle, the Africans found it hard to accept at that time.

Another form of enterprise in which Africans were launching out was in trading cooperatives – for instance, for the buying, transport and sale of wattle bark – but they generally broke down through inexperience, and disputes would arise about the assets. More success was to be had with passenger buses which by 1939, as I recall, had begun to operate under licence.

The *boma*

There was a great change in the typical *boma* or district headquarters in the African areas.[9] In 1914, about half a dozen bachelors comprised the full European strength even in the larger stations, and a married officer was a rarity. In 1939, however, the European official community alone, with its wives and children, often exceeded 40 and the little compact stations had grown into respectably sized townships. When I once asked a Roman Catholic padre why the Pope didn't allow them to marry he replied with a question: Was a district station where the officers were all bachelors more peaceable than a station where one of them was married? I did not reply, but I saw his point. However wistfully one may sometimes have sighed for the old days, the district station had grown older, and we had grown older too. In 1911 the latest promoted district commissioner had less than five years' service; in 1920 it took eight years; and in 1942 there were some very able district officers still waiting for charge of a district after 19 years' service.

On the lighter side of life, there were now tennis, golf, cricket, and rugby football clubs in most major centres, while the number of association football teams, overwhelmingly African, was amazing. The Arab and African Sports Association, started in Mombasa in 1933,

9 For readable accounts by colonial officials of lives now difficult to imagine, see among many others, R. O. Hennings, *African Morning* (London: Chatto & Windus, 1951); Charles Chenevix Trench, *The Desert's Dusty Face* (London: Blackwood, 1964); Terence Gavaghan, *Of Lions and Dungbeetles: A 'Man in the Middle' of Colonial Administration in Kenya* (Ilfracombe: Stockwell, 1999); Oliver Knowles, *Back Seat Driver: Memories from the End of Empire* (Brighton: Pen Press, 2008).

quickly spread over the colony and produced athletes of high calibre. All these activities played an important part both in the social life of the country and in bringing the races closer together. A further development by 1939 was that travel for social purposes had become much easier, with most European and Asian families owning their own motorcar. Many could therefore aspire to an annual holiday at the coast to relieve the grind of farm, commercial or official life, and home leaves after each 30 months' tour were no longer the necessity they had once been.

Population

Population was rising among all races. European numbers increased about six-fold to around 25,000 in 1939 and Asians, with Arabs, were at least 100,000. Although there was no full census until 1948, there were enough data available to suggest that the African population of Kenya increased slowly at first from about 3 million when the protectorate began until, having recovered from the set-back sustained in and after the First World War (including the cession of Jubaland to Italy), it had reached a figure of around 3,400,000 by 1931. In the early days of the Protectorate an abiding factor tending to keep the increase low was the very high rate of infant mortality. It is impossible to say how long a time elapsed before better health conditions began to have an effect in reducing this, for, before the census of 1948, there was never a count of children made. They were assumed in the annual estimates to be constant at 37 per cent of the total population and adults were estimated from the hut tax register. Meanwhile the rate of annual increase had been gradually gaining momentum and, by the end of that period, had reached about 2.5 per cent. Continuing at that rate the African population had topped the 4 million mark by the outbreak of the Second World War. The later census counts of 1948 and 1962 supported these conclusions and showed that the annual increase rate of 2.5 per cent had been maintained.

Compared to the total area of Kenya these figures gave only a low density rate but, because the proportion of fertile and well-watered land was small, the bulk of the population was living in rather high density conditions. In the Fort Hall district in 1939 the people were living at a density of 343 to the square mile, which gave an average of only 9 acres to a family of five. Similar conditions existed in most of the leading districts, and parts of Nyanza were definitely overcrowded. While there was nothing desperate about the situation, it was certainly difficult and was bound to get worse unless the general expansion of industry could proceed at a pace sufficient to absorb the increase in the population. It was clear that energetic measures would therefore be required in economic planning.[10]

A difficulty besetting any economic development was that the men with the capital and experience to start the new enterprises necessary to broaden the basis of the economy were Europeans or Indians. Thus the more progress that we made in developing new industries, the more opportunity it gave to politically-minded critics to claim that Africans were being exploited to provide labour for alien advantage. This was far from the fact. The labour department, which came into being in these years, was tackling the task of labour relations with vigour and fair-mindedness in conditions that were not always easy.[11] By the end of the period, labour conditions had greatly improved on all the leading estates in the quality of housing, more balanced rations, and in medical care. Furthermore, the trades and professions in which Africans could themselves take part were slowly being expanded.

Soil erosion

Before 1914 soil erosion as a result of over-grazing and trampling by domestic livestock was rarely mentioned as constituting a menace, and even in the Northern Frontier and Turkana, it was only vaguely referred to as the encroachment of desert conditions from the north.[12] Ten years later, however, the denudation being caused by excessive accumulation of livestock in all the native reserves was not only causing acute concern but was universally recognised as the greatest problem confronting the field administration.

Cattle, sheep and goats were pre-eminently a sign of wealth and status in tribal life, and as many of them were kept as could be afforded. As grazing was a common right over all uncultivated land, tribesmen set themselves no limit on their stock and consequently, except where the tsetse fly stood guard, the land became heavily overgrazed. Young boys

---

10 For Fazan's interest in population growth and related matters, see Appendix III.

11 For which see Clayton and Savage, *Government and Labour*; additionally, for the period after the Second World War, see Frederick Cooper, *Decolonization and African Society: The Labor Question in French and British Africa* (Cambridge: Cambridge University Press, 1996).

12 Another subject with a large literature. The best Kenyan case study, set within wide comparative reading, is David M. Anderson, *Eroding the Commons: The Politics of Ecology in Baringo, Kenya 1890–1963* (Oxford, James Currey, 2002). For a recent cause for hope, see Mary Tiffen, Michael Mortimore and Francis Gichuki, *More People, Less Erosion: Environmental Recovery in Kenya* (Chichester: Wiley, 1994).

herding goats cut down acacia trees or lopped off branches for the goats to feed on. Firewood became scarce and was used up, shade disappeared, river banks started to cave in and collapse and their beds became wide and sandy. The result was that the stream became a torrent in the rains and a trickle in dry weather until, eventually, one had to dig to get water.

It was not all the fault of African improvidence.[13] Although some tribes, like the Masai, certainly had too many cattle for their needs, others, like the Akamba, had no more than their reasonable requirements demanded but, nevertheless, they had too many for their land. With the population and livestock continually increasing and the land becoming more and more impoverished the problem became most disturbing and offered no short solution.

The bride-price system whereby the father received a stated number of cattle for his daughter on her marriage was often blamed as a contributory cause and it probably was to some extent. A change over to cash, however, would not have resulted in noticeably fewer cattle being kept, for they were valued more than pay, but it might have had a limited effect in that some cattle were kept alive for bride-price long after they ought to have been killed.

Compulsory culling, though often urged, was not practicable, but extensive propaganda was employed, including a mobile cinema, to illustrate the evils of soil erosion and show workable means of conservation. A useful start was made with the introduction of better hedging and contour ploughing, afforestation on the brows of hills, the construction of dams and wash-stops, and the protection of vegetation along river banks. But the main problem was the commonage, so long as everyone could run his cattle and small stock on any uncultivated land. A solution that was attempted was in the fencing and paddocking of private land and the better conservation and distribution of water supplies. The only real solution, however, amongst the traditional tribes, was education, example and unremitting perseverance.[14]

---

13 An example of the frequent differences of opinion between British officials and settlers; most of the latter would blame African improvidence in this instance.

14 The solution to over-stocking was in fact rather different, namely the local meat market. As African peasants were forced by population growth and land shortage to concentrate increasingly on cultivation only, they increasingly bought in beef (previously a rare delicacy in their diets) from other ethnic groups who specialised in pastoralism.

PART III

Government in the African Lands

9

The Field Administration

By 1914 most government stations had been established, and their numbers remained fairly constant at about 35. Five of them were also provincial stations (Mombasa for the Coast; Kisumu for Nyanza; Nyeri for the Central province; Nakuru for the Rift Valley; and Isiolo for the Northern Frontier), while the district commissioner of Nairobi had a special status. The Northern Frontier and Turkana district stations, again, were not typical, being more concerned with the preservation of law and order than with the provision of amenity services.[1]

Almost all the original district *bomas* began and continued for a considerable time as one-man stations. At first called collector and afterwards district commissioner, he was in sole charge of everything – the administration, treasury, police, prison, stores, even the medical stores, buildings, water supply, survey, post office, roads and everything else, including, where possible, the furtherance of trade. This was all done with the assistance of about three Asians – a clerk, a police sub-inspector, and a medical 'compounder' – about 40 African police ranks, a number of porters and some station transport – normally in the shape of ox-wagons, oxen and a mule or two, until motor transport came in about 1923 in the more accessible parts.

There was also a small but indispensable service of messengers who afterwards grew into the tribal police. Like other elements in the colony's district administration this service also may have had its roots in tribal custom. Its first adaptation for use on an extensive scale was probably in the Meru district in the first decade of the century when,

---

1 Berman, *Control and Crisis*, is the standard work on Kenya's field administration, based partly on the recorded memories of retired officials. Fazan was the first of these to be interviewed by Berman, in 1968. For accounts by officials themselves see note 9 in Chapter 8. Cashmore, *Studies in District Administration*, is indispensable for the period before the First World War.

few Africans being able to read or write, the district commissioner, E. B. Horne, organised a body of district messengers to convey his orders to the chiefs and to assist them generally as jacks of all trades. By 1910 they were in use all over the country and were known as tribal retainers, or, more colloquially, *askari kanga*. They had then no regular uniform but usually they wore a discarded police jersey completed with a loin cloth or *kanga*. They were a necessary supplement to the regular police force whose strength in a district was seldom sufficient to do more than provide a garrison for the station and safari escorts.

Apart from being cheaper, they had local knowledge and, consequently, they kept in much closer touch with the people than was possible for the regular police recruited from all parts of Kenya. They were a body comprised largely of the sons or close relations of chiefs and headmen, and so they remained throughout the period of British administration. Until the service obtained official recognition under the title of the Tribal Police in 1929 and its powers were protected by ordinance, it had always been the nurseling of the provincial administration and had been fostered by successive district commissioners, at first with very scanty support and much criticism from headquarters. In the troubles that were to come later they very amply proved their worth.

In the early days the collection and forwarding of supplies was a major preoccupation but, as trade became established and problems of supply became less absorbing, the whole reason and existence of the little *boma* was to establish and maintain good relations with the Africans of the district and lay the foundations for peaceful development. With this extended function it was therefore a great relief to the district commissioner when district and departmental officers began to appear and take over some of these functions. However, a very senior provincial commissioner, C. W. Hobley, had warned against the danger of officers administering each other, and so as to preserve a common objective, it was the practice in most districts for a periodical meeting to be held between the district commissioner and the departmental officers.

By 1914 or shortly afterwards, administrative staffs had risen to the level which they maintained with little alteration until after the Second World War. Districts in Kenya were never graded as I believe they were in India, but there were a number of major districts like Kiambu, Fort Hall, Machakos, and most of those in Nyanza Province. Such senior districts normally had an administrative cadre of one district commissioner and two to three district officers, while intermediate districts, like Nandi, for example, had a district commissioner but seldom more than one district officer. There were also a number of districts, for instance at the coast and in Masai, where the district commissioner was lucky if he was allowed a district officer at all. On the coast, however, there was the considerable advantage of the Arab officers maintained under the provisions of the treaty with the Sultan of Zanzibar.

Departmental staff came much more slowly. The supply of departmental officers usually depended on the particular needs of the district and resources available; but, as regards the major services common to every district, the allocation tended to follow the same general lines as the provision of administrative staff. For instance, a police officer was posted to most senior districts but there were very few at other district stations before 1924. The *bomas* themselves grew steadily until by 1939 the compact little stations had become fair sized townships, not that there was much to boast about in the appearance of the offices and housing. Even if the country was being run on a shoestring one could not but wonder why something a little less ramshackle could not have been afforded. Despite appearances, however, it was from the district station and nowhere else that direct association was maintained between the government and the people.

Administrative officers held judicial powers over two separate ordinances – the Courts Ordinance, first, second, or third class according to experience, and the Native Courts Ordinance, later called the African Courts Ordinance, under which they dealt in their administrative capacity with cases coming up for revision or an appeal from the Native Tribunals. There were thus, in effect, two separate systems, but they met at the top in a common right of ultimate appeal to the Supreme Court.

Ordinarily, all cases arising between Africans in the tribal areas – African Lands – would be heard by Native Tribunals. The exceptions were where the parties were of different tribes or where the offence, if proved, might require a sentence beyond the powers of the tribunal to impose or, as occasionally happened, where the matter under complaint lay outside the normal experiences of tribal life. The great majority of tribunal cases were concerned with marriage relations, disputes about bride price and inheritance or about cattle and goat exchanges, but the most complicated and difficult were about land. A district officer could revise the judgment of the tribunal in any case and, if that did not satisfy the parties, it went ultimately to the Supreme Court.

Before an administrative officer was confirmed in his appointment – which usually happened at the end of his second year – he had to pass the colony's law examination. Until then he had only third-class magisterial powers, which meant that he could not impose a term of imprisonment of more than six months. As he became more senior he would be granted second-class powers and, at the discretion of the chief justice, might be awarded first-class powers after a minimum of nine years service. The Supreme Court maintained a close supervision throughout: monthly returns had to be made to the registrar, and the Supreme Court could call for the record of any case and either confirm or quash, or reduce the sentence or direct a retrial before the same or some other magistrate.

The most common classes of criminal case with which a district commissioner or district officer had to deal directly in his magisterial capacity in the tribal areas were grievous hurt, homicide, and stock theft – for lesser crimes went in the first instance to the native tribunals, while cases of murder or homicide were heard only as preliminary enquiries and committed for trial by a judge of the Supreme Court. He would generally arrange to hear them on circuit, and advantage would be taken of his visit to seek general advice.

By contrast, work of a judicial nature which the district commissioner or district officer had to do in the non-African areas of his district was mostly confined to petty cases arising under the Masters and Servants Ordinance of 1910, afterwards amended and restyled the Employment of Natives Ordinance. These were often irritating and time-consuming.[2] The more important cases occurring in the non-African areas – the White Highlands or in the towns – were generally heard in the town magistrate's court at provincial headquarters, especially civil cases when both the parties were non-African. Lay magistrates were thus spared most of the complexities of British civil law, but it was quite enough for them to unravel the puzzles which arose under native law and custom.

As departmental staff for districts gradually became available, medical services, which were the most urgently needed, were accordingly the first to receive attention. Two doctors, two nursing sisters, and sometimes a sanitation officer comprised the normal allowance of European staff for a major district, and there might be an Asian sub-assistant surgeon. Hospitals were provided at district and headquarters, and, at shared cost with the local native council,

2 It was, however, much worse than irritating for Africans convicted under this ordinance; see David M. Anderson, 'Master and servant in colonial Kenya 1895–1939', *Journal of African History* 41 (2000), pp. 459–85.

dispensaries, dressing stations and, in a few cases, maternity centres were built at divisional centres in the district and staffed with African dressers and nurses. Also, at the initial expense of the local native council, there was generally a motor ambulance attached to the hospital at district headquarters to serve the whole district. But these changes came slowly. Occasional mobile dressing stations circulated where distances were great and population scattered. They were often no more than a carload of medicaments and appliances staffed by one African dresser and a 'donkey boy'.

A special effort was made in conjunction with the public works department to provide district stations with pure water supplies. Care was also taken to prevent camps and transit centres from becoming sources of infection, which had caused serious problems in the past, while propaganda among villagers to provide themselves with household latrine pits had considerable success. The almost crusading zeal of individual medical officers had astonishing results, but they did not always endure once the spur had been removed. One undoubted success in the health campaign was that Africans lost their reluctance to come forward for treatment. Indeed they often became so keen that they pressed for *sindano*, the needle, whether an injection was required or not.[3]

The major tropical diseases were kept in check. Malaria was almost banished from the towns and lessened in trading centres.[4] In the countryside a certain amount of avoiding action was taken by drainage of swamps, instruction regarding the clearing of village sites and the banks of streams, and the free issue of quinine. Outbreaks of bubonic plague, which had once been common, now occurred very rarely and, when they did so, prompt and effective action was taken with the energetic cooperation of the chiefs and people to prevent their spreading. Although the species of tsetse fly which is the vector of sleeping sickness to humans was never quite eliminated from the areas which it infested on the shores and islands of Victoria Nyanza, the incidence of the disease was greatly reduced and regular inspection enabled cases to be detected in the early and curable

3 For the popularity of injections following the visible success of the Salvarsan-based treatment of syphilis and yaws in the 1920s, see Luise White, *Speaking with Vampires: Rumor and History in Colonial Africa* (Berkeley, CA: University of California Press, 2000), p. 100.

4 Kenneth S. Ombongi, 'A history of malaria control policy in colonial Kenya, 1897–1963' (University of Cambridge: PhD dissertation, 2000).

stage. This improvement in public health was not the achievement of the medical department alone. Better education, better agriculture, and better administration through the chiefs and headmen had also played their part.

Government was very slow to provide either money or staff for educational services. The preoccupation of the tiny education department before 1914 was with the children of parents in government service. The task of educating the people at large was left to the Christian missions, which was, of course, confined to their own adherents. The CMS and the Church of Scotland rated education highly from the start but, by contrast, the Roman Catholics then appeared to take the view that they should not be distracted from teaching the gospel. As for the government, it did no more than convene occasional meetings of mission representatives.

The 1914–18 war had been over for several years before government was able to make any effective provision for financing African education and, even then, resources were very small. The method adopted was by grants to missions, allocated through central and provincial education boards. In the course of time, however, when funds were a little easier to come by, it became clear that the government would have to take a more direct part and have at least a few schools of its own. There was a danger that, if everything was left to the missions, they would pull different ways and, furthermore, a channel of education must be open for children who were not adherents of any mission. For the rest, the grants to missions were continued and the sums gradually increased but, along with the increases, the schools were made subject to closer inspection.

There was a time in the early 1920s when the European settlers were pressing strongly for the accent in education to be placed on artificer training.[5] They urged, on the one hand, that a broad syllabus of education would result in a host of semi-educated malcontents most dangerous to society, while, on the other hand, they pointed out that there was an immense demand for skilled workers. Policy was much influenced by these considerations. It was founded on the idea that the education which a child received at school must be something which would enable him to turn his hand to a useful occupation when he left. Although apparently realistic, it was a policy that was not sufficiently broad-based to be more than a facet of the educational system. It did not show a sufficient realisation of the very wide field that would be

5 This controversy can be followed in King, *Pan-Africanism and Education.*

open for the educated African with the expansion of the general economy or of the need which already existed for the training of teachers. Above all it failed to recognise the vital importance of producing Africans with alert minds capable of contributing to their own and their country's improvement. Nevertheless, it was important that Africans with a smattering of education should not regard themselves as a class apart, too good to work with their hands. That is why the department's first ventures in direct education were orientated towards the production of artisans: the technical school at Machakos and the more ambitious Native Industrial Training Depot at Kabete. There were, moreover, some excellent secondary schools which had been provided by the missions as at the Alliance High School (Alliance of Protestant Missions),[6] at Maseno (CMS), at Kikuyu (CSM) and at Nyeri, Tala, and Kabaa (Roman Catholic). It would have taken a government secondary school many years before it could have competed on equal terms.

A powerful new influence came in with the establishment of local native councils in 1924.[7] It became apparent very quickly that what they wanted was higher education. They clamoured to have the schools built from their own contributions whether they yet had the children fit to be enrolled as pupils in them or not. They wanted to be equal to the white man and they demanded it with intensity. District administration now had a delicate task on hand but gradually a compromise was reached. In most senior districts the councils were allowed to build the schools and then hand them over to the department to be staffed and conducted as primary schools in the first instance, the director of education undertaking to set no limit to what they might eventually become. At the same time agreement was reached as to how future contributions from local native councils should best be devoted. A notable feature of the clamour for schooling was that the councils showed themselves at least as ready to vote money from their rates for the education of girls as for boys. This was welcome evidence of their desire to improve the amenities of domestic life, for African men were often criticised for making their women work too hard.

6 B. E. Kipkorir, 'The Alliance High School and the origins of the Kenya African elite 1926–1962' (University of Cambridge: PhD dissertation, 1969).

7 Kenya's African local government was more progressive than in many British African colonies, partly as a means of securing African development without challenging settler influence over central government policy and expenditure.

A further development of importance began in Kikuyu in 1929. This was the independent church and school movement which started with the breakaway from the Church of Scotland and gospel missions over the female circumcision issue.[8] Once these schools had accepted grants and a measure of inspection and control, one could see some advantage in the fact that they had been a spontaneous growth. But during the 1930s they were still a very doubtful factor.

Another question of importance was language. There was no dispute that small children should be taught in their own tongue. After the elementary stage Swahili, being the lingua franca of the country, was taught as a subject, but there was a difference between government and mission schools to the extent that the language in which the teaching was given was Swahili in the former and the tribal language in the latter. A little later in the curriculum English was taught as a subject and, in advanced classes, was used as the medium of instruction. There were many critics, especially among those who did not know Swahili, who would have denied it a place either as a medium or as a subject. It was, however, a prime necessity to the making of the country that the inhabitants throughout should be able to understand each other, and it was not practicable at this period to universalise English. Swahili had had a good start. It came easily to the Bantu tribes, who were the majority, and although it was a foreign language to the others, it was of more use to them in getting along with their Bantu neighbours than a smattering of English would have been.

***

Before 1910, which was the approximate date when an effort was first made to introduce the cultivation of cotton, Africans in upcountry Kenya grew only for their own requirements or for barter at customary markets within walking distance from their homes. If they had any surplus they sold it to the trading centres which by that time had been established in government *bomas* and some of the chiefs' locations. African wants for trade goods at that time being largely confined to blankets and brass wire, there was little incentive to grow more crops than the family needed for food. Indeed the first export trade to reach any significance in African areas beyond the coast strip

8 As already noted, Kikuyu 'independency' preceded the female circumcision crisis, even if it expanded greatly thereafter.

was not any sort of cultivated produce, but the hides and skins of fallen cattle and goats.[9]

It was a hand to mouth economy, and none of the crops on which the Africans mainly relied for food – millets, yellow maize of a rather poor quality, *choroko* beans, bananas, sweet potatoes etc. – had much export potential. Even when cotton was introduced it was only in the lake areas of Nyanza Province that it seemed promising, but it proved exhausting to the soil and never had more than a mediocre success. It thus became a main task for the agricultural department to try, by patient experiment, to improve the quality and increase the variety of African produce and find suitable cash crops for the diverse conditions of the tribal lands. For this purpose it was thought better to employ the department's limited number of trained staff on experimental research work rather than dissipate their strength by posting them to districts. It was not until about 1926, therefore, that agricultural officers could be spared for the latter purpose. In the course of the next decade, most of the major districts were to be provided with one, but until then the administrative officers did the job.

It was hoped to stimulate Africans to grow produce for market beyond their own food requirements by an indirect approach through trade goods. If their wants could be increased and they could be induced to buy implements such as hoes and mattocks or domestic items such as hurricane lamps, boxes with locks, kettles and mugs, they would gradually see the point of increasing their output of produce. Propaganda of this kind worked if not pushed too hard, but a watchful eye had to be kept on the Indian *dukas* to see that inexperienced Africans got fair value for the crops they sold. Some things, like bicycles, caught on amazingly well. In a very few years almost every Kikuyu or Luo seemed to have one. The demand for ploughs came slower but, once the idea had been accepted, they were bought up as quickly as oxen could be trained. In some areas, indeed, where hand cultivation might have been preferable, there were almost too many of them vexing the soil. Despite these changes, however, the

9 The best study of agrarian change among Kenya's Africans is Kitching, *Class and Economic Change* (which relies greatly on Fazan's 1932 economic survey of Kikuyuland, reproduced in abbreviated form as Appendix III). For a comparative history of two areas of Nyanza under Fazan, see Robert M. Maxon, *Going their Separate Ways: Agrarian Transformation in Kenya 1930–1950* (Madison, NJ: Fairleigh Dickinson University Press, 2003).

range of things which were regarded as necessary to the enjoyment of life was still surprisingly small, and, for as long as it remained so, no spectacular advance in the growing of export crops could reasonably be expected.

Some of the traditional methods of agriculture were most destructive, causing widespread soil erosion in many areas. Examples of such methods were the habit of strip cultivation down the sides of hills instead of along the contours, and the wanton destruction of trees by shifting cultivation and uncontrolled burning. Though reluctant to change their habits the Africans appreciated the need for an effort to arrest the decline, and native councils and tribal authorities gave the government their cooperation. The local native council of Machakos, for example, voted 1 shilling on the rates for soil conservation in the first year of its existence and opened a number of nurseries for the raising of tree seedlings.[10] After 1926, when agricultural officers began to be posted to districts, it became possible to intensify the effort both in this and other ways. Trees were planted on the brows of hills; weirs were set in water courses, hedges and ditches were established along the contours of hills and, where it appeared necessary in hilly districts, extensive bench terracing was constructed.

Building dams and making reservoirs made progress in these years. It was work in which Africans were keenly interested and was generally carried out by six-day free labour called up under the Native Authority Ordinance, with paid labour being used for difficult parts, such as the spillway. When I was at Kitui in 1927, it was proposed to build a dam on the border of two locations, but no one had the expertise to forecast its success. When I put it to the two chiefs in *baraza* that it was not more than an uncertain proposition, the senior of them said: 'If a man has a barren wife, does he refuse to sleep with her? We will try.' And so they did. And happily it proved to be productive.

Research by district agricultural officers about the improvement of crops and planting methods was mostly carried out in selected plots set apart for the purpose by the local native council. They used, at first, to be called demonstration plots but, for reasons not hard to guess, it was found prudent to give them another name, such as 'experimental' or 'seed-raising' plots. The result of this research was that gradually quality was greatly improved over a wide range of crops and new varieties were introduced. Seed was issued to Africans showing interest

10 Tiffen et al., *More People Less Erosion* is a study of Machakos district.

and the agricultural officer made frequent tours of the district to inspect and advise. Similar methods were adopted for the improvement of poultry and dairy produce. A greater variety and better quality of food for the inhabitants of the district being thus assured, exchanges, without payment of fee, took place at the customary barter markets which existed in all large centres of population.

Kenya was fortunate in its wide variety of weather and climate. Although severe food shortages occurred, their effect was greatly mitigated by one area being able to help another and, thanks to improved marketing methods and transport facilities, the risk of famine conditions occurring over a wide area was greatly reduced. Particular attention was paid to the growing of cassava and other drought-resisting crops.

Markets for produce intended for export were established alongside the larger barter markets. They were constructed from funds voted by the local native council, which recuperated itself from stallage fees. Immediately inside the gate, the weighing and grading of the produce usually took place. Thereafter, upon payment of an inspection fee, the vendor was free to sell at any one of the stalls which he found facing him in a semi-circle, the idea being that no stallholder should have an advantage. The stallholders were all African and, indeed, local opposition to any but Africans buying in these markets was intense. As for the grower, he was free to take his produce to a general trading centre and sell it to an Indian if he preferred.

Annual returns of African produce exported showed large increases both in quantity and value, but they did not distinguish between what was exported abroad and what was sold in other parts of the country. Sesame, groundnuts, cotton and pyrethrum were among the principal crops exported – and there were many minor items – while large quantities of maize, beans, and potatoes were sold internally in the towns, or as rations for African labourers on farms. Millets, grown in very large quantities, were mostly consumed internally in the district, and were often used for beer.

It was not until the latter half of the inter-war period that Africans were allowed to grow coffee. Since 1925, when the Kikuyu Central Association had come into being, the restrictions on growing coffee had been a hot political issue. Being the country's major cash crop, it was represented that the prohibition was designed to limit the economic capacity of the reserves so as to maintain a large supply of labour for European farms. The reason for the restriction was, in fact, fear that African-grown coffee would be inferior and probably diseased, and thus the reputation of Kenya's premier export crop would be ruined.[11] The wisdom of the prohibition could scarcely be disputed while there were no agricultural officers posted to African districts, but some relaxation of the ban was necessary afterwards. Limited amounts were then allowed to be grown under licence and close supervision. By 1939 the experiment had proved successful and, with proper precautions, restrictions were relaxed. It was, however, not until after the war that Africans participated in the industry to a substantial extent.

As a crop considered suitable for African farming, tea had rather a similar history. There was, however, not the same degree of opposition to their being allowed to plant it nor was much desire shown by the Africans to do so. A few years after the Second World War, an active campaign to introduce it as the main economic crop for Africans in high-altitude areas was launched, apparently with success.[12]

The farming of livestock by Africans was limited by the fact that large tracts of the African lands were infested with the tsetse fly *Glossina morsitans*, which was fatal to cattle.[13] It constituted one of the major problems of the country, and few districts were entirely free. The campaign against it was supervised by experts sent from Nairobi, only manual labour being locally supplied. Results obtained showed that, by windbreaks, spraying and other methods, selected areas of land in tolerably favourable conditions could be virtually cleared of fly, but they could not be guaranteed against its reappearance if attention was relaxed. The drawback was that the cost of the operation generally exceeded any economic return to be expected from it. Prospects of any spectacular success were, therefore, not hopeful although clearing was possible, and there were breeds of cattle which, although not immune, appeared to acquire a degree of tolerance. Meanwhile, the fly was at least performing a useful function in conserving the land.

Far-sighted European settlers welcomed these signs of advance in the native reserves, but they were taken as a grievance by the

11 Historians would place equal emphasis on labour-supply, price competition and quality fears as reasons for banning African coffee growing before the mid-1930s. By then African coffee growers had long demonstrated their competitive capacity in neighbouring Uganda and Tanganyika.

12 Fazan's optimism was well placed; Kenya now claims to be the largest tea exporter in the world.

13 The best study of the disease problems of black and white pastoralists in Kenya is Richard Waller, '"Clean" and "Dirty": Cattle disease and control policy in colonial Kenya, 1900–40', *Journal of African History* 45 (2004), pp. 45–80.

more myopic.[14] It was represented that the more profit an African made from his *shamba* the more reluctant he would be to leave it for work on a settler's farm. It was true, indeed, that the settler might have to increase wages, but it was equally true that he would be getting a better labourer. It could not be to the ultimate good of the whole community that any section of it should be held back. Such a policy would be as economically fatal as it was indefensible morally. This was a point that had been very clearly appreciated by that strong administrator, John Ainsworth, when he was provincial commissioner in Nyanza before the First World War. His version of the 'dual policy' was that Africans should have a free and equal choice between cultivating their own land or going out to work, but he refused to have them 'stagnating in their reserves'. The labour problem was, in fact, a question of balance. There was ample manpower to supply the demands of industry and farming outside the reserves, and enough useful work to be done inside them to keep those who remained behind reasonably busy and, indeed, as initial reluctance about leaving home diminished and working conditions on farms improved, much less was heard about labour shortage.

The charge of 'stagnating in the reserves' was very frequently heard. The traditional division of work between man and woman, leaving fighting and bush clearance to the men and cultivation to the women, had left the men with too little to do after the British government had stopped tribes fighting each other,[15] and the delimitation of reserves and increase of population had reduced the scope for clearing fresh land. Another reason for the charge was due, perhaps, to the fact that there was too little variety in crops and farming method. With all farmers there are peak periods of work and times when work is slack, but if the farmer plants a variety of crops requiring different attention, if he also farms livestock and poultry and if steps have got to be taken to protect the land, conserve fertility and keep grain stores and sheds in proper repair, the idle or

---

14 The next two paragraphs are another section of Fazan's meditation on land allocation and its relation to economic development. The reference back to his first provincial commissioner, Ainsworth, could be seen as a recollection of a simpler time when Kenya was so empty of people and improvement that there seemed to be ample room for 'progress' on either side of the racial divide.

15 'Tribes' had never fought each other; each ethnic group was too loosely organised for that, lacking the necessary policy-making machinery. Their young warriors could as well conduct raids within their own ethnic group as against their neighbours. Raids were rarely carried out over more than a day's fighting range.

comparatively idle periods are reduced. That is what the agricultural department was trying to bring about in the African lands. Compared with the women, the men still had too little to do but, with the introduction of better farming, the disparity had been greatly reduced by the end of the inter-war period.[16]

The agricultural department had certainly not found all the answers by the end of the 1930s. They were, for instance, still searching for the best rotation of crops for the various types of soil and climate. As far as I know they were never able to improve much on the native practice of planting different crops all mixed up together on the same land just as, to take a parallel, large numbers of different species of game can graze or browse together without damage on land which, if made over to an equal weight of cattle or single species of game, would soon show signs of exhaustion. In this and other ways, African methods were often found to be sound practice.[17]

★★★

Except for the ox-wagon track that usually connected the district station with provincial headquarters, there were, before 1914, virtually no roads in African reserve districts.[18] Even a road for ox-wagons was normally fit for nothing else, for it was just a sea of churned up mud and ruts and travellers on foot, mule or bicycle kept off it and used the native tracks. Internal roads between locations were the work of district administration. Each was built by unpaid six-day labour[19] or with the aid of a small grant from the public works road allocation. Later on, when native councils had been established, the cost of any material which had to be bought or any labour which had to be paid was shared out more or less equally between them and government. At first the

16 Kitching, in *Class and Economic Change*, Chapter 1, agrees with Fazan that much of the rise in African production was achieved by women increasing their labour time.

17 An example of Fazan's liberal cast of mind. Many Europeans despised the African habit of mixed planting – but it was an effective and cost-free method of limiting the risks of soil erosion; mixed stands of crops also gave shade against the tropical sun.

18 Edward W. Soja, *The Geography of Modernization in Kenya: A Spatial Analysis of Social, Economic, and Political Change* (Syracuse, NY: Syracuse University Press, 1968), traces the growth of Kenya's road and other communications networks.

19 Government required up to six days per quarter, or 24 days per annum, of so-called 'communal labour' from able-bodied males, mostly to create and maintain local communications. This requirement lapsed in the 1920s when Local Native Councils began to pay hired labour for the purpose.

roads were mere footpaths about eight to 12 feet wide, side-marked by little ditches, quite useless for drainage, but at least showing where the road was supposed to be. Rough bridges over water-courses were made by felling trees, but wide streams had to be waded or crossed on stepping stones, although there were occasional wickerwork bridges. These tracks were later widened to make them fit for motor transport. A camber was put on them and drainage provided. Most bridges, however, were merely cement-topped drifts over which the water poured when the river flowed. Right up to the Second World War motoring on district roads in the African lands was something of an adventure.

Transition from foot safaris to motor cars came rather abruptly about 1925. For the next few years there were many inexperienced drivers negotiating the hazards of sand or mud in unroadworthy cars on uncarworthy roads. Long processions of porters (generally 22 in number to an officer's safari) became a thing of the past. They had been a great waste of labour and certainly the chiefs and headmen were glad to be rid of the duty of keeping camps clean and providing for the necessities of a full-scale safari. But this mark of progress had its obverse side. The old foot safaris were cheerful affairs and not unduly hard on the porters, who often marched along singing. One generally stayed two or three days in camp, and, besides the official *baraza* which may have been the purpose of the safari, one had a good look round and many discussions. Officers were not paid to run races through their districts, and the times when one was least hurried were the times one learnt most.[20] As far as the Africans were concerned, they naturally liked to know when an officer was coming and did not care for having him swoop upon them unawares. There was also advantage in that when an officer came he used to stay long enough to get the *shauris* settled instead of doing just the one thing he came for and off again with a wave of the hand. There was also something in the very nature of the motorcar that engendered a spirit of restlessness. Efforts were therefore made to keep officers out on safari for a respectable proportion of their time but, gradually and inevitably, it dwindled from a half to a third, and from a third to a quarter. Only the agricultural officer was able keep moving more than this, and even he tended to do it by a series of day visits. The

---

20 This memoir is itself evidence of how much an officer could learn about his district from its inhabitants while on foot safari.

rest of the administrative and departmental staff were meanwhile getting their heads too deeply buried in files.[21]

The description given in these pages has tended to follow the major and more developed districts, but equally valuable work of a more pioneering and adventurous kind was still going on in the remoter and less frequented areas. The motorcar and the aeroplane were, however, quickly removing both the distinctive character and the loneliness of these places and life in them was becoming more like that in the rest of the country.

21 This observation reflects a growing complaint by colonial officials, especially after 1945 – that the time they had to spend at their desks dealing with 'paper', thanks to an ever more complex interdepartmental bureaucracy, endangered the personal rapport with 'people' they had once enjoyed on foot safari; see Berman, *Control and Crisis*, p. 331.

10

African Authorities

In the early years of the protectorate many problems had been encountered as the headman system was applied generally to African lands.[1] Appointed under the Village Headman Ordinance of I902, their duties were initially limited, but they were soon to play an energetic part in the recruitment of labour, and the Courts Ordinance of 1907 established tribunals which operated under their control. The result of this rapid development was that there were several unsatisfactory appointments and a good deal of corruption while, at the same time, headmen often did not enjoy much popular support. The government saw its way round the problem by drawing into the tribunal system the councils of elders which traditionally met to adjudicate on disputes between families, a process which was accorded official approval by the promulgation of the Native Tribunal Rules of 1911. In the following year the Native Authority Ordinance consolidated this arrangement of separate executive and judicial functions, extending also the power of chiefs and headmen. By amendment to the Native Authority Ordinance in 1924, the local councils of elders, which traditionally debated matters of general concern, received full recognition and, thereafter, the three types of African authority were used to administer African lands: chiefs and headmen representing the executive element, native tribunals

1 Kenya's colonial chiefs, whose executive powers had little historical precedent, have been much studied. See especially, W. R. Ochieng', 'Colonial African Chiefs: Were they Primarily Self-seeking Scoundrels?' Chapter 3 in Ogot, *Hadith 4: Politics and Nationalism in Kenya* (Nairobi: East African Publishing House, 1972), pp. 46–70; Robert L. Tignor, 'Colonial chiefs in chiefless societies', *Journal of Modern African Studies* 9 (1971), pp. 339–59; idem, *Colonial Transformation*, Chapter III; Clough, *Fighting Two Sides*; chapters by Marshall S. Clough, William R. Ochieng' and A. T. Matson in B. E. Kipkorir (ed.), *Biographical Essays on Imperialism and Collaboration in Colonial Kenya* (Nairobi: Kenya Literature Bureau, 1980); Berman, *Control and Crisis*, pp. 208–18.

representing the judicial element, and African district councils representing the deliberative, budgeting and bye-law making elements. The system was stabilised during the 1930's and other than steady modernisation, no major changes took place, although it was very severely tested in Mau Mau years.

By the Native Authority Ordinance 1912 and its amendments, 'headman' was the only title under which African authorities were appointed. It made no distinction between grades. 'Chief' was a courtesy title, as were the various other terms used to describe particular grades of such authorities. Nevertheless, the term chief was used and it generally meant the chief of a location, of which there were on average about 16 to a district. These locations were usually subdivided into three or four sub-locations under headmen, and those again into quite small units (*itura* = ridge in Kikuyu; *mlango* = clan sub-unit in Nyanza) each under a petty headman sometimes called a *muruka*. In major districts in which a divisional organisation existed, as in Central province, 'senior chief' meant the head of a division or group of locations, and one of them may have been senior chief of the district.

Among the Bantu and Nilotic tribes, who together made up nine tenths of the population, the resemblance to pre-existing forms of authority was close up to locational level. Beyond that, much had to be improvised. In the case of most such tribes, the Kikuyu providing the only large exception, clans were found in territorial areas sufficiently compact to form administrative units. True, there were enclaves of other clans found among them and some clans, such as the Tiriki of North Nyanza, were of mixed origin; but for the most part, the government locations were so drawn as to correspond with the clan lands, except in a few cases where a clan was so large as to cover two or three locations – e.g. Gem or Maragoli in Nyanza. On the other hand there were some clans so small that two or three could be combined in one location.

The clans near Lake Victoria, both Bantu and Nilotic, were large, with populations up to 50,000 in some cases. Some of the clans of the Meru tribe of northern Kenya were comparable. In nearly all such cases there were clan leaders of influence who could well be called chiefs, and some of them could trace their ancestry through several generations of leading men. Although there was no one comparable to the Kabaka of Buganda, having a retinue of ministers and an organised parliament like his *Lukiko*, the clan organisation was sufficiently developed in most cases to provide an adequate nucleus on which to build.

The Kikuyu, having entered their present lands in a succession of settlements by family groups, had no clan chiefs or separate clan areas. When Teleki passed through in 1887 he found a series of petty leaders called *athamaki* claiming suzerainty over *itura* or ridges, and from the experiences of John Boyes it is clear that these *athamaki* were often fighting with each other. By introducing locations and appointing chiefs government made an innovation but, in doing so, it usually drew the boundaries in such a way as to combine a number of neighbouring ridges and, where practicable, appointed the most prominent of these petty leaders as locational chiefs. It is probable, in any case, that such development would have come about. Such things as prayers for rain had necessarily to be conducted on a territorial basis and there were certain venerated places to which the inhabitants of an area would resort for the purpose. Names had already been given to certain wide areas, such as Mathira, Othaya, and Tetu, which afterwards became administrative divisions under senior chiefs.

A divisional organisation with three or four divisions to a district, each containing a number of locations, had many advantages for ease of administration. In order to avoid jealousies, however, the post of divisional chief was not made strictly by appointment. He was chosen from the locational chiefs by agreement and usually by seniority. He retained charge of his own location and became *primus inter pares* rather than superior in his relation to the other chiefs in his division. He was convener and had first right of speech at divisional *barazas*. Any government announcement, local native council by-law or chief's order issued under the provisions of the Native Authority Ordinance would be announced by him. Proof of such announcement had to be given before anyone could be convicted of a breach of orders. Their manner of issuing orders was often very vivid. I remember an occasion when Senior Chief Koinange was issuing three orders to his people. He had a bowman beside him and, as he gave each order, he cried out: 'That is an order as surely as this arrow flies.'[2] At the word, the bowman shot his arrow far out over their heads. And the orders were obeyed.

The very fact that the Kikuyu had so little previous organisation meant that the divisional scheme was introduced without any friction and worked smoothly from the start. In Nyanza, however, where the clan organisation was strong, locational chiefs, being of different clans, did not always take kindly to being grouped into divisions, unless it was in some modified form with the chiefs presiding in rotation.

---

2 Daniel Ostendorff, 'The Koinange dynasty and the development of Kenyan politics' (Oxford University: DPhil dissertation, forthcoming) will reflect, among other things, on the relationship between Koinange and Fazan.

The provincial commissioner would attend the selection or election of a chief, but in the case of a sub-locational headman the district commissioner would preside. The normal procedure was that a *baraza* would be held, at which candidates were proposed and seconded. Up to half a dozen might appear to have substantial backing and, unless there were strong reasons why anyone should be vetoed as unacceptable, all were allowed to stand. The candidates had to affirm publicly that they would be loyal to the man elected, whichever of them it might be. An adjournment of a fortnight or so might sometimes be allowed and, at the appointed date, each candidate stood behind his peg in the ground and supporters ranged themselves in line behind the man they favoured. If any candidate then saw that he had no chance, he dismissed his followers and told them to go and back their fancy among the others. Eventually, the lines would be reduced to two or, at most, three. There would then be a count and, if there was no overall majority, those in the least favoured line would disperse and join one of the other two. Things seldom got as far as that, however, and the elected candidate on the final count would be appointed on six months' probation. By this method hereditary claims got as much consideration as the electors chose to accord them. Sometimes the son of the former chief was chosen, sometimes one of the headmen and occasionally a distinguished outsider. Often the old chief's son would be appointed a *muruka* in his father's sub-location, while a senior headman would be chosen as chief. But this method was not always used. There was a risk in some cases that several small sections of a clan would unite for the occasion and having tipped the scales would then split up again leaving the new chief with no substantial backing. In such cases the provincial commissioner would make the appointment himself on the best advice that he could get.

The first and most important of the duties of chiefs and headmen was to represent the views of their people. As government servants, however, they also had to represent government to the people as well as the people to the government. They were in fact the heads of the 'protected government' vis-a-vis the field representatives of the 'protecting government'. They had very wide powers accorded to them under the Native Authority Ordinance. They might take necessary measures to prevent the spread of disease, restrict excessive drinking or dancing, forbid the planting of noxious plants and the possession of noxious drugs, control the movement of African families or their livestock from one jurisdiction to another, require able-bodied Africans to undertake communal labour up to a stated limit for public purposes in their location, and for almost any other purpose of good government. They were, besides, the principal means of helping the district commissioner to carry out his numerous duties and for enforcing observance of the byelaws passed by the local native council. Further duties which fell to the chiefs to perform varied from helping the police to make arrests to the conducting of a post office. The chief was expected to interest himself in all the activities of his area, be a coordinating centre for all government or native council staff posted there, and keep the district commissioner advised on the current feelings of his people on any matter of special interest. He also had the unpopular task of collecting, or supervising the collection of, hut and poll tax and native council rate in his location. For this duty he was assisted by a tax and rate clerk and the work was checked by the district revenue officer.

As time went on, headquarter offices were built for divisional chiefs and, in some cases, for locational chiefs also. Senior chiefs were provided with clerks and an allowance of 'tribal retainers'. These latter were for many years of rather doubtful status but eventually they obtained recognition as part of the tribal police. Operating partly as police and partly as messengers, they were a kind of semi-official adjunct to the tribal police stationed at district headquarters, with a maximum of about half a dozen to a senior chief. By 1939 these centres were beginning to grow. Court buildings for the tribunals were generally established, and any African field staff of the various departments operating in the division – agricultural instructors and assistants, veterinary scouts, dispensary dressers, etc. – were generally located in the neighbourhood. Produce markets and African-owned shops soon followed and, in one way and another, the centres grew.

With the rapid increase of their responsibilities, some chiefs proved more adaptable than others. Some replacements had to be made, especially in the early days when the chiefs had no clerks. Later on, when this deficiency was made good, it was often found that, if the clerks were kept up to the mark, some of the old illiterate chiefs, who would otherwise have had to retire, still had the best hold on their people.

Unfortunately the growth in the responsibilities of the chiefs was not matched by any comparable increase in their pay. In spite of some increases it still remained pitiably small. For instance, three first-grade chiefs in Nyanza Province, each with a population over 35,000, were drawing an average yearly salary of £126 each and sub-locational headmen in charge of populations of over 2,000 drew an average of only £18 a year, which was less than the pay of a European's house servant at that time.[3] Even making *all* due allowance for the financial

3 Fazan seems to be referring to the later 1930s.

straits in which the country found itself throughout the inter-war period, it is difficult to understand – considering how much the peaceful and orderly administration of the African areas depended on the loyalty and efficiency of the chiefs and headmen – why, in matters of pay, government at headquarters in Nairobi should have rated their services so lightly. It was a major mistake and, if more had been done to build up the authority and prestige of the chiefs in these years, much trouble might have been avoided later on. Too little was done to enhance the dignity of the chiefs or make a government career attractive to leading Africans. It also ensured that there was a constant temptation for them to try and make something on the side.[4]

***

The organisation of the chiefs and headmen was a fairly natural adaptation from what pre-existed among the Bantu and pure Nilotic tribes. The same cannot be claimed in the case of the Nilotic/Hamitics – the Masai and the Kalenjin group – whose traditional authorities were the *laibons*.[5] They could be described as a priestly caste or clan, a little like the Levites of ancient Israel, with a priest/king or chief *laibon* at their head. Most famous of these at the time when the British came was Lenana, chief *laibon* of all the Masai, with whom the treaty of 1904 was signed, and Masikonde, who also signed the treaty as *laibon* of the Purko clan. Less influential than the *laibon*s, but nevertheless an essential pillar of the system, were the *laigwenan*, heads of the warrior age-group. They also signed on behalf of the Masai clans.

It is doubtful whether suitable machinery for the administration of Masailand could have been fashioned out of the *laibon* system, but the issue was still alive in the late 1930's, and so far as I know had not been finally closed before Kenya became independent. The *de facto* position was that the Masai clans were administered by a headman chosen by themselves. As for the chief *laibon*, there was a tendency to use him when his influence appeared likely to be helpful, but otherwise to leave him to his spiritual functions. This ambivalent approach was of

4 '[M]uch trouble might have been avoided later on.' For an argument with which Fazan might have agreed – that chiefs' corruption, especially in land cases, generated Kikuyu resentment prior to the Mau Mau insurgency, see Throup, *Economic and Social Origins*, Chapter 7.

5 For their power among the Maasai, see Richard D. Waller, 'Kidongoi's Kin: Prophecy and Power in Maasailand', in David M. Anderson and Douglas H. Johnson (eds), *Revealing Prophets: Prophecy in Eastern African History* (London: James Currey, 1995), pp. 28–64.

doubtful prudence, so, in effect, he passed into honourable retirement as far as any executive functions were concerned. There were no serious dissentions and, indeed, relations with the Masai remained generally friendly throughout the period of British rule. Transition was not so easy with the Kalenjin group of tribes – the Nandi, Kipsigis, Elgeyo, etc. Attempts to adapt their *laibon* system as a practical means of administration in modern conditions had no success,[6] and the practice of ruling through chiefs and headmen had therefore to be adopted as for the rest of the country.

The African district councils[7]

The family group was the basis of African society, and the clans and tribes were built up from them. The elders of the group would meet in conclave for the discussion of affairs, and the senior head of the senior family would normally preside. There was no essential difference whether the group was a small one or a whole clan or tribe, although meetings of elders of a whole tribe would have been extremely rare.

This organisation was found in different stages of development when the British arrived. Some tribes were much more loosely connected than others as between their various clans and groups, but there was always something recognisable as a council of elders – variously known as *kiama*, *nzama*, *bura*, *tuiyet*, etc. – with a headman presiding. In the taking of decisions, the council, rather than the headman, was the essential element. In general, all heads of families could participate in discussion but, among tribes which had an age-group system – which broadly covered all the tribes which practised circumcision – there was seniority among grades following each other roughly seven years apart. When the time came for the then operative senior age grade to become emeritus – in their early 70s or perhaps a little sooner – the main voice in affairs was passed on to the next grade. It could also happen that a comparatively young man, being the head of an influential family group, or otherwise outstanding, might be admitted to their circle. It

---

6 Indeed, they tended to act as patrons of dissidence, for which see Anderson, 'Black mischief'.

7 Unfortunately, the only general history of African local government in colonial Kenya, Monone Omusule's 'Political and constitutional aspects of the origins and development of local government in Kenya 1895–1963' (Syracuse University: PhD thesis, 1974) was never published. Fazan's survey here is therefore especially useful. He will presumably have been able to refer to his own *Report on the Relations between Government and Local Native Councils* (Nairobi: Government Printer, 1938), which as a research student this editor borrowed from him (and returned) in 1962.

was not a gerontocracy, but they could rightly be called elders. The locality over which they had effective influence corresponded generally to a location, sub-location, or, in some cases, only a ridge.

After the Protectorate was declared, district commissioners made use of these assemblies when visiting locations, both for consultative purposes and for announcing orders. It became the practice, in all districts where it was feasible, for general *barazas* of chiefs, headmen and leading elders to be called to district headquarters on an occasion of particular importance, and for a few prominent persons of the younger generation also to be invited. Thus there arose, in many districts, the nucleus of a district council. It was a natural development from the old *kiamas*, and it occurred in several districts independently and almost spontaneously, without much intervention. There were no signs, however, that it would have grown as an indigenous institution if the British had not come.

Such councils as came about in this way had no defined legal status before 1924. The district commissioner consulted whom he liked and there was at first no regular membership or record. In Nandi a council hall was built in 1916, presumably from contributions, and in South Nyeri a council of 15 members held its first meeting in January 1917. The members comprised eight government headmen, five members of the senior *kiama* initiation, one Roman Catholic and one member of the Church of Scotland. In Central Nyanza a quarterly meeting of chiefs was instituted in 1920. In Fort Hall district an African advisory committee was formed in 1922 of 17 members, of whom three were nominees of mission societies, and regular minutes were kept.

These councils, where they existed, were succeeded in due course by statutory local native councils – afterwards African district councils – for which provision was made in the Native Authority Amendment Ordinance of 1924. It provided that they might be appointed by the governor-in-council for any district or part of a district and should consist of the district commissioner, assistant district commissioner, if any, and such headmen or other natives as the governor might appoint. The appointments of the African members were to be for three years but renewable at the governor's pleasure, and the district commissioner was *ex officio* chairman.

The duties of the council included the passing of byelaws for certain enumerated purposes, which may be described generally as purposes of social service, the tendering of advice to government on matters of local concern, and the administration of the council's revenue. Subject to directions from the governor-in-council, the provincial commissioner exercised general supervision. The councils were provided with opening balances by allocations from the Native Trust Fund and certain accumulated rents derived from leases of land in their jurisdiction.

Recurrent revenue was to be secured from rates voted by themselves, from rents, fees and royalties on land in their areas, from grants made with consent of Legislative Council and also from donations and bequests. By the end of 1925, 23 councils had been gazetted. Two of them combined and, when war broke out in 1939, there were 22.

Apart from the district commissioner and district officers the membership of the councils was exclusively African. The average membership was about 35, the nominated having a slight preponderance in most councils but not in all.[8] By no means all the nominated members were chiefs or headmen. The object of nomination was to preserve the balance of the council so that all shades of responsible opinion should be properly represented. The elected members were generally chosen on a locational basis. It was not easy to organise these elections by secret ballot in an illiterate community, so it was left to the ingenuity of district commissioners to do so. There was one who surmounted the difficulty by having the three candidates sit blindfolded while voters, one at a time, indicated the man they favoured. The proceedings of these councils were orderly and respect was shown to chiefs. Nevertheless, the atmosphere of the early meetings was most evocative. Most elders in those days still wore tribal dress, while the premises were guarded by tribal police whose spears and decorative uniforms still had a tribal character. Almost all the members were eloquent and quite without diffidence. When the issue had been made clear, the quality of debate was high. Some of the best orators were the old men dressed in skins. Even those who had less to say would interject a sharp remark, for instance: 'Kameo is like a louse in the blanket; he has been irritating us all morning.' Votes were seldom taken at these meetings. The members preferred to adjourn to talk things out, and announce a unanimous decision later. They did not like to be hurried, and expressions such as 'This matter will require much careful thought' often ended the debate for the day. In spite of their unhurried attitude, and in spite of the fact that no other subjects evoked such interest as the subsistence and travelling allowance to be paid to members, the councils nevertheless achieved a creditable output of work and admirably fulfilled their prime purpose as a mirror of public opinion.

---

8 The Nyanza Province Local Native Councils were unusual in having unofficial majorities from the start – in 1925, before Fazan was their provincial commissioner; see Omusule, 'Political and constitutional aspects', p. 195.

The expression used in the ordinance was that the governor 'established' councils, whereas the corresponding expression in the Tanganyika legislation was that the governor 'recognized' them. It was a very important distinction, for in the latter case there was an implication that the councils had pre-existing powers independent of government, and disputes would arise as to what they may have been. The Kenya councils, having only the functions conferred on them, were simply a local government operating under the supervision of the provincial and district administration. The intention was that, as the councils proved their capacity, further functions of local government should be entrusted to them progressively, and further sources of revenue be made available.

The financing of local native councils by a self-imposed voluntary rate was a new departure as far as the East African group of colonies and protectorates was concerned and does not seem to have existed in the West African group either. The principle appears to have been first advocated by G. V. Maxwell, chief native commissioner from 1921 to 1930, who copied it from Fiji, whence he had come on transfer. The fact that it was the councils who decided on the rate to be imposed for the year, subject to sanction, undoubtedly gave the members a feeling of responsibility towards their electorate. It became a common practice for them to ask for an adjournment after the first debating of the budget so that they might have time to consult their constituents. Some councils preferred to appoint a sub-committee to examine the budget, after which an interval of two months or so would be allowed before it was again debated. The councils were popular from the start and proved quite ready to rate themselves. In fact, they had to be restrained from overreaching, and it was deemed prudent that, in these early days, the annual rate imposed for a major district should normally be about 2 shillings per adult male, and about half that for the minor districts. At least ten times these amounts were being voted in 1960.

Government, though cautious, was inclined to let the councils have their head in the spending of their money. Machakos council, for instance, to contain erosion in the district, paid for the services of a European reconditioning officer and African assistants who were largely employed on the raising and distribution of tree seedlings – this despite the superstition that, if a man planted a tree, he would die when the tree reached his own height! Also, like other districts, they spent freely on education. There was an understandable urge towards the spectacular and in the first decade of their existence the councils met almost the whole building costs of three hospitals and paid for extensions to several others. They also spent some £40,000 on school buildings and nearly all provided themselves with council halls.

The policy of allowing the councils to be free-spending with their money in the first few years not only kept them keen, but also helped the administration to learn their aspirations. It had a further effect in that it induced government to recognise the need for spending more on the African areas from the general revenues of the colony, for they could hardly allow themselves to be outdone by the African councils. In the upshot, and for whatever reason, the government spent much more in this decade on services to African areas, particularly education and health, than it had ever done before.[9]

After the first few experimental years, it became obvious that, unless some guiding lines were laid down for the division of functions between government and the councils, anomalies would result. After consideration by two government committees, lines of policy began to emerge. As regards amenity services, such as education and public health, it was agreed that the proper sphere of the councils was in the provision of basics. Attempts were made to draw a line for each such service and consider how it could be progressively raised in accordance with the resources and experience of the councils. On the contentious question of roads it was decided that trunk and main roads should be the sole concern of government, while the councils would undertake responsibility for minor roads with the assistance of a grant on something like a half-and-half basis.

A question was raised concerning law and order services centred round the chiefs and headmen, tribal police and the like. Government accepted the major responsibility for paying them, but the issue was principally about their status: whether they would be regarded as having mainly central or local functions. Depending on the outcome of this issue the question then arose as to whether they ought to be shown in the government budget and paid directly or in the native council budget and be paid mainly by grant. As I recall, chiefs were considered central and headmen local.

These functions having been defined, the next problem was how the councils should be provided with adequate resources to meet their growing commitments. It was clear that their commitments would increase much faster than any addition that could be expected in the yield of the council poll rate through increased population, and

9 Fazan appears to be referring to the 1920s, of which the latter years saw marked economic growth.

frequent upward revision of the rate would be resented. Fixed grants would be open to the same objection and any upward revision would require the sanction of legislative council on each occasion. It was better, therefore, that the councils should be granted sources of raising revenue which had some expectation of expansion, if such could be found, rather than fixed grants. These were not easy to find. Receipts from rents were increasing, but only slowly. Tribunal fees were coming in well but were largely earmarked revenue. Neither a direct tax on livestock nor a cultivation tax on West African lines seemed feasible, but market dues looked more promising, and there were possibilities in various kinds of licensing and registration fees. Although these and other sources were being explored for what they might be worth, it seemed fairly clear that the annual poll rate and grants would have to remain the principal source for a number of years to come.

It was not without a tussle that government agreed to the councils receiving the fines inflicted by native tribunals in cases arising under the Native Authority Ordinance, for it was thought that the tribunals might be tempted to impose excessive fines for their profit. Only when government was satisfied that the tribunals and the councils were completely different bodies in membership and all respects did they yield the point. Although it was not a very satisfactory way of financing local government, fines nevertheless added substantially to the revenues.

The total surplus revenues of the councils stood, in 1939, at an encouraging sum of about £100,000. Although this was only about a fifteenth of the total of 20 years later, it was at this time that sure foundations were laid. Despite this success, it was to be regretted that the councils of the Coast and Rift Valley provinces and of the extra-provincial districts of Masai and Turkana, when compared with those of the Central province and Nyanza, had not been able to show so useful a record of progress. This was both because of lack of funds and because of the difficulty inherent in dealing with sparse populations living on indifferent land. These areas thus presented a special problem. Although it seemed possible that, if something in the nature of an equalisation fund were started at provincial level, a rich province might be able to carry its poorer districts, it was clear that, where a whole province was lagging the only recourse was to government grant. The problem highlighted what was perhaps the most serious criticism of the local native council system in Kenya: that it tended to widen the gap between advanced and backward districts and that no comprehensive scheme was worked out for advancing the latter or was even closely considered. No colonial development funds had been made available, yet the country had had to weather two acute periods of worldwide depression besides an abnormal succession of seasonal troubles of crop failures, flood damage, drought, and locusts.

The native tribunals, afterwards called the African Courts[10]

It is not entirely a valid criticism that the distinction between a 'council' and a 'tribunal' did not conform with native custom, because the same elders used previously to operate in both capacities. Formerly, when elders met for debating matters of general concern, a full attendance would be expected, but, when they met for adjudicating a dispute between families, the group elders on both sides would probably settle it, possibly with the addition of representatives from the clans to which both sides belonged.

The traditional assemblies of tribal elders that used to meet for the settlement of claims between litigants came to be known as native tribunals and were so styled in the Native Tribunals Rules of 1911 published under the Courts Ordinance. These were repealed in 1930 on the ground that they were 'obsolete, obscure, or inapplicable' and were replaced by the Native Tribunals Ordinance, which sufficiently covered existing practice and gave scope for future development. It also gave powers to tribunals to try cases of disobedience to the lawful order of a chief. These powers were afterwards expanded under the African Courts Ordinance to widen the range of offences with which the tribunals might deal.

There is no reason to suppose other than that the petty tribunals of *mbari* elders and the like meted out substantial justice successfully and with little fuss in accordance with tribal custom.[11] When in due course the time came for these small bodies to give place to locational tribunals for each chief's area, care was taken that every ridge should be represented on the tribunal and that all major transactions should be accompanied by a ceremony in the presence of witnesses, among whom children should be included. In such circumstances very little could

10 Fazan may well have had in his possession the highly critical report by the legally-trained Arthur Phillips, *Report on Native Tribunals* (Nairobi: Government Printer, 1945), which investigated, among other failings, undue chiefly influence over tribunal decisions. For a general study of the African courts system at an East African rather than Kenyan level and not available to Fazan, see H. F. Morris and James S. Read, *Indirect Rule and the Search for Justice: Essays in East African Legal History* (Oxford: Clarendon Press, 1972).

11 The next two paragraphs refer to Kikuyu legal procedures in particular.

happen without at least one member of the tribunal having a fair knowledge of the case before it came to court.

In the sifting of evidence the parties in dispute were usually set facing each other, and the case was conducted by a method of confrontation. Each disputant checked off his arguments in turn with the help of a bundle of twigs and made his points, throwing down a twig for each point made. The other picked it up and made his reply. The elders sat round and watched closely, occasionally interjecting a question or comment, while sometimes, when one of the parties argued too wildly, there was a shout of laughter. It was the same way with a witness and his interrogator. The method was very effective, and it seldom happened that the decision of the elders was at fault on an ascertainable point of fact. When twigs or clay images were used to represent cattle or goats, as they often were, an elder collected those on each side, and at the end of the case one bundle was set off against the other and judgment was given. If a genuine doubt remained on the facts, the parties might be allowed or required to take an oath. Should a man refuse he would lose his case. If both took the oath, the case would normally be adjourned for divine vengeance to overtake the party forsworn. Such an adjournment is something I have never seen except in land cases, for there was at that time a dread of the consequences of false swearing. There were two principal forms of oath, but one of these was stopped by government. It consisted of the ceremonial beating of a goat to death while praying that the same fate might befall the swearer if his oath were false. The other was an oath on the *githathi* stone (pumice) accompanied by symbolic gestures.

Although it was often remarkable how accurately the details were remembered of transactions which had taken place many years before, attempts were made to impose a limitation to prevent ancient cases from coming to court. But it often happened that a recent claim itself depended on an old transaction. For instance, in a claim for bride price for a girl recently married or about to be married, it might be contended that her father never paid the bride price for her mother because it was a runaway match, so admitting both her maternal grandfather and her mother's legitimate husband (if any), or their successors to the claim.

Court fees in the early days, generally a goat each, were deposited by both sides before the hearing of the case and, to show that there was no favour, were consumed by the elders at the end of it. Later changes introduced the more conventional practice of civil courts, whereby costs followed judgment. Further changes were also wrought. The elders were no longer regaled and they received a fixed fee for attendance, paid by the African district council out of accumulated fees of court. With the introduction of fixed payment, and also as a precaution against bribery, it became the practice for cases to be heard by panels of about five elders chosen by lot from the total membership. If it should happen that an elder with particular knowledge of the case was excluded, he could be called on as a witness.

There were frequent complaints, especially in the early days, that the tribunal had been bribed. Although one could never rule out the possibility of favouritism or family intrigue, they seldom stood up to investigation. It was clear, nevertheless, that a regular method of complaint and appeal must be devised.

The provincial commissioners were responsible to the governor for all matters relating to the establishment, organisation, and administration of the tribunals. In the course of time organisations were evolved in both Nyanza and Central provinces with an impressive hierarchy of locational and divisional tribunals and a central appeal tribunal for each district. All these were subject to inspection and supervision by the district commissioner and his administrative staff, who could call for and, if necessary, revise any case. A right of appeal lay successively to the district commissioner, provincial commissioner and, ultimately, through a case stated by him, to the Supreme Court.

Although the number of appeal processes may seem extravagant, in practice the judgment of the divisional tribunal was accepted in about four fifths of the cases. The appeal tribunal and the district officer's revision then disposed of most of the rest. Thus, out of some thousands of cases heard in his district, the district commissioner would probably not be troubled with more than 40 or 50 coming to him on appeal in the course of the year, and the number reaching the provincial commissioner would not exceed 30 or 40 for the whole province. Land cases were the most troublesome because it was difficult to keep them short. As a check on bogus claims, however, special provision was made in Central province that the tribunals must not hear land cases until the opinion of the elders of the family groups concerned had first been obtained and recorded.

Some of the cases coming up before the district commissioner on appeal were intricate and time-consuming. Often their subject matter was slight and they interfered with administrative work. But nevertheless, one tried hard to see that right was done, down to the last goat. Yet final judgment could not always be delivered without misgivings. Where families had reciprocal relations of gift and counter-gift, frequent inter-marriage, and mutual transactions stretching back for generations, it was not in their interest that relations should be severed.

The success of the tribunals was evident from the fact that they disposed annually of thousands of cases that would otherwise have swamped and bewildered the magistrates' courts. A greater justification of them was that they settled their cases with a conservative but not too obstinate regard for the old tribal custom. It was a compact and logical system of great value for the preservation of family life and discipline, although it was coming under ever-increasing pressure from forces which could not be gainsaid. The first was the introduction of a money economy, with emphasis on individual wealth in place of a currency in cattle and goats, which were under family group control. The second was the breakdown of clan or family group land holdings into small family homesteads. These developments, whatever their benefits, were nevertheless resulting in the disintegration of tribal life with its clan and family sanctions. By protecting custom as far as was reasonable, the tribunals were thus lessening the shock of impact and enabling custom to adjust itself progressively to new conditions.

NOTE: An account of those aspects of tribal custom, which commonly arose as issues before the native courts – about marriage, inheritance, property and tribal discipline – can be found in Appendix II. These were the customs that used to hold tribalism together and are now rapidly disappearing.

PART IV

Land

11

Agrarian Problems of the African Lands

During the inter-war period land tenure achieved such importance both as a political and an economic issue, especially among the Kikuyu, that no fair account of the major problems of the time could be given without according it prominence.[1] The purpose of this account, therefore, is to illustrate the practical difficulties encountered in ensuring Africans a secure tenure and peaceful possession of their land, whether of tribal land, clan land, or group, family, or individual land, and the steps that government had been able to take to that end up to 1939.

When the British Protectorate was declared over Kenya there were no rigid boundaries between tribes nor, within the general area inhabited by a tribe, were there any definitive boundary marks to indicate the limits of clan lands or the holdings of family groups. Custom and long use had caused certain spheres of influence to be respected and sometimes, where tribal disputes had occurred, a settlement had been reached with reference to some natural feature. It was similar with clan and family units. Family groups might claim exclusive rights resting on some basis of first user or legitimate succession and might sometimes have blazed a tree or, with due ceremony, have planted shrubs or lilies to mark the limits of the claim but, for the most part, claims followed the banks of streams to their point of confluence or to the next group holding further down the ridge. Villages and areas of cultivation could be enclosed but, subject to these and a few other exceptions, there was very little visible evidence to

1 The discussion that follows, in which Fazan concentrates on Kikuyu land issues, does not differ in principle from the findings of Sorrenson, *Land Reform*, or A. Fiona D. Mackenzie, *Land, Ecology and Resistance in Kenya, 1880–1952* (Edinburgh: Edinburgh University Press, 1998), the latter of which focuses on Fort Hall/Murang'a district.

suggest that the tribal land was other than a general common and the fact that grazing was a common right gave colour to that view.

It is not to be wondered at in these conditions that government concerned itself very little with private rights at this stage but concentrated on the preservation of inter-tribal peace. Provincial and district boundaries were drawn and occasionally altered with some regard to tribal areas, although most districts contained elements of more than one tribe, and the leading tribes were spread over more than one district. Internally in the districts locational boundaries were drawn in rough conformity to the areas of clan occupation and headmen were appointed accordingly but seldom, if ever, was a man required to move his home because he happened to be living in the area of another tribe or clan. When the preservation of peace so demanded, government might have to intervene to settle a tribal dispute but, except in acute trouble, it was generally best to leave the parties to settle it for themselves.

In the early days of British administration, when the making of roads and tracks, and the siting of camps, trading centres and markets were a main concern, questions of private ownership of land hardly entered the picture at all. If a road in the making passed through crops, either compensation would be paid to the owner of the crop or the road would wait until the crop had been reaped, for most tribes practised a method of shifting cultivation. Only if land was taken for a permanent building was there need for discussion, the matter being talked over with the headman and elders in *baraza*, for nobody yet claimed private ownership of unoccupied land. Internal disputes about gardens or crops and the distribution of cultivation rights on inheritance were settled by the elders in traditional fashion, but private rights over 'bush' land were never an issue at this time.

The same was also true, in general, when larger areas were alienated for such purposes as towns, settlers' farms or mission stations. The local population was protected by the Crown Lands Ordinance of 1900, which provided compensation for those who preferred to leave, for huts and crops and for general disturbance, but not for unoccupied, uncultivated land. There were certain cases in Nairobi, however – of which the CSM land grant of 1905 is the best example – where Kikuyu living on the site had claimed *githaka* rights, and accommodation with them was reached before title was granted.

Government was very slow to accept that anything in the nature of private rights existed in the tribal conception of land tenure beyond a simple right of user. Until 1920 the official and judicial view was that private rights, as distinct from common rights to pasturage and village occupancy, did not extend beyond a right of continued usage of land actually cultivated and a limited area round it marked out for near-future cultivation; and that cessation of cultivation for more than three years voided the right. There was, however, a growing doubt as to whether this attitude was right. In 1899 Mr Justice Cator had written: 'It has sometimes been asserted that the Kikuyu acknowledge individual ownership of land, but I have heard this view contradicted.' And the word *githaka* used in the sense of a land claim occurred in a dispatch to the Foreign Office in the same year. In 1913, the governor, Sir Henry Belfield, directed that an enquiry should be made but when, in the same year, J. O. W. Hope, a senior provincial commissioner, was appointed to mark out land in the Limuru area for European farms and award compensation to any Africans displaced, he never so much as heard the word *githaka* mentioned, although the area was afterwards admitted to have been part of the Kikuyu tribal land and it might have been expected that every possible argument would have been brought forward against its loss. Hope himself stated years later that he had been completely ignorant of the existence of any such system.[2] But, with the better organisation of the native tribunals which occurred about this time, more information was now coming to hand.

Under the Crown Lands Ordinance of 1915, all land in Kenya outside the dominions of the Sultan of Zanzibar was declared to be Crown Land, including the African tribal lands, then called 'native reserves'. The reason advanced for their inclusion was that 'if such lands are vested in the Crown it will be possible for the Crown to regularise their occupation in the interests of the natives thereon, giving them real and definite right to the land'. The intention was good, but, through ignoring the fact that rights already existed and were being used, it misfired badly. In 1921, Sir Jacob Barth, the Chief Justice, gave judgment in a case concerning *githaka* rights: Isake Wainaina Gathemo and another v. Murito Ndagera and others. He stated that as an effect of the Kenya Order-in-Council 1921 combined with the Crown Lands Ordinance 1915, 'all the native rights in such reserved lands, whatever they were under the *githaka* system, disappeared'. This caused dismay, which was only partially mitigated when he explained that his statement did not mean that the Africans had no rights in lands which were entitled to the protection of the courts, but that such rights had not yet been so

2 Fazan's references to Judge Cator and Mr Hope show that he had his copy of the Carter Commission's *Report* by his side, pp. 81–2.

precisely ascertained that the protection of the courts could yet be extended to them.[3] The native tribunals, which, until then, had been doing good work towards sorting out land claims, were thus placed in an awkward position. If the Supreme Court had no jurisdiction, then the tribunals, being subordinate to it, had none either. In practice, however, they continued to hear land cases as before but, for a short period of years until jurisdiction was restored to them under the provisions of the Native Courts Ordinance, their decisions, where actual ownership as distinct from use was claimed, had to rank as advice to the district commissioner in his administrative capacity, not as judicial findings.

Partly, no doubt, as a result of Sir Jacob Barth's judgment, the '*githaka* question', which had hitherto been treated too much as an academic issue about tribal customs, suddenly sprang into great prominence when, in 1922, the Young Kikuyu Association under Harry Thuku agitated for the granting of land titles. The agitation emphasised that there was a need for a firm basis to regulate a system of land rights and at last this was realised. Investigations which had already been going on for some years by individual district officers and missionaries were now pushed forward urgently. Committees to report on tribal land customs were appointed for most of the principal tribes, and at least the existing facts were ascertained. Among the results was the *Report on Kikuyu Land Tenure*, produced in 1929, in the preparation of which witnesses of the Kikuyu, Embu and Meru tribes gave valuable help.[4]

An important point which had emerged clearly was that, although the Kikuyu were now laying great stress on the *githaka* and were very insistent that it should be used as their basis of land tenure, only a very short time had elapsed, at most a couple of generations, since *githaka* had come to mean anything except 'bush' and had acquired a technical significance as a land claim. It was by no means as stable a concept as was being represented: that the *githaka* was a sort of half-way house

---

3 This 'Barth judgment' is quoted in all scholarly histories of the 1920s.

4 Fazan seems to have forgotten the earlier Kikuyu Association, founded in 1919, which acted as a chiefs' trade union. Perhaps his memory was occluded by his own hostility towards the association in the later 1920s, when as District Commissioner Kiambu he felt that his chiefs should have been content to limit their expression of political views to sessions of the formally constituted Local Native Councils, of which most were members *ex officio*. See: Confidential note of a meeting at Government House, 21 November 1930, called to discuss Fazan's handing over report, on leaving Kiambu: Kenya National Archives: PC/CP. 8/5/1. For the 1929 committee, see above, Chapters 7 and 11.

between clan and full private ownership. What the Kikuyu wanted was that the *githaka* should be accepted as the basis of land tenure and that a system of private land ownership should be evolved from it. Government had sympathy for these aspirations and accepted them in principle.

That was approximately the position when the Kenya Land Commission of 1932–3 was appointed under the chairmanship of Sir Morris Carter with very comprehensive terms of reference. Its principal recommendations have already been mentioned. Of those recommendations relating to private land-holding and the development of a system of land tenure within the native lands, three of them were cardinal, namely:

(1) 'that the native lands as defined in the Report should cease to be Crown Land and should be styled the "Native Lands", the "*nuda proprietas*" being deemed to lie with the native population generally but subject to the sovereignty of the Crown and its general powers of control;'

(2) 'that within the several blocks of the Native Lands the inhabitant tribes, groups, families and individuals should have all the rights and powers in respect of land which they have under native custom (as it is or may become either by natural evolution or by rule made under the Lands Trust Ordinance or any other ordinance) in so far as they are not repugnant to the Lands Trust Ordinance or rules made or to be made under it or to any other law or ordinance of the Colony;' and

(3) 'that Government should be given wide powers of control under the Ordinance, which should include a power to make rules for the regulation, development and guidance of land tenure in the Native Lands, but that such rules should only be made after an elaborate procedure of consultation, to be prescribed in the Ordinance, had first been followed.'[5]

As regards the first recommendation, while it appreciated the native impulse which had induced government to declare these areas Crown Land, the commission observed, with some understatement, that 'to deprive a man of his rights in land for the sake of protecting him is a

5 In recommendations (1) and (2), Fazan paraphrases paragraph 1639, p. 418 of the Carter Commission's *Report*; (3) appears to summarise paragraphs 1655–7 on pp. 421–2. These recommendations followed Fazan's minority view in the report of the 1929 committee on Kikuyu land tenure.

method of procedure which is liable to be misunderstood'.[6] The second recommendation made clear that the native lands were not exclusively reserved for the particular tribe or tribes whose name they bore, so protecting minority groups, recognising the existence of private rights, and rendering the whole situation more fluid and adaptable. The third recommendation, the requirement that rules should only be made after long deliberation meant, in effect, that for many years to come more would be accomplished by consultation and agreement than by legal enforcement.

The Kenya Lands Trust Ordinance of 1934, which was framed on the commission's recommendations, distinguished between the 'protective' need and the 'development' need in the administration of the native lands. The protective need was assigned to a Lands Trust Board, whose principal duty was to watch over the integrity of the boundaries and see that any subsequent alterations or exchanges were made fairly and in strict accordance with the provisions of the ordinance. The development need was to be the sole responsibility of the Kenya government, to be conducted through the provincial and district administration. It was subject, however, to a right of the Lands Trust Board to make representations to the secretary of state if it considered that government was failing in this regard to do its duty.

The Kikuyu Land Tenure Committee of 1929 had found it possible to state of the *githaka* system that 'it is the greatest possible tribute to its worth that there are several places in the Nyeri and Fort Hall districts where one may stand and see more than a thousand acres at a stretch with scarcely an acre uncultivated, and the disputes which occur, though complicated and troublesome, are surprisingly few'.[7] While the first half of this assessment was undoubtedly true, the second half suggested a degree of stability which was afterwards found to be incorrect. Indeed, when the Kikuyu *mbari* submitted their claims to the Kenya Land Commission in 1932, it was found that practically the whole Kikuyu country was covered at least two deep in rival *githaka* claims and, in several cases, the same piece of land was claimed by three or more contending groups. It was thus clear that very careful steering

6 This piece of official irony comes from paragraph 1636, p. 418 of the Carter Commission *Report*.

7 Colony and Protectorate of Kenya, *Report of the Kikuyu Land Tenure Committee* (Nairobi: Government Printer, 1929), p. 10, paragraph 22.

would be required before the *githaka* system could be pronounced a viable system of land tenure.[8]

Similar problems existed among other tribes, and even in tribes that had previously been free of land problems, the planting of permanent crops such as tea, coffee, wattle, sugar cane or sisal was soon to create them. It was in the Kikuyu districts, however, that the problems arose most acutely.[9] Rival claims to land were sometimes so large as to amount to a political dispute about seigniory rather than an agrarian one about usage.[10] Indeed they were treated as such – as an administrative matter to be settled by the district commissioner after discussion with the chiefs, headmen and elders on both sides and whomever else he considered it right to consult. Where the issue was genuinely agrarian and concerned some private *right-holding* or crops, it went before the native tribunal of the location concerned, who referred it to the group elders on both sides for an opinion before passing judgment. Thence, if necessary, it could be referred to the district commissioner or beyond through the normal channels of appeal. This arrangement was satisfactory to the extent that the judgment settled the matter immediately in dispute, but no very permanent result could be expected when there was no adequate mapping; when one could never be sure that the parties in court included the real right-holders; and where third-party interests were not represented. But at least substantial justice was being done in a way which was understood and respected. The *mbari* elders and the original tribunal court were generally familiar with the land and details of the dispute and, if a case came up on appeal, some of the members of the divisional appeal tribunal would usually be sent to visit the land. As time went on and education spread, it was

8 Fazan is correct to point out the contradictory claims to property recorded from the various Kikuyu *mbari* (which were lineage corporations or 'houses' with many affiliated dependants rather than purely family descent groups), one of the many hurdles in the way of racial equity and the tenurial reform that Fazan judged necessary to African agricultural well-being.

9 The observations that follow help to explain why the provincial administration was so hesitant in the matter of African land tenure reform in the 1930s and 40s.

10 Fazan's use of the medieval English term *seigniory* (found throughout the 1929 committee report) usefully illustrates the difficulties found by British officials in trying to understand African tenures. Their natural instinct would have been to cast back to the history they half-remembered from school or university. But feudal notions of seigniory needed, first, a king with sovereign powers over land, secondly, lords who swore him homage in return for an allocation of land and, thirdly, clear obligations to tenants below them. None of these elements, except in very variable terms the last, applied to Kikuyuland.

increasingly expected that a sketch and possibly a photograph of some prominent feature on the land should be provided.

Reluctance to mark out boundaries was already disappearing. Advice was given to *githaka* heads and component right-holders in selected areas to mark out their boundaries by hedges—except, of course, where the boundary was a stream—and to use a different method to show whether it was a *githaka* boundary or an internal family right-holding. It was not expected that many of them would do so at first, but it was hoped that the practice might grow, even at the occasional risk of bringing disputes to a head. Although a record of court decisions could be kept and some attempt be made to plot them roughly on a map, no survey or register of right-holdings was practicable at that time, but with the increased planting of permanent crops, the position on the land was becoming more definitive.

Some of the right-holdings, especially near Nairobi, were very small—not yet so small as to be uneconomic, but threatening to become so. This was because Nairobi provided the neighbouring tribal areas with the best market for their produce and their labour, and much of the money earned went to the buying of goats and cattle which, in turn, went to the acquisition of wives. The result was local congestion. There did not seem to be much prospect of restraining it until, with social and economic advance, the Africans would find more uses for their money, and status would no longer depend on the accumulation of livestock and large families.[11]

The system of inheritance aggravated the trouble. When a right-holder died his holding was divided between all his sons living on, or claiming rights in the land. Not only did each of them have to have an equal share of the land which had been cultivated but, if land had been cultivated in separate parts—some, perhaps, by a stream and some higher up on the ridge—each part was also divided. It was better in these cases that the shares should be left unmarked for, in that case, there was still hope of common sense prevailing and it might be expected that the *muramati* (*githaka* head) would use his influence accordingly. Nevertheless, it could be foreseen that, unless something was done to ease the situation, many right-holdings would be reduced to totally uneconomic fragments within a generation.

Many suggestions were made for dealing with the problem. Broadly speaking, they all foundered on the question of how to find alternative

11 This passage summarises one of the arguments Fazan had made at greater length in his 1932 'Economic Survey of the Kikuyu Reserves. See Appendix III.

land or fair compensation for superfluous heirs. They were for example:

(1) Primogeniture: but this had been tried in South Africa in the Transkei without much success, although there was comparatively lucrative employment for the junior brothers to be had on the mines.[12] In Kenya there was no such certainty of work on offer. The elders would certainly not have regarded it as fair treatment that the eldest should have all.
(2) The eldest son to succeed to the title but the co-heirs to be allowed to remain on the land. This would help to the extent of keeping the shape of the right-holding intact, but it would not prevent congestion in respect of use.
(3) As in (2) but the principal heir to be allowed to buy out the others at an agreed valuation at any time up to a stated limit, after which they could not be disturbed or bought out against their will.
(4) The land to go to one heir after closed auction between the heirs.

Suggestions (3) and (4) seemed to be on the right lines. The chief objection against them lay in the fact that the principal heir would seldom have the means to buy out the others. To render either of these schemes workable would probably postulate an agreed valuation, recourse to a land bank, and an arbiter. It was thus necessary that for the proper development of the African lands there should be a land bank from which Africans might borrow for approved purposes on proper security.

Tenants were another complication, for according to Kikuyu custom they had no rights over the land they were cultivating beyond a right to reap their standing crops. They could not be evicted from their huts, however, and this expression was generally held to include the village yard and the cattle pen enclosed with it. Nevertheless, there were various ways in which they could be induced, not forced, to leave, though relations between owner (*mwene*) and tenant (*muhoi*) being normally friendly, cases of a man being moved against his will were very rare. The principal disability against which tenants suffered was that they could not build permanent houses or plant permanent crops: at least, if they did, they would have no security.

---

12 The Kenya government had sent Fazan to South Africa for a brief visit precisely to see what could be learned from the experience of the Transkei, later the first of apartheid's Bantustans.

It was not possible, at this time, to attempt any comprehensive solution to these problems, but the end always kept in view was to introduce more fluidity into the land system so that the population should be able more easily to redistribute itself. The most obvious way of doing this was to permit the buying and selling of land, but there were two main obstacles, the first being that tribal custom was against it. Leaving aside questionable transactions with the Dorobo,[13] there was no authenticated instance of any right-holder having sold his land to another with the approval of the elders, but unquestionably the claims of the right-holders in Kikuyu to have this right were gaining ground and the opposition of the elders was weakening. Probably, if this had been the only obstacle, if a start had been made with a few selected areas and if an appropriate method of prior consultation had been devised, the consent of the elders could have been obtained in cases where the need was clearly urgent. Custom was not the only obstacle, however. It would be necessary that the boundaries of the land should be clearly set forth together with a statement of any encumbrances and contingent interests, and that a period for third-party objections should be allowed before the transaction could be registered. Nothing of this kind had got beyond the discussion stage by the end of the inter-war period. Although sales were thus not practicable as yet, there did seem to be a possibility that the custom of pawning land for goats might be extended and, subject to more equitable conditions regarding redemption, be developed into a form of leasehold.

Leaving now the problems of tenure of agricultural land as between Africans, the very important provisions which the Kenya Lands Trust Ordinance of 1934 made for procuring land for public purposes, trade

---

13 A wealth of political disagreement lies behind this aside. Kikuyu elders and their white sympathisers, principally Dr Louis Leakey (see his *The Southern Kikuyu before 1903* (London: Academic Press, 1977, Chapter 4)) argued that, in southern Kikuyuland especially, Kikuyu agrarian colonisers had bought out Dorobo hunting rights in the nineteenth century in a series of private contracts, hallowed by ritual and often guaranteed by inter-marriage. Kenyatta's *Facing Mount Kenya*, Chapter II, expressed a similar view, not quite so convincingly. Fazan, keen to see that what he regarded as progressive development should not be hindered by historically dubious rights of seigniory, was inclined to believe that many of these accounts were politically convenient fictions. Fortified in this view by Dorobo complaints voiced at the Kenya land commission's public meetings, Fazan wrote in its *Report* (p. 93, paragraph 285) that while Kikuyu had indeed acquired Dorobo rights partly by alliance, adoption and payment – as argued by Leakey and Kenyatta – the process was nonetheless carried through 'largely by force and chicanery' – what he here, in his memoir, calls 'questionable transactions'.

and social requirements must now be considered. The position which had obtained under the Lands Trust Ordinance of 1930 was that townships and trading centres situated within the external boundaries of what were then called native reserves were deemed to be excluded from them, and this also applied to land alienated for a public body, generally a mission, for purposes of social service. Apart from giving the map a pock-marked appearance, it had the effect of removing from the African lands all the principal landmarks of their own advancement. True, the government paid over to the local native council—afterwards, African district council—all the rents they received from these sources, but the Land Commission considered that if, in addition, these places were re-included in the native lands, the councils would come to take an active interest and a pride in them. Government agreed, and action was taken accordingly.

As to any land that might be required for such purposes in the future, the commission, following a practice already being tried with success in the Kiambu and Nyeri districts, recommended a process of 'setting apart' and lease. The land would first be set apart by the native council paying agreed compensation to the right-holders either in the form of an outright payment or, if they preferred, by an initial premium and annual instalment. The land having thus been set free from private interests, the council would then let it on lease for the purpose required, fixing the rent at an amount sufficient to recoup themselves for their outlay and their pains. The commission went into details about the manner of fixing the compensation; about a power of enforcement on the lines of the Land Acquisition Act if no agreement had been reached and the need for the service was urgent and sufficiently important to justify the action; and about power for the provincial commissioner to order an outright final compensation to be paid in cases in which annual payments were causing complications. Nearly all of these recommendations found their way into the new Lands Trust Ordinance of 1934. The method proved most useful for the reservation and leasing of small plots for schools and churches, market sites, agricultural experimental and seed-raising plots, locational centres for chiefs, and other similar purposes of administration and social service. When a larger area was in question, as for a new trading centre, and external boundaries had been duly set apart after compensation to right-holders had been agreed, the district commissioner, after consultation with the local native council, would divide the total area into plots to be leased separately, and the council would receive the rents. Existing townships, district stations and trading centres within the boundaries of the native lands were deemed to have been set apart already. In the initial stages of growth the rents would go wholly to the local native council. As they became a little larger and more important, a township committee would be appointed and, at this stage, the council would be expected to pay a contribution towards their development out of the rents which they received. Later, when the township grew to a size and status vaguely described as Class A, a quit rent would be paid to the council, after which the township authority would take over the responsibility for its future development, together with its rents and revenues, under the general supervision of the commissioner of lands.

12

The White Highlands

The setting apart of a specific area exclusively for European settlers' farms, which was the keystone of white settlement in Kenya, has always been a controversial subject. The White Highlands and white hegemony in the political field went so much hand in hand in the short history of Kenya Colony that they have been regarded as one issue. Among the European community there were some who thought the privilege should never have been granted and others who regarded it as sacrosanct.[1] Perhaps the majority regarded it as something valuable in the formative period which should be progressively relaxed as the Colony gained maturity.[2]

---

1 For calm analysis, see Sorrenson, *Origins of European Settlement*; for passionate defence, see Huxley, *White Man's Country*; for dissent among officials, see Norman Leys, *Kenya* (London: Hogarth Press, 1924) and Ross, *Kenya from Within*.

2 This seems a rare example of wishful thinking on Fazan's part, possibly (one can only speculate) in rueful meditation on his unhappiness, expressed officially at the time, at the way in which the Carter Commission's terms of reference, originally concerned only with African needs, were skewed by the Colonial Office towards the rights of white farmers, as discussed in the Foreword. Few if any settlers would have thought that an appropriate degree of 'maturity' was conceivable in their lifetime. Their leaders fought hard to ensure that the 'administrative convenience' by which they had priority in land transactions in the White Highlands since the Elgin pledge of 1906 was transformed into law by the Highlands Order in Council of 1939. They needed this racially-exclusive state support for the maintenance of their land values. Public official acknowledgment that it was time to open the Highlands to a colour-blind land market had to await the publication of the *Royal Commission on East Africa 1953–55 Report* (London: HMSO, Cmd 9475, 1955) – a conclusion that shocked most white settlers – for which see Michael Blundell, *So Rough a Wind* (London: Weidenfeld & Nicolson, 1964), pp. 236–40, 258–9. The necessary government action came later still, in 1959, for which see Sorrenson, *Land Reform*, pp. 196–7. As noted in the editorial Foreword, this later royal commission openly criticised (pp. 53–62) the 'tribal' and 'racial' assumptions of the Carter Commission's (i.e., Fazan's) *Report* that were forced upon it by its terms of reference. See Fazan's discussion in Chapter 16.

From the time of the early explorers there had been vague ideas of possible white settlement and, as the high cost of maintaining the railway began to impress itself upon the British government, these ideas gained greater shape. Lord Lugard mentioned them and Sir Harry Johnston, commissioner for Uganda, confirmed the suitability of the Highlands for European farms. Sir Charles Eliot, commissioner of the East African Protectorate from 1901 to 1904, was an enthusiastic supporter. With almost crusading enthusiasm he wrote in his annual report for 1908: 'Modern East Africa is the greatest philanthropic achievement of the later nineteenth century [...] It is only a few years since East Africa was nothing but a man-hunting ground [...] diversified by interludes of terrible famine [...] With an adequate administration, proper investigation of the resources of the country, and the encouragement of European settlers and merchants I consider it certain that the Country will pay its way.' And so the policy of white settlement began. With the enactment of the Crown Lands Ordinance of 1902, both before and after it, the first wave of settlement took place. It received great encouragement from the declaration of Lord Elgin as secretary of state for the colonies – first made in 1906 and confirmed in 1908 – that: 'Land lying outside municipal limits, roughly lying between Kiu and Fort Ternan should be granted only to European settlers.'[3] To a very large extent this land was unoccupied by any permanent human habitation at the time when the grants were made. The bulk of it consisted of open savannah plains occupied by herds of game among which the Masai intermittently grazed their cattle; and most of the rest was uninhabited and largely under forest or scrub. This description applied not only to the land which subsequently became the White Highlands but also to the grants made for plantation purposes in other parts of the Colony.[4]

By 1908 British settlement had become a small but distinctly hardy growth, although the total number of Europeans in the whole of Kenya at that date, including officials, missionaries, traders and settlers, scarcely exceeded 3,000. The second wave of settlement took place between 1911 and 1913, when the Limuru farms were surveyed and leased and, for the better regulation of grants and titles, the Crown Lands Ordinance of 1913 was enacted. After that date the only large alienations were in connection with the soldier settler scheme after the

3 See Hyam, *Elgin and Churchill*, pp. 418–19.

4 For earlier discussion of this point see above, Chapter 7, note 25, and for later confirmation, see note 8.

First World War. Lord Hailey records that, after 1919, there were no further block alienations of any considerable extent.[5] Closer settlement by means of sub-division of land already alienated was the main feature in the development of the Highlands which took place after that date.[6]

By the Kenya Annexation Order-in-Council of 1920 and the proclamation of the Colony, the future pattern and policy for the development of Kenya was set. The development of the land reserved for European settlement was to proceed side by side with the development of the African tribal lands in a relationship which was conceived as one of partnership. This sentiment found expression in the phrase 'the dual policy'. Whether it contained within itself the seeds of ultimate friction may be a matter of opinion, but it gave fair promise of success and worked well for many years.

Although the actual numbers of the European population did not much exceed 16,000 at that date, the Order proclaiming the Colony was universally accepted by all Europeans as a Charter and an earnest of intention and supporting declarations were later made. In 1921 Lord Milner, Secretary of State, affirmed that:

> After taking into consideration the facts that during the last fifteen years European British subjects have been encouraged to develop the Highlands and that during that period settlers have taken up land in the Highlands on this understanding, His Majesty's Government have decided that the existing practice must be maintained as regards both initial grants and transfers.

---

5 Fazan here refers to Lord Hailey's *An African Survey: A Study of Problems Arising in Africa South of the Sahara* (London: Oxford University Press, 1938), p. 748, which was very probably on his bookshelf. The survey was conducted under the auspices of the Royal Institute of International Affairs, funded by the Carnegie Corporation of New York, and helped by the Belgian, British, French and Portuguese colonial ministries, at a time when the Great Depression's damage to African economies challenged both the moral justification and economic competence of colonial rule. See John W. Cell, *Hailey: A Study in British Imperialism 1872–1969* (Cambridge: Cambridge University Press, 2002); and Helen Tilley, *Africa as a Living Laboratory: Empire, Development, and the Problem of Scientific Knowledge* (Chicago, IL: University of Chicago Press, 2011).

6 One may speculate that in writing this Fazan may have had in mind that this sub-division – and more intensive farming – was precisely what he had in mind for the well-being of African peasantries within their existing reserve boundaries – as the next paragraph appears to confirm.

Winston Churchill, who succeeded him, confirmed this assurance in 1922 stating that:

> We consider we are pledged by undertakings given in the past to reserve the Highlands of East Africa exclusively for European settlers, and we do not intend to depart from that pledge. And it may be taken as a matter which is definitely settled.

Then in 1923 the Duke of Devonshire declared: 'that the British Government approved the principle, adding that 'the reservation of the Highlands to Europeans must cover transfer as well as original leases from the Crown.'[7]

After the Kenya Land Commission of 1932–3 had reported and its report had been approved, the extent of the Highlands was determined and the boundaries were safeguarded by Order-in-Council.

The land in the Highlands, considered over all, could not be classed, initially, as more than second rate; the best land being already in tribal occupation. Mr Alex Holm, one of Kenya's most distinguished directors of agriculture, stated in legislative council in 1928 that: 'the best land and the most fertile land in this Colony has not been occupied by non-native peoples. The natives have been left in the possession of the most fertile land.'[8]

There were, indeed, in the Highlands large stretches of good arable land suitable for plantation crops such as coffee and tea but, by and large, the general character was open plain where it was not mountainous. Before the bulk of it could be used for dairy and mixed farming or even for ranching, it had to be provided with sufficient water

---

7 These three official statements were made in the context of the early 1920s so-called 'Indian Crisis' when the issue of whether white settlers should enjoy a position of privilege over the more numerous South Asian settlers was decided in the white settlers' favour. This was contrary to the recent imperial promises of racial equality in the dependent Empire, made both to mollify the Indian National Congress and to acknowledge Britain's debt to the Indian army in the First World War. See Gregory, *India and East Africa*; Maxon, *Struggle for Kenya*.

8 While one may assume that self-interest lay behind Mr Holm's statement, agronomists nonetheless agree that about 80 per cent of the most fertile and best-watered land in Kenya did indeed remain in African occupation. For graphic illustration, see Survey of Kenya, *National Atlas of Kenya* (Nairobi: Kenya Government, third edition 1970), maps on pp. 19–35, showing rainfall probability, soils, ecological potential, vegetation, crop combinations, etc. And see the earlier discussion in Chapter 7, note 25.

by damming gullies or sinking boreholes. Even then there were problems of soil deficiency and animal and plant diseases to be solved. Years of patient experiment had to be endured both with livestock and with crops before the right types and methods were proved for the different conditions of soil and climate.

The Joint Parliamentary Commission of 1931, commenting on the degree of disturbance caused to the African tribes by white settlement, said that:

> The influx of European settlement at the beginning of the century was encouraged by Government in order to promote the development of areas which, partly owing to their relatively colder climate and partly owing to Masai devastation, were largely unoccupied or in very sparse or irregular occupation. The subsequent expansion of European settlement may have led to some transactions of doubtful fairness. [...] At the same time it would be difficult to find any other instance of a white population settling in a native country with so little disturbance of the original population.[9]

Appointed as a result of that commission, and charged with the duty of defining the boundaries of the Highlands and of the native lands in such a way as to make redress in cases of 'doubtful fairness' as far as possible, the Kenya Land Commission of 1932–3 set itself to examine the position in great detail. They found there were four tribes which, in varying degrees, could claim to have had tribal land within the Highlands boundaries. The area over which the Masai had exercised rights was by far the most extensive, but this question had been settled by the treaty arrangements of 1904 and 1911 and subsequent adjustments, and there was no desire in any quarter to reopen the matter. The other three tribes were the Kikuyu, the Nandi, and the Kipsigis. Although the extent of the tribal land lost by them to the Highlands was a very small part, barely 3 per cent, of the total area and had only been sparsely occupied, its loss was important to the tribes concerned as being land required for their future expansion. This was especially so in the case of the Kikuyu, whose lost land was of good quality and in an area not far from Nairobi where the growth of population was sure to be rapid.

---

9 Joint Select Committee on Closer Union in East Africa, *Report, Together with the Proceedings of the Committee* (London: HMSO, HC Paper 156 and HL Paper 184 of 1931), p. 24.

The Kikuyu native reserve, as gazetted in 1926, comprised 5,207 square miles. The commission found that about 126 square miles not included in this area was land over which the Kikuyu had established effective occupation and that it had been lost to them, mainly by alienation to the Highlands. After exhaustive inquiry the commission recommended that 33 square miles in the general area of the land lost and 205 square miles in the Mwea area to the east of Nyeri district be added in compensation. An area of 383 square miles of the northern Yatta Plateau contiguous to the Mwea area was also to be added in general compensation and as a permanent addition to provide for future expansion and to facilitate the return to the reserve of small family groups who had been living in pockets of the Highlands, either on European farms or elsewhere, but outside the limits of what could be claimed to have been Kikuyu tribal land. A grant of money was also awarded to help resettlement.[10]

After the boundaries of the Nandi Reserve were delimited in 1907, it was found that they included certain land in the Kipkarren and Kaimosi areas which had been alienated as European farms. To compensate for this and in agreement with the Nandi chiefs, the boundaries were extended in 1910 by 70 square miles and guaranteed; but, unfortunately, a mistake was made and further land was alienated after that date. In July 1912, some 17 square miles were taken in the Kaimosi area for farms and, in 1919, a further block of 130 square miles was surveyed for soldier settlers. The mistake would never have been made if, at the time, the Nandi had had the land in effective use. It appears that the area concerned had only been very sparsely occupied at the time of the survey and that a count had revealed only 419 huts, for which compensation had been duly paid. When the injustice was realised it was found possible, by various adjustments, to return the greater part of the area to Nandi use. There remained, however, some 60 square miles for which compensation had to be found. By paying over the rent and stand premia and an additional sum of £5,000 to the Nandi an acceptable, if not wholly satisfactory, settlement was reached. The status of the affected land became native land leased as farms, and the Nandi continued to be entitled to the rents.

10 For editorial comment on these recommendations to compensate Kikuyu, see above, Chapter 7, note 24. Similar remarks apply to the adjustments made with respect to land alienated from Nandi and Kipsigis.

The Sotik farms, covering an area slightly over 200 square miles, were alienated for settlement from land formerly used by the Kipsigis for pasturage but, it appeared, otherwise unused or very thinly occupied. It had been buffer land between them and the Kisii. The commission decided that the claim could be adequately met by granting the Kipsigis, in conjunction with the Dorobo, an area of 148 square miles, under a light covering of forest and known as Chepalungu to the southward of their reserve. Such claims as were put forward by other tribes were, by comparison, trivial, and the commission had no difficulty in dealing with them. Apart from the Highlands there had been other alienations, as, for instance, in the Taita and Taveta areas where grants of land had been made not so much for private farms as for large company-owned plantations. Adjustments were made to the relative Native Reserves to compensate for the degree of disturbance.

As for private claims, care had been taken from as far back as 1895 at the time of the original grants to protect the interests of any African families who might be found to be actually living on the land. In most cases they were compensated by the original grants and left of their own free will, but there were also cases where they remained and were covered by the provisions of the Crown Lands Ordinance, 1902, repeated in the Crown Lands Ordinance, 1915, which stated that land in the actual occupation of natives at the time of the lease should, so long as it was actually occupied by them, be deemed to be excluded from the lease.

Excellent though this provision was in its intention, it caused much trouble. The extent of African rights had never been defined and, as their families multiplied and relations joined them, a position arose where the European title-holder could never be sure how much of the land he could call his own. The confusion grew still worse when the African right-holders on the land became intermingled with imported labour engaged on 'resident native labour' contracts who also began to make land claims. At the same time the African reserves had begun to fill up, and it was no longer so easy as it had been for families who had been living on a settler's farm under a claim of right to find homes with their relatives in the reserves, even if they had agreed to accept compensation and forgo their rights on the farm. The matter was referred as a special term of reference to the commission. They settled it by calculating how much land would be required for the re-accommodation of such persons in their reserves and added it to the area which had been recommended for expansion to satisfy economic needs. In return for this, the rights on the farms were to be expunged. The recommendation was accepted; a senior officer was seconded to superintend the resettlement and a grant of money was made to ease the disturbance.[11]

The total area of the European Highlands as finally gazetted was 16,700 square miles, and the total for the African lands and Native Reserves combined was 52,095 square miles – the figures, in both cases, being subject to verification by survey. The sum total of both together only amounted to one third of the total land of Kenya. In all the rest of it any person was to be free to take up land under the provisions of the Crown Lands Ordinance without distinction of race, except that there were to be certain areas in which only Africans could hold leases and, in the northern frontier districts, the nomadic tribes living in those parts were conceived as having prior but not exclusive rights.

★★★

Except in the Kiambu district, where it was estimated that there were about 8,000 Africans living on the farm land at the time when the original alienations were made, the White Highlands, over all, had been almost entirely without any permanent habitation. In these conditions the early settlers experienced much difficulty in securing labour. There were hardly any Africans who had worked for wages, and few outside the coast belt even knew what money was. Curiosity and hunger were initially the main inducements, and payment might have to be made in

11 Here is another potent cause behind the later Mau Mau insurgency. Over 4,000 Kikuyu, almost all from Kiambu, lived on white farms in occupation of their ancestral lands, having earlier refused compensation and moved elsewhere. The Carter Commission recommended that these occupation rights be extinguished, in return for resettlement on equivalent land elsewhere. This land was found for them in two areas. The first was the Olengurone settlement scheme, a high-altitude forested area on the western wall of the Rift Valley, where peasant farming was ecologically marginal. For the land-usage and inheritance disputes between government and Kikuyu 'settlers', a potent source of political anger in the origins of Mau Mau, see Throup, *Economic and Social Origins*, Chapter 6. The second settlement area was found for those right-holders who lived on 'white' land at or near Tigoni, close to the Kiambu reserve. Throughout the later 1930s, when trying to negotiate an agreed resettlement, the local officials faced arguments by and between Kikuyu leaders and direct action by impatient white settlers, some of whom burned down African homes and drove off their residents – a usurpation of the law that went unpunished. The angry impasse was seemingly solved by resettlement of some right-holders in the Lari forest reserve but on land claimed by other Kikuyu, as the Lari massacres of 1953 tragically proved. See Anderson, *Histories of the Hanged*, Chapter 4, and Breen, 'The Politics of Land', Chapter VII for the grim story of how decent officials had to grapple increasingly forcibly with the contradictions of the Kenya Land Commission's terms of reference, contradictions resolved in blood.

brass wire, blankets or other trade goods. Necessity to earn money for hut tax was a later urge.

In these circumstances the settlers expected government officers to help them find the labour by persuasion, exercised through chiefs and headmen – particularly as it was allowed in the case of public works.[12] It was an unhappy time for officials, between the devil and the deep blue sea. On the one hand they sympathised with the settlers: labour was badly needed if their farming enterprises were to be a success and it would probably be to the long-term benefit of Africans to participate. On the other hand they were loath to exercise the degree of pressure demanded by the settlers, for to do so would not only cause them to antagonise the native population, but it would also make them fall foul of government at headquarters, which in 1908 had ordered that chiefs could no longer use compulsion to provide labour and had insisted that officials explain to Africans that they need not work unless they so wished. That such intervention was necessary to curb the abuses which had existed hitherto was plain, but the question of whether encouragement by officials was permissible and whether chiefs and headmen should be involved in it, though not approved by government, nevertheless remained open.

There was no doubt that in the early years of the Protectorate, despite legislation, methods regarding labour were often crude. Not only did some of the chiefs use coercion in recruitment, but when the workers reached the farms conditions were often poor and their treatment sometimes harsh. On plantations too conditions were bad, especially in sisal where there was the additional hazard of sharp leaves which frequently gave the cutters unpleasant sores. Gradually, though, the problem was eased. As things got slowly better so, little by little, a trickle of volunteers became a stream and Africans returning after a short spell on a farm usually took a short rest and went back again. Professional recruiters had prospered ever since the Masters and Servants Ordinance 1906, but after 1924 their numbers dwindled, although they were still in evidence for several years to come. This was an indication that most farmers had succeeded in establishing a connection and that their labour position had been secured. The fear of conscription for the Carrier Corps during the First World War and the acute food shortage of 1918 played quite a part in bringing this situation about. Significant later developments were the improvement

12 Fazan's account here is a restrained expression of the administrative dilemma.

in roads and transport, which eased the movement of labour, and the introduction of mechanisation on the farms.

It was not without some crises on the way that the labour supply problem was to be surmounted. These came to a head in 1919 with the issue of the 'Northey circulars', which were an attempt to resolve the ambiguities in which officials found themselves with regard to labour but, although no reference was made to compulsion, the forthright tenor of the circulars was enough to cause a great storm, with missionaries at the forefront of the protest. Nothing happened eventually and the ambiguities remained. The circulars were withdrawn and in 1921 Secretary of State Winston Churchill, ordered that officials desist from recruitment although they were still allowed to provide information as to where labour was required.

Although the circulars were too strongly worded in favour of persuasion, it was in some ways a pity that they should have failed so completely, as the field administration badly needed adequate direction on the subject of recruitment. It seems that the objectionable features hinting at compulsion had been added by the Protectorate's vigorous governor, General Northey himself, without reference to the highly experienced chief native commissioner who had drafted the original of the first circular.[13] The missionaries were against the encouragement of labour in any shape or form but it was this veiled reference to compulsion that they especially could not abide, and in this part of their protest they were supported by certain prominent members of the administration who considered it a violation of the protective duty with which they had been entrusted ever since the earliest days of British rule. But if they considered coercion unacceptable, the broad principle of the involvement of officials in encouraging recruitment for private employers was, in prevailing conditions, a more open question. In many areas the African population had been demoralised by the Carrier Corps experience, on top of which had come the still more serious burden of famine and disease. In the circumstances it was therefore important that things should be kept moving at a comfortable pace and that the malaise afflicting the coast should not be allowed to spread through the entire country. This was particularly so in the poorer areas where the tax burden had become intolerable. For these people work on the European farms would not only provide a vital source of income,

13 The 'highly experienced chief native commissioner' was none other than the young Fazan's hero John Ainsworth. The protective anonymity granted him here was noted in the Foreword.

but would also assist the government with the revenue needed to supply medical facilities and other essential services. Meanwhile there would, of course, be no question of allowing European farming to prosper at the expense of African agriculture. That would be quite unethical, besides which it would be robbing Peter to pay Paul and getting the government nowhere.

A factor in the debate which was probably decisive in the final outcome was the scope of the authority of the chiefs, for on them much of the job of recruitment was bound to fall. Furthermore, as the administration was seriously understaffed by the end of the war – I was myself then running two stations at Kilifi and Malindi single handed – there would be little supervision to see that the job was being done properly. The senior officials and missionaries, acutely mindful of the serious abuses of the 1900's, were thus very wary of entrusting the chiefs with such responsibilities fearing, no doubt, that some of them would not be averse to using coercion, accepting bribes and generally using their authority to promote their own interests. So much did this prey on their minds that the missionaries were even prepared to countenance the idea of limited conscription as a preferable alternative. A further complication was that it was considered that unsophisticated Africans were incapable of distinguishing between a suggestion and an order when it was issued by government. In short it was feared that in practice 'encouragement' would simply be compulsion under another name.

That there were grounds for these apprehensions there can be no doubt, and if there was an appreciable risk that the encouragement of labour would in practice degenerate into compulsion, then the order that officials desist from recruitment can only have been right. But whether it was right is a matter for conjecture. To some extent the chiefs had been made scapegoats not only by missionaries, but also by various settlers who were keen to show that life in the reserves was so poor and brutish that work on the farms could only be a relief. In practice matters were rather different. The system of administration through chiefs and headmen was, in fact, not so very unlike any other maturing authority, and although there were some of them who may have been a doubtful quantity, there were many others at all grades who were certainly of high calibre. By about 1920 many of the faults of the system had already been corrected and there was not much wrong with it that could not have been cured with careful supervision and better pay. Furthermore, for reasons already elaborated, there were serious shortcomings in the cautious attitude which, while acquiescing in the fact that African chiefs were expected to fulfil an ever-wider range of obligations, was reluctant to consider them as properly responsible and to accord them commensurate remuneration and dignity.[14]

Though very much diminished by the 1920's the cry of labour shortage continued to be raised for several years afterwards. Locust infestation, drought and economic slump at the end of the decade put added pressure on the system, but by 1932 the troubles had been largely overcome. This was partly on account of the shrewd economic policies and moderation of that straightforward and homely man, Sir Joseph Byrne, who was governor from 1931 to 1937.[15]

In these circumstances the problem of labour supply was eased. The numbers of squatters, including wives and children, living on settlers' farms in the Highlands under cover of 'resident native labour' contracts was stated in the annual report of the department of agriculture for the year 1932 to be 110,570, the great majority of whom were Kikuyu. Besides these, the best part of 100,000 more were employed on monthly labour contracts. Among the latter, according to the report of the Native Registration Department, there were 40,685 Kikuyu alone. The number of Luo, Abaluhya and Nandi, who provided the labour force for the western part of the Highlands, would have been comparable. These numbers continued to increase and, when the Colony ended, the squatters, together with their wives and children, in all probability exceeded 200,000 and, with contract labourers included, well over a quarter of a million.

The squatters were at once a justification of, and a threat to, the White Highlands, for it was quite certain that the land could never have supported anything like the number of inhabitants in so good a state in those conditions as it could when developed as farms. Indeed, the squatters were probably materially better off than their kinsmen at home, for they had their wages as well as an allotment for their huts and gardens and, usually, some pasture for their goats as well. There did,

14 Historians would, in broad terms, agree with this account of the post-First World War labour crisis. See Clayton and Savage, *Government and Labour*, Chapter 4; Maxon, *Ainsworth*, Chapter X; idem, *Struggle for Kenya*, Chapters 5 and 6. Fazan does not make it sufficiently clear, however, that the missionary pressure group would tolerate forced labour only if conscription were put into the hands of supposedly trustworthy district commissioners, not allegedly self-interested and corruptible chiefs.

15 Here is another example of a difference of view between British officials and the white settler leadership. The latter detested what they saw as the dictatorial arrogance of Fazan's moderate, straightforward and homely Brigadier Sir Joseph Byrne, formerly inspector general of the Royal Irish Constabulary and governor of the non-settler colony of Sierra Leone before being promoted to Kenya.

however, appear to be a risk of the squatter position getting out of hand, and there was some need for review. It was sometimes objected that the system tended to bind the labourer too closely to his employer, for if he left his work he would lose his garden plot and, although he would commonly have no difficulty in securing a similar contract with another employer and would certainly be allowed to reap his standing crops, nobody would willingly leave the land he had cultivated and go somewhere else. An objection from the opposite angle was that, when a squatter who had given years of loyal service became too old for useful work, the employer, out of common humanity, was reluctant to turn him and his family away. A kind of prescriptive right could then arise and an accumulation of time-expired retainers, if carried to excess, would be detrimental to good farming.[16]

For reasons of this kind there were suggestions that, instead of the squatters living on the land of their employers, labour settlements should be formed, serving groups of farms. But, if these settlements were to include agricultural allotments, they would have to be of very considerable extent while, if they did not so provide, the existing difficulties would not have been much eased. There was not yet any urgency about it, and it was still an open question when the end of the Colony came.[17]

Labour conditions on farms improved with time. While the settler himself was living in a wattle-and-daub *banda* a high standard for his labour lines could hardly be expected. In 1914 the first labour inspectorate was established by amendment to the Master and Servants Ordinance and rules about labour conditions were made more exacting. The labour department was at first very small and was mainly concerned with registration, but the chief inspector of labour and the provincial labour officers who began to appear in the field in about the early 1930's, did really admirable work in getting conditions improved as regards the housing and rations of labour on farms and seeing that

16 For comment on Fazan's account of squatter history and a bibliography, see Chapter 8, note 1. There is no doubt that squatter resentment of their treatment, which they regarded as a denial of all they had done to develop the White Highlands, was a major source of recruitment to Mau Mau.

17 By the time the labour department made this proposal, after the Second World War, Fazan had retired. Perhaps that is why he did not grasp the depth of the main white settler objection, which was that it would give Africans the right to live as villagers on the White Highlands independent of a labour contract, a most dangerous precedent in the eyes of white farmers. See Clayton and Savage, *Government and Labour*, pp. 305–11.

the piece-work set was reasonable. Also some of the firms which were established in the 20s and 30s, notably the Magadi Soda Company and the tea estates at Kericho, did useful work in setting higher standards.

While the settlers depended on African labour for the rough work, they personally took a very active and vigorous part in working the land. Anything requiring any degree of skill in the early days had to be done by the farmer himself, or at least under his close supervision. The health and well-being of his labourers were in his care, and he was bound by law to keep a supply of drugs. His wife generally took care of the dispensary side and interested herself in the welfare of the women and children. Some of the larger estates kept schools, but this was not practicable on the smaller farms and squatters' children were at some disadvantage in this respect as compared with those in the African lands.

★★★

There was little but subsistence agriculture in Kenya before the settlers came. There was no agricultural export from upcountry and only a very small amount, including copra, from the coast. Food scarcity, amounting to famine in local areas, was a common condition, made worse by the inability of more fortunate areas to help a stricken neighbour. An export trade was being developed by a few, mostly Indian, merchants in the hides of scrub cattle, but practically all other exports were wild, such as ivory and rhino horn, gum copal, beeswax, ambergris, dried shark, and mangrove poles carried coastwise in Arab dhows. These were not promising conditions in which to start farming, but by 1935 or thereabouts white settlement in the Highlands was out of the wood. It had come through its initial labour troubles, had survived two world depressions and a temporarily crippling change in the currency, had carried out the basic work on the farms, and was not excessively dependent on bank overdrafts. The main export crops had been established, and more than the foundation had been laid for prosperous livestock farming.[18]

With established exports in coffee, tea, sisal, pyrethrum, beeswax, bacon, and dairy produce as the principal products, all from the

18 Mosley, *The Settler Economies*, Chapter 5, agrees with Fazan's assessment of the relative efficiency of white farming in the later 1930s, not least because many of the less efficient farmers – 20 per cent of the total – had gone bankrupt in the depression, leaving their farms vacant, and so available for independent, unsupervised, squatter occupation.

Highlands or European-owned plantations elsewhere, and a large number of other important crops, such as wheat and wattle bark, in support, Kenya's economy when war broke out in 1939 was already on a broader basis than that of its neighbours. Uganda cotton and Tanganyika sisal may have shown greater value but, in terms of self-sufficiency, Kenya with all the combined produce of the Highlands and the African Lands was far better off. There were almost no foodstuffs, except sugar from Uganda and a certain amount of rice for the Asiatic population, that it needed to import in war, while it was able to make a considerable contribution in supplies to its neighbours and the Middle East.

In the early days of settlement the aim had been set predominantly on finding suitable crops for export overseas so as to get money into the country. That was the first essential, but since then the conception had changed so that the importance of a sound internal economy ranked equally with export. Kenya was not one of those fortunate countries which could make its way by growing what it needed for itself and then exporting the surplus. The principal exports, in Kenya's case, were crops grown simply for that purpose rather than to fulfil any local need. Nevertheless, the importance of creating a local demand, however small, as a buffer against a sudden slump in world prices was quickly recognized. Strong and successful efforts were made, for instance, to popularise the drinking of coffee and tea among Africans and to encourage processing industries of all kinds and manufacture from local produce. The Uplands bacon factory, the Kenya Cooperative Creameries, and Liebigs canned meat factory at Athi River were three of the major developments at the end of the inter-war period. Unga Ltd was soon supplying bakeries throughout the country with Kenya-grown wheat. By internal self-sufficiency in food and by manufactures from local products – anything from beer to blankets, boots and belts, bricks, tiles, furniture, etc. – Kenya had placed itself on the road to a self-contained economy. These incipient industries were of great service to the whole of East Africa during the war, and their number and range expanded rapidly afterwards.[19]

---

19 For the war economy see John Lonsdale, 'The Depression and the Second World War in the Transformation of Kenya', in David Killingray and Richard Rathbone (eds), *Africa and the Second World War* (Basingstoke: Macmillan, 1986), pp. 97–142. And for later economic history see below, Chapter 16.

It would be futile to compare the respective contributions of the White Highlands and the African Lands to the total economy of Kenya. The Highlands can claim by far the greater export, but African produce went largely to local markets and did not appear in the export returns. The essential relation was one of partnership, for neither could prosper without the other, and the traders also played their part.

★★★

Although the settlers certainly had too much political influence at this time in the sense that their interests were allowed to predominate too much, their influence was not such as to warrant the indignation which Dr Norman Leys and W. McGregor Ross displayed in their books about Kenya in the 1920's, as if some gross injustice had been done.[20] The influence of the settlers may be viewed from both a political and a social stance. The political will be considered first.

In the 1930's, the composition of the Legislative Council was: officials 19 and non-officials 18 – 11 Europeans, five Asians and two Europeans representing African interests. The distribution could be justified at that stage of the Colony's development, for although the two nominees to represent African interests may appear paltry, the chief native commissioner and four provincial commissioners were also under a duty to see that African questions were fully aired. Furthermore, the two representatives, though European, were not disposed to take a compromise position. Nevertheless, the time had come for Africans to have direct as well as indirect representation.[21] As regards the distribution of European seats, Nairobi had two, Mombasa had one and the coast had one. The other seven were settler

20 Diana Wylie, 'Norman Keys and McGregor Ross: A case study in the conscience of African empire, 1900–1939', *Journal of Imperial and Commonwealth History* v (1977), pp. 294–309, emphatically disagrees with Fazan's conclusion here. It would be reasonable to suppose that Fazan is here remembering the vocal criticisms that Leys and Ross made of his Carter Land Commission recommendations, for which see Breen, 'The Politics of Land', pp. 121–5.

21 The question of the governor's nomination, not popular election, of an African to legislative council was under active consideration in official circles in 1939; war then interrupted this discussion. Eliud Mathu – son of a witchdoctor and member of Balliol College, Oxford – was appointed in late 1944. This move was prompted by the official assumption that the African troops who would soon return from Burma on demobilisation would expect their service and sacrifice to be recognised in some such manner. In general terms British imperial war has been a powerful stimulus to political reform.

constituencies in the Highlands. Granted that Kenya was an agricultural country almost entirely dependent on primary products, that did not mean that the predominant voice should be that of the primary producer. Perhaps a greater representation of business interests would have secured a more balanced judgment. While nobody could blame the settler members for stressing those aspects which were of most immediate concern to themselves, the interests of the banker, the merchant and the shipping companies were bound up with the prosperity of the Colony as a whole as seen over an extended period. The Asian representatives, however, tended to redress the balance somewhat in this respect.[22]

If the settlers thus got their own way rather too often when conflict arose, there was not much conscious bias in presenting their case, and frequently they were right. There was, however, some failure to realise the rapid progress being made in the African Lands, and the Africans did not always get their fair share in the distribution of the expenditure estimates in the annual budget. Settlers who took the trouble to tour the reserves in the Nyanza and Central provinces were invariably surprised at the development they saw in progress and, with increased understanding of the needs, more money was voted for African areas. But it was still in smaller matters, such as grants for minor roads and chief's salaries, that greater provision would have been wiser.

Because of the paucity of the white population, the district councils which had been established in 1929 in rural areas in the Highlands were wholly dependent in their early years on government grants,[23] and their activities were principally concerned with roads and hospitals, the latter also aided by private donations. They made no attempt to deal with political matters beyond their legitimate local level. Africans had no votes or representation on them, but the annual rate which was paid by Africans employed or resident in the Highlands was that imposed by the local native council in their home district and, when collected, it was remitted there to be spent on improvements which they would eventually enjoy when they returned home.

---

22 As a senior provincial commissioner Fazan was *ex-officio* member of legislative council in the later 1930s. For the politics of these years, see Bennett, *Kenya, a Political History*, Chapter 8; idem, chapter on 'Imperial paternalism' in Kenneth Robinson and Frederick Madden, *Essays in Imperial Government Presented to Margery Perham* (Oxford: Blackwell, 1963), pp. 141–69; Gregory, *Quest for Equality*, Chapter 2.

23 By contrast with the local native councils, whose revenue came largely from local rates levied in addition to the hut tax that went to the central government.

It was in farmers' meetings rather than the district council that political matters were discussed. They were much more lively affairs. When political issues arose – as they nearly always did, whether they were on the agenda or not – the views expressed were forthright and sometimes extreme. Men living isolated lives and having to travel many miles over rough roads to meetings were inclined to let off steam but, although the views expressed may have been urged with a forcefulness beyond their merits, it would be unfair to say that they exercised an undue influence in the settler direction any more than the African *barazas*, which were quite as outspoken, did in theirs. Administrative officers, while being on friendly terms with many settlers, nevertheless spent so large a proportion of their time in the African areas listening to their views, that there was no great difficulty in keeping a balanced mind.[24]

One can regard the social influence of the settlers either from the comparatively narrow standpoint of their influence within the white community or from the broader aspect of their influence on the Africans. From the first point of view the influence was wholly good. Government officials – and probably missionaries and merchants too – were immensely indebted to the settlers for rescuing them from their little coteries and enlivening their off-duty lives. They preserved the country from the more extreme absurdities of Crown Colony officialdom where people could scarcely run out of the rain for shelter except in strict order of precedence![25] They also helped to make Kenya a country sufficient in itself.

As for their broader influence, it was a hope frequently expressed at the initiation of the White Highlands policy that the existence of a broad, compact block of farms run on European lines would be an example to Africans. It would be ludicrous, however, to suppose that the settlers laid themselves out to be a model. They lived their own lives in a take-it-or-leave-it sort of way without excessive regard for appearances and with a certain effervescence of spirit that befitted a young colony in the making. As for the Africans, they did not miss much and, as between the great majority of settlers and their employees, a mutual regard grew up. While there was much in the farming practice of the Highlands which Africans could not copy

24 Not all British officials possessed Fazan's strength of mind and principle.

25 Settler memoirs often make satirical reference to the bureaucratic absurdities of officialdom! For relevant bibliographies see Kennedy, *Islands of White*; Jackson, *Madness and Marginality*; Lonsdale, 'Kenya, Home County'.

without more experience and capital, the example was not lost on them, and useful beginnings were made by some Africans with the support of the local native councils. They certainly learnt much by working on European farms, both directly as regards farming practice and indirectly by observing the patience and diligence required of the farmer.

That, however, was not the whole picture. The rapid growth of the African populations both by natural increase and the economic pull towards the main centres of trade and development had begun to cause congestion in those parts of the Kikuyu tribal lands which were nearest Nairobi and the borders of white settlement. Although there were other, often better, outlets available both in other parts of the tribal lands and elsewhere in the Colony, there were still large stretches of the Highlands on which little development was yet to be seen in these inter-war years, and it was not surprising that land-hungry Africans should have hankered after them.

There were no noticeable signs of apprehension at this date at the way in which the policy of parallel development of the White Highlands and the African Lands was working out. On the contrary there were good grounds for satisfaction, over the Colony at large, at the degree of progress achieved so far. Nevertheless, a cause of disquiet could be seen in the tendency of the settler community to read more into the pledge about the integrity of the Highlands than had actually been promised. The pledge was that the administrative practice of granting agricultural land in the Highlands only to Europeans would continue, both as to original grants and transfers. The circumstances in which it had been given and more than once reasserted justified the assumption that this practice would continue on a basis of permanence but it did not justify an assumption that it could never be modified or that permanence meant perpetuity. No government could guarantee that, especially in what was essentially a black man's country.

The essential point of the White Highlands policy was that settlers should be able to take up land and farm it in security, pass it on in equal security to their successors and, in regard to the whole area, that the general character of the reservation should be preserved for so long a time as special protection for European farming interests was needed. After that, relying on results achieved rather than special protection, it could be expected that the Highlands would find their appropriate place in the general economy. By 1939 the Highlands experiment had justified itself financially, and the settler community would have been wise to rely more on the strength of its economic position and the need which Kenya had of it rather than to insist too strongly on privilege. Unfortunately there was very little sign yet that they were prepared to forego any particle of it, either then or in the future.[26]

---

26 Fazan here again resumes his meditation on the outcome of the (Carter) Kenya Land Commission of which he was secretary. He regrets, with an uncharacteristic naivety, that settler leaders seized on, as a permanent right, the land allocations defined by the commission when they ought to have been considered as subject to later review. This review – which was more of a revolution – came with the Royal Commission of 1953–5, for which see Chapter 16. The best guide to the division of white opinion on the question of the rights and wrongs of white settler privilege at the time is to be found in the correspondence, in the years 1942–3 and 1955, between Elspeth Huxley and Margery Perham (both known to Fazan), in their *Race and Politics in Kenya* (London: Faber, revised edition 1956). The correspondence was prompted by the fall of Malaya and Singapore to the Japanese – a British defeat that many blamed on the inability of a racially discriminatory empire to generate loyalty in its native subjects.

PART V

The Later Colonial Period

13

The Second World War

The impact of the Second World War on Kenya was very different from the First World War. There was no surprise about it. Dawning apprehension that it would come began to spread in about 1934, and before the end of 1937 it had became a probability. Although instant reactions were of exasperation that this further trouble should strike just as the country appeared to be set for a period of orderly progress, one soon got swept along with the tide and, accepting what appeared to be inevitable, war preparations became a first priority. The Italian conquest of Abyssinia (now Ethiopia) in 1935 brought the idea further to the fore and it seemed certain that, if war came, Kenya would be heavily involved and, on this occasion, would be far more than a side-show.[1]

---

1 Fazan's account of Kenya's role in the Second World War is written with all the authority that came from his being provincial commissioner of Nyanza, the most populous of Kenya's provinces and a major source of military manpower, at its outbreak, and then civil liaison officer with East Africa's armed forces after 1942. He also compiled the *Native Affairs Department Report* of 1945 that covered all the war years from the viewpoint of the provincial administration from which he had now retired. For Kenya's military history at this time, see Moyse-Bartlett, *The KAR*, for details of combat; Ashley Jackson, *The British Empire and the Second World War* (London: Hambledon Continuum, 2006), pp. 197–300 for Kenya's role in the war. Blundell, *So Rough a Wind*, Chapter 4; idem, *A Love Affair with the Sun: A Memoir of Seventy Years in Kenya* (Nairobi: Kenway Publications, 1994), Chapters 7–11; and John Nunneley, *Tales from the King's African Rifles* (London: Cassell, 2000), relate the memories of white officers, in the last of which the hero is Tomasi Kitinya Liech, the author's servant, from Fazan's Nyanza Province. See Parker, *The Last Colonial Regiment*, for the KAR's Kenya-born white officers. For the African experience, see Timothy Parsons, *The African Rank-and-File: Social Implications of Colonial Military Service in the King's African Rifles, 1902–1964* (Portsmouth, NH: Heinemann, 1999); David Killingray, *Fighting for Britain: African Soldiers in the Second World War* (Oxford: James Currey, 2010); and, at first-hand, Bildad Kaggia, *Roots of Freedom 1921–1963* (Nairobi: East African Publishing House, 1975), Chapters 3–5; Waruhiu Itote, *'Mau Mau' General* (Nairobi: East

It appeared probable that an invasion of the colony in force by the Italian army in Abyssinia might be expected almost immediately on the outbreak of war. Seeing that the total strength of trained infantry in the whole of the East African territories was only just over two brigades – six KAR battalions and one of Northern Rhodesia Rifles – with practically nothing in the way of supporting arms and services, much ground might have to be yielded before South African help could arrive. It was vital, therefore, that Mombasa should be held, both to facilitate recovery and later, when the Italian threat should have been disposed of, to enable Kenya to play a part in the wider war. It could even be foreseen that the Mediterranean would not be freely usable for the transport of troops or supplies to Egypt and that Kenya might become a very important base for the support of a front in the Middle East.

In addition to the seven regular battalions, there was a territorial battalion of KAR in Uganda and the Kenya Regiment of European volunteers, which was raised in 1937, had a peacetime strength of scarcely 200. There was also, at Mombasa, a small but keen Naval Reserve (Royal Naval Volunteer Reserve) for harbour defence. As the threat of war drew closer, district commandants of the Kenya Defence Force were appointed in all districts in which there were more than a handful of Europeans.

Manpower committees were formed in all provinces and districts and, in anticipation of conscription, lists were prepared of all Europeans available for military service and of those held essential to be retained in their civil occupations. Asians who had handed in their names were also listed, but they showed little eagerness to come forward. The purpose of the lists was not so much to find men for the army as to prevent a general rush to join the forces, such as had happened in the First World War with chaotic results to the civil economy. It also allowed men to be fitted into any service, military or civil, where they would be of most use. The group farm manager system tried with some success in the previous war was worked out in greater detail and made ready to be put into effect. Air raid precaution schemes were prepared and a little preliminary practice done.

African Publishing House, 1967), Chapter 3. Books about Mau Mau in the 1960s generally name the movement within inverted commas to indicate that it was not so much a self-appellation as a disparaging nickname given by its opponents; the inverted commas have since disappeared. For the war's influence on official attitudes to African welfare, see Joanna Lewis, *Empire State-Building: War and Welfare in Kenya 1925–52* (Oxford: James Currey, 2000).

Preparations were also made for a special additional police training centre to provide a quick training course for the extra recruits who would be required for the expansion of the police force as quickly as possible after the outbreak of war. But while it was possible to make such paper defence plans in anticipation of war, the 'spirit of Munich' and the hope of peace, not to mention lack of funds, prevented much more being undertaken, except in a minor degree.

It was clearly foreseen that, if war broke out, transport for military operations would not be like the previous war. There would be no long, long processions of head-load porterage, and support for mechanical transport would be of a different kind. Tracks would have to be made and kept open, rough bridges built, lorries manhandled through the mud, and lines of communication would have to be protected. Clearance had not yet been given by the East Africa Command to expand or to raise supporting arms and services, but the civil administration was apprehensive that, if no start was made, the experience of the Carrier Corps in the previous war would be repeated, that is to say, large numbers of men would be called up in a hurry with no proper arrangements made either for officering them, or for documentation, equipment, medicine checking, balanced rations, or training. Very heavy casualties from sickness would certainly result. Accordingly, the matter was discussed at a provincial commissioners' meeting with the governor presiding, and it was arranged that a small nucleus of Pioneer recruits should be raised and trained in Nyanza Province. The question of arming them was, at first, a bone of contention but it was agreed that, on the outbreak of war, at least a quarter should be armed; and eventually they all were.[2] The nucleus was only 360 men, but it was at least a beginning.

Matters of supply arrangements were made through the defence committees for the listing of lorries to be commandeered for the use of the Army on mobilization. About a quarter of all lorries were so earmarked. Possibly they were of some use to the Army in the first month or two; but the main effect when the time came was to reveal what a deplorable collection of outworn vehicles were being driven on roads. Fortunately the Army did not have to rely on them for long.

In spite of the disparity between East African forces and the large Italian army in Abyssinia – estimated at 300,000, of whom 91,000 were Europeans – there was no sign of alarm anywhere. On the contrary, the mood of the country erred towards complacency, but

---

2 See below, note 4.

with the still nearer approach of war – in fact when it was imminent – the East African War Council was formed on the basis of the governors' conference. After war was declared its small secretariat was progressively expanded to cope with new duties. Air Chief Marshal Sir Robert Brooke-Popham, the governor of Kenya, was recalled to his military duties and was succeeded as governor by Sir Henry Monck-Mason Moore, who continued as governor of Kenya and chairman of the conference until the end of the war. Sir Philip Mitchell gave up his post as governor of Uganda to devote himself to the central organisation of the war effort as vice-chairman of the War Council and the chief secretary of Tanganyika was seconded to become civil liaison officer with the East African Command.[3] Great care was taken in setting up the governors' conference machinery, to see that civil officers from the other East African territories got the lion's share of senior posts and so mitigate any resentment there might be at Nairobi being made headquarters. There was general agreement that, from both a civil and military point of view, Nairobi was the best centre for overall direction, but this was admitted by the other territories with acquiescence rather than enthusiasm. The organisation proved adaptable and worked smoothly through the war, not only in matters relating directly to the East African forces and their needs but also in coordinating supplies throughout the East African territories, keeping the internal economy efficient, feeding the enormous numbers of prisoners of war after the Abyssinian campaign, sending substantial supplies of maize and other produce to the Middle East, and dealing with a host of incidental problems as they progressively revealed themselves.

***

East Africa, with Abyssinia, was included as part of the Middle East Command under the over-all direction of Lieutenant General Wavell; and the new general officer commanding, Major General Dickinson, arrived by air only 24 hours before war was declared. The outbreak of war, when it came, was something of an anti-climax. The Italians failed to invade, as expected, and nine more months were to elapse before they eventually declared war on the 10th June 1940.

The interval was useful and gave time to prepare. The initial rounding-up of enemy aliens was accomplished without any trouble by

3 For this account Fazan was doubtless able to refer to Sir Philip Mitchell's autobiography, *African Afterthoughts* (London: Hutchinson, 1954).

the police and the defence forces. It was only in Tanganyika that numbers were substantial and it was soon found possible to release most of them as harmless. Meanwhile the reinforcement and expansion of the East Africa forces proceeded according to plan. Two brigades of West Africans arrived and were to stay on through the Abyssinian campaign. The First South African Brigade also disembarked at Mombasa in July 1940, and went into training for bush warfare at Gilgil. Under this cover the expansion and training of new East African formations began. The Kenya Regiment provided officers and non-commissioned officers to bring establishments of the KAR battalions to full war strength, and, in due course, it became specifically concerned with providing officers and non-commissioned officers for new formations. There were of course not nearly enough Europeans of suitable age available locally for the purpose, so others had to be drafted in from Britain and the dominions. Attempts were made to maintain officers with East African experience in a proportion of about a third, and arrangements were also made for new officers without previous experience of East Africa to visit tribal reserves and acquaint themselves with the way that Africans lived at home. They took especial care to learn Swahili and, after a year or so, there was no distinction in fluency to be observed between them and the average officer locally born.

The first East African troops to enter Abyssinia were probably the 'Recces', later the East African Reconnaissance Regiment. Initially an irregular unit conceived and manned entirely by Kenya settlers, they were to achieve a fine reputation in their detached role. Their objective was to rally the Abyssinians in revolt against the Italians and so embarrass their preparations for the invasion of Kenya. For the general organisation of the operation, Wavell chose Colonel D. A. Sandford, a former gunnery officer who, after serving in the Sudan, had taken up farming in Abyssinia and had acted for a time as adviser to the Emperor Haile Selassie, and for raising and training the rebel bands he chose Major Orde Wingate, whose original methods of combating Arab guerrillas in Palestine had greatly impressed him. Colonel Sandford began operations from a base in Khartoum from the date when Italy declared war. Three months later, on the 20th September 1940, he had moved deep into Abyssinia and established his headquarters at a place called Faguta, some 30 miles south of Lake Tana.

During the initial period while the Italians had overwhelming preponderance they succeeded, in July and August, in taking the Sudanese frontier towns of Gallabat and Kassala on their western flank and overrunning British Somaliland on their east. Their southward drive into Kenya was half-hearted and got no further than North Horr in the Northern Frontier province. By Christmas 1940 the position had been stabilised and forces in Kenya, now under General Cunningham, were ready to take the offensive. Besides the South Africans, whose strength by this time had been built up to a division, there were the 21st and 22nd East Africa Brigades, consisting, in effect, of the KAR and Northern Rhodesia Rifles battalions already mentioned; the 23rd and 24th Brigades, consisting of reinforcements sent from West Africa; and the East Africa Armoured Cars, recently formed from half of the 3rd KAR when that battalion was divided into two. Among the supporting troops were the Pioneers. Expanded into two battalions at the outbreak of war, they had not made too auspicious a start. They had been treated as a poor relation when it came to such things as the issue of equipment and weapons and the supply of a sufficient cadre of officers. This had had an inevitable effect on morale, but when reorganised they played a full and valuable part. One of the battalions became a dual purpose infantry and engineer battalion under Colonel Blundell – later styled the 51st East Africa Engineer Battalion[4] – and the other split into three engineering companies.

The prelude to the general offensive, which ended in the total destruction of the Italian armies in Abyssinia, was the recapture of Kassala by General Platt in January 1941. The plan then put into operation in February consisted of three elements: General Platt, with the 4th and 5th Indian Divisions, operating from the Sudan and invading Eritrea in the north; General Cunningham, with the South African and East African divisions, advancing on Addis Ababa from the south; and nationalist irregular forces stimulated by Colonel Wingate spreading havoc in the interior. These latter were encouraged by the presence of their emperor, who was flown in from Khartoum on the day that Kassala was recovered.[5]

The attack from Kenya began with some hard fighting in disputing the passage of the Juba River. Once that line had been turned, the Italian army cracked. The whole coast area to Mogadishu yielded with no appreciable resistance and, on the advance northwards to Addis Ababa, the pace was so fast as to run off the maps which the Survey Units were

4 For the African mutiny that forced the British to arm this unit, previously promised by Fazan as provincial commissioner of the predominantly Luo recruits, see Blundell, *So Rough a Wind*, pp. 50–1.

5 For a firsthand account by a white settler (initially in Tanganyika) and temporary officer, see W. E. Crosskill, *The Two Thousand Mile War* (London: Robert Hale, 1980); also, Michael Glover, *An Improvised War: The Abyssinian campaign of 1940–1941* (London: Leo Cooper, 1987).

preparing at top speed. Addis Ababa fell on the 5th April, barely two months after the defence line of the Juba River had been turned; an astonishing rate of advance over a distance of some 750 miles in a straight line from Nairobi and more like 1,000 actually travelled.

Meanwhile, in the second half of January, the two Indian divisions under General Platt, having cleared the Sudan of Italian forces, had invaded from the north. Here they came up against a very strong natural defensive position on Keren Mountain, held by two regular divisions. Early attacks failed and the Italians put up by far the most determined resistance they displayed in the whole campaign. The position could not be turned, and arrangements for frontal attack had to be prepared in full view of the enemy. Air support was obtained from South Africa and, finally, after preparations lasting several weeks, General Platt's two divisions took the position by direct assault on the 27th March after a battle lasting three days. This broke Italian resistance in the north.

The issue of the campaign was now certain, but mopping-up operations over that vast country lasted several months. The last serious struggle was at Gondar, where the Italians resisted with the best spirit they had shown since Juba and Keren. This was the end of the fighting. It was now the turn of the civil authority to take over. So began the Occupied Enemy Territory Administration, formed from officers who could, with difficulty, be spared from the district administration in East Africa. The whole organisation was placed under the command of Sir Philip Mitchell with the rank of major-general.[6]

Taken all round, the Italians had done miserably. They failed to attack immediately when Italy declared war, when they still had great superiority in numbers and material, and in the whole campaign it appears that they only dropped two bombs on Kenya, both of which fell quite harmlessly in open country near Malindi. Obviously they did not have their hearts in it and indeed in some cases, as at Mogadishu, they seemed almost glad to surrender. The probable explanation was that they were fighting from a base in a hostile country only recently conquered and in constant dread of a rising, and had given hostages to fortune by bringing out large numbers of civilian settlers with their wives and children.

***

6 Mitchell, *African Afterthoughts*, Chapter X.

The total of East African forces engaged on various fronts in the course of the war was very large. Of front-line, fully-trained infantry, not counting holding battalions or depots, there were, by the end of the war, nine East African Brigades (numbers 21, 22 and 25–31 inclusive), each of three battalions, making, with divisional reinforcements and a few unbrigaded units, a little over 30 battalions in all. Seven of them were from Northern Rhodesia, one from Southern Rhodesia, and the rest were KAR, including two of Somalis. Besides these there were two armoured car units, which became the Third Armoured Cars and the Reconnaissance Regiment after its reorganisation. One can also include with the infantry the dual-purpose 51st Engineer Battalion already mentioned. Six field regiments of artillery were also raised, of which one remained in Kenya, one was tragically sunk by enemy action on the voyage to Ceylon, and the other four saw service in Ceylon and Burma.

The 11th East Africa Division and all brigades had their complement of supporting arms and services like field ambulances, engineer companies and supply and transport units. They also had specialist units such as military police, signallers and surveyors. Very large numbers of East Africa Pioneers and Garrison Infantry companies formed from them served in the Middle East. Twenty-five thousand would be a conservative estimate of the total East African forces there from Syria to Tunisia. Lastly, there was the East African Military Labour Service (MLS), again many thousands, whose service was confined to East Africa. There they were used for almost any labour task which had a war purpose about it.

Recruitment of Africans for this great expansion of the forces was done by one of two alternative methods or, occasionally, by a combination of both. This applied particularly to Kenya, but arrangements in the other territories were not far different. The Army would either send out its own recruiting officers among the population or use the machinery set up by the civil administration. Although general conscription had been introduced at the outbreak of war, it was not used to conscript men to the fighting forces. The only unit for which it was used in Kenya was the MLS, and they were not to be employed outside East Africa. They could, however, volunteer for other units. While they were in the holding depots undergoing their habilitation treatment – that is to say, their inoculations, documentation, becoming accustomed to their rations, camp hygiene and simple discipline, and having arrangements for their family remittances made – they were allowed to volunteer for general service in preference to the MLS, provided that they were found fully fit in every respect. Army recruiting officers would call periodically, have the volunteers paraded and make their selection. The rifle and the enhanced estimation they would have in the eyes of their women were the inducements – for whereas the MLS was unarmed, all other services were armed. Thus there was keen competition to be selected.

After leaving their original recruiting and habilitation depots, recruits received training for several months. It was estimated to take about eight months to train an efficient KAR soldier, and rather longer for an artilleryman and some of the specialist units. This ended with brigade training, the principal centres being the Yatta Plateau in Kenya, and Moshi in Tanganyika. The artillery used Lark Hill, in the Kedong valley, or Gilgil. One of the special values of brigade training was that troops from different parts of East Africa got to know and appreciate each other better. Considering the vast area from which they were drawn it is not surprising that the Chinyanja-speaking battalions from Northern Rhodesia and Nyasaland should have tended at first to stick together and look askance at the Kenya, Uganda and Tanganyika battalions, who for their common language used Swahili and yet were a bewildering variety of ethnic groups. It took a little time for prejudices to wear off, but, by mixing battalions from different territories in the same brigade, this was eventually achieved.

Although East African troops were not sent overseas until they had been fully trained, a partial exception to this rule existed with the Pioneer companies sent to the Middle East. They sometimes had to be sent urgently, with inadequate training, but the deficiency was made good, at least to an extent, on arrival in Egypt where further training was given in the central Pioneer depot at Quassassin. Even before the Italian campaign was over, there was an urgent call for pioneers in the Middle East, and, happily, some such needs had been foreseen. By June 1942 there were eight groups of East Africa Pioneers in the western desert, stretching out to Tobruk and beyond, but they still had had next to no weapon training. The subsequent retreat was a severe test for them, but they won commendation for maintaining cohesion and the steadiness of their bearing. From that point onwards their expansion continued, and they fulfilled a rather dull but important support role, some as pioneer labour and some as garrison infantry, for the rest of the war, being widely distributed over the whole Middle East from Syria in the north to Tripolitania in the west. It was work requiring much patience, and they bore the monotony well. Welfare services, both East African and those of the Middle East command, did all that was possible to relieve the tedium. Their morale remained high, and health good.

***

The entry of Japan into the war in December 1941 – coming only about a fortnight after the Abyssinian campaign had come to an end with the fall of Gondar – opened out new fronts and further tasks for the East African forces. The 21st East Africa Brigade was among the first reinforcements to reach Ceylon,[7] which had become a vital naval base after the fall of Singapore in February, and was later followed by the rest of the 11th East Africa Division. There it remained for approximately the next two years as part of the island defences until it moved to Burma.

Meanwhile, in 1942, East African troops became involved in operations in Madagascar, where the French governor-general had taken a pro-Vichy attitude and refused to cooperate in the defence of the island against the probability of a Japanese landing. The threat of Japanese occupation appeared to the British government to be so serious that preventive action had to be taken, even in the face of French opposition. An expedition was therefore dispatched, and the port of Diego Suarez was successfully attacked and occupied by British troops on the 5th May 1942. Further operations were then delayed for some months to give the governor-general a chance to revise his attitude and cooperate willingly with the British. As he remained stubborn, further landings took place in September and, this time, East African troops took part. The principal role was assigned to the 22nd East Africa Brigade under Brigadier Dimoline, which landed at Majunga and advanced southwards towards the capital at Tananarive. The enemy seemed uncertain in their minds whether to offer merely token resistance or to fight in earnest. It was sometimes one and sometimes the other. They mainly adopted delaying tactics but, after two months of this and a battle in which the whole brigade took part, the Vichy troops surrendered on the 4th November. During the discussion on terms, which took place in a wayside hotel, the French officers pointed out that campaign medals were not customarily awarded in France unless the campaign had lasted six months, and it was a day short of that since the landing at Diego Suarez. Brigadier Dimoline thereupon agreed to let the war go on until one minute after midnight; and at the appointed minute the surrender was signed and the medals were safe. The governor-general having now agreed to cooperate, the island continued under French administration, but the East Africa troops, to the strength of a little less than a division under Major-General

7 Now Sri Lanka.

Smallwood, remained until order was restored. The 22nd Brigade then left for Ceylon and, later, took part in the campaign in Burma.

In the middle of 1944 the 11th East African division, now consisting of the 21st, 22nd, 25th, 26th and 28th East African Brigades, left Ceylon and, after a short interval at Chittagong, repaired to Imphal where the Japanese advance on India was being finally halted. Their main role in the subsequent downward thrust through Burma was to reach and bridge the Chindwin River and establish a bridgehead beyond it.[8] All this was duly accomplished, not without some sharp fighting at Jambo Hill, Kalewa, and beyond the Chindwin. At the turn of the years 1944–5 the 28th East Africa Brigade was independently engaged in the direction of Myitkina, and the 71st KAR Battalion (Somalia) inflicted severe casualties on the enemy. The 22nd East Africa Brigade, detached and lent to the West Africa Division after mopping up Japanese detachments on Ramree Island, advanced southwards from Akyab to the Prome Road, which they reached by mid-May, and continued their advance in conjunction with the West Africans until the end of the war.

When the hostilities were over, East African forces in Burma retired to Ranchi where Major-General Dimoline, who had succeeded to the command of the division early in 1945, was faced with the difficult task of keeping the troops contented during the long period of waiting to return home. The same problem also arose in connection with demobilizing from the Middle East but in both cases and, indeed, in all others involving East African troops, the evacuation and subsequent return of the demobilized men to their homes was successfully accomplished without any untoward incident.[9]

***

It is doubtful whether many Africans joined the forces even at the beginning of the war because they thought their homes were in imminent danger of invasion or because they had any great preference

8 For a most readable account of the KAR's role in this campaign, see Gerald Hanley, *Monsoon Victory* (London: Collins, 1946).

9 British Army commanders learned to treat East African troops with a greater consideration of their need to keep contact with home after the mutiny by 22nd KAR Brigade in early 1942; after defeating the Italians in Ethiopia, they were due to embark for Ceylon (Sri Lanka) without home leave. The 22nd Brigade distinguished itself thereafter, as Fazan notes. Individual soldiers were also known to protest, mainly over racial discrimination in pay and conditions; see Parsons, *African Rank-and-File*, Chapter 6.

for a British protectorate as against a German or Italian one. Tribesmen from the southern territories joined just as readily as those from Kenya and Uganda, which alone were threatened with invasion. Though many had genuine regard for the British connection, and expressions of loyalty to the Sovereign, if vague, were sincere, it would not have caused Africans to go to war if they had not been inclined for other reasons. Certainly they did not join out of affection for the British officials or settlers, however cordial their personal relations might have been.

The prime reason they came in – there is no doubt about it – is that they regarded fighting as a man's job of which they had been too long deprived. When intertribal wars had been stopped and families settled down to cultivate year after year on the same piece of land so that there was little fresh clearing to do, the women's work continued unaffected, but men were at a loose end. Football and dances had not filled the gap, and work for the white man was dull. Cattle raiding, though exciting, was apt to lead to gaol, while war seemed just as stimulating and was free for all. They were also encouraged because it enhanced their status in the tribe to enlist.[10]

East Africa's considerable war effort was supported by a corresponding civil and organizational operation. A first task for Kenya was to render itself as self-sufficient as possible and save shipping space by replacing imports with home production. Small factories were started, which afterwards grew, for making clothes, boots, hardware and other things, but though manufacture played an important part, the main feature of the wartime economy was the production and distribution of food. By each territory helping its neighbour – e.g. Uganda supplying Kenya with sugar and Kenya supplying Uganda and Tanganyika with dairy produce – internal self-sufficiency was largely achieved. Quantities also had to be stepped up to feed the Italian prisoners of war and to send a surplus to the Middle East. Besides agriculture, the meat, dairy and fishing industries were all expanded. All this meant hard work at the centre in the organisation of distribution, rationing, and price control. It also meant hard work

10 Parsons (*African Rank-and-File*, Chapter 3), the KAR's social historian, is sceptical of this view; his evidence suggests, rather, that men volunteered largely from poorer regions and for economic reasons. Myles Osborne, *Loyal Sons of Kenya: Virtue, Ethnicity and Martial Race among the Kamba c. 1800 to the Present* (Cambridge: Cambridge University Press, 2014), agrees with Fazan. But some African ideals of honourable warrior-hood were hostile to strict, demeaning, military discipline – which is why East Africa's chief 'martial race', the Maasai, was rarely found in the army.

on the land by the farmers and by the wives of those who had left on army service, both Europeans and Africans. The African women, besides their normal work of tilling and reaping, had to put their hand to ploughing and other work that in peacetime was done by the men. Field administration was also feeling the strain, for whenever a new task appeared and some new branch was started in Nairobi to deal with it or there was a call for more officers to staff the Occupied Enemy Territory Administration, it was always the field administration that was milked. The more work that had to be shouldered, therefore, the less staff there was to do it. There might have been a breakdown but for the loyal support of the clerical and subordinate services and, not least, the chiefs.

At the centre of affairs the staff of the governors' conference had been greatly expanded. Once the war was over, by a process so natural that the transition attracted very little public comment, the East African governors' conference became the East African High Commission, which was later replaced by the East African Common Services Organisation in 1962. It was formally established in 1946 and was charged with the direction, on behalf of Kenya, Uganda, Tanganyika, and Zanzibar, of subjects transferred to it to the extent specified in each case. These included customs and excise, transport, post and telecommunications, defence, income tax, commercial law and research. In conjunction with the powers of the High Commission, the East African legislative assembly was constituted with power to legislate in these matters. Formal association with Northern Rhodesia and Nyasaland ceased at the end of the war, but it had been fruitful while it lasted.[11]

On the civil side it is doubtful whether the war had any profound immediate effect on the Africans, except that the men away with the army were naturally missed and more work fell to the women. Most of the men on army service were bachelors. Leaves were pretty freely granted after the close of the Italian campaign before the troops proceeded overseas,[12] and, from the Middle East, leaves were granted at two-year intervals. Each man was invited, upon enrolment, to nominate a friend, usually a relative, to look after his affairs, and a two-

11 What Fazan here describes as administratively rational, as it was, was also politically contentious, being a new form of 'closer union', in which Africans throughout East Africa feared being dominated by Kenya's white settlers and Kenya's settlers feared being swamped by Africans.

12 After the 22nd Brigade's mutiny, as earlier noted.

way letter scheme was devised by which an *askari*'s letter form had a blank space for the answer to be written, and it was sent back free of charge. In other respects civil life in the tribal lands continued much as usual, except that better prices were obtained for livestock and crops. There may have been more permanent effect in the way of delayed marriages, but not on a scale to attract notice or occasion remark.[13]

As to the effects on the settlers, it is probable that their experiences in the army did them good. The discipline, even the tedium of army routine had been well endured, and the men were conscious of having done well and borne their part with credit along with the soldiers of other countries. They were glad to be home again, and there can be very few who did not feel themselves to be better and more complete men than they were before they started.[14]

It has sometimes been written that resentment was caused by the officers being British and the rank and file African, and distinction made with separate messes between British and African non-commissioned officers. It is a possibility but I never heard any complaint of the kind voiced among any troops serving in active war areas, and only once or twice among units of garrison or supporting troops elsewhere, where the dullness of daily routine must have been irksome. Be that as it may, there was no holding back promotion from Africans for posts for which they had shown themselves qualified. Before the end of the war some African platoon commanders had been appointed with commissioned rank, and these steps were taken without any outside pressure as soon as men with the necessary qualifications appeared.

The wider question of the effect on raw tribesmen of having gone overseas and observed how people lived in other countries – sometimes several countries and all in the space of a few years – requires more analysis. Broadly speaking, East African forces in Burma, Ceylon, or Abyssinia were too busy to regard the local population as more than part of the scenery. In Madagascar, and still more on garrison duty in Egypt, Palestine, Lebanon, and Syria, they had more leisure to look

---

13 Fazan's view that war service had little effect on Africans is widely agreed by historians, although one can point to examples where former soldiers played a radical role in post-war politics, both Bildad Kaggia and Waruhiu Itote being important examples in the leadership of Mau Mau. See their autobiographies, details given above in note 1.

14 Michael Blundell and other Kenya settlers who had been officers in the KAR had also learned to respect their African troops – with, for some, a consequent liberalisation of their political attitudes.

round and, sometimes, to get into mischief. Having had exceptional opportunities of observing the demeanour of East African troops – indeed, having on one occasion been introduced to a visiting general as 'our licensed spy' – I knew of very few immediate consequences that resulted from this cause either abroad or, as far as I could ascertain, at home. By and large the off-duty behaviour of the East Africans was distinctly good. Exceptions were few, and any fears there might have been to the contrary turned out to be groundless.

Apart from any question of discipline or indiscipline, all these crowded new experiences of other countries could have caused some sort of mental indigestion. Even before the war there were many people who thought, rightly, that the pace of development during two generations had wrenched the tribesmen too far and too fast from their traditions, with a bewildering effect that might, one day, produce a sharp reaction. In that case these wartime experiences must have accelerated the pace. Besides, the idea was beginning to stir uneasily that life in Africa after the war could no longer be lived at its own tempo, but would be subject to increasing pressures from the world outside and, like it or not, it would have to adjust its policies to accord with them.

These forebodings apart, the overall effect of the war was wholly good for East Africa. The country had pulled together as never before, and there was better understanding between the territories and between the races. There could be very few people, whether among the armed forces or helping to keep the civil economy and production going, who did not look back on the war period as on a task well done, to which all races and all tribes had contributed. And, apart from the enhancement of morale, there was a material advantage in that the country had greatly increased its reputation abroad and evoked a lively new interest in East Africa.

14

Post-war Settlement and Kikuyu Politics

Waves of settlement in Kenya always followed wars. The Boer war heralded the first, the Kaiser's war the second and, with the end of Hitler's war, came the third.[1] But there was a difference this time. The interest was more widespread, both as regards the countries from which the settlement came and also in the diversity of their aims. Expansion began almost at once. Nairobi hotels were full. A resident returning some three years after the war would have noticed a significant change. People of diverse nationalities appeared in astonishing numbers, not for the most part as prospective settlers but, rather, as tourists who had come to examine openings for investment. It revealed the pattern of the future. It meant that, hand in hand with new settlement on the farms, there would also be capital available for commercial and industrial enterprises to broaden the basis of the economy. Indeed, the 15 years from the end of the war to 1960 were to be marked by unprecedented economic expansion and, at the same time, intense political conflict. They were years of great importance in the development of Kenya into a nation – that is to say, an entity capable of national feeling, however diverse in origin its communities might be.[2]

Political and economic forces were interacting on each other constantly throughout this period. The Kikuyu Central Association (KCA) had been banned at the beginning of the war but, in 1944, the Kenya African Union (KAU) arose out of its ashes. Jomo Kenyatta, the former president of KCA,[3] had been absent from Kenya when KAU

1 A brilliant insight, not fully shared by other accounts of white settlement in Kenya, by authors whose generation has not been so dominated by war as Fazan's.

2 The British Council was among the 'nation-building' institutions of the time, trying, unsuccessfully, to find common cultural ground for Africans, Europeans and South Asians. See Richard Frost's aptly titled *Race against Time: Human Relations and Politics in Kenya before Independence* (London: Rex Collings, 1978).

3 As earlier noted, he had been General Secretary, not President, of the KCA.

was formed but, returning in 1946, was elected its president. He had been away in Europe much of the time since 1931, mostly in England but including a short visit to Russia. He had spent some time studying anthropology at London University and, in 1945, was elected president of the Pan-African Federation with Kwame Nkrumah of the Gold Coast (afterwards Ghana) as vice-president. It is clear, therefore, that he had not been entirely preoccupied with the affairs of the Kikuyu tribe. He was at once pan-African and a staunch Kikuyu.[4] KAU showed something of the same characteristics, being in many ways pan-Kenyan, but always predominantly Kikuyu. Several of the old KCA leaders were included in the central council of KAU and on its branch committees but, to mark its new character as a union for all Kenya Africans, care was taken to include a number of non-Kikuyu, especially Luo, in prominent posts.[5]

The avowed aims of the association were the end of all racial privilege, whether in government or on the land. Although it professed to be against European privilege but not against Europeans as such, there was a strong and increasing element among the Kikuyu that was definitely unfriendly, and the tone of speeches at KAU meetings was hostile and provocative. The principal issue, as always, was land. The extent of land in effective occupation by the Kikuyu, which had been lost to the European Highlands, was assessed by the Kenya Land Commission at approximately 126 square miles, nearly half of which fell within a radius of 25 miles from Nairobi. They had been awarded, in return, some 33 square miles in the Mwea area, in addition to which,

4 West African and Caribbean pan-Africanists in London complained that Kenyatta was more 'staunch Kikuyu' than pan-African: see Ras Makonnen, with Kenneth King, *Pan-Africanism from within* (Nairobi: Oxford University Press, 1973), p. 162. His visit to Moscow had made Kenyatta a convinced anti-communist, as the British secret services were slow to realise; see Bruce Berman and John Lonsdale, 'Custom, Modernity, and the Search for Kihooto: Kenyatta, Malinowski, and the Making of Facing Mount Kenya', in Helen Tilley, with Robert J. Gordon (eds), *Ordering Africa: Anthropology, European Imperialism, and the Politics of Knowledge* (Manchester: Manchester University Press, 2007), pp. 178–80, and Calder Walton, *Empire of Secrets: British intelligence, the Cold War, and the Twilight of Empire* (London: Harper, 2013), pp. 258–62. Kenyatta had not been president of the pan-African federation, but helped to organise its 1945 Manchester conference. His anthropological studies at the London School of Economics, under Bronislaw Malinowski, had resulted in his book, *Facing Mount Kenya* (1938). See also Jeremy Murray-Brown, *Kenyatta* (London: Allen & Unwin, 1972), Part II. The following account of Kikuyu grievances is more sympathetic than anything Fazan may have read in official reports 20 years earlier.

5 Spencer, *KAU*, would not dissent from this view.

for purposes of economic need and future expansion, an area of 383 square miles had been placed at their disposal in the northern part of the Yatta Plateau adjoining Mwea. Even taking into account the relative merits of the land this seemed a fair settlement of old grievances within the range of what was practicable.[6] Nairobi had, however, proved a magnet which had drawn towards it a large influx of Kikuyu both into the city itself and the neighbouring Kikuyu district of Kiambu, where previously the population had been sparse. Its attraction was as a market both for their produce and their labour.

It was also near Nairobi that the first alienations for European farms were made, naturally enough in view of the emptiness of the countryside at the time, and the effect of these factors was to provide the Kikuyu with a grievance which was to be one of the major causes of Mau Mau. They felt that they were being squeezed from their own land, but if there had been no Nairobi to attract them there would have been no severe congestion, and Nairobi was after all a Masai name.[7]

The development of African district councils, which had given Africans a large degree of responsibility in the sphere of local government, was not enough to satisfy their aspirations. Ever since the time of the Parliamentary Joint Select Committee of 1931 they had pressed for direct representation in Legislative Council. Government had tardily conceded this to the extent of one nominated African member in 1944. This could scarcely have been expected to content them for long, and by 1947 Kikuyu dissatisfaction was already being expressed through the instigation of leaders of KAU, by the refusal of women to undertake communal terracing.[8] Agitation was mounting, always with the Kikuyu in the lead, but with considerable support from

---

6 Fazan, its secretary, would naturally defend the Kenya Land Commission's findings and in purely quantitative terms he was right – but that is to forget all questions of sentiment, the coerced loss of property and disruption of intimate social relations with their complex history and continuing obligations, government regulation of settlement schemes, the poorer soils in the resettlement areas, and so on.

7 Indeed, meaning 'Coldstream'. Fazan's criticism of Kikuyu failure to take due account of their colonial advantages interestingly balances his criticism of the white settler failure to share these advantages more widely – an illustration of how the administrative official's position as 'man in the middle' led to a sometimes exasperated desire for more sober rationality on either side of the racial divide.

8 Kikuyu objections to terracing were only loosely connected to wider political dissent. It was hard work, done mainly by the wives of absentee migrant workers, often for the benefit of wealthier Kikuyu; it interfered with normal farming activities and not infrequently had to be repeated when it failed in its purpose of protecting cultivated hillsides against soil erosion. See Throup, *Economic and Social Origins*, Chapter 7.

the Luo and elements of the Akamba and, for reasons of their own, the Somali Youth League. Mass meetings and political 'tea parties' several hundreds strong were now a feature in all Kikuyu districts, at which demagogues were raising their audiences to a dangerous pitch of enthusiasm. It was only a question of time before an open clash with government would be sure to result in fighting and bloodshed, unless strong and appropriate counter-measures were taken with speed.

This happened at Kahura in the Fort Hall district in August 1947. The village green was packed with thousands of Kikuyu men and women in festive mood and colourful in their Sunday best. They listened eagerly to the impassioned orators who had driven up from Nairobi and time and again they burst forth with the shouts and murmurings of a mob. Chief Ignatio Murai, facing the situation with determination, marched boldly into the ring with his two tribal police, arrested two of the ringleaders and took them to his camp. This sobered the mob for a while, but, recovering later, they advanced to rescue the prisoners and were closing in to attack when the police opened fire. One rioter fell dead, another was wounded, and the rest fled.[9] It was an ominous moment, but after this incident KAU exercised more restraint and the government let its meetings continue within the limits of legitimate agitation, rather than drive it underground. That, however, did not prevent an underground wing from being formed. It came to be known as Mau Mau.[10]

---

9 See Throup, *Economic and Social Origins*, pp. 153–60.

10 There is no agreed analysis of the origins and growth of Mau Mau – whose most likely meaning is 'the greedy eaters (of the authority of their elders)'. Fazan's account is therefore as plausible as any, much more so than the conspiracy theory told in the Kenya government's official history, the 'Corfield Report', *Historical Survey of the Origins and Growth of the Mau Mau Movement in Kenya* (London: HMSO, Cmd 1030, 1960). As discussed above, in the Foreword, Fazan had modified Corfield in his own 1961 *History of the Loyalists*. His mature judgment here on Kenyatta's role – as an inspiration to the militants but not their leader – now flatly contradicts Corfield but is a view with which most later historians would agree. It is no longer possible to tell whether Fazan had read any later study before writing his memoir, but his account bears some similarity to that of Rosberg and Nottingham's *The Myth of 'Mau Mau'*, published in 1966. The historiography on the origins and nature of Mau Mau is large and grows yearly. A select bibliography follows: Rosberg and Nottingham, argue – against the majority British view of the time that Mau Mau was a mental sickness – that it was the militant wing of a rational nationalism, over which Kenyatta lost control – a view that Spencer's *KAU* supports with ample oral evidence. Kanogo, *Squatters and the Roots of Mau Mau*, and Furedi, *Mau Mau War in Perspective*, sees it as the revolt of discarded Highland squatters; Throup, *Economic and Social Origins*, also brings in outcast Nairobi and

In the following year, 1948, the number of African members of the Legislative Council was increased to four. This brought the total of African and Asian members combined to parity with European elected members at 11 each. At the same time the official membership on the government side was reduced to 16 so that there was now an unofficial majority for the first time.[11]

Exactly when or by whom the name Mau Mau was first given is not known but it began to be heard about at this time. Underground movements were not new in Kikuyu. This one may have stemmed from as far back as the independent church movement which followed the breakaway from the Church of Scotland mission in 1929. The *Karing'a* (Orthodox), the 'Pentecostals' and other sects had orientated themselves towards what was, in effect, a Kikuyu tribal religion with the deity conceived as inhabiting Mount Kenya, a doctrine in which Mau Mau was steeped. Superstition, with frequent recourse to witchdoctors, was indeed a strong element in Mau Mau throughout. Although they may not have had the same origin, Mau Mau was regarded as an underground adjunct of KAU, and it seemed to the government that the same organizing brains were at the back of both. While KAU sought to gain its ends essentially by legitimate agitation, Mau Mau was planning revolt, to be put in hand if KAU's more moderate efforts should fail.

Along with the independent church movement there was an associated organisation of independent schools. These, in process of time, split into two groups, the Kikuyu Karing'a Education Association, intensely tribalistic and reactionary, which, when the time came, readily supported Mau Mau; and the Kikuyu Independent Schools Association

---

the discontented Kikuyu 'reserve'. Wunyabari O. Maloba, *Mau Mau and Kenya: An Analysis of a Peasant Revolt* (Bloomington, IN: Indiana University Press, 1993) provides a good synthesis; John Lonsdale, 'The moral economy of Mau Mau', Chapters 11 and 12 in Berman and Lonsdale (eds), *Unhappy Valley*, pp. 265–504, emphasises the angry despair of client dependants, whose inability to achieve adult self-mastery (*wiathi*) in marriage and property ownership turned them against their patrons both white and black. Greet Kershaw's *Mau Mau from Below* (Oxford: James Currey, 1997) has the most detailed knowledge of the land history of northern Kiambu and the most convincing discussion of why elders may have surrendered authority to their young, whose ambitions they could no longer assist.

11 Settler politicians had long demanded an unofficial majority – composed of white settlers. They had now achieved their demand but in a most unwelcome, multi-racial, form: If they were to defeat the government benches in future they could do so only in alliance with South Asian and African members of legislative council.

(KISA), which was more genuinely educational in intent. There is no reason to doubt but that the Teachers' Training College founded in 1939 at Githunguri in Kiambu district by Peter Mbiyu Koinange, eldest son of Senior Chief Koinange, was established quite honestly for its avowed purpose of training teachers for the KISA schools so that they might be able to keep pace with the government and mission schools and qualify for grants in aid.[12] But in the tense situation now prevailing, all this was changed, and Githunguri became almost the main planning centre of the movement.[13] At every KAU meeting and at every opportunity, collections were taken, ostensibly for the college buildings but actually to support the campaign.

Much the same thing occurred with the trade unions, whose chairman and officers seemed nearly always to be Kikuyu or Luo. Several of them became very heavily impregnated with Mau Mau and were the main support to its funds. Trading companies, too, which had sprung up in large numbers among the Kikuyu during the war, were readily persuaded to join Mau Mau and boycott non-members.[14] Even social clubs which had started harmlessly enough were systematically infiltrated and turned to account.

The strong arm of the Mau Mau was provided by the 'Forty Group'. These were young men of the age grades circumcised in or after 1940. It is not true, as is sometimes stated, that many of them had served with the East African forces overseas and had returned disaffected with the war. They may have served in the forces in Kenya at the very end of the war, in some cases, but few had seen service overseas.

---

12 While Fazan rightly acknowledges the initial educational ambitions of Githunguri College, one must also remember his respect for its founder, Senior Chief Koinange.

13 This is now more open to doubt. Kershaw, *Mau Mau from Below*, pp. 220, 223–37, 329–30, writes of several Mau Maus, including a 'Githunguri' or 'Kenyatta' Mau Mau that demanded disciplined but non-violent solidarity; and 'Nairobi' and 'Rift Valley' Mau Maus, more committed to violence, which exploited Kenyatta's reputation, but were not subject to his control. The late Greet Kershaw is the only historian of Mau Mau, either Kenyan or expatriate, to have conducted research in Kikuyuland during the Emergency, initially as a Quaker aid-worker.

14 Fazan was correct. The chairman of Mau Mau's central committee, *Muhimu*, was Eliud Mutonyi, lorry owner and charcoal dealer. Fred Kubai and Bildad Kaggia, leaders of Nairobi's militants, were both, among other things, active trade union officials. See Kaggia, *Roots of Freedom*; Dave Hyde, 'The Nairobi General Strike [1950]: from protest to insurgency', in Andrew Burton (ed.), *The Urban Experience in Eastern Africa* c. *1750–2000* (Nairobi: The British Institute in Eastern Africa, 2002), pp. 235–53.

It seems that until about 1950, Kenyatta had hopes that armed conflict might be avoided and that an agreed solution might be reached, resting on the basis of parity of representation in the Legislative Council and the end of restrictions against Africans and Asians buying land in the Highlands. Partly at his insistence a multi-racial Kenya Citizens Association was formed, but it soon foundered on the two rocks of the Highlands and a common electoral roll, for on neither of these points were the Europeans prepared to give way.[15] It was clearly seen that a common electoral roll would soon swamp Europeans and Asians under a flood of African voters for, however high the qualifications for the vote were set, agitation would not cease until Africans had achieved a clear majority and black domination at an early date. The alternative was community franchise with each community electing its own members to the Legislative Council on a basis approximating to racial parity. The Europeans would have preferred this solution and might have supported it as between themselves and the Africans, but it foundered on the Asian question. Even if such an agreement had been reached, it would have been highly fragile and would have tended to make racial distinctions even more pronounced instead of gradually closing the gap.[16]

As to the White Highlands, there were probably few Europeans who would *not* have admitted that the entail of land to the exclusive ownership of any one race, whether white or black, could not be continued indefinitely and that in time the exclusiveness of privilege would have to be modified and eventually fade out. But, seeing how enormously the economy of the country was dependent on the White Highlands and the skilled farming needed to maintain their fertility, and considering also the rights of the settlers to the fruits of their labours and the security promised them, the settler community envisaged the process in terms of generations. However, even on the most gradual basis there was little disposition among the settlers to relax the exclusiveness of their privilege. At most one could say that there was rather less resentment than there had been at a suggestion that, in certain circumstances and with the consent of their neighbours in the

15 Interestingly, and as part of his continuing meditation on how Kenya's land allocation might, with wiser counsels, have been changed over time, Fazan here attributes the worsening political atmosphere as much to white intransigence as to African militancy, a view that few whites at the time would have accepted but which historians would emphasise.

16 An excellent summary of post-war Kenya's political conundrum.

district, a settler might be allowed to sell his land or part of it to an applicant of another race if it appeared that he had the capital and resources to farm the land properly. But settler opinion as a whole was, in practice, still uncompromising and I know of no such concession being granted.[17]

The standpoint of the two sides was thus much too far apart to have given any real prospect of agreement at that time. No more was heard of the 'Kenya Citizens' and, after this setback, KAU became more extreme. There was no longer any attempt at compromise or any concealment about their aims. They wanted self-government for Africans and the end of colonial rule, recovery of the Highlands, no 'colour bar' and higher wages. KAU remained more or less in the open, stepping up agitation to the utmost limit short of open sedition, and sometimes passing it, but Mau Mau, operating underground, was secretly collecting arms and administering oaths, with no holds barred.

Their programme captivated the minds of many thousands of Kikuyu and kindred tribes of the Embu district. It did not have the expected measure of success among other tribes, however, as they suspected that the self-government intended was domination by the Kikuyu and did not relish it.[18] Nor did they see much good coming to them if the settlers left the Highlands because they would not be passed back to the Masai or other original owners, but the land-hungry Kikuyu would get the greatest share. Indeed, no other solution would have been practicable in such an event, for about a quarter of a million Kikuyu squatters, counting women and children, were already there. The rest of the programme too attracted little notice where other tribes were concerned, although the prospect of higher wages had appeal for many and was a factor in gaining considerable support from the Luo tribe. It was not easy, however, to see where these wages would come from if suddenly the settlers left. As for the lifting of the 'colour bar' and the desire to enter European hotels, or send African children to white schools, it seemed predominantly a Kikuyu craving. Nevertheless, there were enough sympathisers and malcontents among the other tribes – particularly the Abaluhya, Luo, Meru, Suk and the Somalis of the

---

17 Not only were settlers unyielding on any relaxation of their racially-protected right of Highland ownership in the foreseeable future, but many new post-war farmers were settled on state-assisted or tenancy terms that assumed a continuing colonial status.

18 British propaganda played on these fears.

Northern province – to be causing government some concern, but the general disposition was to wait upon events.

It is probable that the reference to the colour bar was intended to have a wider implication than the mere abolition of specifications. The intention was to play upon the latent resentment at Africans being in effect third-rate citizens in their own country. However amicable the relations between the races had been, the leading role which circumstances had given to the white man, and the air of superiority which it engendered, must have been galling to the blacks. The plain fact was that there was far too great a disparity between Europeans and Africans, both as regards attainments and standards of living, to make for contentment or permanent security. Insofar as there was a middle class, it was filled overwhelmingly by Asian technicians, shopkeepers, and clerks sandwiched between a white aristocracy above and African peasant farmers or labourers below. It was a difficulty that time and common sense could best solve, and there was very little sign of discontent over the country at large corresponding to the ferment among the Kikuyu, but it was, nevertheless, an unstable situation which Mau Mau exploited.

The first open defiance on a wide scale began with the so-called women's riots in the Fort Hall and Nyeri districts towards the end of 1951. They were not particularly significant in themselves and resulted in nothing worse than the burning of a number of cattle crushes in protest against the veterinary department's anti-rinderpest campaign, but they were exploited by agitators for seditious purposes. There was no indication in the reports for the year that the situation was getting beyond the capacity of the civil administration to deal with it, except a statement from Fort Hall district that KAU meetings were becoming increasingly hostile.[19] In the expectation, however, that things would get worse and that private property would need

19 Settlers bitterly criticised the colonial government for its apparent complacency in face of rising African militancy. Junior officials tended to blame 'paper' and an aloof central government secretariat and/or the governor, Sir Philip Mitchell who, weary after a distinguished career, could not bear to accept that his crowning achievement, Kenya's governorship, might end in disaster. Official admission of this failing is found in the first term of reference for the retired civil servant Frank Corfield, who in 1957 was charged with explaining not only the growth of Mau Mau but also 'the circumstances which permitted the movement to develop so rapidly without the full knowledge of the Government': *Historical Survey*, p. 1. For a first-hand account of the administration's reactions at the time see Chenevix Trench, *Men who Ruled Kenya*, pp. 220–31.

protection, steps were taken to increase the Kenya Police Reserve (KPR) and parallel precautions were also taken to increase the tribal police in the African lands. Most of the men of the European community joined the KPR, or, if young enough to do so, the Kenya Regiment. From about April 1948, when the general increase of lawlessness necessitated special precautions, members of the KPR, although not yet officially called up, voluntarily carried out frequent patrols.

Whether the KAU leaders had yet come down firmly on the side of open revolt is doubtful, but the movement had now gained a momentum which they were unable to restrain. From the beginning of the year there were numerous outbreaks of fire on pasture land, burning of huts and poisoning of cattle on settlers' farms in the Nyeri and Nanyuki districts, and in February there were serious fires on farms in the Timau area. The African press was full of provocative articles and Mau Mau hymns were secretly printed. Scarcely veiled sedition was being preached at 'tea parties' several hundred strong in the Kiambu district. The spear and shield emblem was painted on the sides of Kikuyu buses, and Mau Mau devotees grew beards, presumably in emulation of Jomo Kenyatta for, beyond question, he was now universally accepted as the dominant figure in the movement. That does not mean, however, that he had control of its operations or approved its every feature.

The Mau Mau oath, which initially had been comparatively mild and used with caution, was now being administered wholesale at a fee of 60 shillings which went to the campaign funds with 2 shillings and 50 cents to the oath administrator. It enjoined complete loyalty to the movement and absolute obedience, even if a man were ordered to do murder. It was administered secretly in huts at night with magical ceremonies involving rituals which, as time went by, became increasingly more revolting. As the Mau Mau campaign proceeded, several different types were employed – probably seven – becoming progressively more bestial and nauseating at each successive stage according to the position held and the ruthlessness of the deeds which the oath-taker bound himself to do, if so ordered. They were not traditional Kikuyu oaths such as might have been administered by a properly constituted elder of the tribe under the sanctions of Kikuyu custom. It seems that, although old men were generally preferred, any Mau Mau of the rank of section commander or above could administer the oath. As to the form, the essential feature of the obscenities practised was that they should be against the order of nature. It had nothing to do with Kikuyu custom: it was as much a flouting of tribal tradition as it was a defiance of government.[20]

Oathing in schools was widespread, not only in KISA and *Karing'a* schools, but also in the bush schools started in forest reserves and settlers' farms where teachers were mostly Kikuyu and where influence could be extended to other tribes. Both the children and their parents had to take the oath. If they refused, the children were banished from the school and frequently the parents' huts would be burnt down. Over the Kikuyu country at large the taking of the oath was not confined to willing adherents. Gangs of young thugs from the Forty Group and their like would round them up and they would be compelled to take it by force.

These activities meant, inevitably, that much more information now reached the government, and there is reason to think that the Mau Mau may have overreached and embarrassed the more sober-minded of the KAU leaders who would have preferred, if oathing was to be used at all, that it should be confined to comparatively narrow cells in key places, ready for rapid expansion if and when open revolt should be unleashed. But their hand had been forced and they must now have realised that the revolt was imminent. If they wished to stop it, their only recourse was to an unequivocal condemnation of Mau Mau, or else they must let it have its head. No such denunciation was made.[21]

Counter-measures by government included restrictions against holding meetings or making collections without a permit. A curfew was imposed in the Fort Hall district. There was also introduced a 'cleansing' oath, intended to remove the curse from anyone who had taken the Mau Mau oath and reported it, or had taken it by force, but the attempt to match magic by magic was of doubtful expediency and had little general effect, although it was reported to have brought relief in a few cases. Meanwhile the deteriorating situation had begun to take a further sinister turn: with the murder of informers against Mau Mau. The first recorded case of the kind was on the 15th May 1952, when the

20 This seems to be generally agreed, including by Kikuyu informants. The most forceful statement of this view and, for white opinion the most authoritative, was in L. S. B. Leakey, *Mau Mau and the Kikuyu* (London: Methuen, 1952), pp. 98–101.

21 This is a questionable statement, thanks to doubt over Kenyatta's meaning when in August 1952, at a meeting on the Kiambu cricket ground – *kirigiti* – called to denounce Mau Mau, he cursed it 'to the roots of the *mikongoe* tree', a mythical tree of the underworld. At his trial the judge suggested he was advising Mau Mau to go underground, but Kubai and Kaggia, leaders of the urban militants, later claimed to have threatened to kill Kenyatta should he continue to condemn Mau Mau.

bodies of two Africans, one of whom had given evidence, were found in the Kileleshwa River with bullet wounds and *panga* slashes.[22]

On the 26th July a large KAU meeting was held at Nyeri. Forty lorries full of supporters of both sexes arrived from Nairobi. Flags in the colours of the movement were openly displayed, and the key-note of the speeches was 'recovery of our stolen land'. It was a red-letter day for Mau Mau recruitment and can be said to have marked the point of no return.[23] During these months while this dangerous situation was building up, the governor of Kenya, Sir Philip Mitchell, was absent from the colony on terminal leave pending retirement. For a reason that may have seemed sufficient to the Colonial Office – that two governors cannot be on the payroll at once – his successor, Sir Evelyn Baring, had to wait until that period of leave had expired. When he eventually arrived on the 29th September, he acted with speed. A quick tour of the affected areas convinced him that he would have to report that a state of emergency existed and must be declared forthwith.

On the night of the 25th/26th September over 150 sheep and cattle on farms in the Nanyuki area were maimed so badly by Mau Mau gangs that they had to be destroyed. This horrible act was the work of youths who had only taken the Mau Mau oath the previous night. But then worse things happened. From the 1st August to the 20th October there were, according to a police report, 34 known murders of Africans by Mau Mau. Four headmen were among the victims, and many chiefs received threatening letters. The culminating crime occurred on the 7th October when Senior Chief Waruhiu of the Githunguri division of Kiambu district was murdered as he was being driven home after attending the hearing of an African court appeal case. His way was blocked both in front and behind by two cars drawn crossways over the road while the murderer got out of the car in front and shot him in cold blood. It was a tragic event, for he was able, honourable and an eminently just man.[24]

On the night of the 20th/21st October the governor proclaimed the state of emergency. Many arrests of suspected Mau Mau leaders were made on that and following days. Immediately after the proclamation

---

22 At this point in the memoir it appears that Fazan was summarising his official *History of the Loyalists*, compiled in 1960–1.

23 The verbatim police report of this mass meeting, which Kenyatta found difficult to control, appears as Appendix F in Corfield's *Historical Survey*, pp. 301–8.

24 Many Kikuyu held a different view of Waruhiu. See Throup, *Economic and Social Origins*, pp. 159–61; Anderson, *Histories of the Hanged*, pp. 11–12, 34–5, 55–7.

the Lancashire Fusiliers were flown in from the [Suez] Canal Zone. The 6th KAR arrived from Tanganyika and the 7th from Uganda to reinforce the 4th, 5th, and 26th who were already in the operational area, with the 3rd and 23rd also in Kenya and available. The Kenya Regiment was embodied with its reserves and called up.[25] The Kenya Police was also expanded by calling up the reserve and, within a short time almost every able-bodied settler who could possibly be spared had joined it, as too had many businessmen. The more elderly joined the Home Guard which was now formed and comprised both European and Asian sections. There was, as yet, no African Home Guard, but certain chiefs had, of their own initiative, formed private guards for the protection of their own people, and the same thing was done by several of the mission stations. European farmers living in affected areas had also, for the most part, assigned a share in their defence plan to their more dependable employees.

Emergency regulations were brought into force at once. African newspapers of seditious tendency were suppressed. Special regulations, supplemented as need arose, were applied to the Kikuyu, Embu, and Meru tribes. Curfews were imposed, travelling restricted, meetings and collections virtually prohibited, labour very strictly regulated, and labourers required to carry an employment record card and to be photographed. Photographs too had to be carried by other Kikuyu on their identity cards. Jomo Kenyatta and five other political leaders were committed for trial on a charge of sedition and, after a controversial trial at Kapenguria, which was very protracted, they were convicted as having been leaders of the Mau Mau movement.[26] Many other people were also detained but it was not found possible to deal with all detainees by trial because witnesses were afraid to come forward and it was not thought right to expose them to Mau Mau vengeance. A tribunal was therefore appointed with a retired colonial judge as chairman to hear detainees' appeals.[27]

---

25 Parker's *Last Colonial Regiment* is more thoughtful and more detailed than Guy Campbell's *The Charging Buffalo: A History of the Kenya Regiment 1937–1963* (London: Leo Cooper, 1986).

26 See John Lonsdale, 'The trials of Jomo Kenyatta: Breaking and making an African nationalist', Chapter 11 in Peter Coss (ed.), *The Moral World of the Law* (Cambridge: Cambridge University Press, 2000), pp. 196–239.

27 And of which Fazan was a member.

15

The Mau Mau Revolt[1]

The first phase of the emergency lasted nearly six months from the 20th October 1952, when it declared, until the end of March, 1953. It was a period when both sides were building up their strength.[2] It is easier now than it was at the time to discern the Mau Mau plan of campaign. The prevalent expectation was that, to the extent of their

1 This account of what is now generally called the Mau Mau war relies heavily on the *History of the Loyalists* which Fazan had compiled in 1960–1 from earlier district accounts. For extended comment see the Foreword. While his analysis of the war's changing character would be accepted in outline, few would now agree that the insurgents had planned a long campaign. Relying on past precedent, they probably hoped that Britain would dismantle white-settler supremacy immediately British troops had been sent in. That the insurgents had one overall command structure and strategy is also debatable. Mau Mau has generated as large a historiography as any other episode in Africa's decolonisation. What follows is a very select bibliography. For the army's campaign, with evidence from the rediscovered 'migrated archive' at Hanslope Park (with files on the abuses that Fazan deplores below), see Huw Bennett, *Fighting the Mau Mau: The British Army and Counter-insurgency in the Kenya Emergency* (Cambridge: Cambridge University Press, 2013). For the legal, social, and political aspects of the war, see Berman, *Control and Crisis*, Chapter 8; Maloba, *Mau Mau and Kenya*; Daniel Branch, *Defeating Mau Mau, Creating Kenya: Counterinsurgency, Civil War, and Decolonization* (Cambridge: Cambridge University Press, 2009); David Anderson, *Histories of the Hanged*; and Caroline Elkins, *Britain's Gulag: The Brutal End of Empire in Kenya* (London: Cape, 2005) – published in the USA as *Imperial Reckoning: The Untold Story of Britain's Gulag in Kenya* (New York, NY: Henry Holt, 2005). Elkins' high mortality estimates are refuted by John Blacker, 'The demography of Mau Mau: Fertility and mortality in Kenya in the 1950s, a demographer's viewpoint', *African Affairs* 106 (2007), pp. 205–27. The insurgents' accounts of their war are discussed in Marshall S. Clough, *Mau Mau Memoirs: History, Memory and Politics* (Boulder, CO: Lynne Rienner, 1998). Varied views are found in E. S. Atieno Odhiambo and John Lonsdale (eds), *Mau Mau and Nationhood: Arms, Authority and Narration* (Oxford: James Currey, 2003).

2 Bennett, *Fighting the Mau Mau*, sees the British blindly lashing out while 'building up their strength'. Initial counterinsurgency reflected ignorance of who 'the enemy'

capability, the Mau Mau would concentrate on terrorist attacks on the lives and property of Europeans in a swift attempt to drive them off their farms, while at the same time conducting a terrorist campaign against loyalists in the Kikuyu districts. Events soon showed, however, that the Mau Mau had laid their plans for a long, rather than a short campaign, and that their primary object was to achieve complete domination of their own home districts, that is to say the three Kikuyu districts (Nyeri, Fort Hall, and Kiambu) and, a little later, Embu and Meru. This they proposed to do by a combination of two methods: firstly by a terrorist campaign conducted by small gangs against chiefs, headmen and other centres of loyalist resistance; secondly, by the formation and training of strong groups in the Aberdares capable of making attacks in force.

The leadership of the militant wing of Mau Mau, wherever engaged – whether in Kikuyu lands or in the mountains and forests of the Aberdares and Mount Kenya – was claimed by Dedan Kimathi. He was described by police as being a former secretary of the Thomson's Falls branch of the KAU and a former clerk of the Tetu Dairies, Nyeri, and at least for the first two years of the Emergency his leadership appears to have been complete and unchallenged. Though speaking English well, his education and subsequent career had been marred by persistent unruliness, but he was possessed of a very forceful personality, hardihood and resource and had risen to prominence as an oath administrator and leader of the Forty Group. He had a fancy for titles, appointing himself Field Marshal of the 'Land Freedom Army' and at periods when he judged the Mau Mau morale to be in need of a fillip he would distribute correspondingly high-sounding promotions to his subordinate leaders.[3]

---

were. The random brutality that resulted, Bennett argues, created a culture that frustrated later efforts to curb the security forces' use of illegitimate violence. For this argument applied to late-colonial emergencies in general, see David French, *The British Way in Counter-Insurgency 1945–1967* (Oxford: Oxford University Press, 2011) who reports, on p. 156, the extraordinary number of 430 African suspects 'shot trying to escape' in the first six months of the Emergency.

3 The chief witness to Kimathi's autocratic leadership is Karari Njama, in (with Donald Barnett) his *Mau Mau from Within: Autobiography and Analysis of Kenya's Peasant Revolt* (London: MacGibbon & Kee, 1966); a similar picture is drawn in Ian Henderson, with Philip Goodhart, *The Hunt for Kimathi* (London: Hamish Hamilton, 1958). Maina wa Kinyatti (ed.), *Kenya's Freedom Struggle: The Dedan Kimathi papers* (London: Zed Books, 1987) translates captured documents. Despite the editor's politically corrected, Marxist, introduction, the actual translations retain the ring of truth.

Meanwhile, other leaders were responsible for the passive wing. Mau Mau cells had been formed in almost every place where considerable numbers of Kikuyu were employed, especially in Nairobi and Thika, as the main centres of supply, and at suitable places on routes used for the movement of recruits. The duty of these cells was to harbour recruits and insurgents in hiding, fit them out, and see to their onward transmission to the active Mau Mau; after the declaration of the Emergency, this system expanded into an elastic organisation of district, divisional locational and sub-locational committees, for each of which there was a parallel committee in Nairobi. There was also an organisation of Mau Mau courts exercising a jurisdiction of extreme severity both in Nairobi and in the reserves. A further elaboration of the system was the provision for substitutes to replace leaders who had been arrested, and even substitutes for substitutes. Little initial difficulty was experienced by the insurgents in supplying themselves with food. They made themselves comfortable in living in underground dugouts, and they had girl companions whom they used as carriers for bringing up supplies. They even had improvised hospitals and kept supplies of penicillin and other drugs obtained from dispensaries (before they were controlled) or purloined from the government hospitals.

Considerable stores of arms and ammunition had been accumulated during the two or three years before the Emergency, partly by illegal purchases, partly by thefts from individuals and largely by theft of supplies from military installations at Mackinnon Road, Nanyuki and Gilgil. A further source from which ammunition was obtained was from the scenes of battle of the Abyssinia campaign. A self-confessed Mau Mau 'general' who was captured at a later stage in the Emergency, admitted that, in the capacity of a driver for the Locust Control, he had found it very easy and lucrative to run ammunition to Mau Mau in his government vehicle. At such places as Jigjiga, where there had been heavy fighting, children used to bring it to him by the handful. Homemade rifles also began to appear, made partly from stolen springs and half-inch piping, of very primitive design but afterwards somewhat improved. Nevertheless, the *panga*, a kind of machete in universal use in local agriculture, and the *simi*, a short straight Masai sword, remained the principal weapons of Mau Mau all through the Emergency.

On the government side the Lancashire Fusiliers were deployed mainly in the Rift Valley and the foothills of the Aberdares, while the KAR battalions were distributed over the three Kikuyu districts and the Nyeri/Nanyuki area, stiffening the resistance of the loyalists and conducting constant patrols. Under their protective screen it was possible to build up and train the forces of local resistance. Concurrently the district administration was expanded on the basis of two district officers helping the district commissioner at his headquarters, and one district officer at each senior chief's division. In conjunction with them, but a little later, the Kenya Police established divisional units.

It was always clear that the defeat of Mau Mau could only be accomplished in such a way as to produce lasting peace when the majority of the Kikuyu turned against it. Meanwhile, the immediate difficulty was to form a home guard and coordinate the scattered islands of resistance when a preponderance of the *athigani*, the young men who made up the traditional warrior element, had themselves taken the Mau Mau oath. At this time the elders and the middle-aged were still either loyal or, at least, uncommitted, and after much thought it was decided to make use of the able-bodied among these older age groups and such of the *athigani* as were deemed loyal after careful screening. In this way the organisation was built up which became known as the Kikuyu, Embu, and Meru Home Guard. It began with the resistance groups formed voluntarily around chiefs and headmen for mutual protection, and with watch and ward groups formed for the same purpose by certain mission stations. The ruthless methods of Mau Mau in enforcing the oath and punishing recusants, sometimes by death, had compelled them to seek protection in this way. By March 1953 the Guard was 15,000 strong and later rose to 22,000 when fighting intensified.

From the outset the Guard had to rely very largely for its support on the tribal police, whose strength was now expanded from a total of 240 for the whole of Central province to 800 by the enrolment of half the chief's messengers. Even so, they were a small force to face the responsibilities thrown upon them. They were never absorbed in the Guard, but two tribal policemen were normally posted as strengthening to each guard post, and their patrols were constantly moving between them. Sixty-three of them were to die in the coming battles, yet throughout they discharged their duties admirably.

Initially, the guard posts were not very strong. Huts were easily burnt and, even when the posts themselves began to be safe, surrounding families including the wives and children of the Guards, had scanty protection. This problem was not solved finally until much later when it became necessary to concentrate these families into protected villages. Meanwhile, the guard posts were progressively strengthened by deep and wide ditches set with pointed stakes in the bottom and ramparts with stockades protected with fences and barbed wire. They were enlarged so as to afford refuge to others besides the immediate members and families of the Guard, and patrols from them were organised to give some measure of protection to the countryside.

The loyalists were armed, initially, only with spears and *simis*, bows and arrows, the firepower being provided by tribal police. This was because of doubts about the loyalty of the Guards. Initially, it had been formed warily, only from persons who had not taken the Mau Mau oath, although from about the middle of 1953 onwards the provision was relaxed, and many men were recruited into the Guard who had taken the Mau Mau oath, but had subsequently taken the cleansing oath or had publicly confessed. Where the Guard had been raised hastily, however, there had been cases of infiltration, so apprehensions about the security of the force lingered on, especially in the European farming areas where it was only slowly that a system of guard posts, with headmen and tribal police, could be built up, as in the reserves. Despite these apprehensions, however, General Hinde, who had been appointed to take charge of all military operations, gave authority in March for 20 per cent of the Guard to be armed with rifles.

Active operations by Mau Mau in this first phase were mostly in the Kikuyu districts, including Embu. Meru was not yet much affected. The insurgents were not yet strong enough to attack a defended post but, working in small terrorist gangs of a dozen or so, and seldom more than 20, they waylaid loyalists in the open or burnt down their huts at night. Chiefs, headmen and tribal police were the principal targets. In the five months from the declaration of the Emergency to the middle of March three chiefs, seven headmen or sub-headmen, and four tribal police were killed, and three other chiefs and five headmen were unsuccessfully attacked. Only one of these attacks was in any sense a battle. Several of the headmen and some of the chiefs were unable to stand the strain and had to be replaced, but there were many who stood firm and resisted, often in the face of very great danger. It was their staunchness that enabled the Kikuyu Guard to be built up and eventually to prevail.

The pattern of attacks on Europeans and, in some cases, Asians continued the same throughout the Emergency. The Mau Mau chose their targets largely at random and, by attacking one household here and another there, they hoped to spread a general sense of alarm and uneasiness. Sometimes the purpose of their attacks was to steal firearms and invariably their method was to take care to be in superior numbers and, where possible, to suborn one of the house servants to let them in. Usually they struck at about 9 p.m. when the householder and his family would he relaxing after dinner and they still had the long hours of darkness before them in which to make their escape. Occasionally they sprang an ambush in the open, especially if they could waylay a farm manager carrying the month's wages for the farm employees in his car.

The position of European farmers in the Central and Rift Valley provinces was not enviable. Nearly all of them had relied predominantly on Kikuyu for their labour force, and there was no doubt that most of these had taken the Mau Mau oath. To discharge them all would have brought farming operations to a standstill, and their return to Kikuyuland, by swelling the ranks of the discontented, would have made administration still more difficult. Most employers tried to compromise, taking a chance with many of the less suspect of their employees, so that production was kept going and the Kikuyu labourers went on with their jobs so far as Mau Mau allowed them to do so.

On several occasions Asian shops in or near the Kikuyu districts were raided and property taken, while in Nairobi more ambitious safe-breakings and robberies took place. African-owned shops were left unmolested, provided that the owner took the oath and agreed to serve only Mau Mau members. European- and Asian-owned shops were not entirely boycotted but Mau Mau orders forbade any African to buy beer or cigarettes, except the home-made Kikuyu substitute, to wear European style hats or to travel in any bus or taxi owned by anyone not a Mau Mau supporter. Asian shopkeepers in trading centres, if they wanted to be free of Mau Mau raids, had to be careful about supplying non-Mau Mau customers. The fact that all these orders were obeyed implicitly is not surprising when one considers how very severely the secret Mau Mau courts punished offenders. At a later stage in the Emergency, when the sites of these courts were discovered and the neighbourhood searched, large numbers of corpses were found with ropes round their necks. The Mau Mau method of keeping order, both within the forest and over all the affected area, was by reign of terror.

In the face of this provocation the government took counter-measures including the levy of a special tax of 20 shillings against the Kikuyu, designed to help pay for the Emergency. Power was reserved to district commissioners to excuse it in the case of individuals believed to be loyal or in the case of whole locations in recognition of good behaviour. This imposition followed successive orders which had been issued by government in December and January 1952–3 by which all the 128 Kikuyu independent schools were closed because almost everyone concerned, both the school committees and the children, were believed to have taken the Mau Mau oath. After a short interval, 97 of them were re-opened, some of them under the auspices of mission societies and the rest under the government's district education boards.

Mau Mau retaliated by issuing notices prohibiting children from attending these schools. In some cases the notices stated that any children breaking the order would have their legs and arms cut off and that their parents and teachers would be beheaded. Some of these notices purported to be issued 'by order of the Mau Mau Marshal Court, Head Office, Mount Kenya'. Several mission schools were attacked in this period, the worst instance being on Christmas Eve when seven Africans were murdered at Kagumo School in Nyeri district[4] and, by the end of 1953, 27 teachers had been killed in Nyeri, Fort Hall, Embu and Meru districts, and 55 schools destroyed. It is certain, however, that Mau Mau did themselves harm by these measures. The children stayed away for a time, but so great was the keenness of the Kikuyu for education that, as soon as the risk abated a little, they went back and the schools continued open, not always in the same places, but where they could be given a measure of protection.[5]

Further regulations, which had been imposed in the months after the declaration of the Emergency, included restrictions in the use of vehicles and bicycles and the control of hotels, shops and markets, all of which were subject to closure for short periods of time. There were also communal fines imposed, initially in the form of stock levies but, later on, in cash. Land belonging to Mau Mau could be confiscated under the Forfeiture Ordinance and from February 1953 it had become a criminal offence to supply Mau Mau with food, drink, clothes or medicine.[6]

The immediate impact of most of these restrictions was to stimulate Mau Mau recruitment, although in time the population wearied of them as they became increasingly disenchanted with Mau Mau. In this respect the most serious consequences were felt as a result of the labour controls. The 'repatriation' of labour from European farms began in 1952 when all the Kikuyu, Meru and Embu labourers of the Leshau ward of Ol' Joro Orok[7] were sent back to the reserves wholesale as an example to the others. Later only those labourers who failed the screening test or refused to be photographed were repatriated, but the

4 For a vivid account, see Anderson, *Histories*, pp. 72–6.

5 For both the experience of a school at the time and the futures of its students, see David P. Sandgren, *Mau Mau's Children: The Making of Kenya's Postcolonial Elite* (Madison, WI: University of Wisconsin Press, 2012).

6 Anderson's *Histories of the Hanged* analyses these and other measures whose formal legality had to be created by exceptional Emergency regulations.

7 At the northern end of the high Kinangop/Nyandarua plateau on the eastern wall of the central Rift Valley, south of Thomson's Falls/Nyahururu.

numbers were enormous and very many also left of their own accord. In addition to these, there were many suspicious characters who did not qualify to be detained, who were sent back to the reserves from Nairobi and other places. There were also 'repatriations' from Tanganyika and Uganda. As a result of these regulations, security was strengthened in the European farmlands even though a number of Mau Mau cells still remained. On the other hand, thousands of Kikuyu, Embu and Meru returned to the reserves without homes to go to and many went at once to join the Mau Mau activists. Urgent measures were taken to provide central reception camps in each district and a series of smaller local centres were established. But, whatever measures were taken, an influx of displaced people on such a scale could not be conducive to law and order. Even though they provided useful labour for the construction of guard posts and other emergency tasks, there is no doubt that their presence in the reserves helped to sustain the groundswell of Mau Mau opinion, and the vocal Nairobi element and students from Kampala gave the movement a greater intellectual impetus. It was not until 1955 that there was to be any movement back into the Highlands.

★★★

Before the end of March 1953 the Mau Mau began the second phase of their campaign to dominate their home districts. While continuing their terrorist attacks on individuals, the burning of huts at night and compulsory oathing, they now felt themselves strong enough to engage the guard posts in direct attacks.

In the middle of March a rumour spread that the Mau Mau might launch a large-scale attack on the loyalists in the Lari location of the Chura division of Kiambu district. All chiefs were alerted, the civil population warned to keep close watch, and arrangements made for constant patrols by tribal police and Kikuyu Home Guards, supplemented by Kenya Police. Unfortunately a company of the 23rd KAR, which had also been available, had to be withdrawn to deal with a riot some 50 miles away at Athi River. At about 9 p.m. on the night of the 28th March, several fires were observed from Uplands police post, seeming to cover the whole Lari area. All available forces were rushed to the scene. They arrived too late to prevent the massacre. The terrorists, afterwards found to be mostly from the Githunguri location, had made widespread simultaneous attacks on villages throughout the area, setting the roofs of huts alight and slaughtering the occupants as they emerged, men, women and children. The few tribal police and 50 or so Home Guards who were present were unable to repulse the attack, but when reinforcements arrived, the battle continued all night and many terrorists were killed before the gangs made good their escape. A police report issued a week later gave the number of victims, including women and children, as 97 killed, 29 wounded, and 46 missing. Ex-chief Luka and 26 members of his family were killed within the space of his own small village. This unprovoked attack, so far from helping the Mau Mau cause, horrified all but the most depraved of the population. Many of the insurgents too were revolted, and waverers rallied to the government side. Although the burning of huts at night continued to be a favourite practice of the Mau Mau throughout the Emergency, they never again attempted a general massacre on this scale.

It is well to consider so appalling an outrage in the light of the fact that it was little more than a couple of generations since the days of tribal warfare when the Masai would raid the Kikuyu and wipe out whole villages. The Mau Mau had heard, too, of many ruthless things done in the recent war and saw no distinction between indiscriminate bombing from the air and the slaughter of families by slashing them to death with *panga*s. One must remember also that there was a great deal of religious fanaticism about the movement and its *Karing'a* origin. They had been very free in quoting the Old Testament in defence of tribal customs and took very literally Jehovah's injunction to 'slay and spare not'.

There was also a special reason why the family of Ex-chief Luka was attacked and exterminated with such ferocity.[8] Along with six or seven other families they had accepted an exchange of land at the time of the demarcation of the boundaries of the White Highlands and, on the recommendation of the Kenya Land Commission, had been given an area cut out from virgin forest. It had never been Kikuyu country but the right-holders on the ridges below had probably regarded it as the

---

8 Fazan here gets to what historians consider the origins of the Lari massacre: the 'Tigoni exchange' whereby Kikuyu 'right holders' on land surrounded by white farms were in the late 1930s resettled on forest reserve land next to the 'reserve'. The problem originated in the land alienation in the Limuru area noted in Chapters 2 and 12. Fazan had proposed the exchange when district commissioner of Kiambu in 1930 and got the Carter Commission to endorse it. Thereafter, as Provincial Commissioner of Nyanza, he could only advise from afar on the implementation of the move. For elaboration of Fazan's analysis, see Anderson, *Histories*, Chapter 4, and Branch, *Defeating Mau Mau*, pp. 55–9. Both note, as Fazan did not, that the retaliatory killings of alleged Mau Mau outnumbered those first murdered by Mau Mau. There were two Lari massacres, not one. For Mau Mau revulsion against the first massacre, see Itote, *'Mau Mau' General*, Chapter 18; and for the reputational risk run by an officer for not joining in the second, see Parker, *Last Colonial Regiment*, p. 265.

natural extension area which their descendants would one day use. Although this had happened 20 years previously without protest at the time, it is notorious that Mau Mau was frequently made an excuse for paying off old scores.

On the same night as the Lari massacre, a legitimate operation of war was skilfully carried out about 15 miles away. A group of about 40 Mau Mau, dressed in great coats to resemble police, raided the Naivasha police station after 10 p.m. and opened fire on the sentries. They ransacked the police station and broke into the armoury, getting away with 30 rifles and 15 machine carbines, while other members opened the police cells and released the prisoners. They also seized two police lorries and were loading ammunition and stores into them when a party of Lancashire Fusiliers arrived and dispersed them.

In the first week in April the 1st Battalions of the Buffs[9] and the Devonshire Regiment arrived to reinforce the Lancashire Fusiliers and complete the 39th Brigade. Shortly afterwards General Hinde appointed Lt Col P. A. Morcombe, who had commanded a KAR battalion during the war and had also had experience of guerrilla warfare in Malaya with the Suffolk Regiment, to be director of the tribal police and the Kikuyu Guard. The district commissioners retained operational command of them but deferred to him in all matters relating to defences, equipment and training. The beneficial effect was soon apparent and the Guards henceforth were much better armed.

Operationally the first four weeks of April were quiet. The opportunity was taken to strengthen defences, while sweeps were undertaken by the KAR into the Aberdares[10] to keep the Mau Mau on the move, probe their positions, and, in conjunction with the tribal police and guard patrols, to harass their supply routes. Both for this purpose and for the protection of the civil population all huts were moved back a mile from the forest fringe, and the intervening strip was declared a prohibited area.

In the last week of April the Mau Mau attacks on guard posts began in earnest in the Nyeri and Fort Hall districts. They continued until the end of July and then tailed off. Kiambu district was left unmolested, owing its immunity partly to the fact that the main routes for forwarding recruits and supplies ran through the district and also that it contained, or was uncomfortably close to, the main centres of Mau

9 Nickname of the Royal East Kent Regiment, disbanded in 1961.

10 Now the Nyandarua Mountains.

Mau planning. As for the Embu and Meru districts, their plans there had not yet passed the oathing stage.

There were 17 recorded attacks on defence posts in these two districts between the 22nd April and the 31st July. In ten of these cases the attack was repulsed and in seven the posts were overrun. There were also several occasions when clashes took place in the open, and ambushes were frequent. Although the guard posts attacked represented only a small proportion of their total number, the strain for the guards of constantly being on the alert was very wearying. There were frequent alarms when the defenders had to stand to, either under direct threat of attack or in readiness to help some other post that was being assailed. Food was short, *shambas* went uncultivated, there was constant anxiety and the men themselves, nearly all of them, were beyond military age. As a matter of principle the Guards were unpaid, because it was essential to be a voluntary effort and be seen to be so. The number of Guards armed with rifles was increased to half. They were given some instruction in their use and they were assisted with food supplies and other essentials from Nairobi. The wonder is not that they sometimes failed, but that, in the circumstances, they did so well.

No detailed description of these events need be given, though a few notable incidents should perhaps be mentioned. On the 28th April the guard post at Ruathia on the forest fringe was attacked at night in pouring rain by a gang of 50 and overrun when the defenders' ammunition had run out. Two tribal police and four guards were killed. Headman William escaped but four days later he was killed in an ambush along with a sergeant of the Kenya Regiment. Less than a week after that another determined attack was made at night on Othaya police station in Nyeri district. The raiders had a Bren gun with them and advanced firing right up to the wire and did not break off the action until 16 of their number had been killed. They then retired, leaving four of their wounded and the Bren behind.

On the 7th June and following days Operation Epsom, a large-scale sweep in the Aberdares, was mounted by the security forces, in which the Buffs, Devons, Lancashire Fusiliers, KAR, Kenya Police, Tribal Police and Guards all took part. This was succeeded by a second operation, Royal Flush, the object of which was to round up any Mau Mau dislodged by Epsom from the Aberdares and driven back into the Reserve. On this occasion the Tribal Police and Guard had the leading role. Meanwhile, in the Reserve, attacks on chiefs and headmen continued. On the 27th June Headman Sospiter's post was attacked and burnt out. He escaped but, on the 30th, Headman Thigira of Mununga, a favourite son of that indomitable old man Senior Chief Njiri, was ambushed and killed.[11]

It was now decided to recruit a number of Akamba retired non-commissioned officers from the KAR to bolster the morale of the Guard. They performed the task admirably, and many were promoted to sergeant major. At this time, too, the Kenya Regiment ceased its operational role, and its British ranks were distributed as district officers (KG) to take charge of groups of guard posts. Within a year there were 200 or more at work in the affected districts. Although the strain on the administration was thus somewhat relieved, the shortage of trained and experienced officers was to create a few problems of its own.

On the 1st July, Nyeri district sustained a severe blow in the death of Chief Reuben of Kirimukuyu, who was caught in an ambush and slashed to death.[12] In the following two weeks a European inspector of police was fatally wounded in the course of an action near Ngaini School and Kigumo post in the Fort Hall district was attacked by a large and well-armed group which advanced in three separate waves after doping themselves with bhang. The guard held out for over two hours until all ammunition was exhausted. The last wave of assailants succeeded in cutting the wire and broke in. Eighteen of the defenders were killed and 23 were carried off. The following morning a similarly named post, Kagumo, some 20 miles south of Nyeri, was attacked and overrun after strong resistance. One tribal policeman and 12 guards were killed.

---

11 For Senior Chief Njiiri's revenge, another retaliatory massacre not mentioned here see Branch, *Defeating Mau Mau*, pp. 61–2; also, Anderson, *Histories*, p. 264; Elkins, *Britain's Gulag*, pp. 78–9; and Bennett, *Fighting the Mau Mau*, p. 216. Fazan's *History of the Loyalists*, p. 38, on which his memoir is here based, was similarly silent. This, in turn, relied on the 39-page typescript 'History of the Kikuyu Guard' by Jock Rutherford, edited by John Pinney (DC Fort Hall), in 1957 – a copy of which is in Oxford's Rhodes House Development Records Project collection, Mss.Afr.s.1915(2). Rutherford's history is published by David Lovatt Smith as *A History of the Kikuyu Guard 1953–1955* (Herstmonceux: Mawenzi Books, 2003). In these official accounts at the time, we see British reluctance to criticise or discipline atrocities committed by the Kikuyu Guard, for fear of alienating the sometimes doubtful loyalty of essential allies in the war against Mau Mau. For this concern at the highest level, see Charles Douglas-Home, *Evelyn Baring, the Last Proconsul* (London: Collins, 1978), pp. 250–6, 260–1, 287–99; and French, *British Way*, pp. 171–2, for Njiiri's bewilderment at attempts to discipline the Kikuyu Guard. See discussion in the Foreword and, below, for Fazan's added, retrospective, reason for reticence; namely, to do nothing to hinder the reconciliation subsequently proclaimed by the post-colonial government.

12 Kirimukuyu's home guard, like others, was composed of wealthier farmers, teachers and traders: Branch, *Defeating Mau Mau*, p. 68.

On the night of the 26th the guard at Gacharagueni in Fort Hall district saw the torch flashes of Mau Mau preparing to attack. A prompt sortie was decisive and the would-be assailants suffered severe losses. The following night Headman Kiarie's post in Fort Hall location 1 was attacked and most of the guard bolted. A tribal policeman, who later received the George Medal for bravery, posted himself at the main gate and, despite Mau Mau rifle and Bren gun fire, almost single-handedly prevented the raiders from entering until, seeing the headlights of approaching relief, they abandoned the attack and made off. On the last day of the month in location 14 of the Fort Hall district, Chief James Kiru and Assistant District Officer Jerome Kihori were ambushed and killed at a road block. Both were highly capable and the latter was a 27-year-old Makerere graduate.

After two further attempts on guard posts in August, both repulsed, direct attacks in force slackened off for a time, and the Mau Mau confined their activities to short raids, ransacking shops in trading centres and driving off cattle from European farms. Frequent clashes took place with the guard patrols so that raiding parties were compelled to fight in the open.

In one of these the noted gang leader Matenjagwo was killed and his authority was assumed by Kago, one of his former lieutenants, who had already established himself independently and was to prove the boldest and most resourceful leader that Mau Mau produced.[13]

The methods which had proved so successful in fighting Mau Mau in their own home areas now began to be applied to the European farms. The Kenya Police established strong posts, and labour on farms was concentrated in defensible positions. African headmen were appointed for group farm areas, each with a posse of Tribal Police and a guard post. The same kind of thing was done in Nairobi, where breakings into shops and warehouses had been sharply on the increase. Thirty headmen were appointed for African wards, supported by 200 Tribal Police.

★★★

13 Fazan's high opinion of Kago is shared in all memoirs of the war, British and Kikuyu; Kago's differences with Kimathi over sexual and other disciplines had forced him out of the forest into the more dangerous operational area of the Kikuyu reserve.

Under the accepted convention respecting the relations between military and police, it was not permissible for the Army to take offensive operations in the Kikuyu tribal lands, since officially there was no war, but only a State of Emergency. They might only act in support of the police when called upon by them to do so for the prevention of crime. This meant, in effect, that they could search huts and make arrests of suspected persons but must then hand their captives over to the police. This was the position obtaining generally throughout the country but there were exceptions. Mount Kenya and the Aberdare Mountains and an additional strip of land 1 mile wide at the foot of them where they bordered with the Kikuyu tribal lands were proclaimed prohibited areas and anyone found there was automatically committing a crime. Here the Army might operate without hindrance from anything, except the wild fauna and the density of the forest, to hunt down Mau Mau or drive them back into their homelands where the police and guards could deal with them. In the early months of the Emergency little progress had been made by the Army in the Aberdares because of the density of the bamboo forest. Nothing was attempted beyond occasional raids, using game tracks, and the Mau Mau always had ample warning of their approach, time to set ambushes or, at need, to evacuate their hide-outs and vanish. No attempt could yet be made by the troops to establish a permanent presence. But, with the arrival of fresh forces in September 1953, it became possible to move over to the offensive in a more positive way.

The first battalion, the Black Watch, relieved the Lancashire Fusiliers in August, and in the following month, the 49th Infantry Brigade, consisting of the Royal Northumberland and the Inniskilling Fusiliers, arrived by air. General Sir George Erskine had been appointed in June to the overall command of the security forces with authority to report directly to the War Office, thus by-passing the Middle East Command, and General Hinde continued with him as his deputy director of operations. It was now possible to proceed to a comprehensive plan for crushing the Mau Mau both by crippling them in their main centre of planning and supply, which was Nairobi, and by attacking them in their main base of operations, which was the Aberdare range, and forcing them out into the open. Both these plans demanded some months of preparation. To purge Nairobi, which had become a Mau Mau stronghold with all its principal committees centred there, thousands of arrests would have to be made and there had to be due provision in advance for the construction of detention camps and for their supply and staffing, and also secret advance preparation for the screening of suspects. As regards his plans for fighting in the Aberdares, General

Erskine arranged for a regiment of Royal Engineers to be flown out for the making of roads through the forest. He also arranged for a squadron of RAF Harvards and, later, a squadron of Lincoln heavy bombers to be flown out for the location and bombing of the Mau Mau hideouts and bases.

In August, as a last chance, government made the rebels an offer. It was conveyed by leaflets dropped from the air and undertook that anyone who surrendered carrying a green branch in his hand would be immune from prosecution for his part in Mau Mau, provided that he had not committed murder. Mau Mau discipline was so strong that the immediate effect was negligible but, later, when they were scattered by air attack, individuals who had grown tired of their forest existence sometimes took the opportunity to desert and after living for a while foraging in the prohibited strip along the forest edge, would pluck up courage to surrender.

The last quarter of the year saw some increase of Mau Mau activity, with renewed attacks on guard posts, but no longer with the same intensity. They now began to turn their attention to Embu district where the guards were less trained and the defences weaker. But the posts held out and only one was overrun, an action in which the much respected Chief Fausto was among those killed.

***

Unexpectedly the Mau Mau offensive flared up again in January 1954, and continued intensively until May. The insurgents did not yet appear to be suffering from shortage of men, for they were able to mount attacks in strength of 300 or more, and sometimes in more than one area at a time. But they were no longer able to maintain this strength without resort to press-gang methods. They were also finding difficulty in obtaining supplies as readily as before from their passive wing. Although they continued to attack guard posts, in fact in greater strength than before, they had to choose their objectives with care. They selected those posts which lay close to their supply routes or otherwise interfered seriously with the passage of recruits, ammunition or food. To ensure the cooperation of their passive wing in the reserves, which had become lukewarm through their lack of success, they intensified their campaign of terrorism, compulsory oathing, and the burning of huts. Schools and schoolteachers were particular objects of their attention. The buildings, being mostly temporary and roofed with thatch, were easily burnt and in the Embu district alone more than 100 were destroyed in the course of the year.

The fighting was no longer confined to the Nyeri and Fort Hall districts. All districts of the province now had their share and the threat to European farms was accordingly increased. An account of the Mau Mau attacks on European or Asian homes would serve little purpose, but an exception may be made in the case of the raid on the farm of P. E. Grimwood in the South Kinangop on the night of the 13th January. The attack began about nine o'clock that evening, when a gang of between 60 and 100 terrorists raided the labour lines. On hearing the firing Grimwood's wife telephoned the police post at Njabini just before the wire was cut.

Meanwhile the terrorists, after setting fire to the labour lines where they killed one man and wounded another, turned their attention to the house. With bugle and whistle calls and armed with automatic weapons and home-made grenades, they advanced to the attack, threw a grenade into the kitchen, smashed windows and doors, climbed onto the roof and tried to force an entry. While his wife stood guard, Grimwood rushed from room to room, using his rifle and keeping the terrorists at bay. Just as he was running short of ammunition, four policemen arrived and engaged the gang, who diverted their fire and then made off. In their flight they ran into an ambush which had been set by the remainder of the police patrol.

There were also several spirited actions between security forces and Mau Mau in January and early February, in one of which, near Karatina, General China, Waruhiu Itote, was captured. He was rated third in the Mau Mau hierarchy after Dedan Kimathi and Stanley Mathenge, and had command over several 'battalions' in the Mount Kenya forests. In consequence of a report by him that many of the insurgents now wanted to surrender, overtures were made and on the 30th March, Mau Mau representatives appeared at Nyeri for talks with the chief native commissioner and the army chief of staff. After what appeared to be a promising start the talks came to nothing, but it was now clear that large numbers of rebels in the forest were only held there by fear, possibly of both sides.

Meanwhile, on the 17th February, Mau Mau made their most ambitious effort of the whole revolt. A very large group led by Kago started from the neighbourhood of Thika in the morning, and advanced on Kandara, one of the three divisional centres of the Fort Hall district, and a main base for the storage of ammunition and supplies. It had also a strongly defended police post and the alarm was given only just in time for the defences to be manned. The raiders ransacked and set fire to a number of houses outside the perimeter of the police post, including offices, stores, Tribal Police lines and the houses of four British officers. Then with great suddenness the tables were turned.

Police officers who had been out on patrol returned with their men, and were shortly followed by other police and troops from Thika and Fort Hall. The assailants, in full retreat, lost 40 men, killed or severely wounded. Next morning, when contacted again on Mununga Ridge, they suffered further loss.

A determined effort, aptly named Operation Anvil, was now carried out in Nairobi in an intensive drive to round up Mau Mau and restore order.[14] In spite of many screening operations the number of Kikuyu in the city had continually increased, and they were now three quarters of the total African population there. The headquarters and principal committees of the Mau Mau organisation were known to be in Nairobi, and something like a reign of terror among Africans not actively supporting them prevailed. Hold-ups were a commonplace and murders very frequent, but practically no information was reaching the police. The intention to take drastic action was announced on the 24th April, and the operation of rounding up and screening continued for the next four weeks. Twenty-seven thousand Kikuyu who failed to pass the test were interned at specially prepared centres, whence, in due course, they were filtered back to their homes in the Reserve through a system of works camps. This dealt a shattering blow to the Mau Mau organisation. Control thenceforward passed to the men in the forests and disintegration and rivalry in command were the natural result.

On the 5th March the Mau Mau struck a bitter blow in the Fort Hall district when the district officer of the Kangema division, James Candler, was ambushed and killed. As he and his escort of tribal police were returning home in the evening they came under heavy fire near Mihuti trading centre. While covering the withdrawal of his men, he was hit by one burst of fire and then another. His last act was to hand over his gun to a tribal policeman to prevent its loss to Mau Mau and order him and the rest of the escort to make good their escape. Candler had always been outstanding in building up resistance, and an example of his initiative was the formation of a highly mobile rover section of picked Tribal Police which, disappearing sometimes for weeks on end, would harass the Mau Mau with stealth and surprise, thus beating them at their own game.[15]

14 Anderson, *Histories*, pp. 200–12, gives a full account of Anvil; Walton, *Empire of Secrets*, p. 249, puts it into the context of imperial counterinsurgency more generally.

15 Jimmy Candler was a hero-figure for the administration and Kenya Regiment. A school rugby-player, he had escaped from a prison-of-war camp in Italy, to fight alongside anti-Fascist partisans: see Chenevix Trench, *Men who Ruled Kenya*, pp. 189, 262–3; Lovatt-Smith, *History of the Kikuyu Guard*, pp. 40–1; Parker, *Last Colonial Regiment*, p. 327.

On the morning of 28th March members of Kago's group dressed in police and tribal police uniforms appeared at Headman Kiarie's guard post at Kiriaini in the Fort Hall district and tried to persuade the guards to come out and join them 'to look for a gang'. The headman's suspicions were aroused and, as he attempted to withdraw the moat bridge, the raiders opened fire. Many more then appeared from all sides and succeeded in exploding grenades inside the post, one of which killed the headman. The four defending riflemen held out until all ammunition was expended, when the attackers then forced their way in and demolished the post. Only two of the defenders escaped. Police reinforcements then arrived and the attackers made off. Large numbers of Guards took up the chase and, by evening, 23 of the raiders were killed or severely wounded. Contact was then lost for a time but re-established on the night of the 30th. During the remainder of the night and into the afternoon of the next day a running fight continued. With the help of a platoon of Inniskillings, which by then had joined the pursuit, further casualties were inflicted. The Mau Mau dead included Kago himself, shot by a tribal policeman.

In this action District Officer Ian Paterson was killed. A fortnight later, another district officer, Richard Wood-White, was killed in action in the same district. He had set off with two tribal policemen in pursuit of two Mau Mau when they ran into a large gang near Gakurwe. The two police were killed outright and Wood-White was wounded in the shoulder while attempting to save their rifles. Headman Daciano came to his assistance but, before they had gone far, Wood-White was killed. The headman escaped through thick bush. Reinforcements then arrived and dispersed the gang.

Mau Mau attacks continued into May and then ceased as far as armed posts were concerned, but tip-and-run raids and ambushes continued. An order from Dedan Kimathi written about this time fell later into the hands of the police, admitting that Mau Mau was now too weak to attempt further attacks on guard posts. That was the beginning of the end, but two and a half more years were to elapse before the complete finish came.

The last phase of the revolt began in about September 1954, when serious offensive operations by Mau Mau had almost ceased. The revolt was virtually over but the remaining insurgents had to be worn down and rounded up, until the last remnant was captured. It ended in December 1956 with the capture of Dedan Kimathi by Tribal Police as he was attempting to cross a ditch which had been dug along 50 miles of the forest edge.

The only notable features of this phase were those of organisation. Concentration of the Kikuyu population into protected villages had begun in parts of Nyeri district in 1953.[16] The primary object in the first instance had been to enable a watch to be kept on doubtful characters and prevent their helping Mau Mau, but it was soon realised that they had equal value for the protection of loyalists when provided with guard and observation posts. All districts of the province took up the plan. A strict curfew was observed. Cattle were driven to pasture under armed escort and, as far as possible, agriculture was similarly protected. Village schools were brought inside the enclosure. From first to last the process took about two years and it was applied, in general, to all exposed locations.

By the middle of 1955 the general population had veered decisively to the government side, and were now prepared to turn out in their thousands in support of sweeps by the security forces. In the changed circumstances it was no longer necessary to retain as many as 22,000 Kikuyu, Embu and Meru guards, but there was more need for fully-trained mobile patrols and combat units. The tribal police was therefore increased to 1,800 men, and a Tribal Police reserve was formed by a selection of the best from the Guard, the remainder of which was run down at the discretion of district commissioners to the number required for watch and ward duties. This both increased the efficiency of the forces needed to cope with the changed circumstances and also forestalled the potential danger of a decline in morale of Guards; for courageously as they had fought in the struggle for the reserves, there was always a threat of indiscipline when frustrations mounted, and, although there was no longer very much danger of desertion, several had taken to the life of vagrants, eking out a precarious existence in and around the prohibited strip.[17]

Meanwhile a new type of combat unit had taken the field after some months of intensive preparation. These were the pseudo-gangs, comprised of captured Mau Mau now operating under the general control of the Special Branch. Any apprehension as to the wisdom of the experiment was soon dispelled for, disguised as Mau Mau gangs, they fought with astonishing bravery and with no desertions.[18] The Kenya

16 Elkins, *Britain's Gulag*, Chapter 8, argues that villagisation was the most brutal price Kikuyu paid for Mau Mau; Branch, *Defeating Mau Mau*, pp. 107–15, shows that protected 'loyalist' villages fared little better than punitive 'Mau Mau' ones.

17 This is not the whole story behind the disbandment of the Kikuyu Guard in early 1955; Fazan returns to the more pressing reasons below, as discussed in the Foreword.

18 Frank Kitson, *Gangs and Counter-gangs* (London: Barrie & Rockliff, 1960) and Parker, *Last Colonial Regiment*, pp. 288–314, 331–2, for complementary accounts of the pseudo-gangs; Bennett, *Defeating the Mau Mau*, pp. 152–9, 243–6, summarises the story; for reference to personal memoirs, see Lonsdale, 'Kenya: Home County', p. 109, footnote 58.

Police and the KPR, both of which had been enormously expanded since the beginning of the Emergency and had given valuable support to the district administration throughout, were now able to divert the greater part of their attention to the protection of the towns and the Highlands.

In an effort to restore normal conditions, the African tribunals, which had been inoperative in the affected districts since the beginning of the acute phase of the emergency, were now re-established. Large numbers of detainees were filtered back through works camps to their homes by a process which involved careful screening, open public confession of their Mau Mau past, and a fine of 60 shillings to the African district council in token of sincerity.

When all active resistance had ceased, the governor, Sir Evelyn Baring, resigned. In spite of his own increasing ill-health he had seen the Emergency through to its successful conclusion and normal conditions of peace and security restored.[19] A considerable period of time, however, was still to elapse before an official end to the Emergency could be proclaimed. Establishment had to be reduced to normal size, and many thousands of detainees had to be released, rehabilitated, and restored to their homes – a process which demanded patience and caution and could not be rushed. Finally, three full years after the arrest of Dedan Kimathi the new governor, Sir Patrick Renison, was able to declare the Emergency officially over, on the 12th January 1960.

★★★

The intention of the above description has been to present the Mau Mau revolt as a military campaign fought out in battles; and so far as possible without distorting the picture, mention has not been made of atrocities, or at least they have not been dwelt on. It is common knowledge that they occurred, but no lingering over these tragedies will help the sufferers; and besides, I fully respect the desire of the

19 Douglas-Home's biography, *Evelyn Baring*, pp. 243–4, 251, 253, 258–9, 275, 281, 285, 299, does not support Fazan's apparent inference that Baring resigned on health grounds once military victory was won; on the contrary, while Baring was never strong and his indecision often criticised, his health had been protected by the appointment of a deputy governor, Frederick Crawford; his five-year term of office was also extended by two years, to late 1959, when he was aged 56. The British government, under parliamentary attack for counterinsurgent brutalities, was anxious to preserve the public appearance of confidence in Baring, lest the whole apparatus of authority collapse under scrutiny. Moreover, Baring was himself keen to embark on what was called the 'second prong' of counterinsurgency, the economic developments discussed in the next chapter.

government of independent Kenya to approach the future in a spirit of amnesty and good will.

The matter, though, cannot be wholly set aside for the purposes of this account, for it had political consequences. As well as the savage and unprovoked attacks by Mau Mau on civilians and their homes, there was also constant anxiety about the treatment of detainees by unruly elements in the security forces, and while by far the former was the most sensational, it was the latter that caused the most searching questions to be asked. In some of the guard posts and a few camps, especially those where the most obdurate detainees were held, there were incidents of prisoners being beaten and mistreated, and allegations were made of a few Mau Mau suspects having died under interrogation while in custody of the Guard. Further, there was reason to believe that there were instances of violence and extortion where certain members of the Guard had used their power to pay off old scores. Another cause for concern was the sanitary condition of the camps where outbreaks of fever claimed several lives.[20]

---

20 Fazan notes two different sectors of the counterinsurgency campaign: the detention camps, under the colony's prisons department; and, among the fighting forces, the Kikuyu Guard, for which his old service, the provincial administration, was responsible. The often disgraceful conditions and punitive abuses in the detention camp 'pipeline' have received increasing exposure with the emergence of archival evidence. The earliest firsthand account, Josiah Mwangi Kariuki, *'Mau Mau' Detainee* (London: Oxford University Press, 1963), told how detainees were at times able press for (temporary) relief of harsh conditions; Wambui Waiyaki Otieno, *Mau Mau's Daughter: A Life History* (Boulder, CO: Lynne Reinner, 1998), Chapter 5, remembered unremitting brutality and sexual violence – what Elkins, *Britain's Gulag*, called the continued war behind the wire, with white officers and black staff determined to exercise control over detainees equally determined to resist illegal confinement. Derek R. Peterson, *Ethnic Patriotism and the East African Revival: A History of Dissent c. 1935–1972* (Cambridge: Cambridge University Press, 2012), Chapter 10, has complicated Elkins' analysis with discussion of how detainees conducted self-criticism and corresponded with their wives, in an effort to re-examine the moral basis of their society – an effort that in one case Fazan, as member of the committee to review detainees' appeals, regarded as 'sincere fanaticism' (Peterson, p. 228). Two 'rehabilitation' officials had contrasting recollections of what 'worked' – force and negotiation, respectively: Terence Gavaghan, *Of Lions and Dung Beetles: A 'Man in the Middle' of Colonial Administration in Kenya* (Ilfracombe: Stockwell, 1999) and James Breckenridge, *40 Years in Kenya* (Bridport: Creeds, 2002). Anderson has followed up his earlier inquiry into counterinsurgent 'crimes of punishment' (*Histories*, Chapter 7) with research prompted by the successful Mau Mau legal case for British reparations; this research was made possible by the release of the 'migrated archive' of secret late-colonial files from Hanslope Park into the National Archive (formerly the Public Record Office or PRO) at Kew, to be archived in the series FCO 141. See D. M. Anderson, 'Mau Mau in the high court and the "lost" British Empire archives: Colonial

It is abundantly clear that there was never any policy of systematic torture of detainees by government, and not one case has been established of an order to abuse a prisoner having been given on good authority.[21] On the contrary, the government and Army chiefs took care to maintain law and discipline at all times. In April 1953 the government delivered a stern public warning to its officials concerning the treatment of detainees and their property and General Erskine, likewise, gave warning to the Army and police in no uncertain terms that maltreatment of civilians and prisoners would not be tolerated. Putting words into action, scores of prosecutions were subsequently brought for the mistreatment of prisoners. It was clear, however, that the legal process was not the most efficient way of dealing with the problem because, as with Mau Mau cases, evidence was hard to gather and also, perhaps, because it was felt that excessive zeal to prosecute and harsh penalties might lower morale and only serve to increase indiscipline. The eventual result was that a second amnesty offered to the Mau Mau in January 1955 was also applied to the Guard under

conspiracy or bureaucratic bungle?' *Journal of Imperial and Commonwealth History* 39 (2011), pp. 699–716, for an indication of what will emerge about the sometimes atrocious lengths to which officials, policemen, soldiers and prison warders felt driven in order to dominate when the legal institutions of power, never sophisticated, reverted to brute force under insurgent attack. Fazan goes some way to explain the loss of discipline; Bennett in *Fighting the Mau Mau*, deepens the analysis, in stressing the legacy of the ignorant anger of the first phase of counterinsurgency and, later, the growing acceptance by the higher command that to restore discipline in the security forces, both white and black, would require sanctions that neither British troops nor Kikuyu Guard were likely to tolerate. Denials and covers-up were the inevitable consequence. Some British conscripts had little sympathy for settler landlords and were reluctant to shoot, and the loyalty of 'loyalists' always needed tender care, frequently averted eyes and, at times, official collusion or perjury. For the high-political calculus of denial, see Philip Murphy, *Alan Lennox-Boyd, a Biography* (London: I.B.Tauris, 1999), pp. 150–5. For the inevitability of escalating violence, see Branch, *Defeating Mau Mau*. For solidarity between former district officers and their Kikuyu allies, see David Lovatt Smith, *Kenya, the Kikuyu and Mau Mau* (Herstmonceux: Mawenzi Books, 2005). French, *British Way*, pp. 132–7, concludes, after comparing casualty rates in 11 late-colonial or post-colonial emergencies from Palestine to Borneo, that British conduct in Kenya was the 'most vicious' of all, if much less so than French conduct in Algeria.

21 While there may have been no government *policy* of systematic torture, the archival evidence now becoming available leaves little doubt that it became a *practice* that the government, increasingly, found it had to tolerate. For firsthand white admissions of this fact see Robert B. Edgerton, *Mau Mau: An African Crucible* (London: Collier Macmillan, 1989), Chapters 5 and 6; Parker, *Last Colonial Regiment*, pp. 367–8.

the same terms.[22] Meanwhile, at field level, district commissioners made strenuous efforts to weed out unsuitable temporary officers in camps and guard posts. The same efforts were also made by the inspector general in the KPR. As for the conditions in screening and detention camps, although it was argued that some of the illness was caused by external infection, there was no denying that they were insanitary and efforts were made to clean them up, with better equipment and proper inspection. The result was a marked improvement in sanitation and health.

For all these efforts the fact remains that throughout the Emergency there were persistent complaints about the treatment of Mau Mau suspects and detainees. Many of them must have had a factual basis – although there were several attempts by Mau Mau to fabricate evidence – and there can be no doubt that successful convictions only represent a part of the problem. This recurrent indiscipline attracted criticism but, more than that, at a time of slender parliamentary majorities in Britain, it provided opposition members with the opportunity to embarrass the government. This came to a head in March 1959, when the scandal of the Hola camp broke shortly before the British general election.[23] At Hola camp in Coast province a number of the most intractable rebels were detained where they refused to co-operate with the camp authorities at all. In an effort to coerce them into work a riot broke out which was beaten back with batons leaving 11 dead. In the subsequent political furore it was not so much these deaths that were at issue as suspicion of a 'cover-up' for, most ill-advisedly, the camp staff had initially reported that the tragedy had been caused by polluted water. No evidence was produced to show that the administration of the colony was culpably party to this conspiracy,[24]

---

22 As discussed in the Foreword, Fazan made no mention of this second amnesty in his *History of the Loyalists.*

23 For the Hola massacre's place in the wider history of British decolonisation, see Robert Shepherd, *Iain Macleod, a Biography* (London: Pimlico, 1994), pp. 154–61. Ronald Hyam, *Britain's Declining Empire: The Road to Decolonization 1918–1968* (Cambridge: Cambridge University Press, 2006), pp. 263–4, argues (in an oracular echo of Murphy, *Alan Lennox-Boyd*, p. 203) that 3 March 1959, the date of both the massacre and the declaration of emergency in Nyasaland/Malawi, might be the 'single fateful date which signalled the moral end of the British empire in Africa'. For that same 'moral unease', see Blundell, *So Rough a Wind*, p. 256.

24 There had been no riot; camp warders had beaten detainees for refusing to work. Fazan's careful phrasing, 'not culpably party', to describe government's initially false information that the deaths had been caused by polluted water, not by illegal beatings, has been refuted by Anderson, *History*, p. 327.

but the opposition lost no chance to hound the Conservative government of the day and the colonial secretary in particular. Inevitably the storm passed, but the government had had an anxious moment and the prime minister, Harold Macmillan, and aspiring young Conservatives may well have formed a definite view at this time that the colonies were not worth the fuss.

★★★

There are discrepancies in the estimates of casualties incurred during the Emergency but the number of Mau Mau killed in action was probably rather more than 10,000, and nearly half of them were accounted for by the Guard and Tribal Police. Against this the security forces lost nearly 600, the great majority being Africans. There is no reliable estimate of the number of civilians killed by Mau Mau. There were probably at least 2,000, but not more than 3,000, and of these, 32 were European and 26 were Asian. The number of convicted terrorists executed during the Mau Mau campaign was just over 1,000. The great majority of these were for the offences of murder, oath administration in its most serious forms, the illegal possession of firearms and explosives, and supplying Mau Mau. In the later stages of the campaign, as restrictions were eased, the mandatory death penalty was lifted from a number of offences. This was partly because of doubts which had been raised about the quality of the evidence in a number of firearms cases.[25]

When hostilities had ceased, everyone but a handful of irreconcilables was immensely pleased that it was all over and it left surprisingly little bitterness behind. As the trouble subsided, however, many questions still remained to be answered. Those which need here to be considered concern the nature of the war and the strategy of either side.

As to the first question, it is beyond dispute that the campaign had an element of civil war in it. Even at a personal level it was most distressing that of the two leading Africans I knew best and, perhaps, respected most, one should have been allegedly implicated in the plot to kill the other.[26] But despite the fact of African fighting African, the loyalists could not have held out by themselves without the Army and police at their backs. Only in the latter phases, in 1955 and 1956, could it be said

25 See Anderson, *Histories*, for the capital punishment of Mau Mau convicts. Fazan's estimate of up to 3,000 victims of Mau Mau murders is calmer than lurid estimates of up to 30,000 at the time – a figure quoted in military circles.

26 See the discussion of Chiefs Koinange and Waruhiu, above, Foreword, note 61.

that Kikuyu public opinion was firmly for the government and that the loyalists, by themselves, or with little outside support, were strong enough to drive the Mau Mau out.

Whatever the strength of the loyalists as against Mau Mau, the choice they faced was never one between British rule and self-government. There could have been few Africans, if any, who could not have hoped for the latter. The differences arose as to how it should be achieved and even among the Kikuyu there were divisions between those for whom it was an immediate aspiration and others who favoured orderly change.[27]

The first group were mainly young men who were easily influenced by agitators and worked up into a state of indignation by highly exaggerated stories about stolen land. The other group was essentially comprised of chiefs and headmen who, with later support from the elders, saw Mau Mau as a flouting of tribal custom as much as of law and order; and there were many besides those with local vested interests who ranged themselves readily in their support. In the middle were perhaps the majority, who were mainly in sympathy with Mau Mau aims but waited to see how things would go and, finally, disgusted with terrorism in its extreme forms and longing for a return to a more peaceful life, rallied to the government side. In shaping loyalist opinion, another element that should not be overlooked is the influence of the Christian church. Some of the most outstanding loyalists were staunch Christians appalled by the Mau Mau excesses, and there were one or two cases of true martyrdom.[28]

As to the Mau Mau and government plans of campaign, the most curious feature of the former is that they never attempted any major act of sabotage. For instance, the main piped water supply to Nairobi, exposed for a considerable part of its length, ran through Kikuyu country, but no attempt was ever made to damage it. Nor, beyond nuisances such as thefts of telegraph wire, were any serious attempts made to damage main communications. It certainly is not the case that Mau Mau failed to think of these things. Probably the chief reason why they refrained is that they realised that such acts would damage

---

27 Fazan was unquestionably correct in this opinion, as could not have been admitted in his 1961 *History of the Loyalists*; elite 'loyalists' went on to win the politics of independence, to the lasting advantage of their descendants. Many 'loyalists', however, (Branch, *Defeating Mau Mau*, pp. 126–30), were poor, powerless, and neglected.

28 This is as plausible summary of the differences in Kikuyu opinion as one can find.

themselves as much as the government and that the repercussions throughout the country would alienate them from the sympathy of other tribes; for they were well aware that outrages such as Lari had seriously undermined their chances of building a wider basis of support and had put paid to any hopes of attracting help from sympathisers living outside the country.

On occasions of civil insurrection government is seldom allowed to be right, whatever it does, and there has never been any shortage of criticism of the government plan of campaign. Of all its policies it is probably the detention camps that have occasioned the most disquiet, even though the authorities were well aware that detainees should be constantly filtered back into the community and, to that end, had provided craft instruction in the camps. I have often wondered, though, whether the government could not have been adventurous. It was a view I held at the time and still maintain, for my experience in Germany after the Second World War had taught me how essential it was to keep the tap running. Further, it seemed to me that although the attempts to negotiate an amnesty with the insurgents were a failure, there was a chance that if one or two of the senior and influential detainees had been released for talks and also allowed to take part in approaches to Mau Mau, far better results might have been obtained. None of the young men who formed the leadership of the active Mau Mau had any significant influence before the hostilities, but there were some among the detainees who were of high standing in the Kikuyu tribe and were respected for their moderation. Although these senior detainees may have thrown in their lot with Mau Mau, it is almost certain that some of them were disturbed, if not horrified, at the turn events had taken, and could possibly, on release, have exercised a highly beneficial influence among their people.

16

Economic Development[1]

The political tensions which culminated in the Mau Mau revolt, and for a time caused great damage to farming in the Central and Rift Valley provinces, did not cause more than a temporary lapse in the influx of new capital and post-war expansion. New enterprise and investment was tentative only for a while but, as soon as it became evident that government was determined to suppress the revolt and had the power to do so, confidence was restored. After the four years' disturbance

1 Fazan did well to devote a chapter to post-war economic development, a process that continued into the first decade and more of independence, causing talk of 'the Kenya exception' to more general postcolonial African failures. Historians differ over causes and outcomes. A starting point must be the weak tax base of a poor colony, limiting its capacity to fund loan expenditure or provide a profitable field for direct private investment; see Leigh Gardner, 'An Unstable Foundation: Taxation and Development in Kenya 1945–53' in Daniel Branch; and Nic Cheeseman and Leigh Gardner (eds), *Our Turn to East: Politics in Kenya since 1950* (Berlin: LIT Verlag, 2010), pp. 53–76. There are opposing views on what was built on this uncertain base. On the positive side, scholars have noted the economically nationalist policy of the late-colonial state. See Berman, *Control and Crisis*, Chapters 6, 7 and 10; Michael McWilliam, 'The Managed Economy: Agricultural Change, Development, and Finance in Kenya, 1945–1963', in D. A. Low and Alison Smith (eds), *History of East Africa* Vol III (Oxford: Clarendon, 1976), pp. 251–89; Kitching, *Class and Economic Change*, Chapter XIII; Robert L. Tignor, *Capitalism and Nationalism at the End of Empire: State and Business in Decolonizing Egypt, Nigeria, and Kenya, 1945–1963* (Princeton NJ: Princeton University Press, 1998), Chapter 9; and David Himbara, *Kenyan Capitalists, the State, and Development* (Boulder, CO: Lynne Rienner, 1994), Chapter 4. Others have added that this entrepreneurial state role was supported by international capital's interest in raising productivity in both smallholder farming and the urban workforce, seen in the extension of African-grown coffee and tea and the growth of urban trade unionism. Smallholder prosperity and urban labour 'stabilisation' were also complementary parts of an explicitly political project – to reduce the migrant labour flows between the two sectors that had assisted the spread of the Mau Mau. For this perspective, see in particular, Michael Cowen, 'Commodity

caused by Mau Mau, recovery was swift. Some of the principal directions of expansion were in the extension of the wharves and docks at the port of Kilindini; the new Nairobi airport; the great improvement in main roads throughout the country – a process which had received much impetus from the magnificent work of the Italian prisoners of war, who had worked as if in their own country and had shown the Public Works Department a thing or two; the search for oil, not without some favourable indications; the beginning of the oil refinery at Mombasa; the intensive development of electric power resources; much improved water supplies in the main towns; and some development of heavy industry, of which the chief example was cement production in quantities sufficient for Kenya's needs and for export to Uganda too.

All sections of the population were increasing fast. There was only one of Kenya's ten leading towns that did not double its population between 1948 and 1962. The figure for Nairobi rose from 118, 276 to 266,700 and for Mombasa from 84,746 to 178,400. The European population, which stood at about 45,000 at the end of the post-war rush, had reached something like 65,000 by 1960.

Nairobi, along with Mombasa, was the barometer of the economy, although it sometimes reflected hope of things to come rather than actual prosperity in being. It was also, with the growing influence of the [East African] High Commission, in a fair way to becoming the political, as it already was the commercial, hub of East Africa. But despite its importance, it had been an untidy town from the start and was worse at the end of the war. Apart from the landscape, a few good buildings, and a passable lay-out on generous lines, it had little to show

production in Kenya's Central Province', in Judith Heyer, Pepe Roberts and Gavin Williams (eds), *Rural Development in Tropical Africa* (London: Macmillan, 1981), pp. 121–42; Alice Amsden, *International Firms and Labour in Kenya 1945–1970* (London: Routledge, 1971); Frederick Cooper, *Decolonization and African Society: The Labor Question in French and British Africa* (Cambridge: Cambridge University Press, 1996). For the opposite view, that an unequal neo-colonial alliance between multinational capitalists and a weak African ruling class continued a colonial interest in an 'underdevelopment' that supplied primary products to the world market, see Colin Leys, *Underdevelopment in Kenya: The Political Economy of Neo-colonialism 1964–1971* (London: Heinemann, 1975). Leys moderated this criticism in 'Learning from the Kenya Debate', in his *The Rise & Fall of Development Theory* (London: James Currey, 1996), when he had learned more about Kenya's own entrepreneurs. Whether these were primarily South Asian or African is disputed between Himbara, *Kenyan Capitalists*, and Michael Cowen and Scott McWilliam, *Indigenous Capital in Kenya: The 'Indian' dimension of debate* (Helsinki: Institute of Development Studies, 1996).

in the way of architecture or aesthetic features and the war had added a succession of storage dumps and barbed wire fences extending a couple of miles or more out into the Athi Plains. Indeed, it seemed no great exaggeration when a writer to the *East African Standard* described Nairobi on the eve of its receiving city status as a 'wen on the face of Africa' – but most people found it a lively place.

Two events brought the first big change. One was that, in 1949, the council raised a loan of £1.5 million which was several times over-subscribed. The other was the arrival, scarcely less significant, of Peter Greensmith, who took charge of the beautification of Nairobi's avenues and open spaces. The most spectacular outcome was Princess Elizabeth Way,[2] which, running right through the town and the best part of the way to the airport and bordered with bougainvillea standards and flowering shrubs, must have been one of the most beautiful highways in Africa. The same treatment of beauty combined with utility was applied wherever possible to all main thoroughfares and island roundabouts in Nairobi.

New amenities and cultural facilities added in this post-war period included the national theatre and cultural centre, several new hotels and clubs, social and athletic facilities, including the multiracial United Kenya Club and, outside the town, Mitchell Park with its many beautiful trees and the Nairobi National Game Park. The King George VI Memorial Hospital, the Kenya High School for Girls and the various faculty blocks of the Royal University College were among the fine public buildings completed or undertaken in this period.[3] Many other large new buildings – shops, hotels, offices and banks – put a new face on the town, so that Nairobi could, by 1960, compare very creditably with any other city in tropical Africa. Indeed, by any standards, it had become an attractive place with a sense of energy and purpose about it. Between the former limits of the town and the airport a new factory and industrial area had been planned and was growing fast, more or less on the site of the old army dumps, and, in connection with it, a new residential quarter, mainly occupied by Asians, had come into being.

The usual difficulties were experienced in finding suitable quarters for Africans at rentals which they could afford to pay, and these were enhanced in the case of Nairobi by the immense increase in the population. It was hard enough to find accommodation for the workers,

---

2 Now Uhuru Highway.

3 Park, hospital, and college are now Jamhuri Park, Kenyatta Hospital and the University of Nairobi.

but no sooner had a room or a share of a room been found for one of them than all sorts of unemployed relatives would squeeze themselves in. The city council and, before it, the municipal council had done their best with housing schemes, but the rapidity of expansion had always outrun their efforts. Unauthorised, or at least irregular, shanty settlements had grown up outside the municipal limits. These were partially demolished as counter-measures in the Mau Mau rising. Meanwhile, the council stepped up its efforts to provide housing for Africans genuinely employed in the town and, with the help of government, took such steps as were possible to keep vagrants away. But the problem was perennial.[4]

In all the other towns and most of the trading centres throughout Kenya, similar but more modest developments were taking place. The typical Indian *duka* ceased in these years to be an unsightly shack of wood and iron. Well-built shops along properly tarmacked and curbed streets were now the common form. What was of more significance was that Africans were slowly but surely finding their way into trade. While they were seldom found as principals in general goods stores, they frequently had their own repair shops for motorcars and bicycles and many were doing responsible work in garages and a few owned petrol pumps. Cobbling and leatherwork was another trade they favoured.[5]

African cooperative companies had been quite common with the Kikuyu before the war, but too often they ended in quarrels and breakdown between the parties.[6] After the war, with more success,

4 For the conflict, often fought by bulldozers, between the ingenuity of the poor in building their own shelter and the city authorities' efforts to provide cheap housing in orderly neighbourhoods, see Andrew Hake, *African Metropolis: Nairobi's Self-help City* (London: Sussex University Press, 1977); and chapters by Achola, Anderson, Lonsdale, Frederiksen, and Atieno Odhiambo in Andrew Burton (ed.), *The Urban Experience in Eastern Africa c.1750–2000* (Nairobi: British Institute in Eastern Africa, 2002).

5 Kenneth King, *The African Artisan: Education and the Informal Sector in Kenya* (London: Heinemann, 1977) and idem, *Jua Kali Kenya: Change and Development in an Informal Economy, 1970–95* (London: James Currey, 1996) pay tribute to the entrepreneurship Fazan noticed. Possibly because the Kikuyu men with whom he had worked earlier were often so disapproving, Fazan failed to see women's role in trade of various kinds, for which see Luise White, *The Comforts of Home: Prostitution in Colonial Nairobi* (Chicago, IL: University of Chicago Press, 1990) and Claire C. Robertson, *Trouble Showed the Way: Women, Men, and Trade in the Nairobi Area, 1890–1990* (Bloomington, IN: Indiana University Press, 1997).

6 For passionate Kikuyu agreement with this statement, see Henry Muoria, 'What should we do, our People?' (1945), in Wangari Muoria-Sal, Bodil Folke Frederiksen, John Lonsdale and Derek Peterson (eds), *Writing for Kenya: The Life and Works of Henry Muoria* (Leiden: Brill, 2009), pp. 137–251.

Africans of several tribes – predominantly Kikuyu, Akamba, Luo, and coast Swahili – were running their own bus and general transport companies, and a few were acting as middlemen, loading produce at local markets and transporting it to the railhead. Cooperative ventures actually dealing in produce, for instance in wattle bark, were fairly common, but they were not often successful. They usually got into debt and, as with so much that Kikuyu handled, became involved in politics to the detriment of business. Nevertheless, however much they might initially take the wrong course, these incursions into trade by Africans were a symptom wholly to be welcomed.

Along with the increasing incidence of Africans in trade there was a rapid development of African trade union activity, which first manifested itself on any great scale in the Mombasa dock strike of 1947.[7] Embryo trade unions started by Indians had been formed in the mid-30s and, from as early as 1937 the government had taken measures to foster their development.[8] They had great attraction to the Kikuyu and Luo tribes, partly, no doubt, for their value as a political weapon. So to ensure that the unions were properly run and also to guard against loose-knit political associations masquerading under their cover, the government took care to maintain a register of bona fide unions. However, it did not stop unregistered unions from operating, and in 1950 matters came to a head when the East African Trades Union Congress was proscribed.[9] As it happened, government measures to prevent groups of political extremists from exploiting organized labour did not impose a serious check on the nationalists' cause for, during the Mau Mau and its aftermath, while there were no political parties, bona fide unions were allowed to remain in being and were to become the main focus and point of dissemination for political ideas. Although the unions were weakened during the Mau Mau by the detention of

7 Frederick Cooper, *On the African Waterfront: Urban Disorder and the Transformation of Work in Colonial Mombasa* (New Haven, CT: Yale University Press, 1987) for the Mombasa story; this study reinforces the 'positive' perspective on relations between the state, capital, and trades unionism in late-colonial Kenya, while showing the strains between them.

8 Makhan Singh, *History of Kenya's Trade Union Movement to 1952* (Nairobi: East African Publishing House, 1969) for the Sikh contribution to Kenya's trade union history; see also Gerard McCann, 'Sikh communities in Southeast Asia and East Africa, *c.*1870–1970' (Cambridge University: PhD dissertation, 2009), pp. 214–21, 238–42.

9 Hyde, 'Nairobi general strike'.

many of their members, their organisation remained intact, and the Kenya Federation of Registered Trade Unions (later the Kenya Federation of Labour) founded in 1952, was, under the skilful guidance of Tom Mboya, to become an important organ of political opinion.[10]

Over all, and in spite of Mau Mau, these post-war years to 1960 saw, by the end of them, great increase in all the major farming activities in the Highlands, the African Lands, and, in a more modest measure, on the coast as well. The many years of patient endeavour which the settlers had devoted to their farms in the Highlands were now showing their full effect. As one gazed over wide prospects of developed farms and homesteads stretching out over the valleys for miles, one could not help but admire what they had achieved.

In the African Lands there had not been, since the later 1930s, any question of holding back any type of agricultural production from any area where it could profitably be grown.[11] Except in Kikuyu, where the Mau Mau rising had caused devastation for the four years of its duration, there was everywhere great advance. The field officers of the agricultural department devoted the greatest part of their attention to African Lands and even Mau Mau contributed indirectly – for the concentration into villages, which was originally undertaken for protection against their attacks, greatly facilitated the demarcation of private family land holdings and, where necessary, the consolidation of fragmented holdings into viable blocks. Thus the whole appearance of the Kikuyu country was changed. In place of innumerable clusters of single-family hutments scattered all over the landscape there were now planned settlements with populations up to about 3,000, which were already being called towns by the inhabitants. There were 110 of them in the Kiambu district, absorbing virtually the whole population, and arrangements in the other districts were similar. It was a golden opportunity for planning

10 For changing British attitudes to Mboya, from hostility to courtship, see David Goldsworthy, *Tom Mboya: The Man Kenya Wanted to Forget* (London: Heinemann, 1982), Part 2; Keith Kyle, *The Politics of the Independence of Kenya* (Basingstoke: Macmillan, 1999), pp. 75–86, 108, 119–20, 130–1.

11 This is certainly true. See, for example, David Anderson and David Throup, 'Africans and agricultural production in colonial Kenya: The myth of the war as a watershed', *Journal of African History* 26 (1985), pp. 327–45; Lonsdale, 'The depression and the Second World War'; Kitching, *Class and Economic Change*, Chapter IV.

the intervening farmland and consolidating fragmented holdings and fortunately money was forthcoming.[12]

A Royal Commission – the East Africa Commission of 1953 under the chairmanship of Sir Hugh Dow – had been appointed by royal warrant and was enjoined, having regard to the rapid rate of increase among the African population and the congestion on the land in certain localities, to 'examine the measures necessary to be taken to achieve an improved standard of living, including the introduction of capital to enable peasant farming to develop and expand production and frame recommendations thereon...'.[13] Coincidentally, a plan named after its principal author, the Swynnerton plan, had been prepared locally for the furtherance of African agriculture, especially in the planting of cash crops and the development of peasant farming on small family holdings. With the publication of the Royal Commission's report in 1955 and the grant by the British government of £5,500,000 which followed, it became possible to put the Swynnerton plan into energetic operation.[14]

Almost everywhere in the Kikuyu districts the local inhabitants were firmly in favour of the proposals, but a period of at least six months was

12 This policy was the logical, if rushed and, in part, punitive conclusion of what Fazan had called for in his minority report of the Kikuyu Land Tenure Committee of 1929 and had got the Carter Commission to recommend in 1934. For the fullest account of land reform, see Sorrenson, *Land Reform in the Kikuyu Country*, Parts 2 and 3. For an enthusiastic account, see Elspeth Huxley, *A New Earth: An Experiment in Colonialism* (London: Chatto & Windus, 1960), Chapters 15 and 16; for the darker side, Elkins, *Britain's Gulag*, Chapter 8. Branch, *Defeating Mau Mau*, pp. 120–5, shows how land consolidation and registration filled a counterinsurgent need for rewards and punishments, as part of a class-forming policy in search of the reliably-sturdy Kikuyu 'yeoman', another romantic medieval borrowing, like the 'seigniory' of 1929.

13 The commission was appointed in response to the concern expressed by Kenya's former governor, Sir Philip Mitchell, about the race between population growth, agrarian productivity, and ecological degradation. The quotation comes from the royal warrant of 1 January 1953 in the preliminary pages of the commission's *Report*, p. ix. As noted in the Foreword, Fazan met the commission's chairman, Sir Hugh Dow, at an early stage of the enquiry. The record of their conversation does not suggest that Fazan's views had any great influence on the commission's thinking.

14 Roger Swynnerton, then deputy director of agriculture, gathered all projects already under discussion into a 'plan'. For differing assessments of the 'agricultural revolution' this may have encouraged, see Huxley, *A New Earth* for the view that the land reform and technical assistance generated a generally beneficial revolution in productivity; Judith Heyer, 'Agricultural Development Policy in Kenya from the Colonial Period to 1975', in Heyer et al. (eds), *Rural Development*, pp. 90–120, for the greater importance of the expansion of tree crops, coffee and tea, among African growers; and Kitching, *Class and Economic Change*, Chapter XI, for the sceptical view –

given over to explanation before a consolidation plan was prepared in any area. Fewer obstacles were encountered than expected and, in the course of the next two or three years, practically the whole of the three Kikuyu districts had been covered. But the demand for private land holdings with registered title did not stop with the Kikuyu, for it quickly spread to other tribes. By 1959 schemes had been applied to favourable parts of the Meru, Elgon, Elgeyo and Marakwet districts and interest was spreading in Nyanza Province and even in Uganda.[15]

The broad plan of consolidation, as applied in the Kikuyu districts, was that a proportion of the land concerned – in some cases, a fifth – was taken for the village centre, roads, commonage, and village allotments, and the rest was divided between right-holders in proportion to the size of their original holdings, each receiving his land in a single block. These blocks differed greatly in size, from upwards of 100 acres to less than an acre. Consolidation did not, by itself, deprive anybody of land rights.[16] Tenants who appeared to be adversely affected were given compensation, or village allotments, or both. Collateral relatives of the registered owner did not lose their rights, but legislation was contemplated to guard against properties becoming too congested by a multiplicity of heirs succeeding on the death of the registered owner. It was clear, however, that until the country was more industrially developed so as to offer alternative means of employment for superfluous right-holders, limitations of this kind could only be introduced with great caution.

When the consolidation of a block was completed, farm layouts were prepared with the assistance of agricultural officers and their staff of African supervisors and instructors. A safe proportion would first be reserved for subsistence crops, pasturage, and fallow. The remainder would then be planned for appropriate cash crops, frequently coffee or, in higher areas, tea or pyrethrum. The earliest schemes were started in

---

based largely on the researches of Michael Cowen – that the Swynnerton era merely confirmed a tendency for 'better farmers' to rely on their off-farm employment to fund the purchase and improvement of land, while smallholders without such off-farm income were excluded from any benefits, falling over time into the ranks of the labouring poor.

15 So fulfilling Fazan's minority vision in the *Report* of the 1929 Kikuyu Land Tenure Committee.

16 This statement fails to take into account the confiscations of some Mau Mau 'terrorists' land, the inability of some Mau Mau detainees to attend local land adjudication committees, the natural inclination of such committees to heed the claims of wealthier, more influential, local worthies, and a tendency for the individualisation of property to neglect previous obligations to women, widows especially.

Nyeri district in 1949; others followed and, in spite of the setback during the Man Mau years, there was an impressive acreage of tea and coffee by the end of the first decade of the scheme, sufficient to attract eulogistic notices in the local newspapers. Even bearing in mind the dangers of planting more than could be adequately supervised, a satisfactory start had undoubtedly been made. This applied not only to farming operations but also to the conservation work done on the land by means of bench terraces, wash-stops, hedging and ditching and, in the more pastoral area, the making of dams. An immense amount remained to be done, but the advance had been notable.

There was also a danger that too rapid an increase in the planting of coffee, tea, or other permanent crops by inexperienced growers might result in neglect, deterioration, and possibly disease, which would greatly damage Kenya's reputation in the markets. There was need not only for supervision on the land but also for research. For this and parallel purposes the East African Agricultural and Forestry Research Organisation had been established on an inter-territorial basis as a bureau of the High Commission to supplement the work of the Kenya Agricultural Research Board and the similar organisations of the other territories; and the East African Veterinary Research Organisation was set up to perform a similar service for the livestock industry. Both these organisations were quartered at Maguga, about 15 miles from Nairobi, and conveniently near to them was the Interterritorial Bureau for Animal Health which undertook far-reaching projects directed towards the eradication or control of animal diseases over wide regions of Africa. It was, at that time, part of the Commission for Technical Cooperation in Africa, an intergovernmental organisation of which Great Britain, France, Belgium, Portugal, South Africa and Rhodesia were the founder members, but with the coming of independence, great changes were clearly impending, and the Food and Agriculture section of the United Nations Organization later took it over.[17]

Fisheries research was another of the functions for which the High Commission was responsible. Because there was no export to places outside Africa, the fishing industry did not get its fair share of notice in the trade returns but within the East African territories it was a major enterprise. It was only after the First World War that the need for spending substantial sums on research and a more comprehensive organisation of the industry, both marine and lacustrine, was fully

17 This internationalisation of technical assistance to Africa was characteristic of the late-colonial era, as Britain relinquished sole responsibility.

appreciated. From the first the fishing industry had been almost entirely in the hands of Africans or Arabs as far as active operations were concerned, although Indians provided much of the capital and collected a large share of the profits. Timber was another of the basic industries to be greatly expanded. This applied not only to cedar, *podo*, *mvuli* and other valuable kinds of wood which were enough to meet all current requirements for building and furniture, but researches were also being made to find uses for other sorts which had not yet found a market. Mining and prospecting for minerals also continued but, apart from an occasional flare-up of interest, there was no spectacular development.

Last but by no means least of the natural resources industries was game preservation and the national parks. It would be impossible not to admire the wild animals and birds of Kenya or fail to find life happier because of them.[18] Nevertheless, there was a time in the early days of settlement when less was heard of the aesthetic pleasure they caused than of the potential menace wild antelope constituted to livestock farmers by the spread of tsetse fly and ticks. The government game department was small, and it was only gradually and with the help of a small band of enthusiasts that a balanced system of game management was evolved. It came to be recognised almost as a sacred trust that the various species must be preserved for the study and enjoyment of posterity and – a consideration of more immediate practical appeal – that they could become, through tourism, a premier source of revenue.

There was a substantial increase during these years in large-scale activities conducted by marketing boards and cooperatives in major products such as coffee, tea, sisal, meat, dairy produce, maize and wheat, and there was also marked development in industrial enterprises like factories, foundries, saw mills, breweries and the commercial exploitation of products such as Magadi soda ash or trade goods like Coca-Cola. There was also a very welcome increase during these years in subsidiary industries based on local products, or the processing and marketing of them, and in research directed to the discovery of new uses for by-products. Among these minor activities were handicrafts such as furniture-making from local timber, wood carving, boot and shoe-making and leather work of all kinds from local hides and skins,

18 See Edward I. Steinhart, *Black Poachers, White Hunters: A Social History of Hunting in Colonial Kenya* (Oxford: James Currey, 2006) for the long history of the national parks idea; and, for a personal account by a park warden – and former district officer in the Kikuyu Guard – David Lovatt Smith, *Amboseli: A Miracle Too Far?* (Herstmonceux: Mawenzi Books, 2008).

tanning from local wattle bark or mangroves, blankets from local wool, sisal products like carpets, rope and twine, canning of local produce, paints and dyes, traditional weaving and wicker work, pottery and milling. All these industries, great and small, were operating to support Kenya's main industry of farming and, at the same time, to offer alternative means of employment and thus to some extent relieve congestion on the land.

In the professional services which were vital to a young agricultural country – public health, education, and veterinary and agricultural research – Kenya had been exceptionally fortunate for a Crown Colony, especially in the higher strata of these services. The trouble was, however, that practically all the top posts requiring degrees were filled by Europeans and the technical diploma grades below them were mainly filled by Asians. This was not a healthy state of affairs in a predominantly African country, especially as the same thing was true of other professions, such as engineering, architecture and the law.[19]

It was obvious that great expansion and intensification of all these services would be required as soon as the revenue could afford them, and from all points of view it was desirable that Africans should be trained to qualify for the technical grades and, as soon thereafter as possible, for full professional status. This had long been recognised, but the process was slow, especially while funds were lacking. All the East African governments and, particularly, the High Commission, were fully alive to the problem and were taking such steps as they could. The conception of a composite University of East Africa with a college established in each of the territories and each of them specialising in a different range of subjects was being planned at this time and a start had been made. Medical training at Mulago College in Kampala was to be a speciality of Uganda, in addition to the all-round syllabus at Makerere. Legal training was to be offered at Dar es Salaam in Tanganyika. The Royal College in Nairobi was similarly to sponsor engineering, while the High Commission concentrated on veterinary, agricultural and forestry research at Muguga and the Scott Laboratories, both near Nairobi. Probably the whole conception postulated a greater degree of co-operation than was likely to be obtained indefinitely between the territories and, eventually, each of them would demand self-sufficiency

---

19 For professional training in East Africa, see John Iliffe, *East African Doctors: A History of the Modern Profession* (Cambridge: Cambridge University Press, 1998); for midwives, Lynn Thomas, *Politics of the Womb: Women, Reproduction, and the State in Kenya* (Berkeley, CA: University of California Press, 2003).

with all-round development. But it was a good start, although it could be foreseen that a long time must elapse before fully qualified Africans in these professions could be provided in substantial numbers and that Europeans would meanwhile continue to be indispensable, especially in research work.

Training to technical standards was more nearly in range and there were several places where instruction to diploma level was being given. As to general education, thanks largely to the missions, competent African teachers were coming forward in increasing numbers. It would be a long time, however, before anything like universal education could be contemplated in a country where population was rapidly expanding, parents were unable to afford the fees, and government resources were slender.

The children of all races were increasing fast. Certainly, by comparison with former days, they were thriving, and no race had made such strides forward as the Africans. Admittedly, one did not have far to go to find hunger and deficiency diseases even in the best districts, and some of the more remote areas were much the same as they had been but, regarding the country as a whole, the progress made in half a century was quite astonishing, considering that most of it had been done from the country's own resources, which had been built up from nothing. During this period, however, new money was at last forthcoming both from colonial development grants and from Kenya's own expanding revenues. The £5.5 million which Britain had made available for African agrarian development at the instance of the Royal Commission had been generally welcomed, seeing that it would enable the productive capacity of the Africans to realise its potential and play a full part in the economy, and that it would go far to dispel legitimate grievances Africans may have felt that their needs in this respect had received less than their fair share of attention.

There was, however, another aspect of the Royal Commission report that was not so well received, not least by the settler community. It was their recommendation that 'the Governor's approval to leases of land between persons of different race should be freely given'.[20] While this went further than many of the settlers would have been prepared to concede at the time, it was the context rather than the recommendation itself that caused alarm. So long as confidence remained, there would have been no need to expect any great number of such transactions for there was not at this time a large number of Europeans who wanted to

20 Royal Commission *Report*, p. 358.

dispose of their land, Africans with the capital to buy, or Asians who genuinely wanted to be farmers. But the tenor of the report showed that the commissioners were opposed to the concept of European Highlands and African Lands. They were, indeed, emphatic in dissociating themselves from it altogether: 'it will be gathered from the general tenor of our Report that our own approach is very different. [...] we think it necessary to encourage the breakdown of tribal and racial boundaries.'[21]

This was the first clear warning that the settlers had that the White Highlands policy was to be abandoned, and naturally it caused resentment. Certainly the time had come, and was overdue, for relaxation in the rigidity of the exclusion, but the commission's proposal seemed to go beyond what was immediately necessary and, coming at a time when things were just settling down to peaceful development after Mau Mau, their comment on the general policy appeared needlessly provocative. In purely economic terms there was little need for dissatisfaction with the way in which the Highlands policy was working out, whether looked at from the point of view of the settlers or, indeed, of the Africans, for even if the whole area of the Highlands had been thrown wide open to general settlement, it is doubtful whether it would have supported a much larger population than the quarter of a million or so, mostly Kikuyu, that was there already as resident labour on the farms.[22]

The fact is, however, that the problem was essentially political, not economic. The rapid growth of population in the African Lands had caused the Kikuyu and, to a lesser extent, other tribes to cast envious eyes on the European Highlands, yet they had been slow to make use of the facilities open to them in other parts of the Colony for spreading themselves wider. They had made practically no effort to take up land

21 Royal Commission *Report*, pp. 55–6; the commissioners here emphasised their opposition to the 'tribal approach' of the Carter Commission, Fazan's commission, an approach that had been required of it in its terms of reference.

22 Fazan here continues his meditation on the ethics and efficiency of Kenya's land allocation policy. The comparative economic and welfare potentials of different types of farming in Kenya's highlands – whether well-capitalised estates with labour forces, co-operative farms, independent smallholdings, etc. – have been much disputed and remain unresolved, being dependent on the state of markets for different crops, technical changes, the efficiency of government support services and so on. In the 1950s there were certainly plausible arguments to the effect that large white farms could support a larger African population in the Rift Valley area than African smallholder settlement.

on lease either in the 'native leasehold areas' or in any part of Kenya, such as the coast or the Tana Valley, where no racial restrictions applied, and in their own districts the drift of population was always towards, rather than away from the centres of greatest density.[23] True it was that there had been a fair amount of infiltration by family groups into unoccupied land in various parts, and quite large numbers, mostly Luo and Abaluhya but not Kikuyu, had migrated, a few at a time, to Uganda and Tanganyika. But in spite of these available outlets, the eyes of Kikuyu politicians were always on the European Highlands. And indeed it was right enough that, as Africans emerged to play an increasingly important role in modern Kenya, a system based on European ownership and African labour in so large an area in the heart of the country, however useful it may have been in the early days, could not be upheld as a principle any longer. Nevertheless, it was only just to the European owners that there should be no abrupt reversal of practice.

The Royal Commission did not intend that farming by Europeans should be ended in Kenya. What they intended was that there should be a closer integration of farming activities throughout the country and that, progressively, racial and tribal privileges should disappear. Such a policy, if given time to prove itself, might increasingly have won support among the settlers, although it would not have won much acceptance from the Africans in regard to their tribal lands. Yet despite these intentions, the tenor of the report caused much uneasiness among the European community and a consequent depression in land values. Comfort, however, could be found in the fact that the Kenya office in London continued, with the approval and support of the British government, to invite new settlers with farming experience to come to Kenya, and in 1958 the then secretary of state, Alan Lennox Boyd, gave the following reassurance: 'H.M. Government are not likely to lend themselves to encouraging people to come if they intend to betray them or their predecessors.'[24] There was not therefore, any widespread loss of confidence.

23 This criticism, if criticism it is, runs counter to Fazan's earlier observations about a rational tendency for migration to areas of greater economic activity, even at the cost of greater congestion. The Native Leasehold Areas tended to be in less populated, because less fertile or less healthy, areas, and had poor communications and other facilities.

24 While I have no doubt that such an assurance was given I have been unable to trace its source.

PART VI

Towards Independence

17

The Lancaster House Conference and the End of the Colony[1]

Ever since the end of the war, continuous efforts had been made to make the structure of government more democratic. In 1947 a chairman had been appointed, later called the speaker, to preside over the Legislative Council, a duty previously discharged by the governor and now gratefully relinquished, and in 1948 an unofficial majority had been granted. In 1954 the colonial secretary, Oliver Lyttelton, produced a constitution, a special feature of which was that it created a council of ministers. There had been a quasi-ministerial system in operation since the end of the war, whereby selected members, not all of them officials, were appointed by the governor to preside over departmental groups. This was now confirmed in the constitution, and the members concerned were given their proper designation of minister. Eight of the ministries were assigned to members from the unofficial ranks – four to Europeans, two to

1 The two best political narratives here are B. A. Ogot, 'The Decisive Years', in B. A. Ogot and W. R. Ochieng' (eds), *Decolonization and Independence in Kenya 1940–93* (London: James Currey, 1995) and Kyle, *Politics of the Independence of Kenya*, except that both, like others, exaggerated (p. 63 and Chapter 7, respectively) the settler influence on the 'regional' or *majimbo* constitution preferred by Kenya's smaller ethnic groups, as opposed to the unitary constitution espoused by the stronger groups, especially the Kikuyu and Luo. For the African drive for *majimbo* see David Anderson, '"Yours in the struggle for Majimbo": Nationalism and party politics of decolonisation in Kenya, 1955–64', *Journal of Contemporary History* 40 (2005), pp. 547–64. Bennett, *Kenya, a Political History*, Chapters 12–14, remains, despite its age (1963), a reliable and admirably concise account. For contrasting autobiographies of political leaders in these years, see Blundell, *So Rough a Wind* and Oginga Odinga, *Not Yet Uhuru.*

Asians and two to Africans.[2] In other respects the Lyttelton plan had something of the air of a stand still. The principle of parity was not openly assailed but the African members demanded, as a condition of their agreement, that their members should be directly elected instead of being nominated by the governor after consultation with the African district councils.[3]

Before the elections were held it was agreed that the number of African constituencies should be increased to eight so that all major tribes could be properly represented. Preliminary arrangements and the preparation of voters' rolls took up most of 1956, and the first African general elections were held on a qualified franchise early in the following year. Eight Africans were duly elected but, since only persons who were accounted loyal (i.e. who had not sided with Mau Mau) were qualified to vote in the Central province, there was no Kikuyu among them. That seat fell to a Meru.[4]

In 1958, Alan Lennox-Boyd succeeded Lyttelton as secretary of state and soon reached the conclusion that further modifications were necessary. Taking advantage of a provision in the Lyttelton constitution which allowed the secretary of state to intervene, he increased the ordinary African seats to 12, and additionally provided for 12 'specially elected members' – four Europeans, four Asians and four Africans – to be appointed by the Legislative Council itself, all members voting together on a common roll. He also made proposals for a Senate, the

---

2 Fazan's memory was at fault here. Among the unofficial ministers there were five Europeans, two Asians and one African (but there were also two African under-secretaries). Lyttelton had wanted two African ministers but failed to persuade the European politicians. See Oliver Lyttelton, *The Memoirs of Lord Chandos* (London: Bodley Head, 1962), p. 407; Blundell, *So Rough a Wind*, pp. 154–61.

3 'Parity' refers to the racial (im)balance of representation on the unofficial benches of the Legislative Council. Before 1948, European un-officials had outnumbered others (Asians and Arabs). For the next ten years, until 1958, Europeans enjoyed 'parity' with all other un-officials (Asian, Arab and African), as unofficial numbers rose from 22 in total to 32. In 1958, in response to African parliamentary opposition, the 'Lennox-Boyd constitution' decisively broke white parity, giving Europeans 18 seats while 30 were for others, 18 of them for Africans. See Table 1 in Appendix 2 to D. A. Low and Alison Smith (eds), *History of East Africa*, Vol III (Oxford: Clarendon, 1976), pp. 558–61.

4 For details of these elections, which were more significant (in giving Africans a constitutional leverage they had not had before) than they seemed at the time, see Geoffrey Engholm, 'African Elections in Kenya, March 1957', in William MacKenzie and Kenneth Robinson (eds), *Five Elections in Africa* (Oxford: Clarendon, 1960), pp. 391–461. Ogot, 'The Decisive Years', pp. 54–9; Branch, *Defeating Mau Mau*, Chapter 5.

principal initial function of which would be to see fair play and point out if any proposed new legislation discriminated to the disadvantage of any race. These changes put an end to 'parity', but the more moderate section of the European community accepted them as in line with the current need and as a necessary step in the evolution of a multi-racial society which they now accepted as the aim towards which all must work. Acknowledging this, a new political party – the New Kenya Group (later the New Kenya Party) – was formed under the leadership of Michael Blundell, who resigned his post as minister for agriculture in order to devote himself to this purpose. As against this, the right-wing element of settler opinion, which considered that parity had been surrendered too early, and too many concessions had been made, was marshalled as the United Party under Group Captain Briggs. He was too uncompromising to make a successful negotiator but he commanded considerable support among the settlers and could be relied upon to put their case with force and sincerity. Amid all the talk about Africanisation or multiracialism there was no doubt that they were going to need a resolute spokesman, but the settler community at least hoped that the Lennox-Boyd dispensation was to be the end of concessions for a protracted period so as to give time to adapt to the new basis.

This was the state of affairs when Iain Macleod took over as colonial secretary in 1959. It had been announced that a constitutional conference on the future government of Kenya would be held in London in 1960, and he urged all delegates to come to it with open minds. In deference to this appeal no considerable attempt was made to form the two settler parties into a team which could have put up speakers by agreement to voice both the extreme and the more moderate views of the European community from a common platform and without too much divergence. This omission was to prove a serious handicap at the conference table, for it was later made to appear that there was no common cause, that there was more divergence than was really the case, and that nobody represented the European community as a whole. As against this, the African representatives presented a united front with Ronald Ngala as chairman and the Luo trade-unionist, Tom Mboya, as secretary. This was despite sharp differences existing between many African leaders. At the conference itself, which opened at Lancaster House in January 1960, it soon become clear that, whoever else had come to it with an open mind, it was not Macleod. From the outset he made it plain that his one object was a swift transition to a parliamentary constitution elected on a common roll franchise. The proceedings of the first day had a shattering effect, multi-racialism was as dead as European hegemony; the future was to be African rule.[5]

The composition of the Legislative Council, as finally determined, was to be 33 members elected on a common franchise (who could be assumed to be all Africans), ten elected Europeans, eight elected Asians and two Arabs, making 53 members elected on a common roll. Additionally, four Europeans, four Asians and four Africans would be elected by the members voting as an electoral college. The governor was to have power to appoint additional members but this, in effect, would probably extend only to two or three officials. As for the council of ministers, it was to be composed of four nominated officials and eight appointed from the non-official members: four Africans, three Europeans and one Asian. This constitution was intended to last for an extended trial period after which, depending upon its successful working, internal self-government would be conferred and, ultimately, independence.

Briggs and his group were helpless and could do no more than stage a token walk-out when, in the absence of Kenyatta, Peter Mbiyu Koinange was admitted as a legal adviser.[6] The Blundell group tried to cooperate in the hope of reaching some semblance of agreement, but the course of debate, so far as one can judge, consisted of nibbling at the framework without any major assault being launched or concession obtained. The nearest approach to one was an agreement that the European members should be elected by a double process – a primary election on a community basis, after which any candidate securing 25 per cent of the total votes would proceed to a second election on a common roll. This at least ensured that nobody could be elected to a European seat without a substantial amount of European backing but the probable result would be that, if three Europeans qualified in the

5 Fazan's critical view of Macleod reflects the shock of most Kenyan Europeans at the time. For Macleod's view of the need to accelerate decolonisation in East Africa – when Britain was already leaving its more valuable West African colonies – see Robert Shepherd, *Iain Macleod, a Biography* (London: Pimlico, 1994), Chapter 8.

6 To meet the African demand for his presence while appeasing the settlers, Koinange – who had survived in political exile as a milkman in north London – was admitted to Lancaster House but not to the conference chamber itself. The Colonial Office's permanent secretary, Sir Hilton Poynton, adapted a nursery rhyme to the occasion: 'Mau Mau milkman, have you got a pass? Yes sir, yes sir, but only second class. Good for the cloakroom, good for the loo, But not for the Music room among the chosen few.' Quoted in Nigel Fisher, *Iain Macleod* (London: Deutsch, 1973), p. 146.

primary election in the order A, B, C, they would emerge from the second election in the order C, B, A.

In the intervals between sessions there was frequent liaison contact between the Blundell group and the African delegates in an effort to narrow their differences, but approaches to the Briggs group with the object of presenting a common front were curiously lacking. There was no doubt that Michael Blundell had done his best, but there were many of the European community who thought that, rather than stay for an agreement that was really no agreement, a serious protest, with insistence on an adjournment, would have been more appropriate. Seeing that these drastic proposals, which in their inevitable results would mean the end of the Colony, had been sprung on the conference without prior notice, there was every reason for pressing for a long adjournment – if, indeed it was agreement that the secretary of state was seeking. Admittedly, such a protest would have been unlikely to affect the final result, but there was need for a halt during which the probable effects of the new policy could have been studied more closely, for it was soon evident that the Colonial Office had little appreciation of them.[7]

The Kenya (Land) Order-in-Council followed in the same year as a matter of course and, by regulations under it, put an official end to the European Highlands. A remnant of the privilege remained for a little while longer to the extent that applications for transfer of title to non-Europeans required reference to district and regional boards before approval was granted. The immediate result of the conference and this order-in-council was that land in the Highlands fell to about a fifth of its former value. Before the year was out capital was leaving the country to an alarming degree and many small farmers went bankrupt.[8] Meanwhile, unemployment became severe. The famine of 1961 exacerbated the problem and there was a wave of strikes and

7 For Macleod's own account of his conference tactics, influenced by his knowing that not even the right wing of his Conservative Party would support the conservative settlers led by Briggs, see Ronald Hyam and Wm Roger Louis (eds), *The Conservative Government and the End of Empire 1957–1964 Part I: High Policy, Political and Constitutional Change* (London: The Stationery Office, 2000), documents 160 and 161.

8 Tignor, *Capitalism and Nationalism*, Chapter 11, has studied this aspect of decolonisation in detail and paints a vivid picture of British crisis-management rather than strategic design, trying to reassure the largest British investors rather than small white farmers, in order to shore up African employment, keep an inter-African peace, maintain Kenya's governability and so make it possible to decolonise.

lawlessness. There were still many settlers whose faith in the country was such that they would have preferred to stay, but it was clear that European small mixed farmers would soon be elbowed out. A petition drawn up by the Convention of Associations[9] and signed by the great majority of European landowners in Kenya was addressed to both Houses of Parliament. It asked for land titles to be secured under the protection of a bill of rights or similar document to be written into the new constitution, and for appropriate steps to be taken to stay the disastrous fall which had taken place in land price values and, as far as possible, to restore them. This was not without some effect. Grants were made by the British government in support of a scheme, started in 1961, for the purchase of land from settlers for resale on easy terms to Africans as yeoman and peasant farms. This went some way towards restoring values, at least in those areas affected by them, but heavy losses were sustained nonetheless.[10]

When the new Kenya elections were held in January and March of that year two African parties confronted each other – the Kenya African National Union (KANU) and the Kenya African Democratic Union (KADU).[11] The former was predominantly Kikuyu, with strong Luo support, and was led for the time being by James Gichuru, as stand-in for Jomo Kenyatta until his release from detention. The latter, representing mainly the smaller tribes, was led by the Giriama former schoolmaster Ronald Ngala. Among the waverers the most significant

9 The 'settlers' parliament' – pressure group would be more accurate – between the wars, but recently in abeyance.

10 In a study yet to be superseded, if modified by Tignor's *Capitalism and Nationalism*, Gary Wasserman, *Politics of Decolonization: Kenya Europeans and the Land Issue 1960–1965* (Cambridge: Cambridge University Press, 1976) showed how white opinion divided between smaller farmers – who called for white solidarity in order to bargain better terms for selling up and moving out – and the larger interests that negotiated cross-racial alliances in order to stay on. Whites came together, however, in supporting land resettlement schemes that bought out many smaller white farms, for resettlement by supposedly moderate African 'yeomen' or 'gentry'.

11 George Bennett and Carl Rosberg, *The Kenyatta Election: Kenya 1960–1961* (London: Oxford University Press, 1961) remains the only full-length study. Kyle, *Politics of Independence*, pp. 120–35, shows, based on the good archival evidence since made available, the mixed British reaction to the highly artificial result. What the British regarded as the 'first eleven', the Kenya African National Union won a large plurality of the vote, but they refused to take office before Kenyatta, still feared by the British, was released. So the 'second eleven', KADU, was able to form a government in alliance with specially-elected European members, but could remain in office only because the British promised to release Kenyatta soon, as they did in August 1961.

were the Abaluhya of Nyanza Province and the Akamba, but in the end they mostly went over to KANU. The point at issue between the two parties was that KADU, fearing domination by the Kikuyu or a Kikuyu/ Luo combination, favoured a plan of loosely-connected regions exercising a high degree of internal autonomy, while KANU wanted a strong centralised government.[12]

The second Lancaster House Conference was held in January 1962, under the chairmanship of Reginald Maudling, who had succeeded Iain Macleod as colonial secretary. Its object was to settle the form of constitution. By this time Jomo Kenyatta had been released and, free from all restrictions, was able to take his seat as leader of KANU. The conference lasted several weeks and ended slightly in favour of KADU. It was agreed that there should be seven regions, including one for the Somalis, and that some of their powers should be inherent, not derived. Questions relating to the boundaries were stood over for later determination, and the precise nature of the inherent powers was left undefined. When it came to working them out in detail, the proposals for semi-autonomous regions were found to be too expensive and too elaborate, besides the fact that the majority party, KANU, was totally opposed to the project. So, in effect, the regions became merely provinces under another name, and it was decided that a single public services code should operate for the whole country. The new form of government was to be just as rigid and centralised as the old had been under the colonial office, and it is probable that no other solution would have been practicable. It was sad, however, to reflect that all the long months of debate about safeguards for minorities, a Bill of Rights, reserved powers for the regions and so forth had produced so little result.[13]

The general election of May 1963 produced a KANU landslide; 68 seats as against KADU's 32.[14] After the election four independent

---

12 See remarks on *majimbo* in note 1 of this chapter.

13 Maudling approached this conference with the same pessimistic realism as Macleod. '[Racial] Arithmetic and African nationalism' had ended white supremacy; so that Britain's remaining duties were to negotiate an orderly transfer of power, avoid 'a relapse into tribalism', and secure minority rights via a Bill of Rights and an independent judiciary. He was unimpressed with the 'verbiage' of KADU's case for regionalism. See his two cabinet memoranda of 20 January and 6 February 1962, documents 172 and 173 in Hyam and Louis, *Conservative Government and End of Empire Part I,* pp. 529–32.

14 See Clyde Sanger and John Nottingham, 'The Kenya general election of 1963', *Journal of Modern African Studies* 2 (1964), pp. 1–40.

members immediately crossed the floor to join the government, and during the following six months there were several other defections, including the eight members of Paul Ngei's breakaway African People's Party, who all went over to KANU. Kenya became self-governing on the 1st June, when Jomo Kenyatta was sworn in as the country's first prime minister. There was then a short period of interim government, with Malcolm Macdonald as governor – Sir Patrick Renison having resigned as governor when the decision to release Kenyatta from all further restriction was taken.[15] It was intended that this interim period should be used as a respite during which the new ministers might gain experience in their duties before full independence was granted. It seems to have been envisaged that this stage should last several years, but by now African impatience could not be restrained and a few months saw the end of it. Independence was granted at midnight on the 11th December 1963, and before the next year was out Kenya had proclaimed itself a republic, the posts of president and prime minister being combined in the person of *Mzee* Jomo Kenyatta.[16] Only the Commonwealth tie remained.[17]

Before independence was granted, the choice was given to British officers in government service in Kenya to continue under the successor government or to retire on pension with a gratuity. By far the most elected to go. Those who stayed, except experts in key positions, were soon to regret it, for they were replaced as soon as sufficiently qualified Africans could be found. The gratuities fixed were well received, but it was hard for those who had belatedly to find themselves new careers. Meanwhile, over the country at large, the immigrant communities, both European and Asian, were watching the situation with growing concern. Many of the Europeans had left before independence and even the Asian communities, more deeply rooted and having no other place in most cases which they regarded as home, expressed their anxiety just before independence in a rush to obtain

15 Renison did not resign; he was sacked for being too 'official' a governor at so highly 'political' a time. See his unhappy relations with three secretaries of state in Kyle, *Politics of Independence*, pp. 133–4, 151, 164. Clyde Sanger; *Malcolm Macdonald: Bringing an End to Empire* (Liverpool: Liverpool University Press, 1995), Chapter 37, compares Macdonald the post-colonial diplomat with Renison the colonial official. Both Sanger and Kyle were journalists in Kenya, observing this process, before they became its historians.

16 *Mzee* means both 'old man' and the social status of 'elder', both terms of respect.

17 This critical account ignores the rate of decolonisation elsewhere as a pressure on the British government; for Fazan's reflections on which see the next chapter.

British passports before it was too late. The number so issued covered something like 100,000 Asians – men, women, and children. It must have been more with an eye to allaying their apprehensions than with any expectation of a general exodus that passports were issued with so generous a hand. Otherwise a step so embarrassing to Britain would never have been taken without first making every endeavour to obtain from the incoming government firm guarantees of a secure life in East Africa for Asian families already established there.[18]

As for the European settlers, it seems to have been expected at the Colonial Office that white settler farming would be able to carry on until, progressively, selected farms would be bought out on a basis of willing seller/willing buyer for African small holdings and yeoman farms under the Land Development and Settlement Schemes, and that the grant provided by the British government for financing those schemes would help, in large measure, to sustain values. It was a view which failed adequately to take into account the extent of the crisis of confidence and fall in land values, largely caused by the intensified pressure of African demand to replace Europeans both in offices and on the land. It had been noticed in all Kenyatta's speeches that while he promised fair and equal treatment for men of all races, it was always qualified by reference to the word 'citizen'. It soon became clear that the undertaking only extended to persons who were willing to adopt Kenya citizenship and renounce their own. Plainly the whites were not really wanted and it seemed, as indeed it turned out, that Europeans taking out Kenya citizenship would find it an illusory safeguard. For the most part, therefore, the settlers were only too glad to get their farms included in the million-acre land purchase scheme started in 1961 for the purchase of land in the former White Highlands through the Land Development and Settlement Board for African smallholders and yeoman farmers. Further, thanks largely to the efforts of Sir Ferdinand Cavendish-Bentinck, who pressed the case to the British government, a grant was made shortly before independence for buying out at a valuation the homes of a limited number of elderly persons of 70 years

18 Donald Rothchild, *Racial Bargaining in Independent Kenya: A Study of Minorities and Decolonization* (London: Oxford University Press, 1973), shows that Asians had more reason than whites to fear the natural African desire to 'Africanise' the civil service and commerce. The British concession to white settlers of a choice between Kenyan and British citizenships could not be denied to Asians – although David Steel's account in *No Entry: The Background and Implications of the Commonwealth Immigrants Act 1968* (London: Hurst, 1969), Chapter 5, suggests that little thought had been given to the issue.

old and more who lived in exposed positions or were regarded as a security risk.[19]

Whatever opinion may be held of the policy which started the White Highlands, it was sad that it all should have been so suddenly and unceremoniously swept away. It was a poor requital for all that white settlement had done for Kenya. With the minimum of disturbance to any pre-existing rights, it had been the leading social and economic factor in the transformation of Kenya into a modern state enjoying, at the time of independence, a high and increasing degree of prosperity. The broader-based structure which it helped to create provided the in-coming African government with a more stable foundation than was enjoyed by either of its East African neighbours.

19 For evidence of a belated British panic about the future security of white farmers and the need, therefore, to expand the land purchase and resettlement schemes on the White Highlands, see Hyam and Louis, *Conservative Government and End of Empire Part I*, pp. 543–5.

18

The Wind of Change[1]

It seems probable that the British government had already begun to realise during the war that, when it was over, some reappraisal of Britain's position towards her colonies would be necessary to suit the new conditions. American opinion was always critical and, during the Dulles period and after the Suez incident, it became more so. In the colonies themselves a growing feeling of Africanism, if not exactly of nationalism, was increasingly a factor to be taken into account. The Mau Mau too had its effect, for although to all intents and purposes the revolt had been suppressed by 1956, it had shown that the stability of

---

1 The causes and crises of the end of Britain's African Empire have generated a large and still-expanding literature. The bibliographic commentary that follows refers only to the points Fazan made in 1969. The most generous appraisal of the Empire's end, that it was a sacrifice made to defeat 'Hitler's evil empire', is found in Niall Ferguson, *Empire: How Britain Made the Modern World* (London: Allen Lane, 2003); his argument – that post-war debt forced Britain to play second fiddle to the anti-imperial United States in the subsequent Cold War (but in which the United States conceded that there was some value in the depth of imperial defences), can be found in most histories of decolonisation, of which the fullest is Frank Heinlein, *British Government Policy and Decolonisation 1945–1963: Scrutinising the Official Mind* (London: Frank Cass, 2002). For the influence of 'the city' and the liberation of sterling from the costs of late-colonialism, see P. J. Cain and A. G. Hopkins, *British Imperialism: Crisis and Deconstruction 1914–1990* (London: Longman, 1993), Chapter 11. Hyam, in *Britain's Declining Empire*, broods on the complex frailties of empire and a post-war weariness with global responsibility, a position with which Bernard Porter, *The Absent-Minded Imperialists: Empire, Society and Culture in Britain* (Oxford: Oxford University Press, 2004) would enthusiastically agree. But in his study of the wars of decolonisation, *Imperial Endgame: Britain's Dirty Wars and the End of Empire* (Basingstoke: Palgrave Macmillan, 2011), Benjamin Grob-Fitzgibbon argues that Britain remained fiercely determined, at the cost of much insurgent blood and British treasure, to ensure that independence was won not by militant insurgents such as Mau Mau but by moderate nationalists who were content to remain in the Commonwealth. The argument will continue.

colonial governments could not be taken for granted; and it may well have been a year and probably two or three years before Macmillan's 'Wind of Change' speech in South Africa in 1960 that Britain's decision to shed its colonies was taken. It was not realised, however, that the wind would become a blizzard and that a process which had been expected to last for 15 years at least would be contracted to half a dozen.

One can well understand that, after all the money spent on quelling the Mau Mau revolt – about £55,000,000 of which the British taxpayer paid half – the British government might weigh up the situation and wonder whether the colonies were worth maintaining. It was not just a question of expense, however, for Britain presumably foresaw that it would be spending far more on these territories in the years following independence than in any equivalent number of years before. It may also have been that Britain anticipated ticklish problems arising in some of these countries and so, shaping its policy on Kashmir lines, thought it advisable to hurry on with independence and let the successor African governments settle their difficulties their own way. There was, for instance, the Somali problem in Kenya, the problems of the Upper Nile, the problem of the Tanganyika/Kenya boundary dividing the Masai, the problems of the position of the Kabaka in Uganda, the 'lost counties' dispute between Buganda and Bunyoro, and the problem of relations with Zanzibar. It was a formidable list for East Africa alone. A third possibility is that Britain genuinely thought these colonies were ready for independence. If that was so, their readiness or unreadiness seems to have played little part in the determination of their place in the independence list, for of those most ready, Southern Rhodesia and Nigeria were leading, while one of those least ready was Tanganyika, yet Tanganyika was one of the first to become independent.[2]

With the possible exception of Ghana, there was no unprompted outcry for independence arising spontaneously from the general population of any of the African colonies in the few years before 1960, during which the British decision to off-load them may be presumed to

---

2 That was precisely the point: in the British view Tanganyika would never be 'ready' for independence, it was too poor. To hang on to the territory, however, would only create hatreds; it was better to hand over responsibility while the 'moderate' Julius Nyerere ('courteous' would be more accurate) was still in charge. See John Iliffe, 'Breaking the Chain at its Weakest Link: TANU and the Colonial Office', in Gregory H. Maddox and James L. Giblin (eds), *In Search of a Nation: Histories of Authority and Dissidence in Tanzania* (Oxford: James Currey, 2005), pp. 168–97. And, see Kyle, *Politics of Independence*, p. 57, for Nyerere's role, therefore, as a pacemaker for East African political progress from 1956 onwards.

have crystallised. Some very able African leaders, however, were now appearing upon the political scene and, even without external prompting or inspiration derived from events elsewhere, parties of genuine nationalism were bound to develop soon. It may be, therefore, that Britain, anticipating this, decided to make a virtue of necessity and be seen to confer independence as an act of grace and so reap gratitude for what, sooner or later, it would have to do in any case.[3] If that is so, it postulates that Britain foresaw a necessity of resigning the colonies at an early date when, generally speaking, the situation was well in hand and the atmosphere more friendly than it had been for some considerable time past. Politicians were pressing strongly for the recognition of equal status for Africans, but they were doing it by constitutional means and were gaining ground. There was nothing to suggest acute tension. Energetic training programmes would have to be pressed forward, but there was no need for panic measures.

It had always been appreciated that independence was the goal to which the British colonies in Africa were directed, yet, when Ghana led the way and was granted independence in 1957, the event did not create any particular stir in Kenya.[4] The West African colonies were so much older than the East, in many ways so much more economically developed and, moreover, so comparatively free from the complications of white settlement and Indian immigration that there was no reason to assume this was to be the beginning of a fast-moving series in which all would be engulfed, or that the kind of all-black constitution, which might be suitable for West Africa, would be applied in the very different circumstances of Kenya. If the British government at that time so intended, Lennox-Boyd would surely not have given the assurance he did to the British settlers in Kenya.[5]

---

3 One more of Fazan's many shrewd observations: for this 'Soulbury doctrine', uttered first in 1944 with reference to Ceylon (Sri Lanka), that 'in the long run giving too much and too soon will prove to be wiser than giving too little and too late', a formula that according to Ronald Hyam ran 'like the proverbial scarlet thread through the history of decolonisation', see Hyam, *Britain's Declining Empire*, p. 120.

4 Europeans in Kenya may not have noticed but the colonial government and Africans did. In 1957, the year of Ghana's independence and Kenya's first African elections to the Legislative Council, Baring, the governor, believed Tom Mboya saw himself as 'the Kenya Nkrumah'. In March 1958 Mboya attended Ghana's first anniversary celebrations and enjoyed the prestige of chairing Kwame Nkrumah's All African Peoples Conference in Accra later that year. See Goldsworthy, *Tom Mboya*, pp. 78, 98–100, 106–8.

5 Fazan appears to have forgotten the constitutional pressure, skilfully led by Tom Mboya, that forced Lennox-Boyd to concede political advance in Kenya in 1957–59 – faster than Britain intended; see Kyle, *Politics of Kenya's Independence*, Chapter 4.

The gradual process, beginning with Ghana, was run off its feet, partly by the impatience of other territories waiting their turn and largely by external influences. The Pan-African movement must be accounted one of them. Although it later struck root and became a genuine aspiration among African countries when independence was imminent, its original motivation was external. The first Pan-African Congress was held as far back as 1919 during the Versailles Peace Conference, and the next three were all organised by the black American Dr W. E. B. du Bois, who was also chairman of the fifth, held in Manchester in 1945 with George Padmore, a West Indian, as secretary, and Jomo Kenyatta playing a prominent role. The objective of the movement had at first been equal rights for Africans, but it had shifted progressively to a demand for independence and then to Pan-African unity. Following the independence of Ghana, there was flurry of activity. In December 1958 the first All African People's Conference was held in Accra with Tom Mboya as chairman, and in the same year, in Tanganyika, the Pan-African Freedom Movement of East and Central Africa was formed.[6]

While these aspirations would certainly have had the strong support of Africans generally, the activities of the Pan-African movement did not arise directly and spontaneously from an upsurge of national feeling. They were largely the work of professional politicians living abroad, and the proceedings attracted more attention in the British newspapers than they did in the colonies. Of much more significance was the movement towards decolonisation in the French Equatorial and West African territories. They had been granted virtual independence in 1958, while still apparently acknowledging a close link with metropolitan France, and the dissolution of the Federation of the French West African colonies followed in the next year. These were signs of the times, but there did not seem to be any compulsive reason why the French action, undertaken for reasons of their own and strongly influenced by the fighting in Algeria, should be taken as an example to be followed by Britain. Their experience was, however, a warning of which all metropolitan powers with African protectorates were bound to take heed. The Belgian decision to withdraw from the Congo, announced

6 For a good journalistic account, see Richard Cox, *Pan-Africanism in Practice: PAFMECSA 1958–1964* (London: Oxford University Press, 1964).

just before the Lancaster House Conference and carried out in the following July, may well have been due to that warning and a realisation that, if widespread trouble were to break out in the Congo, their resources to cope with it would be severely strained.[7]

It is unlikely that these considerations, by themselves, would have been enough to induce Great Britain to abandon her colonial responsibilities and confer independence prematurely before the task of preparation was complete and good prospects for the future assured. But they were not the only reasons. The United States of America never took a kindly view of Britain's possession of a colonial empire and may have brought pressure to bear. Certainly the Americans were not averse to interfering in Kenya by the financing of trade unions directly, despite their avowed political aim. Their anti-colonial feeling was born partly of genuine idealism, partly of historical antipathy and not a little of the profit motive and a desire to cash in where Britain left off. Not, indeed, that they had any intention of taking up the mantle of colonial rule; they would use the modern indirect technique of remote control.[8] It would be a mistake, however, to think that America alone was influenced by considerations of economic advantage. The British Empire, from being a great world power, perhaps the greatest, before the 1914 war, had turned in the inter-war years into a commonwealth of nations loosely connected by ties of kinship and trade preference. After the Second World War the current of trade had been veering in other directions, so that while Canada and Australia looked more towards America, Britain had its eyes on Europe and the common market.

Superadded to all these reasons and permeating them, there was a fresh ideology, not new but refurbished, of which Americans were the chief apostles and the United Nations the symbol. It was the revival of the 'liberty, equality, and fraternity' principle at large again in the West after the downfall of the dictators in the war, and even the East gave it lip service. 'Colonialism' did not seem to fit to

---

7 All analyses of the British decolonisation of East Africa make these same points in assessing the influence of French and Belgian policy. See Blundell, *So Rough a Wind*, p. 271, for his incomprehension that a Belgian decision to leave the Congo should have any relevance to British policy toward Kenya. Fazan may well have read Blundell's memoir, published in 1964.

8 An extraordinarily prescient remark, given early twenty-first-century debate on whether the United States is or is not an imperial power.

this pattern and was becoming almost a term of reproach. That, probably, is the true reason why France, Belgium, and Britain lined up together in giving up their African colonies – like the saints in the hymn 'casting down their golden crowns around the glassy sea'. The movement gained momentum and soon there was no gainsaying it. Apparently nothing was to stand in the way of the new Shibboleth of majority rule, the more instant the better.

An expectation, entertained more by the Americans than Britain, was that if colonies were made independent and then supported by numerous gifts and loans, their consequent gratitude would ensure their alignment with the West on the anti-communist front. It was a policy bound to meet with disillusionment, and the Western powers have found to their cost that despite lavish expenditure on the ex-colonial territories, they have been freely subjected to criticism and abuse from the Afro-Asian bloc. In the midst of the conflict of ideologies, who could blame the newly independent African countries for holding out their hand to both sides and, when it suited them, playing one side off against the other. They had reason to suspect that even the most well-intentioned gift was just another bid for their political support in the cold war of capitalist versus communist; so why should they be grateful?

Considering how frail the craft that Britain launched on so rough a sea, one can only be grateful that Kenya has been able to maintain its stability and keep the machinery of its democracy in working order: this is in the face of the awesome problems of building a nation out of heterogeneous and often conflicting tribes, keeping free from involvements in the bewildering intrigues of neighbours, and avoiding being caught up in one or other of the rival ideologies dividing the great powers. The post-war economic expansion of the country has been sustained and, indeed, the general level of prosperity is probably higher than it has ever been. With the support of external aid now much more freely available, bolder financial policies have been implemented than hitherto were justified. New lines of development have been opened and new sources of revenue explored. As for the political stability of the country, it owes a very great deal to the triumph of leadership of its first president, Mzee Jomo Kenyatta. In the years succeeding independence he fostered a spirit of amnesty and oblivion of past enmities, and he succeeded in controlling the exuberance of his own former partisans, the 'Land Freedom Army'. The undoubted firmness of his statecraft, tempered with judicious moderation, went far to ensure the primacy of constitutional government, not only during his own lifetime but during that of his successors too.[9]

9 A warm and generous conclusion by a former colonial official who loved Kenya, written at a time when it was one of the few African countries not to have suffered a military coup, and when the idea of 'the Kenya exception' was a tribute to its economic success. For a more sober assessment of the limitations of Kenya's import-substituting industry and generally undercapitalised agriculture, see D. K. Fieldhouse, *Black Africa 1945–1980: Economic Decolonization and Arrested Development* (London: Allen & Unwin, 1986), pp. 163–73. Hornsby, *Kenya*, pp. 182–97, takes a more optimistic view of Kenya's economy in the later 1960s, noting the comfortable relations between state management and foreign investment; Daniel Branch, *Kenya, Between Hope and Despair* (New Haven, CT: Yale University Press, 2011), Chapter 1, 'Freedom and Suffering', by contrast, emphasises the discontents of economic disappointment after independence, a mood that should not obscure the improvements achieved in basic education and health care – although these barely kept pace with population growth: see Arthur Hazlewood, *The Economy of Kenya: The Kenyatta Era* (Oxford: Oxford University Press, 1979) and Robert Maxon, 'Social and Cultural Changes', in Ogot and Ochieng', *Decolonization and Independence in Kenya*, pp. 110–47. Susanne Mueller, 'Government and opposition in Kenya, 1996–69', *Journal of Modern African Studies* 22 (1984), pp. 399–427, reprinted as Chapter 4 in Branch et al., *Our Turn to Eat*, pp. 77–105, emphasises the post-colonial continuity of a powerful administrative bureaucracy in disciplining Kenya's political life. There are many studies of Kenyatta's Kenya in similar vein, of which the most trenchant is E. S. Atieno-Odhiambo, 'Democracy and the Ideology of Order in Kenya', in Michael G. Schatzberg (ed.), *The Political Economy of Kenya* (New York, NY: Praeger, 1987), pp. 177–201. Fazan would have been particularly pleased with the high quality of some of Kenya's senior administrative officials, carrying on his own work in progress, for which see David K. Leonard, *African Successes: Four Public Managers of Kenyan Rural Development* (Berkeley, CA: University of California Press, 1991).

APPENDIX I

Policy and Theory[1]

There never was any constitution laid down for the colonial empire, and not much definition of final objectives. Where there was so great a diversity of peoples in widely different stages of social development, the natural inclination of Whitehall was to trust the governor on the spot and, when problems of special complexity arose, a commission would be sent out to examine and advise. Although the British government made little attempt to define objectives for countries yet in an experimental stage it was considered advisable that some simple declaration of principle should be given and, when controversial issues of importance arose, it should be developed by policy directives contained in 'White Papers' from the secretary of state.

The general principle laid down by Queen Victoria in Letters Patent was that, in the administration of natives, regard should be had to substantial justice rather than legal niceties, and that tribal customs should be upheld where they were not inconsistent with natural justice or morality. There was no difficulty for Kenya either in upholding this or in accepting the obligation inherited from the IBEA Company to 'improve the material condition of the natives, advance their civilisation and open the territory to lawful trade and commerce'. These precepts were always kept in mind in the field administration as the basis of their work in the tribal lands.

In a country so dynamic as Kenya, however, political argument was never absent for long. Catchwords such as 'paramountcy', 'dual mandate', 'dual policy' and 'indirect rule' arose, each with its devotees. The belief, or at least the hope, entertained by many of the earlier settlers and fostered by Sir Charles Eliot as governor in 1901–4 was

1 Apart from the correction of one minor error, this Appendix is presented, without editorial comment, as a mature reflection on the Kenya he knew by a man better placed than most to distinguish the practically possible from the theoretically desirable.

that they were founders of a British colony in the fullest sense, where white interests would be 'paramount'. This was too unrealistic to last for long. By 1911 that ideal had already faded, but the settlers' leaders were still professing an aim for internal self-government at an early date and the end of colonial office control. The Devonshire White Paper of 1923, with its declaration of the 'paramountcy' of native interests, put an end to those aspirations.

One unfortunate legacy of those days was that, in 1910, Kenya voluntarily surrendered the grant-in-aid. This was done on the advice of the European settlers as a step towards self-government. It was not a large sum, but the gesture entailed acceptance of an obligation thenceforward to balance the budget from the country's own resources. This was far too great a burden and it hampered progress for many years. Although grants and loans were occasionally given for specific purposes, mainly in connection with railways and harbours, it was not until the Colonial Development and Welfare Act was passed in 1940 that really substantial relief was afforded or the colony enabled to embark on any but the most modest development schemes.

It is doubtful whether Britain's traditional policy of self-sufficiency, which had succeeded well in the early colonial days of the British overseas dominions, was really applicable in the case of backward African protectorates which had to depend on agriculture and where the productive capacity of the soil had not yet been proved. A constant struggle to balance the budget inevitably meant that such funds as were available would be devoted to services promising a quick return, while those of a more slowly-maturing benefit would go short. At the worst it could mean exhaustion of the land through trying to force the pace of production beyond what the soil and the climatic conditions could stand. It may, however, have been that, in view of the large number of protectorates, no other policy was open to the British government without an undue burden on the British taxpayer.

In his book *The Dual Mandate* (1922), Lord Lugard used the term to suggest that there was a double duty owed by colonial administrators – first, to the people they were sent to administer, and secondly, to the metropolitan country which had sent them, so that something should accrue to the advantage of both. The objective of gain to the employer would naturally have been present in the minds of the servants of the IBEA Company which, although altruistic in some of its motives, was essentially a trading concern. But after the Crown took over and the Protectorate was declared, no question of financial profit to Britain influenced the actions of field administration in any way whatever. The problem for the administration was simply and solely one of developing the country for the country's sake, and except in war, when all parts of the Empire made sacrifices for the common victory, no other purpose was in their minds.

The 'dual mandate' must not be confused with the 'dual policy' which was something quite different. In the interests of general peace the declaration about 'paramountcy' had been watered down. It was not to mean that African interests were always to prevail over those of the immigrant communities but, where there was a clash on an issue of fundamental importance, then they should do so. This gave rise to a new conception of a partnership of interests known as 'the dual policy'. The Ormsby Gore Commission of 1924 was perhaps the first to give official currency to the phrase, the application in that instance being economic and directed towards an equal encouragement of productive activity in the African Lands and on European farms. To this the Joint Select Committee of 1931 added a rider that 'the dual policy in regard to economic development should have its counterpart in the political evolution of the Territories'.

There was a mistaken disposition in some quarters to assume that the partnership contemplated in the dual policy was between Africans on the one hand and European settlers on the other, leaving Asians out of it; and that it related especially to labour. That was never the intention and nor was it so interpreted by the field administration. The productivity of the African areas was as essential as their labour, and the Asian element in commerce was essential to both. To promote a sense of harmony and interdependence in a multiracial society was always recognised as the fundamental problem. And that is what gave Kenya its peculiar interest.

The doctrine of partnership was fairly generally accepted, but as the Africans became more educated and experienced and lifted their heads higher, acute competition between the communities would be certain to arise, especially in intermediate posts, and it was evident that very careful steering would be necessary if the policy was to have permanent success. By the early 1930s it had become evident that, sooner or later, the colony would attain self-government. It was not until the event was imminent, however, that the ultimate goal was ever defined or any time schedule indicated for reaching it. So during the inter-war years there seemed to be no urgency about the matter. Indeed government, being more concerned with current problems than final aims, was perhaps too apt to assume that it had all the time in the world before it.

Between the wars much thought and effort was being devoted to improving the organisation as well as the prosperity of the tribal lands. The system, which has been described, was designed to meet practical requirements and was not much influenced by theory. In this respect it was sharply distinguished from that of Tanganyika with its widely advertised 'indirect rule' which came into being after the First World War. When Great Britain then undertook the Mandate for Tanganyika it was politically necessary that the new dispensation should be seen to be different from that of the German predecessors. The point where German methods seemed to be most open to criticism from British standpoints was that they had introduced a kind of *gauleiter* system in parts of the territory, if not the whole, by appointing native subordinate rulers, called *akidas*, as government agents above or replacing the traditional headmen. This system was now discontinued and indirect rule came in with a flourish of trumpets.

Indirect rule was always very much a theorist's theory, mistakenly attributed to Lord Lugard. As a governor in Nigeria he had made much use of native authorities as the principal instruments of his administration. There was nothing new in what he did except the singular success with which he did it. Any government in any protectorate where the native population was living in a tribal condition and vastly preponderated was bound to make extensive use of tribal chiefs or other traditional authorities, usually following a series of agreements with the occupant tribes. The fact of Lord Lugard's outstanding success was probably the reason for elevating the method into a theory; but he himself made no such claim. In so far as indirect rule was a theory at all, with a special content and implication of its own, it meant that great care should be taken to make sure that the native authorities through whom the protectorate government ruled were actually those having traditional power in the tribe and that rule should be conducted as nearly as possible in accordance with tribal custom and with minimal interference. No one would have disagreed with this in principle, but, elevated to a code of practice, it had serious limitations. Sir Donald Cameron, who was responsible as governor for developing this method in Tanganyika, had to curb the enthusiasm of his officers, and specifically corrected any impression that native authorities should not be overruled, even when they made serious mistakes. Thus when the first fine enthusiasm had worn off, not much difference remained between Tanganyika and Kenya in practical African administration. They may have been slightly more concerned with conservation of customary methods, while in Kenya the accent was on progressive adaptation, but real difference in practice or outlook faded very rapidly and, by 1939, practically none remained – except in the scale of salaries paid to a few of their senior chiefs.

As to the Africans themselves, it would be difficult to say at what date they began to feel tribalism a restraint rather than a protection. One may perhaps take the transition as beginning significantly in 1923 when the Kikuyu formed a political association.[2] By 1930, most of the leading tribes were clamouring for more and more education. The urge to progress had now taken a very strong grip and the Africans were not at all grateful for any system or political theory which might have the appearance of holding them back. Although the process of adaptation had hurried on extremely fast, it was to become apparent as the years moved on towards independence that assimilation towards British ways was going ahead spontaneously far faster than had been foreseen. This could be seen in almost every aspect of life, whether in local government, the practice of the native courts, land tenure and development, or social relations.

Perhaps the colonial government showed too much concern for basing development on native custom, for it seemed possible, as independence approached, that chiefs, in time to come, would pass under a cloud as relics of colonialism or as symbols of a tribal past which Africans had outgrown and were anxious to forget. Be that as it may, the system of administration the colonial government was pursuing in the tribal lands was the right one for the times and promised as good a hope for stability in an uncertain future as any other would have done.

The White Highlands were of fundamental importance in the implementation of the dual policy and, although they were not so intimately linked that the one could be said to stand or fall with the other, the dual policy as a point of principle was nevertheless dependent largely on the validity of the justification of the White Highlands. It is probable that the White Highlands will always be the central point of debate, whenever the British record in Kenya is called into question, but the issue was not white settlement itself. That was fully justified both by the circumstances in which it started and, teleologically, by its effects. The point at issue was whether it was right to reserve the whole Highlands block under a guarantee that no non-European should acquire agricultural land in it without the governor's sanction – which, by an 'administrative practice', he was instructed to withhold. If that was ever justified, both the justification and the need for the privilege grew less with time. On the one hand, British protection had converted

2 As noted in the Foreword, Fazan seemed to have forgotten the Kikuyu Association (mostly of official chiefs) founded in 1919.

the African population from one which was approximately static to one which was increasing fast both in numbers and capacity, and local congestion was occurring in parts of the Kikuyu country nearest the Highlands. On the other hand the issue of titles to land in the Highlands had virtually been completed in 1919 and, by 1939, the settlers had had 20 years to secure their positions. Except by subdivision, there was little land remaining unallocated that was suitable for European farms. The rest was either mountainous or forest reserve which might better have been made over to a forest commission, or land which could have been resigned without appreciable loss.

In about 1934 a Highlands Board, supported by local boards, was appointed to advise the governor when any question arose concerning the alienation of any land in the Highlands to non-Europeans. It is a matter for regret that the advice given was almost invariably against the application. A more open-handed attitude would far better have suited the requirements of the time, for it should already have been clear that too obstinate an insistence on the Highlands privilege was the surest way of losing it. It was fast becoming an anachronism, more likely to prove a hindrance than a help to the peaceful development of European farming. If the secretary of state had given a clear warning to that effect at the time when the order-in-council proclaiming the boundaries of the Highlands was issued in 1934 and had insisted that, ultimately, European farming in the Highlands must depend for its security on its value to the colony at large rather than on any privilege or pledge, his advice would probably have been heeded and the lasting prospects of European farming would have been vastly improved. The failure to give such notice in good time before tension became acute was a major error. A timely warning and progressive relaxation of the Highlands privilege through the intervening years might have prevented Mau Mau and, in any case, preparing the way would have enabled the final end of the privilege, when it came as the result of the Royal Commission's report, to be accomplished with less of a shock both to the confidence of the European farming community and to the economy at large.

In short, the dual policy of the colonial administration was substantially right during the formative years of the colony, but a sustained effort should have been made, much sooner than it was, to weld it by progressive adaptation into a single policy of development for the colony as a whole which, ultimately, should have no racial compartments.

APPENDIX II[1]

African Laws and Customs

The conceptions about property, marriage, inheritance and internal discipline which lay at the root of African tribal society still retained much of their vitality during the whole period of British rule in Kenya. It was a cardinal principle of the colonial administration to show respect for them to the utmost extent that the interests of good government allowed, and it is necessary, therefore, to examine what these customs were. Although this account is confined essentially only to those aspects which were apt to arise as issues before the African courts, they amounted, nevertheless, to a logical and coherent system of civil law of great value in the tribal conditions which they served.

The notes from which this study has been prepared were all written in district records by former provincial and district commissioners – principally C.W. Hobley, J. B. Ainsworth, H. R. McClure, Sir Charles Dundas, R. G. Stone and A. M. Champion – in addition to my own jottings. I have also used information gleaned from unofficial, mostly missionary, sources; from consultations with Dr Leakey on the Kikuyu, and Archdeacon Owen on the Luo, and from Dr Lindblom's researches into the Akamba. Among the most important of all my sources is the memory of actual cases and discussion with tribal elders.

For the sake of brevity I shall confine my observations mainly to the larger Bantu tribes – Kikuyu, Kamba, Abaluhya, Meru and the Nyika group – and, there being no *Wa-Kadiri* (average Bantu people), I may be tempted, on occasion, to strike an average and only mention

1 References have, again, been kept to a minimum and have been inserted only when Fazan goes into particular detail. This second appendix, like the first, should however be read principally as ripe reflections generalised from a lifetime of hearing cases between Africans, reading his predecessors' notes, and conversations with other white enthusiasts rather than as an ethnographic survey. Fazan distils the kind of administrative wisdom with which district officers heard lawsuits or presented arguments for change.

exceptions where they are of special significance. The customs of the Nilotics in this range of subjects differ in detail from the Bantu but not in principle and, as for the Nilotic/Hamitic group, particularly the Masai, they very seldom troubled the district administration over the conduct of their family affairs.

Among pervasive elements which were to be observed as informing the tribal conception of social justice was the reluctance of the African to admit that he ever parted finally with any property, the possibility of a re-exchange being always kept at the back of his mind. Another point, especially in dealings with land, was the interplay of the seigneurial rights of the clan or group and the usufruct enjoyed by the individual family.

Social relations: Family groups and marriage relationships

'The tribal system [. . .] embodied an unbroken chain of responsibility of the headman for his people, of the head of the Kraal or family to its members, and of every individual of a tribe to his chief.' This quotation from the *Report of the South African Native Affairs Commission* of 1902–5 contained the root of the matter, although in Kenya different words would have been used. One would be particularly chary of using the word 'chief' in this connection, the concatenation of clan groupings being very much looser in Kenya, and especially loose with the Kikuyu because of the haphazard way in which they entered their present land, groups of one clan frequently bypassing those of another. It is necessary, therefore, to bear in mind that, although the system may be referred to as tribal, the centre of gravity was often the clan or sub-clan or large family group rather than the tribe.

Subject to a small exception in the Digo district of the Coast province, all questions affecting marriage and inheritance among African tribes in Kenya went by father-right, the wife going to live at her husband's home and her father receiving the bulk of the marriage price. The fact that one heifer was customarily paid to the bride's mother's eldest brother may argue a pre-existing system of mother-right which had been superseded but, if so, it must have been a long way back for there is no record or tradition of it. Another sign of a pre-existing system of mother-right is possibly to be found in the rules of 'bashfulness' by which a husband was not permitted to approach or even look at his wife's mother and had to avoid the maternal uncle, although he could converse freely with his wife's father.

Clans were split into two sections. Marriages were within the clan but across the sections, the object being to keep the clan together but prevent excessive inbreeding. Polygamy prevailed theoretically in all Kenya tribes but, in practice, only about one husband in seven had more than one wife. There were, however, some who had many, and, except where Christianity may have proved a limiting factor, a husband would acquire as many wives as he could afford. Chief Mumia is reputed to have had over 100.

In a large village where the head had several wives they were considered as forming two alternating groups, however many there were. The practice was not carried so far in Kenya as it was among some Bantu tribes in South Africa, where normally they were called wives of the right hand and of the left hand and had their huts arranged right and left of the village entrance. In similarly large villages in Kenya the huts of the two groups were generally alternated rather than arranged left and right, but there were still the two groups with their separate affiliations.

The same principle which ordained that marriage should be endogamous within the clan but exogamous across the sections of it could be seen reflected between individual families of the kind just described. The object was the same: to cultivate reciprocal relations while guarding against inbreeding. To take an example, one may imagine two large villages I and II, in each of which there were two groups of wives, A and B in village I; X and Y in village II. If a man from A in village I married a girl from X in village II and they had a son, it would be permissible and not uncommon for that son to marry a girl from Y in village II, but not from X. Similarly, if it had been a daughter born to the man from A and the girl from X, that daughter could be married to a man from Y but not to a man from X. From this example it can be seen that the statement quite often made that there was no objection in tribal custom to intermarriage of first cousins is only partially true. They could not marry if a parent of either of them stood in the relation of brother or sister to a parent of the other, but a common grandfather was permissible. The examples given are oversimplified, and it is not intended to suggest that families cultivated such close relations with each other or that there was a continuous see-saw of marriages between them, but circles of several inter-related families could and did develop, and in such cases groups of wives were the precaution taken against too much in-breeding.

Although comparatively few Africans married more than one wife, it is interesting to note how these large families were built up. After a man had married his first two wives and thereby set up the two sides of the family, he would probably wait many years before taking a third for, if he had children by either of the first two, he had to wait until wives had been found for them before taking a third wife himself. She and each subsequent wife could be affiliated to one of the two original houses, presumably according to the source from which the bride price came. It thus happened that junior wives were very much younger than the first two.

Hospitality rules among Bantu tribes extended so far that a visiting fellow clansman was allowed to sleep with one of the host's wives by his permission expressed or implied, but not when he was absent from the village. It was not impossible, therefore, that, if the husband was old, he may never have slept with his junior wives, although any children born to them would be accounted his, so affecting inheritance after the old man's death.

Whether a father could dispose of his daughter without her consent is a difficult question to answer. Undoubtedly the girl's inclination was a factor in the case but, in pre-Protectorate days, it is unlikely that she would have resisted a firm decision by her father, backed by the elders. There is no evidence, however, to suggest that there were many such occasions, and even should there have been there were provisions of custom to allow her to return to her father and mother for a time if she could not get on with her husband, and to stay there until the quarrel was resolved. It is probable, therefore, that parents were considerate in arranging their daughters' marriages and, in later days when it became easy for discontented wives to run away to Nairobi or Mombasa, parents would have realised the folly of a forced marriage.[2]

Among the Akamba, however, there was a custom of betrothal where parents would allow a daughter of very immature age, often as young as six or seven years, to be betrothed and go and live for a time at the village of her intended husband – in the care, it was said, of one of the women there – and part of the bride price was paid in advance to her father. Although it was possible for the betrothal to be ended by return of the proportion of the bride price paid, it would require a very strong-minded girl and an indulgent father to break off the match. The elders admitted that it was a very bad system, but that had not prevented their continued indulgence in it. It is probable that the custom had its origin in, or at least was reinforced by, a practice of lending out children in return for food in time of famine, as being preferable to starvation. The custom in these cases was for the food to be returned at the harvest and the children recovered, but one can imagine that a girl child might sometimes be kept and a process of betrothal started. With the more

2 Kanogo, *African Womanhood*, has much more to say on this and related issues.

diversified economy of later days, however, the greater variety of cultivation and the opportunities for earning wages, the practice had virtually become a thing of the past.

Bride price

The custom of requiring a suitor to pay bride price for his wife was universal throughout East Africa and practically everywhere south of the Sahara. Although often assailed and much misunderstood, it had survived about a century of criticism and still retained vitality. It was an integral part of the tribal conception of civil law and could not be lightly abandoned. It had many merits and, while it also had its defects, they were not inherent but were caused by the impact of a modern civilization, in which individual rights were the chief concern, upon an age-old tribal system in which individual rights were bound up with, and subordinate to, those of the clan and family.

In 1848 Sir Harry Smith addressed a gathering of South African chiefs and obtained from them an oath 'to abolish the sin of buying wives'. Nearly 50 years later the same attitude was still persisting when, in 1897, courts in the Transvaal decided that bride price was a custom inconsistent with the general principles of civilisation, and their refusal to entertain such cases was confirmed by law. Nearly a generation afterwards, in 1922, opinion had completely veered around, with the native sub-commissioners (district commissioners) of the Transvaal unanimously recommending its recognition.

As for 'the sin of buying wives', Africans had a very different conception of the matter. An African of the Kamba tribe, for example, on being asked why men had to pay for their wives, replied that to get a wife without paying for her was 'like slavery'. The paradox posed by the question of why it should be 'like slavery' to marry a wife freely and with her consent, and not so if she were bought was easily explained if the transaction was regarded as being between families rather than individuals. In the one case the woman had gone by consent of her family to live with a man of another family to 'work for him', and equivalent compensation had been paid to the first family to replace her loss. In the other case one family had gained a breeding member at the expense of the other without compensation, as might have happened in a slave raid. Tribal custom could seldom be faulted on a point of logic!

Marriage was regarded as between families, the interest extending beyond the two individuals immediately concerned. It was not only the parental families on each side who were involved but also the respective grandfather groups. The family elders knew no other duty so binding as the preservation of the family strength and, consequently, they were deeply concerned with anything to do with the family livestock. The head of the family group had to ensure that cattle received in bride price were not used as a free asset but were devoted to securing wives to replenish the family strength and compensate for daughters lost. It was, however, permissible for bride price cattle to be exchanged for other cattle which then became subject to the same obligation. It should be noted, however, that the family at large was not concerned with personally acquired or inherited property not originating in bride price – e.g. cattle or goats bought from wages or, in the old days, ivory found.

The amount of cattle, goats or other property customarily paid in bride price differed from tribe to tribe and, even in the same tribe, the average payments fluctuated in accordance with general circumstances. The tribal elders sometimes declared a standard rate and varied it from time to time, as a non-obligatory guide, but the average appears to have been fairly stable through the years. For instance, in 1909, the standard for the Akamba was stated, in Kitui district, at three cows, two bulls and food worth a cow, while in 1928, in Machakos district, it was stated at two cows, two bulls and a variable number of goats. For the Kikuyu it was stated in 1911 at from 20 to 50 goats and a number of sheepskins for clothing and in 1929, at 30 goats and a ram. But parents were free to bargain, and not every girl fetched the same.

It has frequently been stated that, where no cattle were available and there was no money to procure them, an exchange could he arranged, the father giving a daughter in exchange for a bride for a son, the bride price being, as it were, merely a book entry on both sides of the ledger, without any cattle actually passing. But things did not happen so crudely as that. A man with a son and a daughter and no cattle might, indeed, have got the daughter married off in order that his son might be enabled to marry, but the son would have had to wait until the tally of cattle or goats for his sister's marriage had been paid to his father and, even then, it is probable that the father would have had to exchange them for other cattle before paying bride price for his son. It is unlikely that he would have used the same cattle or that the son could have married a girl from the same household. There always had to be witnesses at the ceremony when the bride price was paid over, and they would not easily have been fobbed off with make-believe. In some shape or form the bride price would have had to be paid. I have heard of cases where clay images were used as pledges but, although I have seen such images, I never came across a definite instance. Payment of cash instead of cattle or goats was already becoming common on the coast by

1920 and was spreading upcountry, but it was not yet established there and it was certainly not a method which appealed to the elders. Times were changing rapidly, however, in that respect.

There was a saying that 'Bride price cattle never die', the reason being that, if a cow or heifer paid in bride price died before it had calved, the hide and the meat, or two goats instead of the meat, could he returned and another cow demanded to replace it. Likewise, if a goat paid in bride price died without issue, the skin and the meat could be returned and another goat demanded.

A poor man, seeking to make up bride price with which to marry, could go to a relative who was richer to ask for a loan or exchange on beneficial terms, and there were well understood ways of going about it. He might, for instance, have had a cow and asked the benefactor to give him the full bride price in exchange for it but, while this sometimes used to be agreed in former times, the elders in Kikuyu (from which these examples are taken) cut it down to 12 goats and a ram. This was above the market price but, as the cow had to be replaced by another if it died before calving, the benefactor need not have come badly out of the deal. The completion of the transaction by the payment of the goats and the calving of the cow was marked by a ceremony. One of the 12 goats was killed and both parties had their share of it, as was regulated by custom. There was formerly a custom called *ngarure*, which was no longer enforceable but voluntary, by which, even after the transaction, if the cow calved freely, one heifer calf was given to the original owner.

There were other methods by which a poor man might be helped through the family group to acquire a wife. If he did not wish to part with his cow finally he could lend it to the benefactor who, in this case, would let him have only six goats and a ram. When the cow had thrown a heifer calf or two bull calves to a bull of the new herd, the benefactor kept the heifer calf – or the two bull calves – and returned the cow to the lender, plus one bull calf in the event of its first, having had a bull calf and then a heifer. Another method was that if the poor man had no cow to offer he could ask his benefactor to lend him a heifer which he would tend and depasture and put to a bull of a new herd. When it had a heifer calf he had to send it to the benefactor, whose acceptance would denote that he could now keep the cow and subsequent issue. If it calved very freely, however, he could be asked for one further heifer.

A stranger to the district who was poor and had no senior relative upon whom he could call for help, was sometimes admitted as a dependant in a village and, after a time, allowed to consort with a woman as his wife according to a form of matrilocal marriage without paying bride price; but any children born would not count as his. Such a man was called, in Kikuyu, a *mwendia ruhiu* (seller of his sword). He might subsequently earn the bride price, however, and convert the marriage to the usual form.

Sometimes whole areas became depleted of livestock through disease or some other cause, and in such cases the elders would declare a reduced standard of bride price to be regarded as normal. It was later permissible among most tribes for bride price to be paid in cash at a declared rate of exchange for cattle and goats, but cash payment was disruptive of the system, for the recipient tended to put the money in his pocket, and there was no guarantee that it would be used to recoup the family strength.

Marriage customs

Wedding formalities included various courtesy visits and small gifts and counter-gifts passing between the suitor and the father of the girl. Among the Nyika tribes, if a wife deserted and a question arose about disposal of the children, the elders would at once ask whether the husband had provided *tembo* in the proper strength and amount to be drunk at the wedding, for they regarded it as blessing the girl's fertility. Unless they were satisfied on this point they would not award the children to their father. It may seem harsh and unfair that the award should have depended on such a thing but in fact, if the marriage was regular, the ceremony would certainly have been held and the drink provided. Another custom which was probably universal among all East African tribes was that the bride was supposed to weep and wail as the bridegroom and his friends took her away to his home. Sometimes the pretence of marriage by capture was made more realistic. The girl's father would probably find a heifer tied up in his cattle *boma* one morning and his acceptance would mark his agreement that the play could take place and, in, due course, the capture would be staged.

Christian marriages had already become common by the end of the inter-war years, with bride and bridegroom, best man and bridesmaids all in their best and ready for their photographs. But the fact of the marriage being Christian did not affect the right of the father to receive a bride price. The same was true when an African girl embraced Islam and married a Mohammedan anywhere in Kenya, except in the Coastal ten-mile strip leased from the Sultan of Zanzibar. There, Islamic law ran for marriages between members of that faith, and the pagan father would not be able to make good his claim. The dowry was paid direct to the girl herself and was usually quite a small amount.

If a man's wife died without giving birth to a child, or in first childbirth while delivering a stillborn child, her father usually came to the husband and gave him one cow of the bride price back. This was not obligatory but was regarded as a graceful gesture. If at the time of the death, however, the bride price had not been paid in full, the husband was able to complete it to the extent of two cows and one bull. As time went on and the two cows calved, the husband took a quantity of beer to the father and asked for one of the calves, which was normally given him as a sign of good will between them. This was according to custom prevailing amongst the Akamba; and the corresponding custom in Kikuyu was stated in 1929 by tribal elders to be that, the full bride price then being 30 goats and a ram, the husband should have returned to him any excess which he might have paid beyond 20 goats. If he had paid less, he had to make it up to 20.

If a man was impotent the wife could leave him and return to her father, who had to return the bride price; but if the wife was sterile the husband had no right to return her or claim return of bride price on that ground alone. By mutual consent a man could return his wife to her father before she had had a child on the ground of incompatibility and, if no reconciliation took place, he could recover bride price, but not until she had been married to someone else. If, having returned the girl to her father, he subsequently took her back, there would be an inquiry as to whose fault it was. If it was the girl's fault the husband would be entitled, by Kikuyu custom, to recover a goat from her father on the ground that the hut had been without fire, but if it was the husband's fault, he would have to pay a goat for the insult.

In the old days there was little difficulty about runaway wives. There was a limit as to where they could run and the elders simply ordered their return to their husbands. There was no Nairobi then but, with increased social mobility, the elders had perforce to be more lenient. They could order her return once but, if she deserted a second time, all sorts of complications arose about bride price and children. Unless the husband claimed return of the bride price, which he seldom did, any children which she might bear to her lover were accounted children of the husband, and, when a girl child so born grew up and was married, he became entitled to receive the bride price. Cases were often allowed to drag on like this for years until that contingency arose and a second case about the bride price on the marriage of the runaway's daughter came before the Tribunal. To avoid this constant resurgence of ancient cases the Tribunal slowly came round to the idea that, if the wife could not be induced to return to her husband or if, having been returned once, she again deserted, the correct solution was to order the lover to pay the bride price to her father, whereupon the father returned the original bride price to the husband who retained the original children but had no claim to any born to her by her lover. This had the merit of awarding the children to the natural father, and the further advantage of concluding the case. If the lover failed to carry out the order of the tribunal, he could be charged with the criminal offence of wife-stealing, punishable with a fine, in addition to distraint for the bride price, with imprisonment in the case of default.

If an unmarried girl became pregnant by a lover but remained with her father, the lover had to pay the father 12 goats and a ram by Kikuyu custom, and a similar penalty in cattle among tribes such as the Akamba, whose customary payments were in that currency. This was to compensate for loss of the girl's value as a bride. The father, out of delicacy, would not use these goats towards bride price for a wife for himself or one of his sons but would exchange them for others which could be so used. Finally, when the girl was married, he discounted 12 goats and a ram from the bride price demanded.

Inheritance

When a man died leaving no married sons, his eldest brother became guardian of the estate, the most important items in which, apart from land, were his widows, children, and cattle. As soon as the eldest son was old enough to take a wife, the guardian would find him one, paying the bride price from cattle and goats forming part of the general estate. After the marriage the son would become guardian, but the deceased's eldest brother and the group elders would continue to exercise a general supervision.

The guardian was not able to deprive the widows of any cattle which the deceased may have settled on them in his lifetime; nor could the widows be made to move from their village or huts against their will. But, to the extent to which they agreed, the guardian could, and did, take over charge of their cattle. He was also responsible for the unallocated cattle of the estate. It happened more often than not that all parties were willing for him to take over most of the cattle into his charge, probably for convenience of herding.

The guardian of the estate bought wives for the sons in order of seniority but he could not buy a second wife for any of them until they all had wives. Cattle allocated by the deceased to any one of his wives could not be used to get wives for the sons of any other wife – except, perhaps, in an affiliated house with her consent. Any cattle used by the guardian to buy wives for any of the sons were deducted from their share when the estate came to division. Subject to this, the first son in each house got one beast more than the second, and the second, probably, one more than the third. The rest inherited equally. The unallocated pool was retained meanwhile in the hands of the senior son of the senior wife, not as his own possession, but for use in bride price to secure wives for unmarried members of the family in due order.

In a criminal case at Machakos the distribution of an estate happened to be relevant. Sub-headman Mutyanyaa, an eccentric but respected elder of the old school, was called as an expert witness. He explained that the reason why the eldest and second sons got more than the others was that they had a certain liability. If the cattle of younger sons died the elder sons had to compensate them out of their share, and the second son could apply in like manner to the eldest son. The eldest son, however, could void this liability if he gave the first heifer born to his cattle after distribution to the second son, and the second son could behave in like manner to the third.

The custom about widows was for the senior of them, if she agreed, to take the next junior brother of the deceased for her protector, and any children she had by him were to count as sons or daughters of the deceased husband. The same applied if she took a different protector. If she preferred, she could take any of the junior brothers or, indeed, someone else, but it was expected of her that she would choose a member of the family. The junior widows were also normally inherited by brothers of the deceased but, if they were much younger than the brothers, they could select from the junior generation. It would not have been in order, however, for them to select any son of the deceased, by whatever wife, except for a son of a wife who had never slept with her husband. It was also permissible for a widow to return to her father's village and cultivate the land as she had done when a girl.

Children followed the widows, and any subsequently born were counted to the deceased and addressed by his name. That is to say that a man had his own first name, but was addressed politely as 'son of so-and-so'. When a daughter, born to the widow by her protector, was married, he received the bride price – which afforded a good reason why widows were always expected to choose their protectors within the family.

A widow could not be compelled to leave the village or hut in which she was living when her husband died. Although cattle settled on her by her husband during his lifetime could be used in bride price for a son, she had to be left with sufficient for her maintenance. There were some widows of rich husbands who had quite large property in cattle and goats; they could even, if living alone, buy themselves a 'wife', and any children born to that wife by a lover would count as children of the widow's deceased husband.

There was very little that women could be said actually to own, for they remained minors all their lives. But, especially in the case of widows, it was rather an academic distinction because they were in tolerably secure possession of what their husbands had settled on them or, more accurately, on their 'houses'. As to a widow's personal property, she had nothing much but ornaments and clothes, the hut which had to be built for her – which she kept when her husband died – a bed and other necessaries, and *shambas* to cultivate. Her husband provided the ornaments and returned those her father gave her.

With cash replacing barter in so many of the transactions of African life it was not to be expected that the bride price system of livestock payments would hold out indefinitely against it. In the coastal belt, payment in cash and trade goods had become the regular method, and some of the district officers stationed in African areas welcomed the substitution of cash payments, even advocating this method to the elders on the ground that the accumulation of herds of useless scrub cattle and goats for no other purpose than to bolster up the bride price system was causing grave denudation of the land. It was indeed a fact that bride price cattle were kept with more regard for their beef and milk value than as currency. Nevertheless, if ever payments in cash were to prove the rule and the utility of the bride price system ended, many of the customs that had held African society together in the past would be lost along with it.

Land tenure

The principles of tribal custom in regard to land corresponded closely with those relating to marriage, inheritance and livestock. There was the seigniory of the tribe or clan over their lands as a whole, and there were users' rights enjoyed by individual members. The elders at each level – whether tribal, clan, sub-clan or family group – were responsible for the integrity of the land they occupied.

The key point of the system was the reluctance to let any land pass finally out of the possession either of the clan or of individual groups. Strangers could be admitted as tenants, but they acquired no permanent right. Although land might be lent, it was always redeemable, so long as native custom remained intact. The only admitted exception was where land was surrendered in compensation for a man slain. Within the general scope of this principle there were endless shades of difference between land practices in different parts, depending upon the nature of the land, the character of the occupant, tribe, the manner in which the clans came in, and the period of their effective occupation.

Sparse occupation

While ample land was still available, family or individual rights caused little difficulty, and even tribal and clan right were more seigneurial than agrarian in character. The theory was that the land belonged to God and that the elders of the tribe were the trustees of the land that God had given them. This theory persisted undiminished by defeat or migration. The Nyika, who developed it to a remarkable extent, were demonstrably living a long way from their former homes.

Although tribal and clan boundaries were well understood and mostly respected, they were not precisely defined, except where a river or other natural barrier provided a convenient frontier, or in a local area where there had been a dispute. It was generally preferred to leave things indeterminate while recognising the need for mutual accommodation. Thus it happened that tribal boundaries often converged at salt licks, to which the cattle of both sides had access, and they remained there unmolested even in a state of near war. Likewise, barter markets on tribal borders stayed open in all conditions.

As regards individuals – or families or groups – both the expressed intention to use, and the actual use of previously vacant land, conveyed various rights. Their rights were simply those of user, the cessation of use for a period of X years being taken as abandonment. Rights to land not actually used or marked out for near future use were not recognised or claimed.

A stranger wishing to break up and till bush land in the recognised sphere of influence of another clan was expected to ask permission of the head of the family group most nearly concerned. It was never refused. He would probably make a gift, possibly a goat, and receive a counter-gift, possibly honey, but these were to establish good relations and were never demanded. Where a building site was proposed, a soothsayer would probably be called in and the village built where he advised.

Natural objects such as pools, ant-hills, wild palm trees used for tapping palm wine and trees used for hanging honey barrels were not considered to belong in any sense to the person who might happen to be cultivating the land around them, but the right went to the man who first made use of them. Water rights, however, were not exclusive. In the case of land claimed for cultivation it was usual to make some formal claim, or set some mark. A clearing made round bush land with the intention of burning it off would have been sufficient.

Hunting and fishing rights went by first use. Where the tribe or clan had no known predecessor, no difficulty arose. But where one tribe or clan had settled on land formerly occupied by another, the previous occupants were credited with a kind of spiritual ownership. They may have set a human skull at a weir in the water of a river to safeguard the fishing rights, and in such a case a member of the departed tribe would be called in to remove the curse and start the season's fishing. Similar practice would also have obtained regarding hunting in the forest. Certain trees were particularly venerated and certain high places were used for community prayers for rain. Baobabs at the coast were believed to be haunted by the spirits of dead ancestors, and many highly civilised persons, Arab as well as African, would confess to a certain awed reluctance about cutting one down. The Nyika clans each had their sacred village or *kaya* with a stockade around it. Although built, no doubt, mostly for defence, the *kaya* contained wooden images of departed elders which were set there as guardians.

The favourite method of cultivation common to all agricultural tribes was by bush clearing and burning and then, after a season or two of use, passing on to fresh land and repeating the process. So long as there was fresh land available nothing but the proximity of enemies or the presence of tsetse fly hindered them in this practice. It was, however, a practice that accounted for the widespread devastation of natural forest and parkland.

Most pastoral tribes were thinly spread over the land. The Masai were typical, and a population of a single family of five to the square mile would be a fair estimate. They were stockowners in sure possession of their land and unchallenged by any outside tribe. Apart from the widely scattered rotational grazing areas of each clan, agrarian problems hardly troubled them at all. They did not fence or paddock and they turned deaf ears to proposals that they should organise a system of large ranches where dams and boreholes could be more systematically constructed, and veterinary inspection more easily arranged. There was, however, one small section which had some agriculture but, by and large, the only cultivation by the Masai was done for them by Kikuyu wives whom they had begun to marry in comparatively recent years. They showed little interest in 'progress' and were content to let the white man's civilization pass them by. An old Masai, when asked what he liked best of all things, replied that he loved to sit in the evening, and watch the cloud of dust rising over the brow of the hill as his cattle were being driven home, and see it get bigger as the years went by and his herds increased; some years it got smaller, but that was life. He was content.

Closer occupation

When a certain density of population was reached, say about 80–100 to the square mile, the expedient which all tribes favoured of cutting down the forest when their fields were worn out became more difficult. Shifting cultivation being thus restricted, land practices continued much the same as before but they were better defined. Group lands were often marked by felling trees, setting stones or planting bushes – thorny *Solanum*, *itoka* lilies or otherwise as may have been the tribal custom – but a fence or hedge could only be set around villages, cattle *bomas*, cultivated land or land intended for early cultivation. A space beyond the actual confines of the village could be included for the purpose of allowing bush or trees to grow up, but grazing lands were still common and could not be fenced.

When the head of a family died, the land cultivated by each of his wives was divided between each of her sons. If she had more than one, each son inherited his due proportion of each, for there was no question of one taking one and another taking another. If there was uncultivated land within the recognised sphere of influence of the family or family group affected by the death, it was not considered to be inherited as property, but when in due course it was required for cultivation the eldest son of the senior wife would be the apportioner.

Strangers or relations by marriage were freely admitted as tenants and notice to quit was seldom given. When one of them left, either on notice or more often of his own free will, he could return to reap his standing crops. He was allowed to cut down and remove any trees he had planted but had no claim to any shoots that might grow up afterwards. He could not cut down banana trees but, if any bunches had begun to form he could come back and collect them later.

Except for a really heinous offence he could not be evicted from his hut but life could be made very uncomfortable for him until he chose to go. As the growing of permanent crops was becoming more common, the need for more security of tenure, both for right-holders and tenants, became apparent.

Individual tenure

Under cover of their *githaka* system, land tenure among the Kikuyu became mainly a question of private rights exercised by small family groups or even individual families. There was no longer any effectual control by the tribe or clan. Insofar as any supervision over land transactions remained at all, it was exercised by the senior member of the family group living on the *githaka*, who was sometimes called the *muramati*. The *githaka* itself, representing the total holding of the group, was generally confined to a single ridge or part of a ridge between two rivers or streams, and the claims to it were based on an original hunting right alleged to have been exercised by an ancestor while the land was still under forest. The word meant bush land or forest, and variants of it were found among most of the Bantu tribes of East Africa. Apart from the Kikuyu, it was only in the *butaka* system of Buganda that it appeared to have acquired a technical significance as a land claim. Elsewhere, it kept its original sense of bush or 'no man's land', a curious starting point for a system of land tenure.

The nine main clans of the Kikuyu were formed before they ever entered their present homes. Immigrating from the North East, they entered their new land, not in compact clan blocks but by individual families of different clans passing over each other to lands of their own choosing with little or no regard for cohesion. That this haphazard occupation should have been possible attests that the land was largely free of previous occupation. According to their own account, they found the whole area north of the Chania River, which now comprises the Nyeri and Fort Hall districts, uninhabited. There are, indeed, faint traces of a legendary people called by the Kikuyu the Gumba, who lived in holes in the ground, a few of which have been discovered. They seem to have been a very shy people, and legend has it that they disappeared suddenly in a single night. Some say they turned themselves into pelicans and flew away.[3]

The country, with its ridges and well-watered valleys, was almost by natural intent predestined for family holdings. It was practically all forest when the Kikuyu first came. At that time they were not agricultural people but lived mainly by hunting and bee-keeping, and individual families claimed hunting rights along the ridges, resting their claim on first use. When, in due course, they turned to agriculture and cut down or burnt the forest, they continued to use the fiction of hunting right to support their land claims. The concept of right of user was thus ingeniously extended.

---

3 For later discussions of Kikuyu origins, see Muriuki, *History of the Kikuyu* and Lonsdale, 'Contests of time'.

The original *githaka* holdings had been large, covering whole ridges between streams flowing down the Aberdares to their point of confluence. In typical cases the land on a *githaka* was held in individual right-holdings by the component families, but there would be a residue left undistributed in the hands of the *muramati*. Over time, through inheritance and increase in the number of right-holders, the undistributed middle became used up and, well before the Second World War, there was practically none of it left in the Fort Hall and Kiambu districts. Although a *githaka* did not customarily split on inheritance, it was plain that, as between the tendency of the *aramati* to become landlords and of the right-holders to assert independence, that the scales were coming down on the side of the right-holders.

Apart from exceptional cases in the Kiambu district, the principle continued to hold that land must not he sold or permanently bartered away. But, as already stated, it could be pawned on a basis of redeemability, subject to permission of the elders. The essential nature of the transaction was a loan of goats to a man, generally a poor man, who needed them for making up bride price and he in turn pledged a piece of land temporarily in exchange for the loan. It was not permissible under native custom, as it then stood, for the approach to be made the other way round. To do so would be an insult.

The elders would not allow a man to pledge land for more goats than he would be able to repay. The rule of redemption was that if the man who lent the goats cultivated the land while it was in his hands, he would, on redemption, get his goats back without their increase. If he had not cultivated the land, however, he would get them back with their increase. The arrangement was that for the increase enjoyed from land, the borrower of the goats was entitled to their increase. No question of 'might have cultivated' came into it; it was just settled on the facts, and was a very good example of the basic principle of tribal customary law.

While former custom was generally averse to the setting of boundaries except where a dispute had arisen, they were later marked out much more freely, and it was important that witnesses, including young men or boys, were present at the ceremony that had to be held. Similarly the old rule that pasture land was common and could not be fenced was later replaced by one that allowed for it to be enclosed. It could not be enclosed completely, however, and a way round had to be left, however awkwardly placed. But small paddocks for partially stall-fed cattle were now to be seen and were accepted as an innovation without complaint. It was also permissible for a *githaka* holder, for the purpose of resting over-grazed land, to put a curse on it against any cattle entering there, and when the grazing recovered the curse was removed by his driving his own cattle in.

The Kiambu district lay south of the Chania River. Unlike the Nyeri and Fort Hall districts on the north side, it had not been free of previous occupation. Dorobo bushmen were hunting over the ridges when the Kikuyu came in, possibly about the middle of the nineteenth century. In this case the Kikuyu did not claim to have been the first users, but they asserted that they had obtained the hunting rights by legitimate acquisition from the Dorobo. The character of these transactions has been much disputed. The conclusion of the Kenya Land Commission about them was that they consisted 'partly of alliance and partnership; partly of adoption and absorption, partly of payment, and largely of force and chicanery'.[4] At any rate it is clear that by the time Count Teleki passed through in 1887, the Kikuyu had already supplanted the Dorobo and had established themselves securely along the ridges. The grandsons of these Dorobo who were still living in the district not unnaturally felt themselves jockeyed out of their land. They coalesced with the Kikuyu but were fairly easily distinguished. They were seldom heard to complain openly, but they spoke wistfully of the past.

No doubt, to begin with the Dorobo did not realise that they had lost the land for good. But they failed to redeem it, partly because it was of little use to them after the forest had been cleared, and also they had no chance. It is generally agreed, however, that something claimed by the Kikuyu to have been a final payment was organised by chief Kinyanjui in respect of the southernmost part lying south of the railway. Though doubtless wise, it was a definite departure from native tribal custom. On the strength of this precedent, the Kikuyu of Kiambu district began to claim that they had a custom of outright sale, and Fort Hall district soon began to follow suit. While the elders in Kiambu district supported this contention, it is doubtful if they would have approved the practical application of it if any right-holder had actually attempted to sell his land, and they certainly would have resisted any sale to a stranger. It was a right asserted but not yet fully admitted or exercised when war broke out in 1939.

It was clear then that further modifications were needed before a viable method of land tenure could emerge, but there were many difficulties. The principle that grazing land was common to all meant that there was no check on overstocking, for there was nobody who would limit the numbers of his cattle to make room for somebody else's.

4 Carter Commission *Report*, p. 93, paragraph 285.

The move towards enclosure and private paddocks was auspicious, but the process was very slow and, meanwhile, exhaustion and denudation of the soil continued. Another problem was that the absence of a right to buy and sell prevented families from extending their holdings when their fortunes or their numbers increased, or poorer families from contracting them. Moreover the system of inheritance was leading to excessive subdivision and fragmentation. The absence of a right to purchase or lease land for any extensive period was also a serious obstacle to obtaining land for a public or semi-public purpose, such as a trading centre, a church or a school, or even a facility to erect telegraph poles. Mining rights, too, were a problem. In fact the whole system had become far too rigid for modern requirements. The need for registration of private right, both of right-holders and of tenants, and for the more definite demarcation of boundaries, was becoming ever more apparent with the planting of permanent crops and the building of more substantial houses. The rights – or cancellation of rights – of co-heirs long absent from the land were also demanding attention. It was suspected too that the *githaka* system had always demanded a degree of convenient forgetfulness to make it workable and it was hoped that registration would set the matter straight.

Legislation introduced in implementation of the Land Commission's report of 1933 helped to resolve some of these problems, especially in providing an acceptable method of leasing land for public purposes. But it was not until much later that definite administrative and legal machinery was introduced to enable right-holdings to be consolidated, a check to be put on the number of permitted subdivisions and to provide a process for the adjudication and registration of titles and the definition of tenants' rights. Indeed, independence was granted to Kenya before the enactments had passed beyond the drafting stage.

Order and discipline

It is frequently stated that there was no criminal law under African tribal custom, but that it was merely a branch of their civil law. It was the case, rather, that elders conceived their duty to be not in judging the degree of criminality of an action but in keeping the balance true between contending clans or family groups and in acting generally in the interests of good discipline. No question of praise or blame affects their judgment. Their view was that, if a moral offence had been committed, divine vengeance would probably exact retribution, but, should a question of purification or of propitiation of ancestral spirits be involved, the elders on both sides would consume a sacrifice and peace would be restored.

There was a regular tariff for fixing compensation for death or bodily injury. It differed between tribes but appeared to remain fairly constant through the years. In two lists for the Kitui Akamba, one made in 1909 and the other in 1934, the assessment was constant in each case for the death of a man at 14 cows and a bull; for a woman at seven cows and a bull. For the loss of an arm or a leg the earlier list showed seven cows and a bull; the later, six cows and a bull. For the loss of both arms or legs, the earlier list showed 14 cows and a bull; the later, ten cows and a bull. The scale for minor injuries showed no significant change.

The reason why the compensation paid for the death of a woman was greater than the bride price paid on her marriage, seeing that in both cases there was the same total loss to the family strength, was that there was a wider spread of recipients in the case of death. Whereas only the fathers and, to the extent stated above, the maternal uncle would receive in the case of marriage, all the affiliated houses would be entitled to a share in the case of death, all being in the same measure affected

In pre-Protectorate days no distinction was made, whether the killing or injury was by intent or accident. To understand the reason for this, it is necessary to regard the matter as between different clans or family groups rather than individuals or small families. It would have been pointless, for instance, to order Cain to pay blood compensation for the killing of Abel, since Adam could probably have found himself both payer and receiver. Furthermore, it is quite possible, that the whole system was designed to prevent fighting breaking out between clans or sections of a clan or tribe when a member of one had suffered death or injury at the hands of a member of another, whether intentionally or otherwise. The fact that among the Kikuyu land was sometimes surrendered instead of cattle supports this intra-tribal interpretation of the transaction. But whether or not this was the case, the relatives of the person who had caused the injury contributed to the compensation, and the party receiving it shared out with his. When the slayer and the slain were members of the same family or small family group, the matter was probably settled within the circle without insistence on the full tariff, although there might have been a purification ceremony and sacrifice. I recollect only one such case in which a man had sent a boy on an errand who was a relation but not a member of the immediate family. On the way the boy was bitten by a snake and died. The native tribunal ordered the full blood compensation to be paid, but I believe that, in the end, it was cut down to half.

After the Protectorate was established cases of murder were tried by British High Court judges operating under the Indian Penal Code until 1930 and, after that, the Laws of Kenya, which followed British procedure. This meant, for the Africans, a departure from the principle of communal responsibility to an individual basis, and it took some time for them to appreciate the change. When a murderer was executed, the relatives of the murdered man preferring cattle were apt to regard the execution as a waste, on the other hand if there was an acquittal on the ground of insufficient evidence the relatives of the man killed were reluctant to forego their claim for compensation, and the feud between the families would persist. In the latter case acrimony was not tempered by the fact that the degree of proof necessary to establish guilt in a murder trial was greater than the degree necessary to decide a question of civil compensation.

In cases of theft, Akamba elders awarded compensation seven times the value of the cattle or small stock stolen. This may seem extremely severe, but in the old days there was practically no sneak-thieving for there was no purpose in stealing a cow from the family bride price pool. It was a question not of sneak-thieving but of raiding as between clans or rival sections of a clan, and the man caught was not the only one responsible. All the family therefore contributed to pay the penalty, and the man whose cow was stolen would share out the compensation with others of his family whose cattle, being kept in the same *boma*, had been equally exposed to risk. He would get his own cow back – or equivalent, if it was not recovered – and no more than his fair share of the rest.

It appears that among the Kikuyu, sneak-thieving of sheep and goats was more common. In 1911 H. R. McClure, then district commissioner of Nyeri, observed that, if the stolen animals were recovered alive, the thief was let off lightly with a fine of one sheep to the owner and one extra to the tribunal, and this covered the lot, however many had been stolen. If they had been eaten, however, the fine was ten times the number consumed to be paid entirely to the owner, and all who had taken part in the feast had to contribute. In one case quoted the owner of a stolen bullock received 200 sheep in compensation. It would certainly have been beyond the capacity of the feasters to provide 200 sheep of their own, but the burden would have been shared out among all the members of their families. Indeed, the practice has long survived that any man sentenced in court to pay a fine could look to his relations to help him out, possibly as a kind of insurance against a misfortune that might happen to anybody. Whereas ordinary wizards – rainmakers and the like – were considered respectable and useful members of society under old tribal custom, a man who practiced black magic, that is to say a man who was credited with the power to cast a spell on another so that he died, was condemned, if detected, to instant death by stoning. This was the only class of case in which the death penalty was imposed.

Naturally, this had to be stopped after the Protectorate was declared and such cases had to come before British courts. But unless something very definite like attempted poisoning could be proved, and I know of no such case, there was little or nothing that could be done. To convict such a man of the very minor offence of carrying charms merely gave him an advertisement, and in any case it was not easy to classify a wizard's ordinary stock in trade of charms and powders as either 'black' or 'white', for the same charm might serve for a suitor courting a girl or for a man proposing to perjure himself in court.[5]

The ancient sanctions of tribal society, with its various rites, taboos, initiations and age grades, sufficed to maintain the internal discipline of the community. With the advent of British rule and new ways, however, these had inevitably broken down to a greater or less extent, and a problem of discipline was arising. Curiously it was the tribes which in the past were best organised for war that seemed to preserve their respect for their elders and traditional mores rather better than the rest.

Among the Masai the young warriors, or *moran*, used to live in *manyattas* apart from their elders and were organised in companies under their own leaders, or *laigwenan*. The Kalenjin group of tribes – Nandi, Kipsigis, Elgeyo etc. – had rather similar organisations in the past, but less pronounced. The Masai *moran* were allowed to have girls with them or visit them in their *manyattas* but they were not supposed to have full intercourse and might not marry. Internal discipline of its kind was strict and Spartan, the whole object of their existence being preparation for war or raiding. There was a senior and a junior age grade and considerable rivalry between them; the seniors taunting the younger and provoking them to prove themselves by particularly brave and lawless acts before they succeeded to the higher grade.

In the case of such *manyattas* as were allowed to continue after the Protectorate was declared, the total period which a *moran* spent in training was two years, after which he retired to a life of respectability. With the cessation of tribal wars, however, they ceased to serve any useful purpose, but on the principle that it was better to adapt than suppress, some district commissioners experimented with the possibility of converting them to educational uses somewhat on the

5 For the difficulties in reconciling African witchcraft beliefs with British ideas of justice, see Richard Waller, 'Witchcraft and the law in colonial Kenya', *Past and Present* 180 (2003), pp. 241–75; Katherine Luongo, *Witchcraft and Colonial Rule in Kenya, 1900–1955* (Cambridge: Cambridge University Press, 2011).

lines of 'Outward Bound' courses. It was a commendable attempt but probably hopeless from the start.

The decay of the warrior system deprived these young men of their chief employment, and the Masai, in particular, were slow to accommodate themselves to a life more in keeping with modern requirements. There was not, however, any observable increase of indiscipline in the internal relations of tribal life or any sign of disrespect towards their elders. In that respect the tribal taboos had held. But cattle theft continued as an individual pastime, or in teams of two or three, and was not much abated.

Among the Bantu tribes, the *thingira* and *simba* huts in which the young men lived were no more than a shadow of what may once have been a warlike organisation and, correspondingly, the behaviour of the young men towards their elders became a frequent cause of complaint. The fault, however, was not all with them, for it was inevitable that a cleavage between the generations should appear, having regard to the different circumstances in which they were reared. In the old days everyone knew his place through ancient custom, including initiation and age grade rites that had not changed for centuries. Furthermore, parental discipline by the head of the household was very severe and, except in cases of extreme cruelty, was always upheld by the elders. Young men, therefore, did not speak out of turn and wives did not run away, but it was not expected that this state of affairs could continue in face of the profound changes that British rule brought. However, to support the old traditions a little while longer, disrespect to elders was included among the subjects with which the tribunals were authorised to deal as breaches of tribal custom.

The above account is intended to illustrate the principles informing the conduct of African social life in the range of subjects, with which the tribunals most frequently had to deal. Reference to subjects that, although important, were not essential to that purpose, have therefore been omitted. Among such subjects were the age grade system, the significance of circumcision, adoption and rebirth for those tribes which practised them, totemism, magic and witchcraft. Religious beliefs, however, deserve special note.

Students of African taboos have sometimes been so carried away by their enthusiasm as to lead one to suppose that an African's life, from birth to death, was so beset by all manner of superstitions and fears that he could scarcely conduct a rational existence. That was not the case. While superstition certainly had a much more prominent place in African society than in Europe, there was no reason to suppose that Africans were often deflected from their intended course of action.

I have had men pointed out to me who were said to possess the evil eye, and I have seen Africans, even partly educated Africans, scared by the dread of it. But I have only known of one case where the fear seemed to have a permanent effect. I have also known of about three cases of death where witchcraft was credibly alleged, but it was impossible to say whether the men died through the fear of it or whether they were ill and died from some other cause. Although the fear of magic was probably greater when tribalism was strong, it was far from being a spent force: when allied to politics it could still be very potent, as was to be seen in the Mau Mau rising. In normal private life, however, it was not as all-pervasive as some anthropologists would have one believe.

A much stronger influence than magic, and certainly more constructive in shaping African life and character, was the belief in ancestral spirits. It seems to have been a kind of two-way traffic, for so long as the ancestor was remembered, so long did his influence endure. Great men in the tribe also continued to shed a benign influence and some became legendary heroes, like Gikuyu and Mumbi, the Adam and Eve of the Kikuyu, or Ramogi, the first ancestor of the Luo. It appears that these spirits were capable of being offended but they were nearly always protective and friendly, so that when a man was seriously ill, the spirits of his ancestors were believed to contend for his recovery against malignant spirits, possibly of old enemies who were trying to pull him down. At the head of this spiritual world there was a conception of a tribal, and also it seems, a universal god. These two conceptions were so blended as to be thought of together as one – just as Jehovah of the Old Testament appeared sometimes as a tribal deity and sometimes universal.

APPENDIX III

Kenya Land Commission Economic Evidence (Kikuyu) Memorandum

AN ECONOMIC SURVEY OF THE KIKUYU RESERVES

Mr S. H. Fazan, O.B.E. District Commissioner

EDITORIAL NOTE: *This memorandum, completed in late 1932 when Fazan was district commissioner of Kiambu in southern Kikuyuland, is valued as a major source of evidence by economic and social historians of colonial Kenya despite the fact that it is flawed by the lack of statistical services available to an impoverished colonial administration in the grip of the 1930s depression. In the original volume of evidence to the Kenya Land Commission, p 1099, a senior government statistician commented that* 'Mr. Fazan's guesses are as good as any which could be made by anybody else' *and that* 'his guesses are naturally better than any I could possibly put forward'. *In any case Fazan's is the only accessible evidence we have for the time and place; what modifications one makes to his findings are a matter for historical judgment, informed by hindsight; we know what came next, Fazan did not. It is as well to remember the basis of his evidence: namely, his own sharp-eyed, experienced, observation and the data and opinions offered him by his colleagues. The memorandum has therefore to be read as the best that an intelligent and conscientious member of a colonial government could, with great care and observant attention, produce at that time; it tells us as much about 'the official mind', its conventional assumptions and limited expectations, as about the condition of Kikuyuland in the early 1930s.*

Those historians who have placed greatest reliance on Fazan's survey make the following criticisms of his data. He almost certainly underestimated the size of the 'average' Kikuyu household – as did all other official measurements at the time, gathered on hut-tax expeditions; he therefore underestimated the size of the Kikuyu population. This underestimation, in turn, meant that household acreage was smaller than he supposed but that the total amount of cultivated land was greater. If his estimates were to some, unknowable, extent misleading in these respects, he was also silent on two other matters of interest to the social and political historian. First, he said almost nothing on the division of labour between men and women. It is now generally agreed that the intensification of women's labour in the twentieth century was the foundation of African agricultural growth under colonial rule – at least before the spread of such smallholder tree crops as coffee and tea in the 1950s. Second, while Fazan cautions his readers, repeatedly, that the 'average' household on which he bases his figures was a statistical fiction, by making no attempt to estimate the extent of household inequality he may have left the impression of a more even distribution of acreage and wealth than existed in reality. This in turn may (one cannot be certain) have hidden the degree to which wealthier households sold produce to poorer ones, whose buying power would have depended on their male and female wage labour both within and outwith Kikuyuland.[1]

The original memorandum, 69 pages long with appendices, was published in the first volume of The 'Carter' Kenya Land Commission's Evidence, *(Government Printer, Nairobi: 1933), pp. 971–1039. The three volumes of evidence, which have been well described as Kenya's Domesday Book, are to be found in the University Libraries of Cambridge, London, Nairobi, Oxford and Princeton, as well as the Library of Congress in Washington DC and the British Library, London. Since Fazan was secretary to the Land Commission and the main author of its report, his memorandum was more influential than most in shaping the commission's findings.*

The memorandum has been severely cut in this edition. Fazan's forecasts of conditions in the 'Kikuyu reserves' in 1947 and 1962, and the administrative measures which he recommends in consequence, as well as many points of lesser detail, are summarised in italics, as nearly as possible in Fazan's prose style; where direct quotes are included in the summarised passages they are rendered in Roman script. *As explained in note 18, Fazan's forecasts turned out to be wrong in most respects, thanks more to the ambitions of Herr Hitler than to the failings of Mr Fazan. They nonetheless show how an intelligent official saw the rather daunting future and* 'the task of administration', *which was* 'to ensure that this [future] state of things does not arise.' *Fazan's four appendices,*

1 Kitching, *Class and Economic Change*, pp. 35–9; Mackenzie, *Land, Ecology and Resistance*, pp. 130–2.

(pp. 1033–9) which show how he calculated the figures presented in the memorandum's several statistical tables, have been omitted.

The original page numbers are indicated in bold, in square brackets, so that readers can get a sense of the relative severity of different cuts and can the more easily compare this edited version with the original should they have access to the latter. Where changes have been made to correct minor errors or omissions in the original this is clearly indicated, in bold and in square brackets. The one exception to this rule relates to chapter numbers. In the 'contents list' on page 971 Fazan numbered his chapters in 'Hindu-Arabic' numerals but then switched to Roman numerals in subsequent chapter headings; in this version all his Roman chapter numbers have been changed back to 'Hindu-Arabic'.

Editorial comment is confined to notes. Fazan's memorandum had ***no*** *footnotes.*

–o0o–

[971] The area under review in this survey is the Kiambu Native Reserve, the Fort Hall Native Reserve, and the Tetu, Mathira, and Othaya Divisions of the South Nyeri Reserve. That is to say, it is the three administrative districts, minus Keruguya. I shall refer to this area as "Kikuyu Proper", simply for the sake of having a name for it, and not with any wish to raise the question whether the natives of Keruguya (i.e. Ndia and Kichugu) are racially full Kikuyu or not. The reasons for omitting Keruguya are partly the different nature of the country and partly the lack of reliable information about it.

My object in writing this paper is twofold: First, that it may be of use to the Commission which will deal with the native lands; secondly, that it may be of use in working out a policy of development suitable to these reserves.

There are two essential bases on which any policy of agrarian development must rest – the one social, and the other economic. This may sound like a truism, but it becomes worth stating when one reflects that the Report on Land Tenure in Kikuyu is at its strongest on the social or anthropological side, and attempts no systematic study of the economic question. It is hoped that this paper may do something to adjust the balance.[2]

The argument will be as follows:

2 Fazan here takes the opportunity to reinforce the arguments behind his 1929 minority report for the Land Tenure Committee. See the discussion in his memoir, above, Chapters 7 and 11.

Part I – The Present

Chapter 1 The Population
Chapter 2 Present Agricultural Production
Chapter 3 The Economics of the Household: The Family Holding
Chapter 4 The Economics of the Household: The Family Budget
Chapter 5 The Question of the Adequacy of the Reserve to the Present Needs of the Population

Part II – The Future

Chapter 1 The Probable Density and Distribution, Fifteen Years Hence and Thirty Years Hence
Chapter 2 [*a*] The Probable Increase in Agricultural Skill, and the Probable Development of the Reserve at These Periods
[*b*] The Position as It May Be Expected to Affect the Household Budget
Chapter 3 The Question of the Adequacy of the Reserve to the Probable Needs of the Population at These Periods

Part III – Remedies

Chapter 1 The Results to Be Expected from Agrarian Adjustment within the Reserve Boundaries, and the General Nature of Such Adjustments
[972]
Chapter 2 The General Nature of the Results that Might Be Expected from any Addition of Land to the Reserve.
Chapter 3 The Potentialities of Interpenetration

Important Note. – I wish to make it quite clear that in the first two parts of this memorandum I shall attempt nothing but an impartial appraisement of the facts. Any mistakes which I may make will be the kind of mistakes that one might make in mathematics, and I shall most sedulously avoid any colouring of the argument to fit any particular point of view or policy.

In the third part of this memorandum it is inevitable but that personal opinions must be stated; but my object is to keep the discussion in the plane of principle, and to express only such opinions as one might be entitled to express on points of agrarian principle after some degree of special study of the subject.

I especially disclaim all intention, so far as this memorandum is concerned, of recommending that any particular area should or should not be added to the reserve. In so far as I have views on the subject, I shall find another place in which to state them. I wish to do nothing that might detract in any way from the value of this essay as an exposition of the principles rather than the specific issued involved.

Part I – The Present

Chapter 1 – The Kikuyu Population

No serious inquiry into the agrarian development which will be suitable to the Kikuyu can possibly be attempted without a previous economic survey. The starting points for such a survey must be the character and the extent of the land and the character and the tendencies of the population.

[**CUT**: *16 lines explain that all statistics* 'may be accepted as the closest estimate which it has yet been possible to make.' *Fazan is fairly confident of his figures for the present population, less so of his estimates of the rate of increase.*[3]]

The following table shows the total population. It must, however, be noted that the Keruguya area, which is shown in the table, is outside the scope of our survey, and attention is drawn to the footnote, which shows the adjustment necessary.

[973]

3 Fazan's caution about his future projections was wise; they were far below the figures recorded by the censuses of 1948 and 1962 – for which see note 17 below.

Table 1 The total population: Estimate of the total population for all Kikuyu in 1931.

	Men			Women				
	Married	Single	Total men	Married	Single	Total women	Children under sixteen	Total population
Kiambu Reserve	21,976	6,626	28,602	31,137	903	32,040	43,387	104,029
Fort Hall Reserve	32,793	21,916	54,709	43,707	567	49,274	67,869	171,852
Nyeri Reserve (including Keruguya)	35,935	24,417	60,402	65,374	752	66,126	91,093	217,621
Total resident in reserve	90,754	52,959	143,713	145,218	2,222	147,440	202,349	493,502
Total resident outside the reserve	20,513	11,614	32,127	32,415	486	32,901	45,167	110,195
GRAND TOTAL	111,267	64,573	175,840	177,633	2,703	180,341	247,516	603,697

NOTE: Since the Keruguya Area will not be included in the present economic survey, it is necessary to record that the total population for Nyeri alone (without Keruguya) is 121,210.[4]

It will be noticed that the number of Kikuyu living outside the reserve exceeds 110,000, and is more than the total population of the Kiambu Native Reserve.[5]

[974] The table which follows shows the density of population:

Table 2

District	Area in acres	Resident Kikuyu population	Acreage per head of resident population	Non-resident population (i.e. Kikuyu living out side reserve)	Acreage per head if non-resident population were to return
Kiambu	254,720	104,029	2.45	37,256	1.80
Fort Hall	373,120	171,852	2.17	40,073	1.76
Nyeri (without Keruguya)	194,560	121,210	1.60	18,303(?)	1.39
TOTAL	822,400	397,091	2.07	95,637	1.67

[CUT: *A 14-line note cautions against too great reliance on the figures, especially for Nyeri district, whose boundaries were subject to periodic change.*]

The Structure of the Family

The following table shows the structure of the family:

Table 3

			Unmarried			
District	**Householder**	**Wives**	**Men**	**Girls**	**Children**	**Total**
Kiambu	1	1.41	0.30	0.04	1.98	4.73
Fort Hall	1	1.48	0.69	0.02	2.07	5.26
Nyeri (without Keruguya)	1	1.82	0.68	0.02	2.53	6.05
AVERAGE OVER ALL	1	1.56	0.57	0.02	2.17	5.32

4 The Keruguya area, now known as Ndia and Gichugu, had earlier been assigned to the neighbouring Embu district. Its omission from Fazan's calculations is of no significance to the general picture.

5 The rate of polygyny at this time can be inferred from the fact that Fazan thought only 1.5 per cent of women to be unmarried while 38 per cent of all Kikuyu men were. Fazan's own comment on the figures is found below, p. 975. Most of those Kikuyu 'living outside the reserve' will have been 'squatters', labour tenants more properly speaking, on white farms.

[**CUT**: *A four-line note repeats the cautions made under Table 2*].

[975] The table confirms the common opinion that, as civilization advances, there is a nearer approach to monogamy, and a better distribution of wives. The distribution in Kiambu, where 77 per cent of the grown men are married, is far better than in Fort Hall or Nyeri, where it is only 60 per cent in each case.[6] Although there are more women in comparison with men in Kiambu District than either of the others, yet the proportion of wives to each husband is less. The individual family or "household" is therefore smaller, and we may expect the process to continue until the Fig. 4.5 is reached, which is the normal average in civilized countries.

The Acreage Available per Family

The table given above (Table No. 2), showing the acreage available per head of population, needs to be supplemented or else it may be misleading. It is far easier to appreciate the position if the figures are presented in the form of the acreage available per household, for, in general, the household is the unit of production.

Table 4 Showing the acreage available per household.

District	Sub-division	Population	Number of households	Average strength of household	Total acres	Acreage available per household
				Persons		
Kiambu	North and Central Divisions	65,207	13,775	4.73	167,040	12.13
	Dagoretti	38,822	8,201	4.73	40.320	4.92
	Ndeyia	–	–	–	47,360	Grazing common
Total for Kiambu District		104,029	21,976	4.73	254,720	11.59
Fort Hall		171,852	32,671	5.26	373,120	11.42
Nyeri		121,210	20,035	6.05	194,560	9.71
TOTAL FOR THE WHOLE AREA UNDER REVIEW		397,091	74,682	5.32	822,400	11.01

6 No historian has questioned Fazan's observations here.

[**CUT**: *In nine lines Fazan notes that the Ndeiya grazing area is shown as uninhabited because its floating population is credited to their home 'division'. 'Household' means a married man and his dependants, as in Table 3.*]

The Rate of Increase

The foregoing table showing population-density (Table No. 2) is convincing proof that the rate of population-increase is a matter of very practical moment. Unfortunately, the data available are not **[976]** sufficient for an absolutely reliable calculation, and a certain margin of possible error must be accorded to the conclusion of this memorandum, which is as follows:

Average annual rate of population increase during the decade 1921–1931.

	Resident population only	**Or**	**Squatters being allocated to districts of origin**
	Per cent		*Per cent*
Kiambu	2.5	Or	2.6
Fort Hall	0.4	"	1.0
Nyeri	0.2	"	1.4
Keruguya	0.3	"	1.4
Squatters	6.2	"	–
AVERAGE FOR ALL KIKUYU WHERE-EVER RESIDENT	1.5	Or	1.5

Comment. – While the average rate of increase among the squatters has been 6.2 per cent over the whole decade, since 1927 it has only been about 1 per cent, or less than its own natural increase, which indicates that, on balance during those years, more persons have returned to the reserve than have left it. While there will no doubt be fluctuations, this is an augury that the amount of relief which the settled area is likely to provide in future for any problem of congestion in the reserve will be strictly limited, and it is more than possible that the reserves will be called upon to provide for an influx of squatters from the settled area.[7]

The figures given in this chapter are clearly very relevant to the question whether the reserve is adequate to the needs of the population, but it is better to attempt no comment until all the factors bearing on the case have been passed in review.

Chapter 2 – Present Agricultural Production

All produce is disposed in one of four ways:—

(a) Consumed internally in the reserve
(b) Exported to settled areas
(c) Exported to other native areas
(d) Exported abroad

Table A shows the consumption in the reserve, and differentiates between districts.

Table B below shows exports according to destination, but does not differentiate between districts. The particulars for the several districts are shown in Appendix No. 1.

Table C shows the total production for each district.

Note. – The items, cattle, goats, poultry, eggs, dairy produce, charcoal, and manure are not included in the tables, but will be considered separately.

[977]

7 Fazan's comment on the recent reverse flow of squatters reflects the fact that white farmers were trying to restrict squatter entitlements to their own grazing and cultivation on white farms in the later 1920s. He understated the problems of the future, since further white restrictions on squatter entitlements in the 1940s, with the consequent attempts by squatters to regain a footing in the reserves, often in vain, were a major cause of the Mau Mau insurrection.

Table A Consumption: Table of foodstuffs consumed *annually* in the reserve (Kikuyu proper) and their value at producer's prices.

Crop	Kiambu	Fort Hall	Nyeri (less Keruguya)	Total	Rate	Value
	Tons	*Tons*	*Tons*	*Tons*	*Sh.*	£
Maize	5.646	6,223	4,390	16.259	55	44,712
Beans	2,813	4,667	3,292	10,777	77	41,491
European potatoes	3,767	3,111	2,195	9,073	44	19,96
Sweet potatoes	5,646	12,446	8,780	26,872	37	49,713
Millets	939	4,668	3,217	8,824	110	435,321
Yams, arrowroot, vegetables and cassava	1,073	1,773	1,250	4,096	37	7,577
Cane	23,117	38,189	26,935	88,241	18	79,417
⋆Bananas	⋆2,404	⋆3,972	⋆2,801	⋆9,177	500	229,425
TOTAL VALUE £	133,163	227,574	160,091			520,828

⋆ Units of 1,000 bunches.

Method of Computation

In working out the figures for consumption in the reserve, it has been assumed that in Kiambu District a family of 4.5 persons consumes—

1½ lb. of maize, ¾ lb. of beans, 1 lb. European potatoes, 1½ lb. sweet potatoes, and ¼ lb. of millet daily; and 2 lb. weekly of either yams, arrowroot, vegetables or cassava; two bunches of bananas a week; and one ton of sugar cane a year.

In Nyeri and Fort Hall Districts, where fewer European potatoes are grown, and where millet enters largely into the diet, the consumption is shown as—

1 lb. maize, ¾ lb. beans, ½ lb. European potatoes, 2 lb. sweet potatoes, ¾ lb. millet daily, and the other items as before.

This diet is supplemented to some extent by meat, eggs and milk, and various herbs, roots, and wild fruits. The supply of meat and milk will be considered below, but the other items have not been calculated.

[978] The total figures have been reached by dividing the total population by 4.5, and considering the result as so many standard families, and multiplying out accordingly. The fact that the average household has subsequently been ascertained to be greater than 4.5 will cause no appreciable error in the result, since it only means that the total households are fewer and the consumption-capacity of each proportionately greater. In terms of a family of 5.32, which Table 3 of Chapter 1 shows to be the average size of family for the area under review, the Table works out at about Sh. 11/60 worth of foodstuff per month.[8]

The composition of a family, as given in Table 3 of Chapter 1, is 3.13 adults and 2.17 children. If we take the consumption capacity of two children to be equal to that of one adult, the consumption capacity of such a household is equal to that of 4¼ adults.

The proportion therefore is that Sh. 11/60 feeds 4¼ adults for a month – an allowance of some cents per adult per day. This seems small until one reflects that it is enough to buy the ordinary ration of maize meal on a farm (2 lb. equals about 7 cents in an average year) and leave about two cents over. And we have not yet taken into account the extent to which the food supply is augmented by occasional meat, and milk and eggs (in the case of the mission element, which eats eggs), and various wild herbs, roots and fruit.

[CUT: *In two paragraphs Fazan explains that he has costed household consumption at producer (market) prices rather than the cheaper barter prices that may have been negotiated between households.*][9]

The following table shows export from the reserve. The manner in which the figures have been obtained is shown in the notes appended to the table, and in Appendix No. 1.

[979]

8 Fazan does not specify how much of this monthly Sh. 11/60 'worth of foodstuff' is the household's own production – for which the cost would have been the maintenance and reproduction of its own labour power – and how much is bought in. It appears, however, that most of the food consumed will have been home-produced except, as noted earlier, among the poorest with the smallest acreages.

9 Fazan's several methods of computing producer prices follow on p. 980.

Table B Export: Table of export from the reserve (Kikuyu proper) and their value at producer's prices.

Crop	Rate per ton	Sold to non-native areas		Sold to native areas		Exported abroad		Total exports	
	Sh.	Tons	£	Tons	£	Tons	£	Tons	£
Maize	55	32,165	88,454	4,740	13,035	—	—	36,905	101,489
Beans and other pulse	77	4,770	18,364	496	1,910	1,297	4,993	6.563	25,267
European potatoes	44	6,437	14,161	436	959	3,100	6,820	9,973	21,940
Sweet potatoes	37	1,080	1,993	4,000	7,400	—	—	5,080	9,398
Millets	110	520	2,860	300	1,650	—	—	820	4,510
Yams, arrowroot, cassava, vegetables	37	541	1,001	900	1,665	—	—	1,441	2,666
Cane	13	1,481	1,333	2,700	2,430	—	—	4,181	3,763
Wattle	35	—	—	—	—	9,017	15,780	9,017	15,780
Bananas (bunches)	50 cts. per bunch	543,000	13,700	—	—	—	—	548,000	13,700
£		—	141,871	—	29,049	—	27,593	—	198,513

[980]

Note. – In working out the figures the principal sources used for estimation are:—

(a) A comparison of the railway returns for the years for which these have been available, and reasonable discretion in interpreting them. It would, for instance, have been absurd to accept the year 1929 as a typical year, or to be bound slavishly to an exact average taken over the years examined. The year 1931, generally speaking, forms the basis of the Kiambu figures, but would not have been suitable for Fort Hall or Nyeri, where considerable food shortage prevailed. In the case of Fort Hall, the years 1927 and 1928 have been the most useful sources of information, all years since then having been, for some reason or other, abnormal.

(b) An examination of the records during the food control period, and especially the record for Kiambu, has enabled it to be determined with great accuracy what proportion of maize exported goes to local settlers and how much of it touches the railway.

(c) Inquiries from millers and prominent shopkeepers have supplemented the above information.

(d) Inspection of markets has afforded the principal basis for determining how much of the various kinds of produce is exported by head-load to other native **[corrected from "natives"]** areas or to squatters in settled areas.

[**CUT**: *In three paragraphs Fazan thanks two agricultural officers, W. Gordon Leckie and C. O. Oates, as well as his fellow district commissioners, for helping to collect information and for critical discussion of his findings. Personal observation by his colleagues is his main check on figures obtained by other means. The figures shown in Table C below do not include any livestock, their hides or dairy produce, poultry, eggs, charcoal or manure. (This excised passages extends half way down page 982.)*]

[981]

Table C Table showing the total produce of the area under review (Kikuyu proper): Total consumed, total sold, and total value, arranged according to districts.

Crop	Kiambu			Fort Hall			Nyeri (less Keruguya)					
	Consumed	Sold	Total	Consumed	Sold	Total	Consumed	Sold	Total	Total amt.	Rate	Total value
	Tons	*Tons*	*Tons*	*Tons*	*Tons*	*Tons*	*Tons*	*Tons*	*Tons*	*Tons*	*Sh.*	£
Maize	5.646	14,159	19,805	6,223	16,552	22,775	4,390	6,194	10,584	53,164	55	146,201
Beans and other pulses	2.818	3,366	6,184	4,667	2,657	7,324	3,292	540	3,832	17,340	77	66,758
European potatoes	3,767	8,543	12,310	3,111	1,170	4,281	2,195	260	2,455	19,046	44	41,901
Sweet potatoes	5,646	2,580	8,226	12,446	2,000	14,446	8,780	500	9,280	31,952	37	59,111
Millets	939	—	939	4,668	800	5,468	3,217	20	3,237	9,644	110	53,042
Yams, arrowroots, vegetables, cassava	1,073	81	1,154	1,773	160	1,933	1,250	1,200	2,450	5,537	37	10,243
Cane	23.117	1,531	24,648	38,189	1,800	39,989	26,935	850	27,785	92.422	18	83,180
Wattle	—	4,071	4,071	—	4,166	4,166	—	780	700	9:017	35	15,780
Bananas (units of 1,000 bunches)	2,404	258	2,662	3,972	210	4,182	2,801	80	2,881	9,725	5C0	243,125
												£ 719,341

[982]

Acreage

The acreage which grows the crops and supports the stock may now be considered. The acreage required to grow the crops by native methods and with the degree of skill at present obtaining is shown in the following table.

The acreages given below have been estimated on the basis of production in the manner made clear in the table. They have been compared with the results obtained by ocular observation and simple surveys of locations. In the case of Kiambu the correspondence was very close, 79,000 acres being the figure obtained by ocular observation, as against 82,569 acres obtained by the "Production" method. In the other two districts, the discrepancy was considerably greater, and in both cases the figure obtained by observation was the larger of the two. While I expect that the truth lies somewhere between the two estimates, I have decided to accept the figures obtained on the basis of production as the more conservative, and, on the whole, the better supported by evidence. It is probable that the difference can be partly explained by *(a)* an insufficient allowance having been made for wattle cut down and used for domestic purposes, and *(b)* a larger barter of grain with the Akamba in exchange for goats than has here been estimated. Neither of these things will make any very material difference to the nature of our conclusions.

[983]

Table D Showing acreage cultivated and how cultivated.

		A. Seasonal crops					B. Perennial crops				C. stock-feed, etc.	D. home-stead	Grand total
				Resultant acres Seasonally distributed									
District	Crop	Total tons produced annually	Yield per acre per season	Long rains	Short rains	Average acreage under seasonal crops at one time	Crop	Total tons produced annually	Yield per acre per season	Average acres under perennial crop	Estimated at half acre per household	Estimated at one-tenth acre per household	Average in cultivation (including homestead)
Kiambu	Maize	19,805	4 bags	28,707	25,757		Sweet potatoes	8,226	1 ton				
	Beans and other pulses	6,184	2 ½	13,605	13,605	44,774	Yams, arrowroot, cassava, etc.	1,154	2 ”	24,609	10,988	2,198	82,569
	Millets	939	3½	—	2,951		Sugar cane	24,648	10 ”				
	European potatoes	12,312	2½tons	2,462	2,462		Wattle	4,071	½ ”				
							Bananas*	2,662	bunches 520				

* In Units of 1,000 bunches.

Table D Showing acreage cultivated and how cultivated.

	A. Seasonal crops						B. Perennial crops				C. stock-feed, etc.	D. home-stead	Grand total
				Resultant acres Seasonally distributed									
District	Crop	Total tons produced annually	Yield per acre per season	Long rains	Short rains	Average acreage under seasonal crops at one time	Crop	Total tons produced annually	Yield per acre per season	Average acres under perennial crop	Estimated at half acre per household	Estimated at one-tenth acre per household	Average in cultivation (including homestead)
Fort Hall	Maize	22,775	4 bags	39,946	22,760		Sweet potatoes	14,446	1 ton				
	Beans and other pulses	7,324	2 ½	16,113	16,113	57,129	Yams, arrowroot, cassava, etc.	1,933	2 ”	42,364	16,335	3,267	119,095
	Millets	5,468	3½	—	17,185		Sugar cane	39,989	10 ”				
	European potatoes	4,281	2 tons	1,070	1,070		Wattle	4,166	$\frac{1}{3}$ ”				
							Bananas*	4,182	Bunches 400				
Nyeri (less Keruguya)	Maize	10,584	3½bags	21,704	11,520		Sweet potatoes	9,280	1 ton				
	Beans and other pulses	3,832	2½ ”	8,430	8,430	30,952	Yams, arrowroot, cassava, etc.	2,450	2 ”	22,825	10,017	2,003	65,797
	Millets	3,237	3½ ”	—	10,174		Sugar Cane	27,785	10 ”				
	European potatoes	2,455	1½ tons	818	818		Wattle	780	$\frac{1}{3}$ ”				
							Bananas*						
								2,881	Bunches 400	TOTAL ACRES CULTIVATED			267,461

* In Units of 1,000 bunches.

[984] [CUT: *The explanatory note to Table D takes up nearly one page of print. Fazan believes that the relatively low yields per acre for grains, pulses, and potatoes are due to* 'the wasteful methods of the natives'. *He deliberately discounts the locust invasion of 1931 (with unknowable effects on harvests). He emphasises the value of column C, 'stockfeed etcetera'. Stockfeed is mainly sweet potatoes, grown for goats. The* 'etcetera' *includes the residue of other perennial crops now out of production, on which goats also feed; thatching grass; trees to supply building poles, and so on.*]

Table E Acreage and utilization showing acreage of "Kikuyu Proper" and the extent to which is cultivated.

District	Sub-division	A Cultivated	B Necessarily fallow	C Cultivable but not cultivated	D Non-cultivable	Total
Kiambu	North and Central Divisions,	55,974	9,666	67,996	33,404	167,040
	Dagoretti	26 595	4,593	2,128	7.004	40,320
	Ndeyia	Negligible	—	6,400	40,960	47,360
Kiambu total		82,569	14,259	76,524	81,368	254,720
Fort hall		119,095	19,577	158,459	75,989	373,120
Nyeri (*less Keruguya*)		65,797	10,588	66,843	51.332	194 560
Total for the area under review (Kikuyu proper)		267,461	44,424	301,826	208,689	822,400

[985]
Note 1. – The land "necessarily fallow" has been assessed as shown here below:—

(1) For every four acres under "seasonal crops", as shown in Table D, one acre of fallow has been allowed.
(2) For every eight acres under "perennial crops", as shown in Table D, one acre of fallow has been allowed.

Note 2. – The land shown as "non-cultivable" is land which is not cultivable by the Kikuyu by the present methods and with their present degree of skill. But considerable portions of this land could be cultivated by persons skilled in dry farming, while there are other parts which could be made productive by terracing.

Note 3. – The acreage under wattle in the three districts is larger than is here presented, but a great deal of it has only been lately planted. There is no production from it, and consequently no means of getting a cross check. It has therefore been decided to leave it out of account.

Other Production (i.e., Production not included in any of the above tables)

By far the most important item under this head is live stock–cattle, goats and sheep. But before considering them it will be convenient to dispose of the comparatively minor items.

Poultry and Eggs – Except near Nairobi and on the borders of the settled area, the Kikuyu keep chickens for meat rather than for eggs. It is only the mission element which eats eggs, and no means exist for taking them long distances to market.

I have no means of saying how many chickens or eggs are consumed in the reserve. All that can be said is that chickens form a very useful addition to the food supply. We need not consider internal consumption in reckoning the family budget, since it is simply an item on both sides of the account. Nor need we consider the acreage necessary to keep the poultry, since they are kept in the homestead, for which allowance has already been made.

It is estimated that the Kikuyu sell about £6,000 worth of chickens annually to areas outside the reserve, the principal market being Nairobi. The allocation by districts is approximately: Kiambu, £3,500; Fort Hall, £2,000; Nyeri, £500. The amount is smaller than one would suppose, because most of the native chickens sold in Nairobi are from Ukamba.

Mr. Leckie estimates that £19,000 worth of native eggs are sold in Nairobi and the Kiambu farm area annually, and that most of them come from the Kiambu Reserve. But there is probably a considerable deduction to be made on account of eggs sold by native squatters on farms and other sources. I do not think that Kiambu Reserve can safely be credited with more than £13,000. The figure for Fort Hall may be about £2,000, and Nyeri £500.

Dairy Produce – Some individual natives make good profits by selling milk to European farms and to Nairobi. But when spread over the whole reserve, these profits would be negligible. They will have to be taken into account in another place, when we are considering the relative financial position of families living near Nairobi and those resident in remoter parts of the reserve.

The internal consumption of milk is considered below under the heading "Cattle and Goats".

[986] *Hides* – The export is almost negligible. Nearly all hides are used internally in the reserve.

Manure – The Kiambu Native Reserve sells about 10,000 tons annually to the settled area, at about Sh. 17 per ton, a total value of £8,500. The amount sold by Fort Hall and Nyeri is almost negligible, but may amount to £1,000 in each case.

Charcoal – The amount of charcoal sold by the Kiambu Native Reserve is estimated at £2,340. The amount sold by Fort Hall and Nyeri is negligible.

Pigs – These are confined to the Kijabe and Upper Kiambu areas. They are a negligible quantity at present, but promise well.

Cattle, Goats and Sheep – The best figures available in the office of the Veterinary Department are from a census made by Stock Inspector Saunders of the Fort Hall District in 1922. His figures are for twenty-two locations, and show 10,396 bulls, 24,280 cows, 4,127 calves. and 63,735 goats and sheep, as being the stock of 24,626 huts. The average household contains 1.48 huts, which gives 0.62 bulls, 1.46 cows, 0.25 calves, and 3.83 goats and sheep to each household. If we assume similar conditions in all three districts – a reasonable supposition – the resultant total stock for the area under review is:—

	Cattle			
	Male stock	Cows	Calves	Sheep and goats
Kiambu	13,625	32,035	5,494	84,163
Fort Hall	20,256	47,700	8,168	125,130
Nyeri	12,422	29,251	5,009	76,734
	46,303	109,036	18,671	286,032

A calculation explained in the note here below indicates that the meat supply which the natives derive from this stock is just under 3¼ lb. per family of 5.32 persons per week. This supply, even when supplemented by occasional chickens, and even if it were distributed equally over the population, which it is not, would not provide a ration which the Health Department is prepared to regard as adequate. On the other hand, it is very unlikely that at any time in the past of which we have knowledge the Kikuyu have ever been in the habit of eating more meat than this.[10]

(*Note.* – It has been assumed that about 70 calves are born annually to 100 cows, of which about 40 die before they are a year old, and are consumed as meat, for which an average deadweight of 30 lb. has been assigned. The remainder matures, and is assumed to balance slaughters and other deaths, since the number of live stock appear to remain about constant. For each mature beast dead or slaughtered, an average deadweight allowance of 180 lb. has been assigned. An **[987]** allowance was then made for 2,000 cattle imported, either on the hoof for slaughter or in the form of meat. The maturing progeny of the goats has been estimated at 50 per cent per annum, and, since the number remains nearly static, are assumed to balance the slaughters and other deaths, and a deadweight of 30 lb. has been assigned. A further allowance was made for 40,000 goats imported, and it is estimated that the other two districts make the figure up to 40,000.)

The daily yield of milk is estimated by the Acting Chief Veterinary Officer at 13,629 gallons (i.e. an assumption that every fourth cow is in milk, and that a native cow yields half a gallon a day).

This allows 1¼ gallons per household per week. Native custom until lately has not admitted of any very extensive use of goats' milk, although it is used for sick persons and occasionally for children.

Captain Dixon[11] points out that the Kikuyu might with advantage kill a greater portion of their male stock, but admits the necessity of keeping a certain reserve of meat supply. He considers that, in all the circumstances, the male stock could safely be reduced by about ten thousand, which would materially reduce the acreage required to support them. But it is admitted, and in fact evident, that the 109,036 cows and 286,032 sheep and goats, together with a reasonable

---

10 This is an important observation: East Africans did not generally slaughter their livestock for consumption other than at moderately frequent ceremonial or hospitable occasions or for warriors before a raid.

11 Captain Oswald Dixon, M.C., acting chief veterinary officer, served in Kenya from 1912 until 1935. Like other government vets he had been commissioned into the army for the First World War campaign in German East Africa (now Tanzania) in order to care for military transport animals, oxen and mules. The first veterinary officer in Kikuyuland, Robert Hammond, was posted to Nyeri in 1939 to encourage the keeping of pigs which, as Fazan notes, 'promised well'. I am indebted to Dr Donald H. M. Fraser for information on veterinary personnel.

number of male stock and calves, are no more than are necessary for the tribe.

Captain Dixon estimates that the Kikuyu Reserve can carry a beast to every four to six acres. In view of the fact that the cattle are driven into the *shambas* after reaping, and derive a good deal of sustenance in that way, he considers that four acres of uncultivated land would be a sufficient allowance per head of cattle.[12]

This would require 436,144 acres for the cows alone. The total acres available according to Table E above are 554,939 (i.e. the total of Columns B, C and D), which would leave a remainder of 118,795 acres after providing for the cows.

Provision for goats appears to be ample. The 37,340 acres shown as "stock feed, etc.," though devoted as to about half of it to miscellaneous purposes, is, as to the other half, planted with sweet potatoes. This land would be capable of supporting up to twelve goats to the acre, provided that the goats also had the run of the neighbouring hillsides which divide the ridges. That accounts for 224,040 of the 286,032 sheep and goats, and there would be no great difficulty in accommodating the remainder on the hillsides, or on the land which has been shown as "necessarily fallow".

But there are still the 46,303 male stock to be considered. Even if this number were reduced as Captain Dixon would advise, there would still be about 144,000 acres required, which is more than is available. It will probably have to be admitted that a certain degree, not yet perhaps a very serious degree, of overstocking exists. That is not because of any unreasonable accumulation of stock by the Kikuyu, **[988]** but because of the inadequacy of the land to support their reasonable requirements under their present methods of animal husbandry and with their present degree of skill in farming.

12 The concept of the land's fixed livestock 'carrying capacity' was a ruling idea at the time, stimulated by a global concern about soil erosion. The concept, rather more political or moral than ecological, took little note of changing seasonal conditions, different ecologies, changing forms of husbandry or market conditions and so on. For full discussions, see Anderson, *Eroding the Commons*, pp. 135–43, 157–89; idem, 'Depression, dust bowl, demography and drought: The colonial state and soil conservation in East Africa during the 1930s', *African Affairs* 83 (1984), pp. 321–43.

No veterinary officer is stationed in Kikuyu, and there is therefore no recent stock census. It would be absurd to base too many conclusions on a census of one of the three districts made ten years ago. But if the estimate was too high, then the available ration of meat is still less adequate than is here supposed, while, if the estimate was too low, then the overstocking is the more serious.

It has been said with some force that a tribe possessing such valuable agricultural land as the Kikuyu cannot expect to develop it under stock, but should rather aim at greater agricultural production, so as to be able to supplement their meat supply by purchase. This postulates an amount of free money and market facilities greater than they yet possess.

[**CUT**: *Eleven lines sum up the economic picture Fazan has described thus far. The next chapter will* 'bring it into focus' *by concentrating on the individual household.*]

Chapter 3 – The Economics of the Household

The Family Holding

In order to form an estimate for the average degree of well-being of an average household in the native reserve, it will be necessary to consider:—

(a) The average family holding.
(b) Earnings in the reserve, which are not directly from agricultural production.
(c) Earnings brought into the reserve from outside, and other facilities derived from the settled area.

Against these things will have to be set-off the necessary expenses of the family.

But in order that the result may not be misleading, due prominence will have to be given to the fact that the average wealth of a household differs greatly according to locality. And it will also have to be borne in mind that, since in all countries it is the few who are rich and the many who are poor, the generality of the people are living at a level below the figure obtained by a general average.

[989] The following table shows the average family holding. The details are extracted from the tables already given in the previous chapters.

Table 1 Showing the acreage cultivated by an average householder, the manner in which it is planted, and the acreage remaining as his share of common grazing for his stock.

	Average acreage per household		
	Kiambu	**Fort Hall**	**Nyeri (less Keruguya)**
Crop	**Household of 4.73**	**Household of 5.26**	**Household of 6.05**
Maize or millet	1.31	1.22	1.08
Beans	0.62	0.49	0.42
European potatoes	0.11	0.03	0.04
Sweet potatoes	0.37	0.44	0.46
Yams, arrowroot, cassava, etc.	0.03	0.03	0.06
Sugar cane	0.11	0.12	0.14
Wattle	0.37	0.38	0.11
Bananas	0.23	0.32	0.36
Total under crops	3.15	3.03	2.67
Total necessarily fallow (one-quarter of above)	0.65	0.60	0.53
Stockfeed, etc.	0.50	0.50	0.50
Homestead	0.10	0.10	0.10
Total agriculturally developed	4.40	4.23	3.80
Proportion of grazing Commonage available per household	7.19	7.19	5.91
Total land of all kind Available per household	11.59	11.42	9.71

[**CUT**: *Fazan explains that the figures given in this table are calculated from earlier tables in the Memorandum.*]

Note. – The figures given in the previous chapter for sales of poultry, eggs, charcoal, and manure show £27,340 earned by Kiambu; £4,000 by Fort Hall, and £1,000 by Nyeri. This increases the total figure for "value of produce sold" by Sh. 25 per household in Kiambu; Sh. 2 in Fort Hall, and Sh. 1 in Nyeri. The very large difference in favour of Kiambu is due to the proximity of Nairobi and a closely-settled European area.

[990] The result of the whole calculation is as follows:—

	Value of produce		
	Consumed	Sold	Total
	Sh.	*Sh.*	*Sh.*
Per household in —			
Kiambu Native Reserve	121	107	228
Fort Hall Native Reserve	139	52	191
Nyeri Native Reserve	160	28	188

Note. – The figures under "value of produce consumed" cover only crops grown and consumed by the family. They do not include the stockfeed consumed by the goats or the firewood used by the family, or any allowance for meat, eggs, or milk consumed.

Comments intended to correct false impressions created by the method of "averages"

It may almost be said that nature abhors an average, and there is a great distinction between the average and the typical. A presentment of an economic picture by averages ought to be constantly corrected by reference to a background of direct experience, and by common sense, and it will be well to consider the more important of the misconceptions that might otherwise arise in the present case.

(*a*) *The Unit of Production* – The unit of production is shown as being a single household. In general this is not very far wide of the mark, but there are qualifications. There is a nexus between families under the tribal system, by which they help each other in various ways as, for instance, in building a house, or in feeding poor relations and it cannot be said that each separate household is entirely dependent on its own production and earnings. Nor is it entirely free from external management and control. Several households often live as right-holders on one *githaka* and are to a certain extent subject to mutual obligations and a common direction. The powers of the *muramati*, as seignieur of *githaka*, differ according to district, and, no doubt, also according to personality. The data of planting seed is largely governed by the predictions of old men of the tribe, who are its meteorological experts. And even in the marketing of crops a large measure of control is exercised by the elders in times of food-shortage. Nor can the household be regarded as entirely compact within itself. Where there is more than one wife, each has separate gardens and the goats which she gets by sale of produce are the property of her "house," and so the family budget becomes divided.

The fact that some families are right-holders (*wenye*) and some tenants (*ahoi* or *athami*) does not very greatly affect the question of production or the household budget. Though first-fruits are sometimes paid, they are in the nature of voluntary gifts and no system of rent has appeared. Evictions cannot take place until after the crop has been reaped.

[991] The employment of labour for a wage or in some species of economic subservience is not common, but is by no means unknown.

While it is therefore broadly true to regard the individual household as the unit of production, these qualifications have to be kept in mind, and, in some connexions, are very important. For instance, any attempt to establish a universal system of independent small-holdings would weaken the bond which connects the family with the *mbari* and the clan, and so disintegrate the only effective co-operative organization which native society has yet devised. A long period of adaptation lies ahead before the Kikuyu will be ready to forsake the protection of their tribal system in favour of more civilized methods, which they must gradually assimilate to their use.

(*b*) *The Size of the Household Unit* – By our method of averages we have shown that the average household is 4.73 in Kiambu; 5.26 in Fort Hall, and 6.05 in Nyeri. The average household over all was found to consist of 1 householder with 1.56 wives, 0.57 single men, 0.02 single girls and 2.17 children. This is an excellent illustration of how, by seeking too meticulously to give an accurate picture, one eventually succeeds in producing a picture of nothing. For where in nature do we find a man with 1.56 wives? The fact is that, though some householders have several wives and put the average up all round, most have only one wife and the typical family is much the same here as it is in England or anywhere else, and consists of a man and his wife, and two children, and a sort of a *quintum quid*, which in order to avoid decimals we may imagine as the services of one young man shared between two households.

It will be noted that the difference between the "typical" and the "average" is small in the case of Kiambu, but considerable in Nyeri, where the wives are not so widely distributed and there are consequently fewer households and more bachelors.

(*c*) **[changed from "(*d*)"]** *Extent of Cultivation per household* – The difference between the average and the typical household reflects itself in the extent of cultivated lands, though not perhaps in exact proportion. It is obvious that the large families cultivate more than the small, and since the typical family is below the average, so also the typical extent of gardens is below the average as shown in the table. But I think that a case could be made out to show that the smaller family is relatively more efficient, and probably cultivates more land in proportion to its size.

(*d*) **[changed from "(*e*)"]** *The shape and General Condition of the Cultivated Lands* – The table conveys the suggestion that the household's gardens are compact. In fact they are nearly always scattered. Sometimes this is because the householder likes to cultivate on different types of soil, a patch of red land, and a patch of brown friable soil, and a patch of swamp. Sometimes it is because he has more than one wife and they like to have their gardens separate. And sometimes it is because he is a right-holder on more than one *githaka*. The fragmentation of holdings which often sets in when these scattered patches are inherited is a major evil of the *githaka* system and similar systems.

[992] Another misleading feature of the table is the allowance made per household for "Proportion of grazing commonage available." This is misleading in two ways: In the first place it might suggest that householders have or can acquire prior rights over definite pieces of commonage and annex them to their exclusive use. This is certainly not the case, but the extent to which it is perhaps very gradually coming to be the case is very well worth study, and an account is given in the Kikuyu Land Tenure Report. Since that report was written a few isolated cases have come to light in the Kiambu and Fort Hall Districts, where natives have lately fenced in lands to make private paddocks. They are persons of considerable local influence and this probably accounts for the fact that there has so far been no complaint. But it is a sign that custom is changing.

The other way in which the expression is misleading is that it suggests that there is something which is known or recognized as "a common." Under the *githaka* system this is not true. No land is common, but certain rights are common, and the right to depasture cattle on any land not cultivated or specially reserved in accordance with custom is one of them. The only real common in the area under review is the 74 square miles of Ndeyia grazing area, which was added to the reserve in 1913, and was not formerly Kikuyu land, and is therefore not subject to the *githaka* system.

The practical effect has been that the *githaka* land in all the most thickly populated areas has been taken into cultivation to such an extent that most of the cattle have been sent away to Ndeyia or some distant location where there is more grazing and consequently the household does not get even the limited amount of milk which would seem, on the figures, to be available.

[**CUT**: *Fazan admits, in reflections over one page in length, that it is* 'ludicrous' *to suppose that the average Kikuyu household has the full range of crops indicated in the table; he has also had to make arbitrary choices about which of the changing phases of the domestic cycle represents the average household at any one moment.*]

[993]

Chapter 4 – The Economics of the Household

The Family Budget

One of the results of this chapter will be to show that the average household in the reserve has remarkably little free money at its command, and it may be thought that I am introducing it as a piece of special pleading to show that the reserve is inadequate to the present needs of the tribe. That is not my intention. The limits of the land available to the tribe do not operate at this stage to constrict the average household income to any sensible degree.

But a study of the household economics of the present is necessary before we can look forward into the future. The extent of the agricultural skill which the population will be able to attain is a very relevant consideration for the future, and will depend on the education which **[994]** it will be able to afford, as well as the implements which it will be able to buy, and the health and social conditions which it will be able to attain. We cannot safely speculate on these things, unless we have a clear idea of its present economic condition.

It is for this reason and not with any idea of special pleading that this chapter must be written. Earnings from agricultural sources have already been reviewed and attention must now be directed to earnings from other sources.

Earnings from Sources other than Agricultural

1. We shall first consider money earned inside the reserve. This falls into three classes:—

(a) Earnings from semi-manufacture—e.g., milling. Also manufacture of toys, ornamented belts, etc.
(b) Earnings from sale of non-agricultural produce to places outside the reserve, e.g., sand, murram, lime, red-ochre.

(c) Wages paid by Government or missions. Payments by the Local Native Council may also be included, if we show contributions to rates as an item on the expenditure side.

It will be noticed that the above classification does not include professional or technical services which natives render to each other, except such as fall under (*c*) and are financed by Government or missions. The reason is that the money which one native pays to another for carriage of produce, or for building a house, or whatever the service may be, is simply money circulating in the reserve and does not augment the total earnings of the reserve as a whole.

In another connexion below it will be necessary to take these matters into consideration, but for the present purpose it will be sufficient to confine ourselves to the three categories mentioned above.

(a) *Earnings from Semi-Manufacture, etc.* – I am advised that items under this class would not exceed Sh. 2 per family per annum, and are more or less equally distributed between the three districts.

(b) *Earnings by Sale of Non-Agricultural Produce* – Although some individuals make large profits under this head, they would not amount to more than 50 cents per household when distributed over the whole of the reserve. The item covers sand, lime, clay, red-ochre, fuel, thatching grass, bamboos, and many other things.

(c) *Wages paid by Government and Missions* – Emoluments under Provincial Administration vote were paid out to chiefs, tribal policemen, hut counters, interpreters, etc., to the total amount of £12,836 for the whole Province. Approximately three-fifths of this may be credited to the area under review. It works out at Sh. 3/44 per household. As nearly as I am able to determine, the amounts paid out in wages to Kikuyu by Local Native Councils in the area concerned is £2,200 or 59 cents per household.

Under the head of Education I find that disbursements made by Government or Missions for teachers' salaries, or wages of menial staff serve to add, when averaged out over all, about Sh. 1/25 annually to the resources of an average household.

[995] The contribution made by the Public Works Department in the shape of wages inside the reserve, paid for the upkeep of "Native Reserve Tracks", adds about 20 cents to the household revenue, and the contributions of all other departments taken together possibly add 10 cents more.

The total of these items is Sh. 5.58 per household.

The total of money earned in the reserve by means other than agricultural is therefore:—

	Per household per annum	
	Sh.	*Cts.*
(i) By manufacture or semi-manufacture	2	00
(ii) By sale of non-agricultural produce	0	50
(iii) By government, mission or local native council wages	5	58
Total (nearest Shilling)	8	00

Note. – It appears that it will be sufficiently accurate for our purpose to regard receipts under this head, amounting to an average of Sh. 8 per household over the whole area under review, as being equally distributed, and to credit the average household budgets of each district with Sh. 8. Actually Kiambu and Nyeri receive rather more from the educational expenditure than Fort Hall, but it would only affect the situation to the extent of a few cents, while Fort Hall has a definite advantage over the others in respect of item (ii).

2. We shall now turn to the consideration of the money earned outside the reserve.

   By far the most considerable item is labour and this must be subdivided into three classes:—

   (a) Daily workers who return to the reserve at night.
   (b) Monthly wage earners, other than squatters.
   (c) Squatters.

(a) *Daily Workers* – The vast majority of these are coffee pickers. An article in *The East African Standard*, dated 14th December, 1931, quoting official returns showed the total yield of coffee for the area served by Kikuyu pickers as follows:—

	cwt.
Fort Hall	35,695
Kiambu	79,250
Nairobi	850
Nyeri North	5,930
	121,735

I am informed by the Coffee Expert of the Agricultural Department that approximately 30 *debbies* of ripe coffee make one cwt. of clean coffee.[13] The average wage paid to a picker is 20 cents per *debbie* picked. The total earnings would therefore be £36,520 or Sh. 9/82 per household.

(b) *Monthly Wage Earners other than Squatters* – This heading comprises men ordinarily resident in the reserve, who are working temporarily for a wage outside it.

[996] The figures of the Native Registration Department show 40,685 Kikuyu native labourers. But these include an enormous proportion of natives who are really squatters, whether they are so shown on returns or not.

I have examined the hut tax lists for all the farm area and had the totals for Kikuyu extracted from them, and I find that on the whole of the farm area there are as many Kikuyu women as men, and in fact rather more. Practically all Kikuyu employed as agricultural labour on farms are squatters or the relations of squatters with whom they live.[14]

Practically the only Kikuyu labourers who are independent units returning to the reserve on the expiry of their contracts are either—

working in townships, or
working on the railway, or
working on the borders of the reserve,

and there is a small addendum for "miscellaneous".

The details as nearly as they can be ascertained are as follows. The Chief Registrar of Natives considers that they are as accurate as circumstances and the state of the records permit.

Item – 9,988 working in Nairobi at an average wage of Sh. 25/92 a month and earning £155,333 a year. And a further 1,500 or thereabouts, of unregistered casuals, whose total earnings in a year are possibly about £12,600.

Item – 2,000 working in Mombasa at an average wage of Sh. 20 a month and earning £24,000 a year.

---

13 A *debe* (Swahili) could be any tin can but here is a 5-gallon petrol can. Daily coffee pickers, walking out across the reserve border to a neighbouring white estate and back again before nightfall, were almost entirely women and children.

14 These remarks apply to all white farms and estates, not just to the coffee estates on the Kikuyu border where day-labourers could be employed.

Item – 1,100 working in other townships at an average wage of Sh. 22 a month, and earning £14,520 a year.

Item – 1,228 working on the railway (besides those already included in figures for Nairobi and Mombasa above) at an average wage of Sh. 16 a month, and earning £11,189 a year.

Item – A constant average of 5,000 working in the Kiambu, Dagoretti, Thika, Fort Hall, Nyeri, Nanyuki, and Rumuruti area (other than squatters or persons resident with squatters) at an average wage of Sh. 14, and earning £42,000 a year.

Item – "Miscellaneous" = Kikuyu who are working for wages in other areas (i.e. not in the reserve nor in Nairobi, nor Mombasa, nor any township, nor in the railway, nor on the farm areas mentioned) and who are not squatters or domiciled with squatters. They are very few and we may perhaps set down 500 as covering them all, and the average wage as Sh. 14 a month, making a total of £4,200 a year.

The total of these items is 21,316 Kikuyu ordinarily resident in the reserve but working temporarily outside it, and earning £262,410 a year.

Note.– From the Population Statement in Table I [*sic*] of Chapter I [*sic*] it is seen that there are altogether 52,959 unmarried natives ordinarily resident in the reserve, and the above figures suggest that the percentage of them who are out of the reserve, wage-earning, at one time is 40 per cent, a figure which the Chief Registrar of Natives confirms as being approximately correct.
[997]

(c) *Squatters* – Table 1 **[changed from I]** of Chapter 1 shows 110,195 squatters comprising 20,518 families of an average strength of 5.37 persons with 1.57 adult males. If they work, as most squatters do, for an average wage of 6 months in the year at Sh. 12 a month, they would earn Sh. 112/04 for the household, and the total earnings of all squatters would be £114,942.

The total earnings from wages received for work outside the reserve are therefore:—

(*a*) Earned by daily labourers who return to the reserve at night	£36,520
(*b*) Earned by men ordinarily living in the reserve, but working temporarily for a monthly wage outside it	262,410
(*c*) Earned by squatters	114,942
	£413,872

[**CUT**: *Fazan here takes a page to discuss the proportions of wages earned outside the reserve that are remitted or brought back to the reserve. Daily coffee pickers, women and children, bring back all their earnings, while monthly wage-earners, all of them men, spend much of their income on their own maintenance at their place of work. Kiambu households, being nearer to Nairobi, benefit more from these workers than do their counterparts in Nyeri or Fort Hall.* **[998]** *Squatter (family) earnings on the 'White Highlands' do not come back to the reserve; squatters nonetheless benefit reserve households by grazing some of their cattle on white farmlands. The 'average' squatter household income is second to that of Kiambu but probably higher than in Fort Hall or Nyeri.*]

Summary showing the extent to which wage-earning outside the reserve affects the budget of the average household in the reserve

	Profit per household			
	In Kiambu	**In Fort Hall**	**In Nyeri**	**Over all**
	Sh.	*Sh. cts.*	*Sh.*	*Sh.*
(a) On account of profits earned by daily workers	22	6 50	2	10
(b) On account of profits earned by monthly wage-earners	40	29 50	38	35
Total average profits by wages earned outside the reserve	62	36 00	40	45

A Note on Profits made by Trading outside the Reserve

Our review of the situation will not be complete unless we consider this matter. There are a good many Kikuyu traders who go into Masai with a very inadequate stock in trade, and eventually return with large profits. But much of this profit is expended in meat which is taken into the reserve and sold for cash. While it augments the meat supply of natives of the Dagoretti area, it does not appreciably affect the monetary position.

A Note on Miscellaneous Receipts

The Kikuyu are a tribe with a very shrewd eye to the main chance and pick up unconsidered profits from sources which no European could hope to estimate. These range from Christmas boxes and the Government vote for "rewards and gratuities" to the tips earned by golf caddies, and the earnings of rickshaw boys and taxi drivers in Nairobi, or the commissions of newspaper sellers, and all manner of "scrounging", legitimate and illegitimate. Whether sufficient of the money won in these ways finds its way into the **[999]** reserve to make any appreciable difference in the household budget, I cannot say. No allowance for it will be included in the calculation although possibly it ought to be.

The Necessary Expenses of the Household

I have no intention of making any close examination of this subject. My only object is to ascertain roughly how much free money the average household has at its command to spend as it likes.

Tax – Table 3 of Chapter 1 shows that an average household in Kiambu contains 1.71 taxable units; in Fort Hall, 2.17; and in Nyeri, 2.50.

The liabilities for tax (at Sh. 12) are therefore Sh. 20/52 in Kiambu; Sh. 26/04 in Fort Hall; Sh. 30 in Nyeri. These figures will be found to be in inverse ratio to the capacity to pay.

Rate – The same table in Chapter 1 shows that there are 1.30 persons liable to pay native council rate in an average household in Kiambu; 1.69 in Fort Hall; 1.68 in Nyeri. With the rate at Sh. 2 in Kiambu, and Sh. 1 in the other two districts, this becomes: Kiambu, Sh. 2/60; Fort Hall Sh. 1/69; and Nyeri Sh. 1/68.

The necessary expenditure in tax and rate is therefore (to the nearest sixpence): Kiambu, Sh 23; Fort Hall, Sh. 27/50; and Nyeri, Sh. 31/50.[15]

[**CUT**: *In half a page Fazan first reminds readers of a household's necessary consumption of food, as detailed in Table A, p. 997. He then considers livestock bought in by barter. This expenditure may amount to Sh. 6 per household in Kiambu, 5/50 in Fort Hall, and 3/50 in Nyeri; it is not possible to know the cost of the clothing and other articles brought home by returning workers.*]

[1000] The results of our examination into the household budget may now be presented in the following table:—

15 Since 1920, after a controversial conversion from the Indian rupee, Kenya's currency had been tied to the pound sterling, at the rate of 20 Kenya shillings (here Sh.) to the pound. There were 100 cents to the shilling. Fazan's English 'sixpence' is therefore 50 Kenyan cents.

The average annual household budget Kiambu (household of 4.73)

Receipts			Payments		
	Sh. cts.	*Sh. cts.*			*Sh. cts.*
1. By produce of the family holding—			1. Consumption of food—		
(a) Grown and consumed	121 00		*Contra 1* (a) opposite		121 00
(b) Grown and sold	107 00				
		228 00			
2. By other earnings inside the reserve—			2. Necessary purchases of live stock in Barter—		
(a) By manufacture, milling, etc.	2 00		*Contra 1* (b) opposite (*Vide* notes above)		6 00
(b) By sale of non-agricultural produce	0 50				
(c) By government, mission, or local native council wages	5 50				
		8 00			
3. By earnings outside the reserve—			3. Taxes and rates—	*Sh. cts.*	
(a) By daily workers	22 00		Taxes	20 50	
(b) By monthly wage-earners	40 00		Rates	2 50	
		62 00			23 00
			Balance of free money— For clothes, housing, furniture, implements, education fees, etc.		148 00
	Sh.	298 00		*Sh.*	298 00

[1001]

The average annual household budget (*continued*)
Fort Hall (household of 5.26)

Receipts	*Sh. cts.*	*Sh. cts.*	Payments	*Sh. cts.*	*Sh. cts.*
1. By produce of the family holding—			1. Consumption of food—		
(a) Grown and consumed	139 00		*Contra 1* (a) opposite		139 00
(b) Grown and sold	52 00				
		191 00			
2. By other earnings inside the reserve—			2. Necessary purchases of live stock in Barter—		
(a) By manufacture, milling, etc.	2 00		*Contra 1* (b) opposite (*Vide* notes above)		5 50
(b) By sale of non-agricultural produce	0 50				
(c) By government, mission, or local native council wages	5 50				
		8 00			
3. By earnings outside the reserve—			3. Taxes and rates—	*Sh. cts.*	
(a) By daily workers	6 50		Taxes	26 00	
(b) By monthly wage-earners	29 50		Rates	1 50	
		36 00			27 50
			Balance of free money— For clothes, housing, furniture, implements, education fees, etc.		68 00
	Sh.	235 00		*Sh.*	235 00

The average annual household budget (*continued*)
Nyeri (household of 6.05)

Receipts			Payments		
	Sh. cts.	*Sh. cts.*			*Sh. cts.*
1. By produce of the family holding—			1. Consumption of food—		
(a) Grown and consumed	160 00		*Contra 1* (a) opposite		160 00
(b) Grown and sold	28 00				
		188 00			
2. By other earnings inside the reserve—			2. Necessary purchases of live stock in Barter—		
(a) By manufacture, milling, etc.	2 00		*Contra 1* (b) opposite (*Vide* notes above)		3 50
(b) By sale of non-agricultural produce	0 50				
(c) By government, mission, or local					
Native council wages	5 50				
		8 00			
3. By earnings outside the reserve—			3. Taxes and rates—	*Sh. cts.*	
(a) By daily workers	2 00		Taxes	30 00	
(b) By monthly wage-earners	38 00		Rates	1 50	
		40 00			31 50
			Balance of free money—		
			For clothes, housing, furniture, implements,		
			education fees, etc.		41 00
	Sh.	236 00		*Sh.*	236 00

[1003] [**CUT**: *On this page, in an unnumbered table Fazan averages the income and expenditure of an average household of 5.32 persons for Kikuyuland as a whole. This table is omitted here since it compounds all the objections that Fazan has noted for averages. The previous tables of district averages are marginally less misleading.*]

[1004–5] [**CUT**: *In these two whole pages Fazan expands on his earlier warnings of the dangers of working with averages: it makes no allowance for different levels of off-farm earnings according to education or skill; it takes no account of different degrees of neighbourly cooperation or of support for widows; it fails to allow for differences in the number of a householder's wives and therefore in the number of wage-earning sons – an inequality most marked in Nyeri district. Nor does the taking of averages measure relative congestion, or explain the paradox that households in the most congested area of southern Kiambu, nearest Nairobi, are also the most well off.*]

[1006]

Chapter 5 – The Question of the Adequacy of the Reserve to the Present Needs of the Population

[**CUT**: *In three brief introductory paragraphs Fazan explains that he will now introduce his own personal observations. These are* 'rather dogmatic' *for the sake of brevity and contrast with* 'colourless' *statistics which, he reminds us, may suffer from much error. If he finds* 'certain deficiencies in the tribal life' *he must consider whether these are attributable to lack of skill,* 'defects in the agrarian system', *or insufficient land.*]

Descriptions of Present Conditions

The area under review, which we have called "Kikuyu Proper", is some 822,400 acres, inhabited by a population of 397,091 persons, living at a density of 309 to the square mile. The population is sufficiently virile to be increasing at a rate of 1.6 per cent per annum over all, but there is a considerable degree of internal movement towards the southern areas, so that the Kiambu District is increasing faster than the others.

The most thickly populated part in respect of the total land available, whether cultivable or uncultivable, is the southern part of the Tetu Division of the South Nyeri District, where there is a block of about fifteen square miles inhabited at a density of nearly 500 to the square mile. The land is exceptionally fertile, but is not very favourably situated in respect of markets.

The Dagoretti area of the Kiambu District appears at first sight to be more densely inhabited, but it is helped out by the Ndeyia grazing area. But if one considers cultivable land only, then it is undoubtedly the most crowded. These people, having for long enjoyed the educational facilities of several principal schools and missions, have a better knowledge of farming methods and the utilization of markets. They are well served with roads and by the main line of the Kenya and Uganda Railway, and are attaining to a degree of well being and independence of mind quite exceptional in Kenya. It is a point worth noting that the division where congestion is most often alleged is in point of material prosperity far ahead of its neighbours.

The average household over the whole of Kikuyu Proper is 5.32 persons, and has 11.01 acres available to its use, of which it uses 3.58 agriculturally (inclusive of homestead and area under stock feed), and has 0.59 acres necessary fallow. The remainder, 6.83 acres, is uncultivated.

Judged by European standards, the Kikuyu is not a good farmer, but he is well above the average of East African tribes. He has begun to respond to the tuition of the agricultural officers, and in Kiambu District the yield of maize to the acre is reported to have increased by twenty per cent in the last six years.

[1007] The produce grown on the 3.58 acres is worth Sh. 192, but Sh. 139 worth of it is consumed by the family, leaving a profit of Sh. 53. This is sufficient to pay the taxes and rates, which work out at Sh. 25/50, and leave a balance of Sh. 25/50, most of which may be regarded as free money at command of the household. These resources are supplemented by other earnings, both inside and outside the reserve, which amount on an average to Sh. 53 per annum.

Notes have already been written to show that the generality of households are living on a scale below the general average, and that there are necessarily cases of elderly persons who are living on a scale below the generality.

These monetary resources appear at first sight to be very inadequate, but there is no other tribe in the Colony which is better off in this respect, and, until the coming of the white man, tribal life was successfully conducted without any money at all.

But the Government and the missions are launched on a campaign of native betterment. The old native huts are giving place to rectangular houses of cedar poles with walls of split bamboos, a roof of banana thatching or corrugated iron, and roughly carpentered doors and windows. They are owned at present by the more outstanding young men of the tribe, generally literate, who are able to command a wage which has enabled them to build these houses and sometimes to erect improved grain stores and to buy a cart. They are not averse to display, and buy themselves an assortment of European clothing. They make or buy rough furniture for their houses, and have a number of cheap plates and cups.

The missions refuse education to nobody, and many, if not most, of the children of the tribe are getting a smattering of education, which teaches them to regard these outstanding young men as exemplars of a standard to which they themselves may attain. But the fact remains that even this modest standard of life could not easily be universalized. The free money which the present household budget discloses is not enough for financing it, and no general means of augmenting resources seems to exist, except either the cultivation of a larger acreage per household or the attainment of better methods which will cause greater production to be secured from the same acreage. Meanwhile the mass of the tribe continue to live in the old Kikuyu huts, which are extremely squalid.

To put the matter shortly, the tribe has enough money to live according to the old standards, but not enough to enable it to attain to the new standards by which alone a healthy people, useful to the Colony as a whole, can be maintained. This lack of money is mainly to be ascribed to a lack of agricultural skill; but at a later stage of this chapter we shall have to consider whether it is also, in any measure at all, due to a lack of land.

We may now consider the food supply. The vegetable diet which the household derives from its gardens may be regarded as satisfactory, and is certainly well ahead of most other tribes, and a great improvement on anything the Kikuyu knew before the coming of the white **[1008]** man. The total of uncultivated land is some 554,939 acres (inclusive of fallow), which supports, as nearly as can be estimated, 109,251 cows, and 46,303 male stock—an average of one beast to 3½ acres. The Acting Chief Veterinary Officer estimates that Kikuyu land can carry one beast to every four to six acres. It is therefore the case that the land is somewhat overstocked.

[**CUT**: *In five lines Fazan queries the wisdom of culling male stock, since there should be a prudent reserve of stock to augment the currently inadequate meat supply.*]

Besides the cattle, there are computed to be some 286,032 sheep and goats. These are supported adequately on the area which each household has under "stock feed", which is mainly sweet potatoes, and on the bushes which grow on the steep slopes between the ridges.

It is estimated that the entire meat supply which is available from these sources, and from an annual importation of 2,000 cattle for slaughter and 40,000 goats, amounts to just under 3¼ lb. of meat per household per week, an inadequate ration even if equally distributed.

But we know that in fact it is not evenly distributed, and it is often the old men, who could best manage without it, who get the greatest share.

[**CUT**: *It cannot be known how far the meat ration is supplemented by chickens; a recent medical survey reported that Kikuyu were deficient in animal protein.*]

The yield of milk from the cows is estimated to be sufficient to allow 1¼ gallons per household per week. But, since a large proportion, probably amounting to more than half, of the cows are kept at long distances from the homes of the owners, much of this milk is enjoyed by the herdsmen, and very little reaches the growing children who are in most need of it. It ought to be possible to supplement the supply very largely by goats' milk, but the Kikuyu have an unfortunate prejudice against it.

Since neither the meat supply nor the milk supply are adequate to the needs of the tribe, it would not be just to attribute the overstocking simply to the uneconomic collection of superfluous cattle, although it is a fact that at present cattle are prized as much for their potential value as bride price as for their meat or milk value, and many decrepit beasts and barren cows cumber the ground.

It is generally admitted by Administrative Officers who know the tribe that there is a marked improvement in physique, which is the more noticeable as one gets nearer to Nairobi. This is partly due to more civilized habits, learnt from Europeans, and partly to the proximity of markets which enables the family to sell produce and accumulate far more free money than is the case in the more remote locations.

[1009] The density at which the people are living has to a great extent prevented the practice of shifting cultivation and frequent fallowing of large stretches of land. While this will ultimately lead to a better and more economic use of land, there is grave risk that, until natives have adapted themselves to the new conditions and realized the necessity of ploughing in and of manuring, there will be very great deterioration of the soil through exhaustion, and signs of this are already apparent.

The tribal organization of the Kikuyu has never been strong. The main clans are scattered in small units. Even the *mbari* or family groups are often subdivided. The process of disintegration is most advanced in the Kiambu District, where it is generally allowed by custom that a man may separate from his cousins and divide the *githaka*, and instances of partition even between brothers are beginning to appear. While these movements in the direction of individualism are perhaps to be welcomed as a sign of progress, nevertheless some embarrassment has been caused by the rapidity with which the old institutions are breaking down and giving place to a civilization imperfectly understood by the people.

Optimum Density

The optimum density of any area cannot be a constant figure, but must vary according to the factors which from time to time come into play, and especially according to the skill and habits of the population. But it is no simple matter of a proportion sum, and it does not always follow that a rise in the level of living demands more land per family or that an increase of population must result in a lower standard of living. It depends on the circumstances of the case. For this reason, it was necessary to give a short character sketch of the people. The factors bearing on the case having now been stated, we can proceed to summarize the issues:—

(i) Is the density of population causing agrarian difficulties, and would they be materially alleviated by a decrease in density?
(ii) Is the density of population causing a deterioration of the soil?
(iii) Is the agricultural production per household less than it would otherwise be on account of the density of population?
(iv) Are the people less well nourished than they would otherwise be because of the density of population?

(i) The First Issue

Inheritance in Kenya is by division between heirs with an undistributed right of seigniory in the hands of the senior heir. This did not in the past lead to excessive subdivision, for the reasons that—

(a) the population, though of an increasing tendency, was reduced by sudden checks, such as famine and disease;
(b) the population, except in the Fort Hall District, was more sparse, and there was more room for subdivision; and
(c) if a piece of land became congested, there was always more land elsewhere to be carved out of the forest, and some of the right-holders could voluntarily move elsewhere.

[1010] Better health conditions, better communications, and the fixation of boundaries have altered the situation, and many right-holdings are becoming excessively subdivided. This is already an evil of considerable proportions in Dagoretti Division and in part of Nyeri District, but is not yet acute elsewhere.

A still greater evil in the system of inheritance is fragmentation. If a man has three pieces of land and three sons, each of the sons inherits in each of the three places, and if a man inherits both from his father and his uncle he soon finds himself the owner of a large number of little fragmented holdings.

It would not be fair to say that density of population is solely responsible. However wide the boundaries of the reserve had been set, the whole of the land would have been claimed as so many *ithaka*, and, however congested a particular *githaka* becomes, right-holders will not readily abandon it in order to settle as mere tenants on the *ithaka* of others. Another cause of local congestion is the "bride price" system, which practically ordains that if a man has three daughters and no sons he will use the bride price received to buy himself three additional wives, quite irrespectively of the size of the holding.

It will therefore be seen that local congestion is ascribable rather to defects in the agrarian system than to lack of land.

(ii) Density and Deterioration of the Soil

It is difficult to resist the conclusion that, while the regular manuring of land and a proper rotation of crops are a better method than the frequent fallowing which is the traditional native system, they take a long time to learn, and meanwhile erosion is proceeding at a rapid pace. Moreover, the Kikuyu have not realized the importance of keeping a proper covering of bush to hold up the wash on the steep hillsides, nor of hedging and ditching. While they are learning these things fast, they will have to learn them still faster if they are to compete with the rapidity of soil-deterioration.

It must be concluded that in this respect the people are more thick on the land than is suitable to their present degree of skill, and therefore over-population exists. But the remedy would appear to lie in the direction of improving their skill rather than reducing their relative numbers either by emigration or by an addition of their land. It is unlikely that an addition of land would alleviate the position at all, for there are large stretches of land not yet taken into cultivation, especially on the western border near the Aberdares,[16] and there is little reason to believe that the surplus population could be induced to migrate from the more congested areas on to any additional land that might be provided.

16 The Aberdare (now Nyandarua) mountains of up to 13,000 feet or 4,000 metres form the western rim of Kikuyuland; while increasingly cold and wet, this rim remains cultivable up to about 8,000 feet.

(iii) Density and Agricultural Production

The Agricultural Officers are agreed that the people would be better employed in more intensive cultivation of their present gardens than in extending their area. Nevertheless, they consider that an increase by twenty-five per cent of the acreage under seasonal crops would not be beyond their capacity, and they also consider that the acreage under wattle could be increased by fifty per cent, allowing as **[1011]** included in the fifty percent the area already planted in immature wattle, which was left out of account. Such an extension would require 44,704 acres, and would reduce very materially the acreage available for stock.

[**CUT**: *In two paragraphs Fazan argues that there is little to prevent Kikuyu from putting more of their land under wattle, since if needed they can graze their cattle elsewhere, and population density is a hindrance only in very specific locations.* [17]]

(iv) Density and the Food Supply

It has already been stated that in respect of vegetable food the Kikuyu are better nourished than most tribes. But they do not get enough meat or milk.

If they were skilled in stall-feeding, they could keep more cattle, and if they had more cash and more markets they could buy more meat. And if they could get over their prejudice against goats' milk, they would have more milk. But conditions being as they are, there is a deficiency in these things in spite of the full stocking of the reserve. This is another indication that the Kikuyu are living at too great a density for their present skill.

[**CUT**: *In seven paragraphs occupying nearly one page, Fazan summarises his findings on present conditions. He reaches two main conclusions: (i) that Kikuyuland is over-populated only in the sense that Kikuyu do not yet have the skill to meet their needs without exhausting the soil, thanks to their poor farming and animal husbandry practices; and (ii) that the inflexibility of their land tenure systems and a lack of marketing facilities are a greater hindrance to improved agriculture than lack of land.*]

17 Kikuyu did indeed increase their wattle plantings; by 1945 most households had planted some wattle (the logs being turned into charcoal for sale as fuel by Kikuyu traders, the bark being bought by large commercial firms for tanning hides) and at its peak in the early 1950s wattle earned nearly Sh. 750 per acre, but over a several-year production cycle. See Cowen, 'Commodity production', p. 124.

Part II – The future

[1012–22] [CUT: *These 10.5 pages are here summarised. They contain two chapters. The one-page Chapter 1 on* 'The Probable Density and Distribution of Population Fifteen Years hence and Thirty Years hence' *assumes a current rate of population increase of 1.6 per cent per annum, rising to 2 per cent by 1941 but declining by the 1950s due to a tendency to marry later. For the sake of simplicity, Fazan assumes a uniform rate of increase of 1.8 per cent. On that assumption, and with the current (1931) population of the three Kikuyu districts being 397,091, in 1947 their population will be 528,131 and in 1962, 690,003. With squatters on the 'White Highlands' now numbering 95,637, in 1947 (assuming no movement in or out) they will be 127,197 and 166,183 in 1962.*[18] *The number of households will increase by 40 per cent by 1947, much faster than population, since* 'a better distribution of wives' *will lead to a decrease in average household size. Average household acreage for all purposes, currently 11.01 acres, will shrink to 7.78 acres in 1947 and 5.6 in 1962. Fazan believes that his 1962 prediction will not come about, thanks to likely Kikuyu emigration among their close neighbours, Embu and Meru, and the ability of the stock-owning Maasai to offer competitive bride-wealth for Kikuyu daughters, so reducing potential Kikuyu fertility.*

The much longer Chapter 2 is on 'The Probable Increase in Agricultural Skill, and the Probable Development at these Periods'. *Fazan starts with two cautions: first, his assumption of constant prices thanks to an inability to predict price inflation and, second, another reminder that his statistical basis is no more than* 'intelligent estimation'.

In 1947, 15 years hence, at constant prices, Fazan estimates that the smaller average household will, purely in monetary terms rather than in overall domestic consumption, be over twice as well off as at present, with a net income of earnings over expenditure of Sh. 220 as against 1931's Sh. 106. This will be due to a 60 per cent increase in the yield per acre of grains and pulses, a great increase in the acreage under perennial crops such as wattle, with a corresponding decrease in other less productive uses such as fallow land and in the amount of grazing needed per head of cattle, thanks to paddocking and the planting of more stockfeed. Fazan also doubts that many more

---

18 Fazan's future population figures turned out to be gross underestimates. The 1948 census, Kenya's first, counted 1,026,341 Kikuyu, of whom 29 per cent or nearly 295,000 were living outside the reserve, most of them squatters. According to the 1962 census there were 1,642,065 Kikuyu living in Kenya, of whom 40 per cent or around 657,000 were living outside their 'home' districts. At both dates Kikuyu had a much larger 'diaspora' outside their 'home' districts than any other Kenyan ethnic group.

Kikuyu than at present will be able to afford ploughs; this constraint will limit the demand for more draught oxen – with their large pasture needs – and farm carts. An important assumption underlies the prediction that cultivation will earn a greater household income, namely that by 1947 Kikuyu will have learned to farm both their less well-watered land and their hillsides – on as yet unbuilt contour terraces. Nonetheless, Fazan warns that the Kikuyu reserve 'will not be entirely sufficient to the capacity of the people', *even if the land were distributed efficiently. And it will not be: Fazan repeats his criticisms of the rigidity and inequities of the* githaka *system, first voiced in his minority report for the 1929 Kikuyu Land Tenure Committee.*

Fazan holds out little hope for increased incomes from poultry and eggs, from hides and skins, or from dairy products and manure: the egg market is nearly swamped, hides and skins will have given way to textile clothing, and Kikuyu will themselves use all the dairy products and manure that they produce. The one hope for expanded sales is for charcoal. He holds out the prospect of a modest increase in wage income, from local government and mission-school employment in the reserve and from day-labour coffee-picking on nearby settler estates, but fears that any growth in employment in Nairobi will not add to the average household income, given the expected rise in the number of smaller households.[19]

Fazan then moves on to the position in 1962, 30 years on from the moment of writing. The population will then be nearly 31 per cent greater than in 1947; the greater employment of wage labour by Kikuyu farmers will mean that while families will be smaller, productive households will remain as large

---

19 These last two paragraphs on estimates of Kikuyu production in 1947 illustrate the perils of economic forecasting. Two vital developments could not be foreseen in 1932, one colonial and the other global. First, by 1935 the Kenyan government, faced with the collapse of settler agriculture in the depression, was forced to take measures to increase African agricultural incomes, with improved marketing arrangements and the first, tentative, relaxation on the prohibition of African coffee planting. Second, and above all, however, Fazan could not predict the Second World War or its economic impact on rural producers. He hopes for a 60 per cent increase in the *yield* of grains and pulses, but could not foretell that wartime shortages would also greatly inflate their producer *prices*, to the advantage of both white and black farmers in Kenya and the disadvantage of urban workers. Kikuyu producers were adept at evading wartime price controls. The end of the war brought the sale of surplus army lorries (often to returned soldiers with their previously unspent pay available to them) so that the expected increase in *draught animals* did not occur – and in any case Kikuyu did, against expectations, abandon oxen for donkeys. Female labour on the *contour terracing* on which Fazan placed hopes created such resentment that historians talk of 'the women's revolt' in the late 1940s. Reform of the *githaka* land tenure system and the registration of individual smallholdings was carried out with speed, in some respects as much a punitive

as in 1947. Despite still greater farming skills, over 10 per cent of the reserve's land will remain fit only for grazing. More optimistically, crop rotation should by 1962 mean that it is no longer necessary to set aside much land as fallow; better milk yields per cow and more stall feeding will reduce the acreage needed for a family's milk supply – but with a presumed end to head porterage more pasture will be needed for draught animals, and goats will still be needed as a meat supply. After these deductions have been made the average household will have just less than 3 acres available for cultivation, as against just over 3.5 acres in 1947. After the rapid increase in estimated yields between 1931 and 1947, Fazan expects a much slower increase after 1947, perhaps 15 per cent all round. The planting of coffee will not make much difference for each household, since the space available after the planting of essential food crops will be so small. So Fazan concludes that household incomes in 1962 will scarcely be higher than in 1947, not least because the demand for wage labour outside the reserves will grow no faster than the African labour supply. He ends the chapter **[1022]** *on a gloomy note:]*

'The devising of an agrarian system which would ensure the best possible distribution of so dense a population would tax the capacity even of the most advanced Governments, however many experts they had to advise them. It is far beyond the capacity of a handful of Europeans administering an African country, not only because they are far too harassed to have the time for expert study but also through lack of material resources. It is impossible to see how intensive cultivation

---

measure as enlightened agrarian reform, during the Mau Mau 'Emergency' when administrative resources were greatly increased. Fazan was quite right about the bright prospects for charcoal (at least until the early 1950s when coffee and tea began to take over) but greatly underestimated the employment prospects of Nairobi, whose productive employment increased greatly during the Second World War. For all these developments, see Kitching, *Class and Economic Change*, pp. 57–73, 108–30; Anderson and Throup, 'Africans and Agricultural Production'; Lonsdale, 'The Depression and the Second World War'; Throup, *Economic and Social Origins*, Chapter 7.

20 Fazan's forecasts for 1962 are as short of the mark as for 1947, thanks to another war, the Mau Mau Emergency, and the imminent prospect of Kenya's independence, neither of them readily imaginable in 1932. A full discussion of this period is found in Chapter 16 of the memoir and its accompanying notes, which provide the relevant bibliography. To take specific points here raised by Fazan: *milk yields* were fast improving in the 1950s thanks to leading Kikuyu upgrading their cattle privately by purchases from white dairy farmers and to the government programme of artificial insemination that crossed (Indian) Sahiwal bulls with local Zebu cows. *Human porterage* (largely by women) was still common but was being replaced by lorries, not draught oxen. *Coffee* – and tea – became a cause of further social differentiation as

can take place on this scale without a system of land registration which would be far too costly to be afforded.[20]

'The extent to which an equal distribution does not take place will be the measure of the distress that will ensue.'

[1023]

[Part II]

Chapter 3 – The Question of the Adequacy of the Reserve to the Probable Needs of the Population at These Periods[21]

Three periods have been taken for examination: the present; fifteen years hence, and thirty years hence. The numerical method which has been followed has not been in all ways satisfactory, and may seem to point too dogmatically to conclusions which are in reality very tentative. They have to be tested against the background of experience and observation, and after all due allowance has been made for possible error the following conclusions seem to be justified:

The Present (1932)

Congestion does not exist as a general condition, but only in certain areas and in certain particulars:—

(a) There are fairly wide areas, which include the whole Dagoretti Division, where the population is living beyond the optimum density in the sense that, if it had more room, the cultivation per family would be greater. Local foci of congestion also occur in locations which are not congested over all.

---

planting was allowed only on holdings of above average size, in order to preserve food security. Despite the population growing faster than waged employment, there were increases in many real wages thanks both to trade union organisation and the diversification of Kenya's economy through international investment. Nor would there be only *a handful of Europeans* in charge, partly because of the great increase in the staff establishments of all branches of government after 1945 ('the second colonial occupation', as it was called) but also because by 1962 a programme of rapid Africanisation had begun. The consolidation and legal *registration* of individually-owned land was indeed expensive but paid for largely by the British government and seen as an essential part of the counterinsurgency campaign against Mau Mau.

21 Fazan's underestimates of future population growth and his inability to foresee the developments mentioned in the previous two notes mean that this chapter has no useful predictive capacity. Its value lies in the insights it gives into the pessimistic cast of 'the official mind' (and one of unusual intelligence) at the time and, in the last sentence of the chapter, its sense of responsibility.

(b) The people are more thick on the land than is suitable to their present degree of skill in methods to combat soil erosion and exhaustion.

(c) The present degree of skill barely permits of the people keeping sufficient stock for its requirements without overstocking and deterioration of the land.

The average developed holding is only about four acres, but stock is run on common pasture which amounts to an allowance of rather more than seven additional acres to the household. As a measure of the standard of life prevailing, it may be stated that the average household appears to get about Sh. 53 of profit from its agricultural activities after feeding itself, and makes about the same amount from other sources.

Such congestion as exists is due rather to lack of skill than lack of land, and an increase of skill may be expected for some years to come to result in a raising of the standard of life, even though the population is increasing.

Fifteen Years Hence (1947)

The average holding will probably be between six and seven acres, but the common pasture will almost have disappeared.

The population would by this time have the skill to develop the whole area under review with a reasonable standard of efficiency, and, given the best possible distribution, the area should suffice. But it is certain that this proviso cannot be fully realized, and to the extent to which it is not realized, local congestion will exist.

If good distribution of population is secured, it would appear probable that the monetary resources of the average household, after feeding itself, will be about twice as great as at present. If the distribution is indifferent the degree of betterment will be less, but it is a safe conclusion that the household of 1947 will produce or earn considerably more money than the household of 1932.

[1024] This does not necessarily mean that it will be better off. The increase in skill will require an increased outlay in agricultural implements, and an increased annual charge for depreciation. Moreover, the modest ambitions of the household of to-day enable it to be contented at small expense, but there is, in my opinion, good ground for thinking that the standard of life which is already being taught to natives will prove to be beyond the means of the generality, and the actual rate of development will be so greatly below their expectations that, although there will be more material prosperity than at present, there will also be more discontent.[22]

Thirty Years Hence (1962)

If the calculations are correct, the population will have reached a density of approximately 537 to the square mile over an area of 1,285 square miles. This density is not vastly greater than that which already exists in the South Tetu Division of Nyeri and in most of the Dagoretti Division of Kiambu. But that such a density should be reached over so wide an area is quite exceptional among African tribes.

There seems to be no reason to doubt but that, unless something unforeseen occurs, approximately this density will be reached, although various minor forms of relief will be found. For instance, there will probably be an increase in the number of girls who are disposed in marriage to the Masai, and there will be relatives who follow them to the home of their husbands. There may also be some voluntary migration to the less congested areas in the northern part of the Province. But the economic pull southward towards Nairobi is very strong, and is not likely to be counteracted at so early a date. In spite of the exceptional density at which the population will be living, it is probable that the average householder will be in a monetary sense much better off than he is to-day, and perhaps not appreciably worse off than he will be in 1947. But he will certainly be poorer than he would be if he had scope to develop his full agricultural skill.

He will probably have reached the standard of skill which would enable him to farm eight acres of land intensively, but he will have to be content with five and a quarter. In other words, the population will be living beyond the optimum density.

If the distribution is even, there will be a general congestion, and, since the people will be forced through lack of land to accept a level of life below their capabilities, they will be discontented.

If the distribution is not even, the local congestions will be the more acute, and there will be distress. The decay of the tribal system[23] will decrease the means of relieving it.

For reasons already given above it seems unlikely that the average family will earn more money from sources outside the reserve than it does to-day.

22 The Mau Mau insurrection proved Fazan right in this.

23 Fazan appears to have in mind patronage and clientage as the core of 'the tribal system', now giving way to 'individualism'.

Perhaps I have not been quite accurate in saying that only five and a quarter acres will be available to a household. As natives advance in civilization, a differentiation of professions will begin to appear, and it will no longer be true that every household is agricultural. **[1025]** The proportion of land available for the agricultural families would therefore be greater. It is worth remarking that in Denmark, the most intensively agricultural of all European countries, only two-fifths of the population are directly employed in agriculture. Naturally, the development of other means of livelihood in Kikuyu will be a much slower growth, but it is certainly not a negligible factor, and some allowance must be made for it.

As congestion approaches, economic necessity will compel later marriages, and the rate of population-increase will decline. But the common experience is that this sort of remedy lags a good way behind the disease.

Ultimately, an equilibrium will be reached, but the danger is that, before it is reached, the standard of life may have been depressed to a point where a low grade population is leading an impoverished life on impoverished soil.

It is the task of administration to ensure that this state of things does not arise.

[**CUT to the end of the memorandum, pp. 1025–39**]

Part III – REMEDIES consists of three chapters that compare the different remedies thinkable in 1932 that might be adopted to ensure that a future in which 'a low grade population is leading an impoverished life on impoverished soil' *does not arise. The chapters discuss, in turn,* 'agrarian adjustments' *within the Kikuyu reserve, the likely results of adding land to the reserve, and the likely consequences of* 'interpenetration' *between Kikuyu and other ethnic groups or tribes.*

In the first chapter, Fazan recognises that populations are likely to cluster where there is economic opportunity – as in the Dagoretti area near Nairobi, or where the land is especially fertile or well watered – as in the South Tetu area of Nyeri district. If economic forces can effect such redistributions of population, what need, he asks, is there of remedial action from government and how might it be effective? **[1026]** *Fazan's answer is that overcrowding, however measured, will lead to the* 'breakdown of tribal authority', *a growth in crime, destitution, and insanitary risks to public health – and so to the need for a more intensive, and costly, administration. Government must therefore forestall such a situation by creating the communications and market access that would spread economic opportunity more widely. Such a solution, however, merely raises Fazan's next question: would the Kikuyu* *system of land tenure allow such fluidity? And his answer is an unequivocal 'no'.*

He lists five defects in what he understands of the Kikuyu 'githaka' *system of tenure, making it* 'unsuitable to modern requirements'*: (i) its concept of* 'spiritual ownership' *– the householder's responsibility to both his ancestors and to the unborn – restricts movement from one's ancestral land; (ii) partible inheritance results in uneconomic holdings among heirs;* **[1027]** *(iii) this tendency is increased by the likely fragmentation of any one household's land; (iv) the common rights to pasture livestock – unlike the private ownership of cropland – encourages the ownership of more cattle and smallstock than the land can carry; and (v) Kikuyu tenancy rights are so insecure that they discourage landowners in congested areas from seeking tenancies in less crowded areas. If these difficulties were not enough, then the desired direction of population redistribution would in any case be in the opposite direction to the poles of economic attraction.*

The second chapter of Part III, thanks to the poor prospects of 'a more even internal distribution' *of population, turns to consider whether any* 'block addition' *of land to the reserve would solve the problem of* 'congestion'*. For clarity of argument, Fazan sets aside other considerations* 'such as the rectification of grievances'.

[1028] *There are two major economic issues, of which the first is whether a block addition of land would offer a permanent solution to Kikuyu congestion. Fazan sees little hope in this, indeed fears that any addition of land – and it would have to be large, which makes it difficult to find – would merely deter the Kikuyu from facing up to the changes that they must make to attain greater economic efficiency: such as* 'sweeping aside' *tenurial restrictions and customs* 'which have lost their uses'*; developing agricultural processing industries; and delaying the age of marriage.* **[1029]** *Fazan sees no sign of the Kikuyu adopting such reforms. The precedents are discouraging: the additions already made to the Kikuyu reserves, the 74 square miles at Ndeiya, added in 1913, and the 205 square miles of the Mwea plains (1929) have simply been used as* 'grazing commonages'*. And he is not enthusiastic about any land usage rules being explored that would override Kikuyu land tenure conventions, whether on a settlement scheme outwith the reserve, or within the reserve.*

[1030] *The second question is whether an addition to the Kikuyu Reserve would be of economic advantage to Kenya as a whole. Fazan thinks not. There is no unoccupied land contiguous to Kikuyuland – other than forests that must be conserved – and to move some Kikuyu to* 'disconnected' *empty land at a distance would be* 'clumsy'*; in any case his previous comments on Kikuyu agriculture suggest that any such enlargement would not lead to any much-needed increase in Kenya's production. So, he asks, might* *interpenetration of tribes* 'kept separate for political and administrative purposes' *provide a less clumsy answer?*

Chapter 3, of just over one page, investigates 'the potentialities of interpenetration'. *Fazan points out that the legal position* 'whether a native can or cannot penetrate into an area reserved for another tribe and acquire land there' *is full of* 'puzzles' – *and he does* 'not much care what the legal answer may be'. *While barriers between one people and another are a* 'political necessity'; *for agrarian purposes* **[1031]** *they should be relaxed as far as is possible without damaging* 'the security and well-being of the occupant population'. *No relaxation of the boundaries between the 'White Highlands' and native reserves, however, is possible without* 'the strictest possible safeguards' *since the respective civilisations are so different. And where there is rivalry between native tribes interpenetration would become dangerous. Such cases are rare, however, and in general interpenetration is beneficial. It helps a growing tribe to expand without agitating for new boundaries. In addition,* 'an infusion of new blood' *is good for a host people who absorb incomers. Less congested tribes like the Maasai can offer good bride prices for Kikuyu girls whose children will learn how to cultivate, so teaching Maasai mixed farming methods that will make better use of their land. Nonetheless, with all these advantages it is well to remember that interpenetration will be successful only insofar as it is very gradual.*[24]

[1032] *Fazan concludes that while he has tried to present an impartial summary,* 'after all this hard work I think I can claim the right to a very short statement on my own account'. *He proceeds to reach four conclusions, that:*

24 'Interpenetration' between different immigrant ethnic groups had been common before colonial rule. It became increasingly contentious – with growing populations, rising land values, and administrative separations – in the colonial period. In recent years it has been the main cause of 'post-election violence', as ethnic immigrants in regions not originally their own are feared as electoral rivals with the potential to exclude their 'hosts' from the state's welfare and development resources. See: Richard Waller, 'Acceptees and Aliens: Kikuyu Settlement in Maasailand' in Thomas Spear and Richard Waller (eds), *Being Maasai: Ethnicity and Identity in East Africa* (London: James Currey, 1993), pp. 226–57; Timothy Parsons, 'Local responses to the ethnic geography of colonialism in the Gusii highlands of British-ruled Kenya', *Ethnohistory* 58 (2011), pp. 491–523; idem, 'Being Kikuyu in Meru: Challenging the tribal geography of colonial Kenya', *Journal of African History* 53 (2012), pp. 65–86; Sarah Jenkins, 'Ethnicity, violence, and the immigrant-guest metaphor in Kenya', *African Affairs* 111 (2012), pp. 576–96; John Lonsdale, 'Kenya's Seven Ages of Ethnicity' in Hiroyuki Hino et al. (eds), *Ethnic Diversity and Inclusive Development in Africa: Searching for the Way Forward* (Cambridge: Cambridge University Press, forthcoming).

(i) *Such occasional local congestion as Kikuyu currently suffer is* 'mainly due to lack of skill'.

(ii) *The next 30 years will see a race between population growth and increasing skill. The latter may take the lead at first, leading to improved standards of living, but thereafter congestion is likely to take over, so causing improvement to slow down, if not to cease.*

(iii) *Exports from the reserve, similarly, are likely to rise for some years and then decline.*

(iv) *This* 'threatened arrest of progress must be prevented' *in the interests of both the Kikuyu and Kenya:*

- *the best means of prevention will be agrarian reform aimed at both security of tenure and* 'reasonable fluidity of movement and occupation' *to the degree that each aim reinforces the other;*
- *a better population distribution within the Kikuyu reserve must be tackled by (a)* 'providing better markets and communications' *and (b) the progressive modification of githaka land tenure;*
- *better internal distribution will not be enough in itself to relieve congestion;* 'some external relief will be necessary' – *preferably by gradual interpenetration, an issue that needs urgent attention, especially with regard to 'White Highland' squatters. Even with interpenetration some more direct extension to the reserve may have to play a part.*[25]

[1033–9] *Four supporting statistical and methodological appendices are omitted.*

---

25 Many of the recommendations in the Kenya Land Commission's *Report* (Cmd. 4556, 1934) echoed the spirit of Fazan's personal conclusions.

Bibliography

Amsden, Alice, *International Firms and Labour in Kenya 1945–1970* (London: Routledge, 1971).

Anderson, David M., 'Depression, dust bowl, demography, and drought: The colonial state and soil conservation in East Africa during the 1930s', *African Affairs* 83 (1984), pp. 321–43.

———, 'Stock theft and moral economy in colonial Kenya', *Africa* 56 (1986), pp. 399–416.

———, 'Black mischief: Crime, protest and resistance in colonial Kenya', *Historical Journal* 36 (1993), pp. 851–77.

———, 'Master and servant in colonial Kenya 1895–1939', *Journal of African History* 41 (2000), pp. 459–85.

———, *Eroding the Commons: The politics of ecology in Baringo, Kenya 1890–1963* (Oxford: James Currey, 2002).

———, *Histories of the Hanged: Britain's dirty war in Kenya and the end of Empire* (London: Weidenfeld and Nicolson, 2005).

———, '"Yours in the struggle for Majimbo": Nationalism and party politics of decolonization in Kenya, 1955–64', *Journal of Contemporary History* 40 (2005), pp. 547–64.

———, 'Mau Mau in the high court and the "lost" British Empire archives: Colonial conspiracy or bureaucratic bungle?' *Journal of Imperial and Commonwealth History* 39 (2011), pp. 699–716.

Anderson, David M., and Throup, David, 'Africans and agricultural production in colonial Kenya: The myth of the war as a watershed', *Journal of African History* 26 (1985), pp. 327–45.

Anderson, David M., and Waller, Richard, *Colonial Crimes* (forthcoming).

Anderson, John, *The Struggle for the School* (Nairobi: Longman Kenya, 1970).

Atieno-Odhiambo, E.S., 'Democracy and the Ideology of Order in Kenya', in Michael G. Schatzberg (ed.), *The Political Economy of Kenya* (New York, NY: Praeger, 1987), pp. 177–201.

———, 'From Warriors to *Jonanga*: The Struggle Over Nakedness by the Luo of Kenya', in Werner Graebner (ed.), *Sokomoko: Popular Culture in East Africa* (Amsterdam: Rodopi, 1992), pp. 11–22.

——— (ed.), *African Historians and African Voices: Essays Presented to Professor Bethwell Allan Ogot* (Basel: Schlettwein, 2001).

Atieno-Odhiambo, E.S. and Lonsdale, John (eds), *Mau Mau and Nationhood: Arms, Authority and Narration* (Oxford: James Currey, 2003).

Beachey, R.W., *The Slave Trade of Eastern Africa* (London: Rex Collings, 1976).

Bennett, George, *Kenya, a Political History: The Colonial Period* (London: Oxford University Press, 1963).

———, 'Imperial Paternalism' in Kenneth Robinson and Frederick Madden, *Essays in Imperial Government Presented to Margery Perham* (Oxford: Blackwell, 1963), pp. 141–69.

Bennett, George, and Rosberg, Carl, *The Kenyatta Election: Kenya 1960–1961* (London: Oxford University Press, 1961).

Bennett, Huw, *Fighting the Mau Mau: The British Army and Counter-insurgency in the Kenya Emergency* (Cambridge: Cambridge University Press, 2013).

Berman, Bruce, *Control and Crisis in Colonial Kenya: The Dialectic of Domination* (London: James Currey, 1990).

Berman, Bruce, and Lonsdale, John (eds), *Unhappy Valley: Conflict in Kenya and Africa* (London: James Currey, 1992).

———, 'Custom, Modernity, and the Search for Kihooto: Kenyatta, Malinowski, and the Making of Facing Mount Kenya', in Helen Tilley, with Robert J. Gordon (eds), *Ordering Africa: Anthropology, European Imperialism, and the Politics of Knowledge* (Manchester: Manchester University Press, 2007), pp. 178–80.

Blacker, John, 'The demography of Mau Mau: Fertility and mortality in Kenya in the 1950s, a demographer's viewpoint', *African Affairs* 106 (2007), pp. 205–27.

Blundell, Michael, *So Rough a Wind* (London: Weidenfeld and Nicolson, 1964).

———, *A Love Affair with the Sun: A Memoir of Seventy Years in Kenya* (Nairobi: Kenway Publications, 1994).

Boyd, William, *An Ice Cream War* (London: Hamish Hamilton, 1982).

Branch, Daniel, *Defeating Mau Mau, Creating Kenya: Counterinsurgency, Civil War, and Decolonization* (Cambridge: Cambridge University Press, 2009).

———, *Kenya, Between Hope and Despair* (New Haven, CT: Yale University Press, 2011).

Branch, Daniel, Cheeseman, Nic and Gardner, Leigh (eds), *Our Turn to East: Politics in Kenya Since 1950* (Berlin: LIT Verlag, 2010).

Brantley, Cynthia, *The Giriama and Colonial Resistance in Kenya, 1800–1920* (Berkeley; Los Angeles, CA: University of California Press, 1981).

Breckenridge, James, *40 Years in Kenya* (Bridport: Creeds, 2002).

Breen, Rita M., 'The politics of land: The Kenya Land Commission (1932–33) and its effects on land policy in Kenya' (Michigan State University: PhD thesis, 1976).

Brennan, James R., 'Lowering the Sultan's flag: Sovereignty and decolonization in coastal Kenya', *Comparative Studies in Society and History* 50 (2008), pp. 831–61.

Brown, Monty, *Where Giants Trod: The Saga of Kenya's Desert Lake* (London: Quiller Press, 2001).

Burton, Andrew (ed.), *The Urban Experience in Eastern Africa* c.*1750–2000* (Nairobi: The British Institute in Eastern Africa, 2002).

Cain, P.J. and Hopkins, A.G., *British Imperialism: Crisis and Deconstruction 1914–1990* (London: Longman, 1993).

Callahan, Michael D., *Mandates and Empire: The League of Nations and Africa, 1914–1931* (Brighton: Sussex Academic Press, 1999).

Campbell, Guy, *The Charging Buffalo: A history of the Kenya Regiment 1937–1963* (London: Leo Cooper, 1986).

Cashmore, T.H.R., 'Studies in district administration in the East Africa Protectorate (1895–1918)' ([Cambridge University: PhD dissertation 1968], Cambridge African Studies Centre Occasional Paper).

Cell, John W, *Hailey: A Study in British Imperialism 1872–1969* (Cambridge: Cambridge University Press, 2002).

——— (ed.), *By Kenya Possessed: The Correspondence of Norman Leys and J.H. Oldham, 1918–1926* (Chicago, IL; London: University of Chicago Press, 1976).

Chenevix Trench, Charles, *The Desert's Dusty Face* (London: Blackwood, 1964).

———, *Men who Ruled Kenya: The Kenya Administration 1892–1963* (London; New York, NY: The Radcliffe Press, 1993).

Church of Scotland, *Memorandum Prepared by the Kikuyu Mission Council on Female Circumcision* (Kikuyu; cyclostyled, 1931).
Clayton, Anthony and Savage, Donald C., *Government and Labour in Kenya 1895–1963* (London: Frank Cass, 1974).
Clough, Marshall S., *Fighting Two Sides: Kenyan Chiefs and Politicians, 1918–1940* (Niwot, CO: University Press of Colorado, 1990).
———, *Mau Mau Memoirs: History, Memory and Politics* (Boulder, CO: Lynne Rienner, 1998).
Colonial Office, *Report of the Kenya Land Commission* (London: HMSO, Cmd 4556, 1934).
———, *East Africa Royal Commission 1953–55 Report* (London: HMSO, Cmd 9475, 1955).
———, *Historical Survey of the Origins and Growth of Mau Mau* (London: HMSO, Cmd 1030, May 1960).
Colony and Protectorate of Kenya, *Report of the Kikuyu Land Tenure Committee* (Nairobi: Government Printer, 1929).
———, *Report on the Relations between Government and Local Native Councils* (Nairobi: Government printer, 1938).
———, *History of the Loyalists* (Nairobi: Government Printer, 1961).
Constantine, Stephen, *The Making of British Colonial Development Policy 1914–1940* (London: Frank Cass, 1984).
Cooper, Frederick, *Plantation Slavery on the East Coast of Africa* (New Haven, CT; London: Yale University Press, 1977).
———, *From Slaves to Squatters: Plantation Labour and Agriculture in Zanzibar and Coastal Kenya 1890–1925* (New Haven, CT; London: Yale University Press, 1980).
———, *On the African Waterfront: Urban Disorder and the Transformation of Work in Colonial Mombasa* (New Haven, CT: Yale University Press, 1987).
———, *Decolonization and African Society: The Labor Question in French and British Africa* (Cambridge: Cambridge University Press, 1996).
Cowen, Michael, 'Commodity production in Kenya's Central Province', in Judith Heyer, Pepe Roberts and Gavin Williams (eds), *Rural Development in Tropical Africa* (London: Macmillan, 1981), pp. 121–42.
Cowen, Michael and McWilliam, Scott, *Indigenous Capital in Kenya: The 'Indian' Dimension of Debate* (Helsinki: Institute of Development Studies, 1996).
Cox, Richard, *Pan-Africanism in Practice: PAFMECSA 1958–1964* (London: Oxford University Press, 1964).
Crosskill, W.E., *The Two Thousand Mile War* (London: Robert Hale, 1980).
de Vere Allen, James, *Swahili Origins: Swahili Culture and the Shungwaya Phenomenon* (London: James Currey, 1993).
Douglas-Home, Charles, *Evelyn Baring, the Last Proconsul* (London: Collins, 1978).
Duder, C.J., '"Men of the officer class": participants in the 1919 Soldier Settlement Scheme in Kenya', *African Affairs* 92 (1993), pp. 69–87.
Edgerton, Robert B., *Mau Mau: An African Crucible* (London: Collier Macmillan, 1989).
Elkins, Caroline, *Britain's Gulag: The Brutal End of Empire in Kenya* (London: Cape, 2005).
Engholm, Geoffrey, 'African elections in Kenya, March 1957', in William MacKenzie and Kenneth Robinson (eds), *Five Elections in Africa* (Oxford: Clarendon, 1960), pp. 391–461.
Fearn, Hugh, *An African Economy: A Study of the Economic Development of the Nyanza Province of Kenya 1903–1953* (London: Oxford University Press, 1961).
Ferguson, Niall, *Empire: How Britain Made the Modern World* (London: Allen Lane, 2003).
Fieldhouse, D.K., Heyer, Judith, Roberts, Pepe, and Williams, Gavin, *Black Africa 1945–1980: Economic Decolonization and Arrested Development* (London: Allen and Unwin, 1986).

Fisher, Nigel, *Iain Macleod* (London: Deutsch, 1973).
French, David, *The British Way in Counter-Insurgency 1945–1967* (Oxford: Oxford University Press, 2011).
Frost, Richard, *Race against Time: Human Relations and Politics in Kenya before Independence* (London: Rex Collings, 1978).
Furedi, Frank, *The Mau Mau War in Perspective* (London: James Currey, 1989).
Galbraith, J.S., *Mackinnon and East Africa, 1878–1895* (Cambridge: Cambridge University Press, 1972).
Gardner, Leigh, 'An Unstable Foundation: Taxation and Development in Kenya 1945–53', in Daniel Branch Nic Cheeseman and Leigh Gardner, *Our Turn to Eat* (Berlin; London: LIT Verlag, 2010), pp. 53–76.
Gavaghan, Terence, *Of Lions and Dung Beetles: A 'Man in the Middle' of Colonial Administration in Kenya* (Ilfracombe: Stockwell, 1999).
Ghai, Y.P. and McAuslan, J.P.W.B., *Public Law and Political Change in Kenya: A Study of the Legal Framework of Government from Colonial Times to the Present* (Nairobi, Oxford University Press, 1970).
Glassman, Jonathan, *Feasts and Riot: Revelry, Rebellion, and Popular Consciousness on the Swahili Coast, 1856–1888* (Portsmouth NH; London: Heinemann and James Currey, 1995).
Glover, Michael, *An Improvised War: The Abyssinian campaign of 1940–1941* (London: Leo Cooper, 1987).
Goldsworthy, David, *Tom Mboya: The Man Kenya Wanted to Forget* (London: Heinemann, 1982).
Gray, Sir John, *The British in Mombasa 1824–1826, being a History of Captain Owen's Protectorate* (London; New York, NY: Macmillan, 1957).
Gregory, Robert G., *India and East Africa: A History of Race Relations within the British Empire 1890–1939* (Oxford: Clarendon, 1971).
———, *South Asians in East Africa: An Economic and Social History, 1890–1980* (Boulder, CO: Westview Press, 1993).
———, *Quest for Equality: Asian Politics in East Africa 1900–1967* (New Delhi: Orient Longman, 1993).
Grob-Fitzgibbon, Benjamin, *Imperial Endgame: Britain's Dirty Wars and the End of Empire* (Basingstoke: Palgrave Macmillan, 2011).
Hailey, (Malcolm) Lord, *An African Survey: A Study of Problems Arising in Africa South of the Sahara* (London: Oxford University Press, 1938).
Hake, Andrew, *African Metropolis: Nairobi's Self-help City* (London: Sussex University Press, 1977).
Hanley, Gerald, *Monsoon Victory* (London: Collins, 1946).
Hay, Margaret Jean, *Fashioning a Modern Identity in Colonial Western Kenya: Struggles over Clothing in the Interwar Period* (Boston, MA: African Studies Center, Occasional Paper 35, 2002).
Hazell, Alastair, *The Last Slave Market* (London: Constable, 2012).
Hazlewood, Arthur, *The Economy of Kenya: The Kenyatta Era* (Oxford: Oxford University Press, 1979).
Heinlein, Frank, *British Government Policy and Decolonisation 1945–1963: Scrutinising the Official Mind* (London: Frank Cass, 2002).
Henderson, Ian, with Philip Goodhart, *The Hunt for Kimathi* (London: Hamish Hamilton, 1958).
Hennings, R.O., *African Morning* (London: Chatto & Windus, 1951).
Heyer, Judith, 'Agricultural development policy in Kenya from the colonial period to 1975', in Judith Heyer, Pepe Roberts and Gavin Williams (eds), *Rural Development*, pp. 90–120.
Heyer, Judith, Roberts, Pepe and Williams, Gavin (eds), *Rural Development in Tropical Africa* (London: Macmillan, 1981).

Himbara, David, *Kenyan Capitalists, the State, and Development* (Boulder CO: Lynne Rienner, 1994).
Hobley, C.W., *Kenya, from Chartered Company to Crown Colony* (London: Witherby, 1929).
Hodges, Geoffrey, *The Carrier Corps: Military Labor in the East African Campaign, 1914–1918* (New York, NY: Greenwood Press, 1986).
Horton, Mark, *Shanga: The Archaeology of a Muslim Trading Community on the Coast of East Africa* (London: British Institute in Eastern Africa, 1996).
Hughes, Lotte, *Moving the Maasai: A Colonial Misadventure* (Basingstoke: Palgrave Macmillan, 2006).
Huxley, Elspeth, *White Man's Country: Lord Delamere and the Making of Kenya*, 2 vols (London: Chatto & Windus, 1935).
———, *The Flame Trees of Thika* (London: Chatto & Windus, 1959).
———, *A New Earth: An experiment in colonialism* (London: Chatto & Windus, 1960).
———, *The Mottled Lizard* (London: Chatto & Windus, 1962).
——— (ed.), *Nellie: Letters from Africa* (London: Weidenfeld & Nicolson, 1980).
Huxley, Elspeth and Perham, Margery, *Race and Politics in Kenya* (London: Faber, revised edition 1956).
Hyam, Ronald, *Elgin and Churchill at the Colonial Office 1905–1908: the Watershed of the Empire–Commonwealth* (London: Macmillan, 1968).
———, *Britain's Declining Empire: the Road to Decolonization 1918–1968* (Cambridge: Cambridge University Press, 2006).
Hyam, Ronald and Louis, Wm Roger (eds), *The Conservative Government and the End of Empire 1957–1964. Part I: High Policy, Political and Constitutional Change* (London: The Stationery Office, 2000).
Hyde, Dave, 'The Nairobi General Strike [1950]: From Protest to Insurgency', in Andrew Burton, *The Urban Experience* (Nairobi: British Institute in Eastern Africa, 2002), pp. 235–53.
Iliffe, John, *Africans: The History of a Continent* (Cambridge: Cambridge University Press, 1995, second edition 2007).
———, *East African Doctors: A History of the Modern Profession* (Cambridge: Cambridge University Press, 1998).
———, *Honour in African History* (Cambridge: Cambridge University Press, 2005).
———, 'Breaking the Chain at its Weakest Link: TANU and the Colonial Office', in Gregory H. Maddox and James L. Giblin (eds), *In Search of a Nation: Histories of Authority and Dissidence in Tanzania* (Oxford: James Currey, 2005), pp. 168–97.
Itote, Waruhiu, *'Mau Mau' General* (Nairobi: East African Publishing House, 1967).
Jackson, Ashley, *The British Empire and the Second World War* (London: Hambledon Continuum, 2006).
Jackson, William, *Madness and Marginality: The Lives of Kenya's White Insane* (Manchester University Press, 2013).
Jenkins, Sarah, 'Ethnicity, violence, and the immigrant-guest metaphor in Kenya', *African Affairs* 111 (2012), pp. 576–96.
Joint Select Committee on Closer Union in East Africa, *Report, Together with the Proceedings of the Committee* (London: HMSO, HC Paper 156 and HL Paper 184 of 1931).
Kaggia, Bildad, *Roots of Freedom 1921–1963* (Nairobi: East African Publishing House, 1975).
Kanogo, Tabitha, *Squatters and the Roots of Mau Mau* (London: James Currey, 1987).
———, *African Womanhood in Colonial Kenya 1900–50* (Oxford: James Currey, 2005).
Kanyinga, Karuti, 'The land question in Kenya: Struggles, accumulation and changing politics' (Roskilde University: PhD dissertation, 1998).

Karanja, John, *Founding an African Faith: Kikuyu Anglican Christianity 1900–1945* (Nairobi: Uzima, 1999).
Kariuki, Josiah Mwangi, *'Mau Mau' Detainee* (London: Oxford University Press, 1963).
Kennedy, Dane, *Islands of White: Settler Society and Culture in Kenya and Southern Rhodesia, 1890–1939* (Durham, NC: Duke University Press, 1987).
Kenyatta, Jomo, *Facing Mount Kenya: The Tribal Life of the Gikuyu* (London: Secker and Warburg, 1938).
Kershaw, Greet, *Mau Mau from Below* (Oxford: James Currey, 1997).
Killingray, David, *Fighting for Britain: African Soldiers in the Second World War* (Oxford: James Currey, 2010).
King, Kenneth J., *Pan-Africanism and Education: A Study of Race, Philanthropy and Education in the Southern States of America and East Africa* (Oxford: Clarendon, 1971).
———, *The African Artisan: Education and the Informal Sector in Kenya* (London: Heinemann, 1977).
———, *Jua Kali Kenya: Change and Development in an Informal Economy, 1970–95* (London: James Currey, 1996).
Kinyatti, Maina wa (ed.), *Kenya's Freedom Struggle: The Dedan Kimathi Papers* (London: Zed Books, 1987).
Kipkorir, B.E., 'The Alliance High School and the origins of the Kenya African elite 1926–1962' (University of Cambridge: PhD dissertation, 1969).
———, *Descent from Cherang'any Hills: Memoirs of a Reluctant Academic* (Nairobi: Macmillan Kenya, 2009).
——— (ed.), *Biographical Essays on Imperialism and Collaboration in Colonial Kenya* (Nairobi: Kenya Literature Bureau, 1980).
Kitching, Gavin, *Class and Economic Change in Kenya: The Making of an African Petite Bourgeoisie 1905–1970* (New Haven, CT: Yale University Press, 1980).
Kitson, Frank, *Gangs and Counter-gangs* (London: Barrie and Rockliff, 1960).
Klump, Donna and Kratz, Corinne, 'Aesthetics, Expertise and Ethnicity: Okiek and Maasai Perspectives on Personal Ornament', in Thomas Spear and Richard Waller (eds), *Being Maasai*, pp. 195–221.
Knowles, Oliver, *Back Seat Driver: Memories from the End of Empire* (Brighton: Pen Press, 2008).
Kuczynski, R.R., *Demographic Survey of the British Colonial Empire, Vol II* (London: Oxford University Press, 1949).
Kyle, Keith, *The Politics of the Independence of Kenya* (Basingstoke: Macmillan, 1999).
Lamphear, John, *The Scattering Time: Turkana Responses to Colonial Rule* (Oxford: Clarendon, 1992).
Leakey, L.S.B., *Mau Mau and the Kikuyu* (London: Methuen, 1952).
———, *The Southern Kikuyu before 1903*, 3 vols (London: Academic Press, 1977).
Le Breton, F.H., *Up-country Swahili* (Richmond: Simpson, 13 editions from 1936 to 1956).
Leonard, David K., *African Successes: Four Public Managers of Kenyan Rural Development* (Berkeley, CA: University of California Press, 1991).
Lewis, Joanna, *Empire State-Building: War and Welfare in Kenya 1925–52* (Oxford: James Currey, 2000).
Leys, Colin, *Underdevelopment in Kenya: The Political Economy of Neo-colonialism 1964–1971* (London: Heinemann, 1975).
———, 'Learning from the Kenya debate' in Colin Leys (ed.), *The Rise and Fall of Development Theory* (London: James Currey, 1996), pp. 143–63.
Leys, Norman, *Kenya* (London: Hogarth Press, 1924).

Lonsdale, John, 'The Depression and the Second World War in the Transformation of Kenya', in David Killingray and Richard Rathbone (eds), *Africa and the Second World War* (Basingstoke: Macmillan, 1986), pp. 97–142.

———, 'Mau Maus of the mind: Making Mau Mau and remaking Kenya', *Journal of African History* 31 (1990), pp. 393–421.

———, 'The Conquest State of Kenya, 1895–1905', in Bruce Berman and John Lonsdale (eds), *Unhappy Valley* (Ohio, OH: Ohio University Press), pp. 13–44.

———, 'The Politics of Conquest in Western Kenya, 1894–1908', in Bruce Berman and John Lonsdale (eds), *Unhappy Valley* (Ohio, OH: Ohio University Press), pp. 45–74.

———, 'The Moral Economy of Mau Mau', in Bruce Berman and John Lonsdale (eds), *Unhappy Valley* (Ohio, OH: Ohio University Press), pp. 265–504.

———, 'The Trials of Jomo Kenyatta: Breaking and Making an African Nationalist', in Peter Coss (ed.), *The Moral World of the Law* (Cambridge: Cambridge University Press, 2000), pp. 196–239.

———, 'Contests of Time: Kikuyu Historiographies, Old and New', in Axel Harneit-Sievers (ed.), *A Place in the World: New Local Historiographies from Africa and South Asia* (Leiden: Brill, 2002), pp. 201–54.

———, 'Kikuyu Christianities: A History of Intimate Diversity', in David Maxwell, with Ingrid Lawrie (eds), *Christianity and the African Imagination: Essays in Honour of Adrian Hastings* (Leiden: Brill, 2002), pp. 157–97.

———, '"Listen while I Read": Patriotic Christianity Among the Young Gikuyu', in Toyin Falola (ed.), *Christianity and Social Change in Africa: Essays in Honor of J.D.Y. Peel* (Durham, NC: Carolina Academic Press, 2005), pp. 563–93.

———, 'Kenya: Home County and African Frontier', in Robert Bickers (ed.), *Settlers and Expatriates: Britons Over the Seas* (Oxford: Oxford University Press, 2010), pp. 74–111.

———, 'Kenya's Seven Ages of Ethnicity' in Hiroyuki Hino, John Lonsdale, and Frances Stewart (eds), *Ethnic Diversity and Inclusive Development in Africa: Searching for the Way Forward* (Cambridge: Cambridge University Press, forthcoming).

Lovatt Smith, David, *Kenya, the Kikuyu and Mau Mau* (Herstmonceux: Mawenzi Books, 2005).

———, *Amboseli: A Miracle too Far?* (Herstmonceux: Mawenzi Books, 2008).

——— (ed.), *A History of the Kikuyu Guard 1953–1955* (Herstmonceux: Mawenzi Books, 2003, second edition 2006).

Low D.A. and Smith, Alison (eds), *History of East Africa* III (Oxford: Clarendon, 1976).

Luongo, Katherine, *Witchcraft and Colonial Rule in Kenya, 1900–1955* (Cambridge: Cambridge University Press, 2011).

Lynch, Gabrielle, *I Say to You: Ethnic Politics and the Kalenjin in Kenya* (Chicago, IL: University of Chicago Press, 2011).

Lyttelton, Oliver, *The Memoirs of Lord Chandos* (London: Bodley Head, 1962).

Lytton, Lord, *The Desert and the Green* (London: Macdonald, 1957).

Maciel, Mervyn, *Bwana Karani* (London: Merlin Books, 1985).

Mackenzie, A. Fiona D., *Land, Ecology and Resistance in Kenya, 1880–1952* (Edinburgh: Edinburgh University Press, 1998).

Makonnen, Ras, with Kenneth King, *Pan-Africanism from Within* (Nairobi: Oxford University Press, 1973).

Maloba, Wunyabari O., *Mau Mau and Kenya: An Analysis of a Peasant Revolt* (Bloomington, IN: Indiana University Press, 1993).

Mangat, J.S., *A History of the Asians in East Africa, c. 1886 to 1945* (Oxford: Clarendon, 1969).

Matson, A.T., *Nandi Resistance to British Rule 1890–1906* (Nairobi: East African Publishing House, 1972).
Maxon, Robert M., *John Ainsworth and the Making of Kenya* (Lanham, MD: University Press of America, 1980).
———, *Struggle for Kenya: The Loss and Reassertion of Imperial Initiative 1912–1923* (London; Toronto: Associated University Presses, 1993).
———, 'Social and Cultural Changes', in B.A. Ogot and W.R. Ochieng', *Decolonization and Independence in Kenya* (Ohio, OH: Ohio University Press, 1995), pp. 110–47.
———, *Going their Separate Ways: Agrarian Transformation in Kenya 1930–1950* (Madison, NJ: Fairleigh Dickinson University Press, 2003).
al Mazru'i, Shaykh Al-Amin bin 'Ali, *The History of the Mazru'i Dynasty of Mombasa* (Oxford: Oxford University Press, 1995).
McCann, Gerard, 'Sikh communities in Southeast Asia and East Africa, *c.* 1870–1970' (Cambridge University: PhD dissertation, 2010).
McWilliam, Michael, 'The Managed Economy: Agricultural Change, Development, and Finance in Kenya, 1945–1963', in D.A. Low and Alison Smith (eds), *History of East Africa* vol III (Oxford: Clarendon, 1976), pp. 251–89.
Meinertzhagen, Richard, *Kenya Diary 1902–1906* (Edinburgh: Oliver and Boyd, 1957).
Middleton, John, *The World of the Swahili: An African Mercantile Civilization* (New Haven, CT; London: Yale University Press, 1992).
Mitchell, Sir Philip, *African Afterthoughts* (London: Hutchinson, 1954).
Moorehead, Alan, *The White Nile* (New York, NY: Harper, 1960).
Morris, H.F. and Read, James S., *Indirect Rule and the Search for Justice: Essays in East African Legal History* (Oxford: Clarendon Press, 1972).
Mosley, Paul, *The Settler Economies: Studies in the Economic History of Kenya and Southern Rhodesia 1900–1963* (Cambridge: Cambridge University Press, 1983).
Moyse-Bartlett, H., *The King's African Rifles: A Study in the Military History of East and Central Africa, 1890–1945* (Aldershot: Gale and Polden, 1956).
Mueller, Susanne, 'Government and opposition in Kenya, 1996–69', *Journal of Modern African Studies* 22 (1984), pp. 399–427, reprinted as Chapter 4 in Branch et al. (eds), *Our Turn to Eat* (2010), pp. 77–105.
Mungeam, G.H., *British Rule in Kenya 1895–1912: The Establishment of Administration in the East Africa Protectorate* (Oxford: Clarendon, 1966).
Munro, J.F., *Colonial Rule and the Kamba: Social Change in the Kenya Highlands 1889–1939* (Oxford: Clarendon Press, 1975).
Muriuki, Godfrey, *A History of the Kikuyu 1500–1900* (Nairobi: Oxford University Press, 1974).
Muoria, Henry, 'What Should We Do, Our People? (1945)', in Wangari Muoria-Sal, Bodil Folke Frederiksen, John Lonsdale and Derek Peterson (eds), *Writing for Kenya: The Life and Works of Henry Muoria* (Leiden: Brill, 2009), pp. 137–251.
Murphy, Philip, *Alan Lennox-Boyd, a Biography* (London: I.B.Tauris, 1999).
Murray-Brown, Jeremy, *Kenyatta* (London: Allen and Unwin, 1972).
Ndege, George O., *Health, State and Society in Kenya* (Rochester, NY: University of Rochester Press, 2001).
Nicholls, C.S., *Red Strangers: The White Tribe of Kenya* (London: Timewell Press, 2005).
Njama, Karari, with Donald Barnett, *Mau Mau from Within: Autobiography and Analysis of Kenya's Peasant Revolt* (London: MacGibbon and Kee, 1966).
Njoroge, Lawrence M., *A Century of Catholic Endeavour: Holy Ghost and Consolata Missions in Kenya* (Nairobi: Paulines, 1999).
Nunneley, John, *Tales from the King's African Rifles* (London: Cassell, 2000).
Nurse, Derek and Thomas Hinnebusch, *Swahili and Sabaki, a Linguistic History* (Berkeley, CA: University of California Press, 1993).

Ochieng', W.R., 'Colonial African Chiefs: Were they Primarily Self-seeking Scoundrels?' in Ogot, *Hadith 4: Politics and Nationalism in Kenya* (Nairobi: East African Publishing House, 1972), pp. 46–70.

Odinga, Oginga, *Not Yet Uhuru* (London: Heinemann, 1967).

Ogot, B.A., *History of the Southern Luo, Volume 1: Migration and Settlement 1500–1900* (Nairobi: East African Publishing House, 1967).

——— 'The Decisive Years 1956–63' in B.A. Ogot and W.R. Ochieng', *Decolonization and Independence in Kenya* (Ohio, OH: Ohio University Press, 1995), pp. 48–79.

——— and W.R. Ochieng' (eds), *Decolonization and Independence in Kenya 1940–93* (London: James Currey 1995).

Ombongi, Kenneth S., 'A history of malaria control policy in colonial Kenya, 1897–1963' (University of Cambridge: PhD thesis, 2000).

Omusule, Monone, 'Political and constitutional aspects of the origins and development of local government in Kenya 1895–1963' (Syracuse University: PhD thesis, 1974).

Osborne, Myles, *Loyal Sons of Kenya: Virtue, Ethnicity and Martial Race among the Kamba,* c. *1800 to the Present* (Cambridge: Cambridge University Press, 2014).

Ostendorff, Daniel, 'The Koinange dynasty and the development of Kenyan politics' (Oxford University DPhil dissertation, forthcoming).

Otieno, Wambui Waiyaki, *Mau Mau's Daughter: A Life History* (Boulder, CO: Lynne Reinner, 1998).

Paice, Edward, *Lost Lion of Empire: The Life of 'Cape to Cairo' Grogan* (London: HarperCollins, 2001).

———, *Tip and Run: The untold tragedy of the Great War in Africa* (London: Weidenfeld & Nicolson, 2007).

Parker, Ian, *The Last Colonial Regiment: The History of the Kenya Regiment (T.F.)* (Milton Brodie: Librario Publishing, 2011).

Parsons, Timothy H., *The African Rank-and-File: Social Implications of Colonial Military Service in the King's African Rifles, 1902–1964* (Portsmouth, NH: Heinemann, 1999).

———, 'Local responses to the ethnic geography of colonialism in the Gusii highlands of British-ruled Kenya', *Ethnohistory* 58 (2011), pp. 491–523.

———, 'Being Kikuyu in Meru: Challenging the tribal geography of colonial Kenya', *Journal of African History* 53 (2012), pp. 65–86.

Pearson, Michael N., *Port Cities and Intruders: The Swahili coast, India, and Portugal in the early modern era* (Baltimore, MD: The Johns Hopkins Press, 1998).

Perham, Margery, *East African Journey: Kenya and Tanganyika 1929–30* (London: Faber & Faber, 1976).

——— and Bull, Mary, *The Diaries of Lord Lugard*, 3 vols (London: Faber, 1959).

Peterson, Derek R., *Creative Writing: Translation, Bookkeeping, and the Work of the Imagination in Colonial Kenya* (Portsmouth, NH: Heinemann, 2004).

———, *Ethnic Patriotism and the East African Revival: A History of Dissent* c. *1935–1972* (Cambridge: Cambridge University Press, 2013).

——— (ed.), *Abolitionism and Imperialism in Britain, Africa, and the Atlantic* (Athens, OH: Ohio University Press, 2010).

Phillips, Arthur, *Report on Native Tribunals* (Nairobi: Government Printer, 1945).

Porter, Bernard, *The Absent-Minded Imperialists: Empire, Society and Culture in Britain* (Oxford: Oxford University Press, 2004).

Pouwels, Randall L., *Horn and Crescent: Cultural Change and Traditional Islam on the East African Coast, 800–1900* (Cambridge: Cambridge University Press, 1987).

Reed, Colin, *Pastors, Partners and Paternalists: African Church Leaders and Western Missionaries in the Anglican Church in Kenya, 1850–1900* (Leiden: Brill, 1997).

Reid, Richard, *War in Pre-Colonial Eastern Africa: The Patterns and Meanings of State-level Conflict in the Nineteenth Century* (Oxford: James Currey, 2007).
Robertson, Claire C., *Trouble Showed the Way: Women, Men, and Trade in the Nairobi Area, 1890–1990* (Bloomington, IN: Indiana University Press, 1997).
Robinson, R.E, and Gallagher, J. A., with Alice Denny, *Africa and the Victorians* (London: Macmillan, 1961).
Romero, Patricia, *Lamu: History, Society and Family in an East African Port City* (Princeton, NJ: Markus Wiener, 1997).
Rosberg, Carl G. and Nottingham, John, *The Myth of 'Mau Mau': Nationalism in Kenya* (New York, NY: London: Praeger and Pall Mall, 1966).
Ross, William McGregor, *Kenya from Within: A Short Political History* (London: Allen and Unwin, 1927).
Rothchild, Donald, *Racial Bargaining in Independent Kenya: A Study of Minorities and Decolonization* (London: Oxford University Press, 1973).
Salim, A.I., *Swahili-speaking Peoples of Kenya's Coast, 1895–1965* (Nairobi: East African Publishing House, 1973).
Sandgren, David P., *Mau Mau's Children: The Making of Kenya's Postcolonial Elite* (Madison, WI: University of Wisconsin Press, 2012).
Sanger, Clyde, *Malcolm Macdonald: Bringing an End to Empire* (Liverpool: Liverpool University Press, 1995).
Sanger, Clyde and Nottingham, John, 'The Kenya general election of 1963', *Journal of Modern African Studies* 2 (1964), pp. 1–40.
Schmidt, Heike I., *Colonialism and Violence in Zimbabwe: A History of Suffering* (Woodbridge: James Currey, 2013).
Shepherd, Robert, *Iain Macleod, a Biography* (London: Pimlico, 1994).
Sheriff, Abdul, *Slaves, Spices, and Ivory in Zanzibar 1770–1873* (London: James Currey, 1987).
Simpson, Donald, *Dark Companions: The African Contribution to the European Exploration of East Africa* (London: Paul Elek, 1975).
Singh, Makhan, *History of Kenya's Trade Union Movement to 1952* (Nairobi: East African Publishing House, 1969).
Soja, Edward W., *The Geography of Modernization in Kenya: A Spatial Analysis of Social, Economic, and Political Change* (Syracuse, NY: Syracuse University Press, 1968).
Sorrenson, M.P.K., *Land Reform in the Kikuyu Country* (Nairobi: Oxford University Press, 1967).
————, *Origins of European Settlement in Kenya* (Nairobi: Oxford University Press, 1968).
Spear, Thomas T., *The Kaya Complex: A History of the Mijikenda Peoples of the Kenya Coast to 1900* (Nairobi: Kenya Literature Bureau, 1978).
Spear, Thomas T. and Waller, Richard (eds), *Being Maasai: Ethnicity and Identity in East Africa* (London: James Currey, 1993).
Spencer, John, *KAU: The Kenya African Union* (London: KPI, 1985).
Steel, David, *No Entry: The Background and Implications of the Commonwealth Immigrants Act 1968* (London: Hurst, 1969).
Steinhart, Edward I., *Black Poachers, White Hunters: A Social History of Hunting in Colonial Kenya* (Oxford: James Currey, 2006).
Strayer, Robert W., *The Making of Mission Communities in East Africa* (London: Heinemann, 1978).
Survey of Kenya, *National Atlas of Kenya* (Nairobi: Kenya Government, third edition 1970).
Sutton, John, *A Thousand Years of East Africa* (London: British Institute in Eastern Africa, 1990).
Thomas, Lynn, *Politics of the Womb: Women, Reproduction, and the State in Kenya* (Berkeley, CA: University of California Press, 2003).

Throup, David, *Economic and Social Origins of Mau Mau* (London: James Currey, 1987).
Thuku, Harry, with Kenneth King, *An Autobiography* (Nairobi: Oxford University Press, 1970).
Tiffen, Mary, Mortimore, Michael and Gichuki, Francis, *More People, Less Erosion: Environmental Recovery in Kenya* (Chichester: Wiley, 1994).
Tignor, Robert L., 'Colonial chiefs in chiefless societies', *Journal of Modern African Studies* 9 (1971), pp. 339–59.
———, *The Colonial Transformation of Kenya: The Kamba. Kikuyu, and Maasai from 1900 to 1939* (Princeton, NJ: Princeton University Press, 1976).
———, *Capitalism and Nationalism at the End of Empire: State and Business in Decolonizing Egypt, Nigeria, and Kenya, 1945–1963* (Princeton, NJ: Princeton University Press, 1998).
Tilley, Helen, *Africa as a Living Laboratory: Empire, Development, and the Problem of Scientific Knowledge* (Chicago: University of Chicago Press, 2011).
van Zwanenberg, R.M.A, with Anne King, *An Economic History of Kenya and Uganda 1800–1970* (Basingstoke: Macmillan, 1975).
Vassanji, M.G., *The Book of Secrets* (Edinburgh: Canongate, 2006).
Waller, Richard D., 'The Maasai and the British, 1895–1905: The origins of an alliance', *Journal of African History* 17 (1976), pp. 529–53.
———, 'Acceptees and aliens: Kikuyu settlement in Maasailand' in Thomas Spear and Richard Waller (eds), *Being Maasai: ethnicity and identity in East Africa* (London: James Currey, 1993), pp. 226–57.
———, 'Kidongoi's kin: prophecy and power in Maasailand', Chapter 2 in David M. Anderson and Douglas H. Johnson (eds), *Revealing Prophets: Prophecy in eastern African history* (London: James Currey, 1995), pp. 28–64.
———, 'Witchcraft and the law in colonial Kenya', *Past and Present* 180 (2003), pp. 241–75.
———, '"Clean" and "Dirty": Cattle disease and control policy in colonial Kenya, 1900–40', *Journal of African History* 45 (2004), pp. 45–80.
Walton, Calder, *Empire of Secret: British Intelligence, the Cold War, and the Twilight of empire* (London: Harper, 2013).
Wasserman, Gary, *Politics of Decolonization: Kenya Europeans and the Land Issue 1960–1965* (Cambridge: Cambridge University Press, 1976).
Watkins, Elizabeth, *Oscar from Africa: The Biography of O.F. Watkins* (London; New York, NY: The Radcliffe Press, 1995).
Weisbord, Robert G., *African Zion: The Attempt to Establish a Jewish Colony in the East Africa Protectorate, 1903–1905* (Philadelphia: Jewish Publication Society of America, 1968).
Were, Gideon S., *A History of the Abaluyia of Western Kenya,* c. *1500–1930* (Nairobi: East African Publishing House, 1967).
White, Luise, *The Comforts of Home: Prostitution in Colonial Nairobi* (Chicago: University of Chicago Press, 1990).
———, *Speaking with Vampires: Rumor and History in Colonial Africa* (Berkeley: University of California Press, 2000).
———, 'Work, clothes, and talk in Eastern Africa: An essay about masculinity and migrancy', in Atieno Odhiambo, *African Historians and African Voices* (2001), pp. 69–74.
Willis, Justin, *Mombasa, the Swahili, and the Making of the Mijikenda* (Oxford: Clarendon, 1993).
———, *Potent Brews: A Social History of Alcohol in East Africa 1850–1999* (Oxford: James Currey, 2002).
Wylie, Diana, 'Norman Keys and McGregor Ross: A case study in the conscience of African empire, 1900–1939', *Journal of Imperial and Commonwealth History* 5 (1977), pp. 294–309.

Index

Abyssinia (now Ethiopia) and Abyssinians, 21, 33, 169, 171, 172–5, 199
Abaluhya people, xxxvii, 20, 39, 191, 245, 262
African Labour *see* Labour, African
Akamba people (*see also* Kamba people), 5, 20, 31, 38, 41, 97, 187, 208, 245, 265, 267, 270–71, 282
Ainsworth, John, xix–xx, xxxvii, 11, 31, 56, 113, 156, 262
America and Americans, 47, 79, 249, 253–4
Arabs (*see also* Zanzibar), xx, 3–7, 11, 20, 37, 42–3, 50, 71, 75
  Arab officers, 11, 64, 65–6, 103
  Mazrui dynasty, 4, 6–7, 14, 61–2
  Oman and Omanis, 4–7, 28
Asians and Asiatics (*see also* Indians), xvii, xxxix, 23, 30, 44, 170, 190, 192, 201–2, 225, 233, 246–7, 258

Bajun people, 63
Baring, Sir Evelyn (Governor, 1952–9), 195, 216
Baringo, 12, 16
Barth, Sir Jacob (Chief Justice), 137–8
Belfield, Sir Henry (Governor, 1912–7), 49, 137
Belgium and Belgians, 10, 53–4, 58, 252–3, 254
Blundell, Michael, 241, 242–3
Boer War, 45, 54, 184
Borana people *see* Galla people
Briggs, Group Captain, 241, 242–3
British East Africa Protectorate *see* Kenya Colony
Brooke-Popham, Air Chief Marshal Sir Robert (Governor 1937–9), 172
Byrne, Sir Joseph (Governor 1931–7), 158
British policy towards Kenya and East Africa, xviii, 18, 19, 256–7
  'Closer union', 81, 82, 151, 181
  Colonial Development and Welfare, 84, 257
  East Africa Royal Commission (1953–5), 229, 234–6, 261
  East African High Commission, 81–4, 172, 224, 233–4
  Elgin pledge (1906), 22–3, 148, 165
  Joint Parliamentary Committee (1931), 83–5, 151, 258
  Lennox-Boyd pledge, 1958, 236, 251
  Milner, Churchill and Devonshire (1921–3), 77–8, 149–50, 156, 257
Buganda, 9, 118, 250, 277

Campbell, W. F. G., 32
Candler, James, 213
Carter, Morris (Judge) *see* Kenya Land Commission
Cavendish-Bentinck, Sir Ferdinand, 247
Chiefs and British rule (*see also* Mau Mau, Loyalists), xxx, xxxviii, xl, 34–5, 110, 120–22, 181, 201, 259–60
  and African society, 118–19, 122–3, 157–8
  Gero, xxxvii

Kinanjui (Kinyanjui), 12
Koinange, 119, 189
Laws relating to, 19, 25, 110, 117–18, 120
Mumia, xxxvii, 16, 17, 264
Murai, Ignatio, 187; Njiri, 208
Waruhiu, 195
Clitoridectomy *see* Female circumcision
Coast province (*see also* Zanzibar), xx, 11, 25–6, 61–73, 267–8, 269, 273
Corfield, Frank, xxix
Coryndon, Sir Robert (Governor, 1922–5), 77

Decolonisation of Kenya and East Africa (*see also* Legislative Council), xix, xxviii–xxx, xxxviii, 220, 239–55
First Lancaster House conference (1960), 241–3
Macmillan, Harold (Prime Minister, 1957–63), xxviii, 220
Macleod, Iain (Secretary of State, 1959–61), 241, 245
Second Lancaster House conference (1962), 245–6
'Wind of Change' (1960), 250
Delamere, Lord, 45
Dorobo *see* Okiek
Dual Mandate, The (Lord Lugard's book), 257
'Dual mandate', 256, 258
'Dual policy', 113, 149, 258, 260–61

East Africa Protectorate (EAP) *see* Kenya Colony
Economic and social geography of Kenya, 36–7, 43–5, 67–8, 128, 150–51
Economic history of Kenya, xxxvi–vii, 13, 18, 30, 44–5, 63–4, 67, 74–5, 81, 88, 160–62, 180–81, 223–36, 254–5
Economic life in Africa, 36–42, 66–73, 93–4, 108–114, 181, 228, 286–340
'Economic Survey of the Kikuyu Reserves' (S. H. Fazan's survey), xxxiv –v, xxxvi, 286–340
Economic research of High Commission
Crops and planting methods, 110, 233
Fishing industry, 231–2
Forestry, 233
Veterinary, 233
Economy
Exports, 13, 44–5, 63, 68, 73, 74, 109, 111–12, 160–61, 298–9
Fishing, 71–2, 231–2, 275
Hunting, 41, 67, 275, 277
Industry and artisanal manufacture, 67, 161, 180, 184, 224, 225, 232–3
Livestock and pastoralism, 36, 38, 40, 44, 63, 64, 68, 72–3, 88, 96–7, 112, 192, 215, 231, 232, 266–73, 75–6, 278–80, 305–9, 326–7
Tourism, 184, 232
Education and training (*see also* Missions), xxiii, xxiv, 47, 90–91, 106–8, 160, 225, 233–4, 325–6
Eliot, Sir Charles (Commissioner, 1901–4), 18, 148, 256
Embu people (*see also* Mau Mau), 20, 191
Emergency *see* Mau Mau
Environment
Conservation, 109, 112, 126, 231, 257, 279–80, 327, 329
History, 110
Soil erosion, 96–7
Erskine, General Sir George, 210–11, 218
Ethiopia *see* Abyssinia
European exploration of East Africa, 7–10, 118–9

Famine and food shortage, 32, 64, 66, 111, 148, 155, 156, 160, 243, 265
Road-building as famine-relief, 64
Fazan, S. H.,
Career, iv–xviii, xix–xxxiv, xl–xliii, 27–35, 82, 157, 222
'Economic Survey of the Kikuyu Reserves', xxxiv –v, xxxvi, 286–340
History of the Loyalists, xv, xxv–xxxiii, xxxix, xl
Observer of African life, xvi, xix, xxxiv–xxxv, xxxvii, xxxix, xlii,

34–5, 36–42, 66–73, 91–4, 108–115, 262–340
Female circumcision, xxi, xxxviii, 78–80
First World War, x, 29, 32, 49–58, 184
Fort Jesus, 4, 6, 11, 28, 61
Fort Smith, 12, 15, 32
Fort Ternan, 17, 23, 148
France and the French, 4–6, 9, 10, 15, 178, 252, 254

Galla people, 36–7, 63, 68
Germany and Germans (*see also* missionaries), 7–8, 10–11, 16
  Allied Control Commission, xxiv, 222
  German East Africa, xxxix, 11, 17, 22, 28–9, 32, 49–58, 259
Gero (Luo chief), xxxvii
Gethin, Richard, 51–2
Ghana, 185, 250–52
Giriama, 21, 68, 244
Girouard, Sir Percy (Governor, 1909–12), 29
Goans and Goanese, 44
Grigg, Sir Edward (Governor, 1925–30), 82
Grogan, Captain Ewart, 45

Hailey, Lord, 83, 149
Hall, Francis, 12, 20, 31–2
Hamilton, Sir Robert (Chief Justice), 28
Hardinge, Sir Arthur (Commissioner, 1895–1900), 14, 62
Health and disease, xxxvi, 30, 32, 46, 57, 64–5, 70–71, 72, 74, 89–90, 104–6, 156–7, 160, 199, 217, 219, 225, 234
History of the Loyalists (S. H. Fazan's report), xv, xxv–xxxiii, xxxix, xl
Hobley, Charles William, 17, 20, 102, 262
Holder, Henry (cricketer), 30
Holm, Alex (Director of Agriculture), 150
Hope, J. O. W., 137
Horne, E. B., 102

Imperial British East Africa Company (IBEA), 11–13, 256, 257
India, 58, 77
  Indian army, 8, 52, 175
  Indian politics in Kenya, 76–7, 163, 190
  Indians in Kenya (see also Asians, Trade), 43–4, 62, 63, 66–7, 75, 93–4, 109, 192
Islam and Muslims (Mohammedans), 3–4, 42–3, 64, 269
Italy and Italians, 37, 169–70, 171, 172, 173–5, 180, 224

Jackson, Frederick J., 17

Kalenjin people (see also Nandi, Kipsigis), 123
Kamba people (see also Akamba), xx, xl, 7, 266
'Kavirondo', 17, 39
Kenya and Kenyans,
  Clothing, 39, 91–2
  Gender, 65, 97, 135–7, 139–40, 142–3, 180–3, 186, 192, 199, 230, 262–85
  Generation, 65, 97, 135–7, 139–40, 142–3, 180–3, 186, 192, 199, 230, 262–85
  Housing, 92–3, 225–6, 325–6
  Kenya African Democratic Union (KADU), 244–6
  Kenya African National Union (KANU), 244–6
  Kenya African Union (KAU), xxxix, 184–8, 191, 193, 195, 198
  Pan-Africanism, 185, 252
  Politicians,
    Kenyatta, Jomo, xxviii–xxx, xxxiii–iv, 80, 93, 184–5, 190, 193, 196, 244, 245–7, 252, 254–5
    Koinange, Peter Mbiyu, 189, 242
    Mboya, Tom, 228, 241, 252
    Ngala, Ronald, 241, 244
    Thuku, Harry, 76, 138
  Politics after the First World War, 75–8
  Press, 93, 193, 196
  Sport, 94–5, 180
Kenya Colony (formerly British East Africa Protectorate), 75, 149
  Administration and government, xvii, 19, 28, 29, 31–2, 47–8, 65, 94, 101–16, 181, 256–61, 287, 337

Changes in, xxxv, xxxvi–viii, 31–2, 88–97
Conquest, xxxvii, 11–13, 14–21, 27, 31–2, 33, 37
Laws relating to Africans, 103–4, 129–32, 138, 216, 280–84
'pacification', xxxvii, 11–13, 14–21, 27, 31–2, 33, 37
resistance, xxxvii, 11–13, 14–21, 27, 31–2, 33, 37
Kenya Regiment, 170, 173, 193, 208
Kenya Defence Force *see* Kenya Regiment
Kericho, 17, 74
Kiambu, xxi, 154, 186, 193, 195, 204, 206, 228, 278–9, 286–340
Kikuyu people (*see also* Mau Mau), 20, 31, 189, 227, 267–9, 270–71, 282
Diet, 295–7, 326–7, 330
Grievances, xv, 11–12, 25, 75–6, 111, 138, 151–2, 165, 185–7, 191, 235–6
Household economy, 15, 286–340
Independent churches and schools, 80, 108, 188–9, 194, 202–3
Kikuyu Guard (KG) *see* Mau Mau, Loyalists
Land Tenure, xxi–iii, 32, 76, 78, 136–9, 140–44, 229–31, 276–80, 293, 312–14, 327–9, 332, 333, 338–9
Political bodies (*see also* Africans, Politics, Mau Mau), 76, 80–1, 138, 184–5
Women's protests, 186–7, 192
Kilimanjaro, Mount, 7, 22, 28–9
Kilindini Harbour, Mombasa, 27, 72, 224
Kinanjui (Kinyanjui) (Kikuyu chief), 12
King's African Rifles (KAR, previously East African Rifles), xx, 16, 19, 21, 48, 50, 53–5, 170, 174, 176–80, 182–3, 196, 199, 207–8
Kipsigis people, 17, 74, 153
Kisii, 20, 32, 50, 51–2
Kisumu, 17, 30–31
Kitui, xx, 7, 20, 110, 281
Koinange (Kikuyu chief), 119, 189
Labour, African (non-domestic), 30, 39, 45, 96, 104, 110, 154–60, 313, 315–9
Working conditions, 155, 159–60, 164–5
Wages, 113, 158, 191
Carrier Corps in First World War, xxxix, 54–7, 155, 156, 171
In Mau Mau Emergency, 196, 202, 203–4, 227–8
Pioneers in Second World War, 57, 171, 174, 176–7
'Problems', xix, 18, 113, 154–8, 176–7, 186
'Squatters' (resident farm labour), 88–9, 153, 158–9, 191, 202, 235, 294–5, 318–9, 331
Trade Unions, 189, 227–8, 253
Laikipia, 22, 23
Lamu, 9, 61, 63, 64, 71
Land (see also White Highlands)
African land tenure (see also Kikuyu land tenure), 135–7, 139–40, 273–80
Alienation of African lands, xv, xxi, 21–2, 23–4, 25, 26, 74, 136, 144–6, 148, 150–54, 185–6
Consolidation and registration, 228–9, 230–31, 280, 333
Islamic tenures, 64
Kenya Land Commission, xiv–xvi, xix, xxii–xxiii, xxiv, xxv, xxvii, xxxiii, xxxiv, xxxvii, xl–xli, 24, 84–7, 139–40, 151–4, 185–6, 203, 279–80, 286–340
Legislation, 25–6, 86–7, 137, 140, 145, 153
Settlement schemes, 1960s, 244, 247
League of Nations, 58
Leakey, Dr Louis, xxii, 262
Legislative Council, 19, 75, 162–3, 186, 188, 190, 239, 242
1954 Lyttelton Constitution, 239–40
1957 African elections, 240
1958 Lennox-Boyd Constitution, 240–41
1961 General Election, 244–5
1963 General Election, 245–6
Leroki (Leroghi) plateau, 24

Leys, Dr Norman, 163
Limuru, 25, 137, 148
Local government in Africa, xxiii, xxxiii, 80, 104–5, 107, 110, 111, 118, 123–9, 145–6, 163
Lokiriama, 33
Lugard, Captain Frederick D. (later Lord), 12, 16, 31, 148, 257, 259
Luhya or Luyia people *see* Abaluhya
Luo people, xvi, xxxvii, 17, 38–9, 185, 187, 189, 191, 227, 285

Macdonald, Malcolm (Governor, 1963), 246
Machakos, xx, 11, 110, 126, 272
Malindi, xx, 4, 63, 157
Martin, James, 31
Masai (Maasai) people, 5, 9, 12, 15, 21, 29, 39–42, 97, 122, 191, 250, 263, 275–6, 283–4, 336
Masai Moves, 21–2, 23–4, 122–3, 151
Mau Mau, xv–xvi, xxiii, xxiv–xxxiii, xxxix, 186, 187, 188–9, 192, 193, 195, 197–224, 249–50, 285
  Atrocity, xxvi–viii, xxx–xxxiii, xl, 202–3, 204–5, 216–20, 222
  Casualty figures, 220
  Civil war, xxv–xxxiii, xxx–xxxiii, xl, 196, 198, 200–1, 204–9, 211, 213–15, 217, 220–2, 240
  Counterinsurgency, xv, xl, 194, 195–6, 197, 199–204, 206–11, 213, 226
  Detainees, xxv, xxxiii, 196, 216, 217, 219, 222
  Emergency, xv, xl, 194, 195–6, 197, 199–204, 206–11, 213, 226
  Home Guard, xxv–xxxiii, xxx–xxxiii, xl, 196, 198, 200–1, 204–9, 211, 213–15, 217, 220–2, 240
  Lari massacres (March 1953), xxiv, 25, 204–6, 222
  Loyalists, xxv–xxxiii, xxx–xxxiii, xl, 196, 198, 200–1, 204–9, 211, 213–15, 217, 220–2, 240
  Operation Anvil, 213
  Pseudo gangs, 215–16
  Villagisation, 200–1, 214–15, 228–9
Mau Mau leaders
  Itote, Waruhiu (General China), 212
  Kago, General, 209, 212–13, 214
  Kimathi, Field-Marshal Dedan, 198, 212, 214, 216
  Mathenge, Stanley, 212
Maxwell, G. V., 126
Meru people (*see also* Mau Mau), 191, 240, 262
Mijikenda people *see* Nyika people
Missions and missionaries, xxiii, xxxviii, 46–7, 69, 79–80, 106–7, 156–7, 221, 262, 269
  American missions, 47, 79
  Catholic missions, 47, 79
  Church Missionary Society, 7–8, 47, 79
  Church of Scotland mission, 47, 79–80, 188
  Livingstone, David, 8–9
Mitchell, Sir Philip (Governor, 1944–52), 172, 195
Mombasa (*see also* Kilindini), xx, 4, 6–7, 14, 27–8, 61, 72, 88, 170, 227
Monck-Mason Moore, Sir Henry (Governor, 1939–44), 172
Mumia (Luyia chief), xxxvii, 16, 17, 264
Murai, Ignatio (ex-senior Kikuyu chief), 187
Murang'a (Fort Hall), 20, 32, 187, 193, 194, 209, 212–14, 286–340

Nairobi, 18, 29, 88, 142, 172, 184, 186, 199, 204, 209, 210, 213, 224–6, 269
Naivasha, 15, 206
Nakuru, 30, 45, 88
Nandi people, 12, 17, 20, 39–42, 152
Nile River, 8, 9, 10, 16, 250
Njiri (senior Mununga chief), 208
Northern Frontier Province, 21, 37, 86, 174
Northey, General Sir Edward (Governor, 1919–22), 50, 54, 156
Nyanza Province and Districts, xix, xxiii, xxxvii, 16, 17, 20, 30–1, 34–5, 76, 81, 109, 163, 171, 230
Nyeri, xxi, 193, 198, 208, 231, 283, 286–340
Nyika (Mijikenda) people, 7, 38, 63, 66, 73, 269, 275

Ogot, Bethwell, xvi
Okiek (Dorobo) people, xxxix, 12, 41, 279
Oromo people *see* Galla people

Partition of Africa (*see also* Scramble for Africa), 5
Pokomo people, xxxvi, 63, 68–71
Pokot people *see* Suk people
Police (Kenya and British East Africa), 21, 171, 196, 200, 206, 209, 213, 216
  Kenya Police Reserve (KPR), 193, 216, 219
  Tribal police, xxx, 101–2, 187, 193, 200, 209, 213–15
Population diversity, 24, 28, 95–6, 224
  African, 36, 95–6, 165, 286–340
  Asian, 36
  European, 27, 57, 75, 148–9
  Racial proportions, xviii, 36
Portugal and Portuguese, 4–5, 10, 28, 44, 61–2

Race relations, 57, 75–7, 93–4, 96, 111, 164–5, 182–3, 185, 190, 191–2, 225, 233, 246–7, 258
Railway *see* Transport and travel
Ravine, Eldama, 12, 15–16, 17
Renison, Sir Patrick (Governor, 1959–62), xxix, 216, 246
Ross, William McGregor, 162

Samburu people, 24, 33
Scramble for Africa 10, 83; *see also* partition of Africa
Second World War, xxiii–iv, 84, 161, 169–83, 184
Seyyid Said Sultan, 4, 5, 6, 61
Slavery
  Abolition, 5
  Slave trade, 5–9, 11, 12, 20, 61–3
  Social and economic consequences, xx, 38, 43, 61–2, 64–5, 71, 148, 266
Somalia and Somalis, 37–8, 58, 68–9, 70, 173, 179, 187, 191, 245, 250
Somaliland *see* Somalia
Sotik, 20, 74, 153
South African War *see* Boer War
South Africa and South Africans, 53, 55, 64, 170, 173–4, 250
Sudan and Sudanese troops (*askari*), 11, 15–17
Suk people, 33, 191
Swahili people and language, 15, 20, 28, 33, 37, 42–3, 63, 69, 71, 108, 173, 177
Swynnerton plan, xxxvi, 229

Taita, 7, 153
Tana River, xx, xxxvi, 63, 68–71
Tanganyika, 48, 77, 83, 173, 250, 259
Taveta, 51, 53, 153
Taxation and expenditure
  Hut and poll tax, 19, 34, 121, 320–23, 325
  Inter-racial imbalance, 84, 91, 127, 156, 163
Tigoni, xxiv, xxxiii
Transport and travel, xxxvi, 29, 44, 101, 114–16, 156, 171
  Air, 88, 116, 224
  Bicycle, 34, 109, 203
  Lake, 30
  Ox-cart and donkey, 15, 29, 44, 114
  Porters and foot safari, 15, 33–5, 54–7, 115
  Railway, 14, 17–18, 28–30, 88
  Road (cars, buses, lorries), 29, 44, 57, 71, 94, 95, 115–16, 127, 136, 171, 195, 224, 227
'Tribalism', xxxv, xxxix
  Detribalisation, 21–4
  'Interpenetration', 339–40
  Laws and Customs, 262–85
  Migration, 37–42, 45
  Pacification, 12, 17
Turkana people and region, xx, 32–3, 37, 86

Uganda, 10, 11, 12, 16, 30, 250

Victoria, Lake, xix, 8, 10, 12, 17, 30, 105

Wars, xxxv, 184, 258
  First World War, 1914–18, x, 29, 32, 49–58, 184

Second World War, 1939–45, xxiii–iv, 84, 161, 169–83, 184
South African (Boer) War, 1899– 1902, 45, 54, 184
Waruhiu (senior Kikuyu chief), 195
Watkins, Oscar, 56
West Africa and West Africans, 126, 128, 173, 174, 179, 185, 251–2
White Highlands (*see also* Land)
Economics, xviii–xix, xxxvi–vii, 18, 24, 44–5, 64, 72, 74–5, 81, 88, 111–12, 113, 150, 157, 160–62, 184, 228, 235, 243–4
Policy and its abandonment, viii, 22–3, 75–7, 85–7, 147–66, 190–91, 234–6, 243–4, 247–8, 260–61, 339
White settlers
Afrikaners, 45–6
Coming after the two World Wars, 49–50, 51–2, 54, 170, 173, 181–3
Politics, xvii, xviii–xix, xxvii–viii, xxx–xxxi, xxxviii, xli, 18, 22–4, 26, 75–6, 82–3, 162–4, 165–6, 181–3, 190–91, 241, 244, 247–8, 256–7
Social life, xix, xxiv, xxxv, 29, 44, 46, 73, 74, 164, 182
In First and Second World Wars, 49–50, 51–2, 54, 170, 173, 181–3
Witchcraft fears, xxxii–iii, 188, 282–3, 285
Witchdoctors, 162, 188
Witu, 10, 61, 63

Zanzibar (*see also* Arabs), 8–11, 250

Plate 1 Porters on foot safari, Nyanza, before the First World War.

Plate 2 Luo warriors, before 1914.

Plate 3 Luo women dancing, before 1914.

Plate 4 Nyanza women, probably from Kisii, visit S. H. Fazan on safari, before 1916.

Plate 5 Luo Chiefs' Retainers or Tribal Police, before 1916.

Plate 6 S. H. Fazan's house, Lokiriama, Turkana, 1915 or 1916.

Plate 7 Transport donkeys, Turkana, *c.* 1916.

Plate 8 Turkana warriors, *c.* 1916.

Plate 9 A Christmas drink, Lokiriama, 1915 or 1916.

Plate 10 Christmas races, Lokiriama, 1915 or 1916.

Plate 11 Oxcart, the normal transport for settler pioneers.

Plate 12 Mombasa docks, 1926.

Plate 13 Mr and Mrs Fazan, shopping in Mombasa, 1926.

Plate 14 A coastal street, 1920s.

Plate 15 Unroadworthy car, 1920s.

Plate 16 Uncarworthy road, 1920s.

Plate 17 The District Commissioner's new house, Machakos, *c.* 1927.

Plate 18 S. H. Fazan with Kamba women charcoal burners, 1920s.

Plate 19 A District Commissioner's Baraza, 1920s.

Plate 20 Kikuyu Ngoma [dance], almost certainly in 1928, to celebrate the visit of Edward Prince of Wales.

Plate 21 The Aga Khan's Golden Jubilee, celebrated in Kisumu, 1937. Left to right, outside the Provincial Commissioner's House: The Aga Khan, Sir Sultan Muhammad Shah; Anthea Fazan, Stephen Fazan, Eleanor Fazan, the Begum Andrée Aga Khan, S. H. Fazan, Mrs Fazan, Mrs Cochrane, Cecil Davenport (a fellow Provincial Commissioner).

Plate 22 S. H. Fazan in full tropical fig with the Governor's lady, Lady Brooke-Popham, 1937.

Plate 23 The new Governor, Sir Robert Brooke-Popham, with his senior officials, 1937. S. H. Fazan, as the senior Provincial Commissioner, is seated at the Governor's right-hand side.